EXPLORING
PSYCHOLOGY

Mapping Psychology 1

We would like to dedicate this course to the memory of Brenda Smith, Psychology Staff Tutor and member of the course team, who died during the final year of the course's production. She had been a Psychology Staff Tutor since 1995, first in Scotland and then most recently in Ireland, but her close association with the Open University stretches back much further than this. She was an Open University student herself and then later returned to teach and was a tutor who enthused and supported very many students throughout their social science studies. At her funeral one of these students spoke very movingly of her warmth and energy and of the fact that she had really 'made a difference' to their lives. She certainly also made a difference to our DSE212 course team, where her commitment to education for mature students was clear in everything that she said and did, and her immensely hard work influenced many of our plans for the teaching and learning strategy of the course and the content of the texts. She contributed enormously at both a professional and personal level, particularly to the early work of the course team, and we hope that her influence on the course will shine through, helping it in turn to 'make a difference' to the lives of all the students who will study it in the coming years.

Mapping Psychology 1

Edited by Dorothy Miell, Ann Phoenix and Kerry Thomas

The Open University

Cover and title page images: Guillem Ramos-Poqui

This publication forms part of an Open University course DSE212 *Exploring Psychology*. Details of this and other Open University courses can be obtained from the Call Centre, PO Box 724, The Open University, Milton Keynes MK7 6ZS, United Kingdom: tel. +44 (0)1908 653231, email ces-gen@open.ac.uk

Alternatively, you may visit the Open University website at http://www.open.ac.uk where you can learn more about the wide range of courses and packs offered at all levels by the Open University.

To purchase this publication or other components of Open University courses, contact Open University Worldwide Ltd, The Berrill Building, Walton Hall, Milton Keynes MK7 6AA, United Kingdom: tel. +44 (0)1908 858785; fax +44 (0)1908 858787; email ouwenq@open.ac.uk; website http://www.ouw.co.uk

The Open University
Walton Hall, Milton Keynes
MK7 6AA

First published 2002. Reprinted 2002

Edited, designed and typeset by The Open University.

Printed in the United Kingdom by The Bath Press, Bath.

ISBN 0 7492 5353 3

1.2

Contents

DSE212 course team

Open University staff

Dr Dorothy Miell, Senior Lecturer in Psychology, Faculty of Social Sciences (Course Team Chair)

Dr Paul Anand, Lecturer in Economics, Faculty of Social Sciences

Peter Barnes, Lecturer in Centre for Childhood, Development and Learning, Faculty of Education and Language Studies

Pam Berry, Key Compositor

Dr Nicola Brace, Lecturer in Psychology, Faculty of Social Sciences

Dr Nick Braisby, Lecturer in Psychology, Faculty of Social Sciences

Maurice Brown, Software Designer

Sue Carter, Staff Tutor, Faculty of Social Sciences

Annabel Caulfield, Course Manager, Faculty of Social Sciences

Lydia Chant, Course Manager, Faculty of Social Sciences

Dr Troy Cooper, Staff Tutor, Faculty of Social Sciences

Crystal Cunningham, Researcher, BBC/OU

Shanti Dass, Editor

Sue Dobson, Graphic Artist

Alison Edwards, Editor

Marion Edwards, Software Designer

Jayne Ellery, Production Assistant, BBC/OU

Dr Linda Finlay, Associate Lecturer, Faculty of Social Sciences, co-opted member of course team

Alison Goslin, Designer

Professor Judith Greene, Professor of Psychology (retired), Faculty of Social Sciences

Professor Wendy Hollway, Professor of Psychology, Faculty of Social Sciences

Silvana Ioannou, Researcher, BBC/OU

Dr Amy Johnston, Lecturer in Behavioural Neuroscience, Faculty of Science

Dr Adam Joinson, Lecturer in Educational Technology, Institute of Educational Technology

Sally Kynan, Research Associate in Psychology

Andrew Law, Executive Producer, BBC/OU

Dr Martin Le Voi, Lecturer in Psychology, Faculty of Social Sciences

Dr Karen Littleton, Lecturer in Centre for Childhood, Development and Learning, Faculty of Education and Language Studies

Dr Bundy Mackintosh, Lecturer in Psychology, Faculty of Social Sciences

Marie Morris, Course Secretary

Dr Peter Naish, Lecturer in Psychology, Faculty of Social Sciences

Daniel Nettle, Lecturer in Biological Psychology, Departments of Biological Sciences and Psychology

John Oates, Senior Lecturer in Centre for Childhood, Development and Learning, Faculty of Education and Language Studies

Michael Peet, Producer, BBC/OU

Dr Ann Phoenix, Senior Lecturer in Psychology, Faculty of Social Sciences

Dr Graham Pike, Lecturer in Psychology, Faculty of Social Sciences

Dr Ilona Roth, Lecturer in Psychology, Faculty of Social Sciences

Brenda Smith, Staff Tutor, Faculty of Social Sciences

Dr Richard Stevens, Senior Lecturer in Psychology, Faculty of Social Sciences

Colin Thomas, Lead Software Designer

Dr Kerry Thomas, Senior Lecturer in Psychology, Faculty of Social Sciences

Dr Frederick Toates, Reader in Psychobiology, Faculty of Science

Jenny Walker, Production Director, BBC/OU

Dr Helen Westcott, Lecturer in Psychology, Faculty of Social Sciences

Dr Clare Wood, Lecturer in Centre for Childhood, Development and Learning, Faculty of Education and Language Studies

Christopher Wooldridge, Editor

External authors and critical readers

Dr Koula Asimakopoulou, Tutor Panel

Debbie Balchin, Tutor Panel

Dr Peter Banister, Head of Psychology and Speech Pathology Department, Manchester Metropolitan University

Clive Barrett, Tutor Panel

Dr Kevin Buchanan, Senior Lecturer in Psychology, University College, Northampton

Dr Richard Cains, Tutor Panel

Professor Stephen Clift, Tutor Panel

Linda Corlett, Associate Lecturer, Faculty of Social Sciences

Victoria Culpin, Tutor Panel

Dr Tim Dalgleish, Research Clinical Psychologist, Brain Sciences Unit, Cambridge

Dr Graham Edgar, Tutor Panel, Research Scientist, BAE SYSTEMS

Patricia Fisher, Equal Opportunities critical reader

David Goddard, Tutor Panel

Dr Dan Goodley, Lecturer in Inclusive Education, University of Sheffield

Victoria Green, Student Panel

Dr Mary Hanley, Senior Lecturer in Psychology, University College, Northampton

Dr Jarrod Hollis, Associate Lecturer, Faculty of Social Sciences

Rob Jarman, Tutor Panel

Dr Hélène Joffe, Lecturer in Psychology, University College London

Dr Helen Kaye, Associate Lecturer, Faculty of Social Sciences

Professor Matt Lambon-Ralph, Professor of Cognitive Neuroscience, University of Manchester

Rebecca Lawthom, Senior Lecturer in Psychology, Manchester Metropolitan University

Kim Lock, Student Panel

Patricia Matthews, Tutor Panel

Dr Elizabeth Ockleford, Tutor Panel

Penelope Quest, Student Panel

Susan Ram, Student Panel

Dr Alex Richardson, Senior Research Fellow in Psychology and Neuroscience, Imperial College of Medicine, London, also Research Affiliate, University Laboratory of Physiology, Oxford

Dr Carol Sweeney, Tutor Panel

Dr Annette Thomson, Associate Lecturer, Faculty of Social Sciences

Dr Stella Tickle, Tutor Panel

Carol Tindall, Senior Lecturer in Psychology, Manchester Metropolitan University

Jane Tobbell, Senior Lecturer in Psychology, Manchester Metropolitan University

Martin Treacy, Associate Lecturer, Faculty of Social Sciences

Professor Aldert Vrij, Professor in Applied Social Psychology, University of Portsmouth

External assessors

Professor Martin Conway, Professor of Psychology, Durham University

Professor Anne Woollet, Professor of Psychology, University of East London

Psychology in the 21st century

Ann Phoenix and Kerry Thomas

Contents

1 Orientation

Psychological ideas are popular in everyday life because the subject matter of psychology is people and, hence, ourselves. Even if you have never studied any psychology before, it is likely that you will have encountered psychological ideas in the media or in discussions with other people. Psychological research findings and their practical and professional application are regularly in the newspapers, on television, radio, and on the Internet. For example, the possible evolutionary origins of behaviour, emotions, consciousness and the brain, and the impact of various therapies, are all recurrent debates in the media in many countries. These public debates help to make psychology a very visible part of everyday life and culture.

Yet, all this media coverage can confuse anyone wanting to find out what psychology is about because psychological knowledge is presented in a variety of ways. For example, 'common-sense' psychological ideas have long been presented in the media. A good illustration of this kind of common sense might be the topic of 'leadership', something that is commonly talked about in everyday language. Television, radio and newspapers often raise questions or offer un-researched opinions on leadership qualities, failures of leadership, why a historical figure was a charismatic leader or why some people seem to have the power to influence cults to engage in dramatic and often self-destructive behaviours. The media also can present rather dubious interpretations of psychology drawn upon largely to support the arguments journalists wanted to make in the first place, as when reporters contact psychologists hoping to get a ready quote about why holidays are stressful or why men hate shopping. More recently, however, and for our purposes more usefully, in many countries there are now books, articles, radio programmes and quite substantial television series dealing in a serious manner with psychological research and debate.

Activity 1

Try to think of examples of psychological topics you have encountered recently in the media. Write these down. Note your reactions to the way they were presented. Do you think they were handled in a serious, balanced way, giving relevant evidence, or were they treated in a superficial and perhaps journalistic manner? Have another look at these notes when you reach the end of this introductory chapter and see if you have changed your views.

As you work through this book you may find support for some of your ideas about psychology, but find that others are challenged because, not surprisingly, psychology is not entirely as it is portrayed in the media. We would like to welcome you to the study of psychology, and hope that by the time you have read this book you will be able to evaluate commonly presented psychological issues in an informed way.

Those of us who have written this book are excited by our subject matter. You will see as you go through the chapters that we have different areas of expertise and interest within psychology. One of the major aims of the book is to introduce you to that diversity and to invite you to share our enthusiasm. A discipline that encompasses such diversity and continues to be dynamic in producing new knowledge and new ways of looking at the world and human beings has much to offer.

1.1 Psychology has wide appeal

Some people will be doing this psychology course to consolidate earlier study and experience and to build a career. Others will be quite new to psychology as a formal research-based discipline. Some will have been stimulated to take a course in psychology by the well-publicized examples of research findings or psychologists at work that are presented in the media. Some will be coming to this course because of experiences in their own personal lives. This may be because they have been touched by especially difficult circumstances which they want to come to terms with, or because they feel the need to understand psychological topics such as identity, personality, relationships, intergroup relations or unconscious motivations. Others may have become curious about basic psychological questions such as how we perceive, the nature of memory, why we forget, and how we can understand the processes of learning. Psychologists working professionally, whether doing research or in their psychotherapeutic practices, can help us to think about such everyday issues.

Whilst no psychology course can promise definitive answers to all the questions in which you personally may be interested, the material in this first book, and the rest of the course, will increase your knowledge and your awareness, and provide ways of thinking about psychological issues of many kinds. In this introductory chapter we want to indicate how we have arrived at the contemporary, multifaceted discipline of twenty-first-century psychology and discuss some of the issues which psychologists debate and study.

Activity 2

Consider the suggestions we made about why people might be starting this course and then list *your own* reasons for studying psychology. Think about this question in some depth; don't stop at just one reason. Try to bring into mind anything that might be of relevance to you, especially at this particular point in your life. If you can, keep these notes until you reach the end of the course and then consider if, and how, the psychology you have studied has illuminated these original goals.

1.2 Psychology has social impact

The relevance of psychology to everyday concerns, and the ease with which it can be popularized and used, mean that psychological knowledge – some of it dubious, some of it accurate – is continually absorbed into culture and often incorporated into the very language we use. Examples of psychological concepts that have entered popular discourse include the notion that we are predisposed, both through evolution and through the functioning of our brains and nervous systems, to behave in certain ways and to have intellectual and emotional capacities and limitations. In many cultures psychoanalytic ideas are commonplace; for example, the centrality of sexuality and its repression, and the idea that Freudian 'slips' – mistakes of action – reveal unconscious motivation. Many people speak of having short-term and long-term memories and recognize that they use different strategies for remembering details of recent and more distant events. And a lot of people now know that it is possible to be fooled into perceiving illusions as real and that things as routine as face-recognition or behaviour-in-groups are extremely complex. Many people have absorbed and take for granted the psychological notion that what happens to us in childhood has an influence on our psychological functioning over the rest of our lives. Ideas about the importance of parenting and parental styles of child rearing have also become part of ordinary talk, with the result that some children now complain about not getting enough 'quality time' with their parents.

These examples demonstrate also how psychological concepts have an impact on the ways in which we think life should, ideally, be lived. Such ideas, and many others, have been influenced by psychological research, even when they are ideas that are not widely recognized as psychological. Furthermore, psychologists are increasingly being called on to give expert evidence on questions as disparate as legal decisions and design issues. It would, therefore, be true to say that psychology has an impact on our beliefs about ourselves and how life ought to be lived as well as on our everyday behaviours.

So far we have highlighted a pathway of influence *from* psychology *to* society. But this is not a one-way street. It is certainly the case that psychological research quite often addresses questions that originate in common-sense understandings. And this direction of influence between psychology and ordinary, everyday knowledge about people has led some to suggest that perhaps psychology is no more than common sense. However, as a field of enquiry, psychology is about much more than common sense, particularly in the way it investigates its subject matter.

Psychological knowledge advances through systematic research that is based on consciously articulated ideas. And psychology is evidence-based. Psychologists may *start* from the knowledge they already have by virtue of being people themselves. This can be knowledge about people and psychological processes that are common in the culture or it may come from personal experiences of dealing with the world. It is these kinds of knowledge that are often called *common sense*. For example, one tradition in the study of personality began from the ordinary-language adjectives that everyone uses to describe other people's characteristics; this will be discussed in Chapter 5 ('The individual differences approach to personality'). And many psychological researchers have chosen research topics and studied them in ways that seem to reflect their own life concerns; you will find a clear example of this in the next chapter on 'Identities and diversities' (Chapter 1).

However, evidence-based research findings quite often contradict the common-sense understandings of the time, and can produce new understandings that themselves eventually become accepted as common sense. For example, in the middle of the last century, it was widely accepted in Western societies that infants should not be 'spoiled' by being attended to every time they cried. Consequently, they were expected to learn to spend time without adult attention. But a wealth of psychological research from the 1960s onwards has reported that even very young infants are able to interact with other people in far more sophisticated ways than had been thought. And it has been found that they develop best when they receive plenty of stimulation from the people around them and their environments more generally. The idea of leaving infants to cry or to spend time alone is now much less accepted than it was. Instead, the notion that they need stimulation has become part of ordinary knowledge about child rearing and generated a multimillion dollar industry in the production of infant educational toys.

Although psychologists may begin from 'ordinary' knowledge or their own preoccupations, they usually start formulating their research questions using the existing body of psychological knowledge (the literature) and the evidence-based research that their colleagues and co-workers are engaged in (see Box 1). Sometimes technological developments can lead to entirely new research directions. These new directions might not have been envisaged through the application of common sense or using older evidence-based methods. One example of such a technology-driven new direction is *neuropsychology* and the increasing application of brain-imaging techniques as a way of furthering understanding of behaviour and mental processes. Other examples are advances in genetics and the decoding of the human genome, as well as computer-aided analysis of videotaped observations.

1 Using evidence: the cycle of enquiry

What do we mean when we say that psychology is an evidence-based discipline? The basic principle is that it is necessary to have some means of evaluating the answers to psychological research questions. Sherratt and her colleagues (Sherratt *et al.*, 2000) devised a 'circuit of knowledge' as a way to help students examine evidence and move away from common-sense reactions to psychological questions. We have used a version of this that we call the cycle of enquiry (see Figure 1).

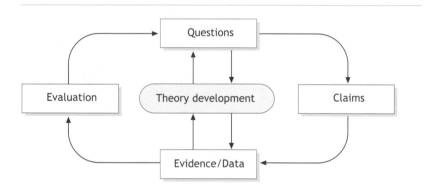

Figure 1 The cycle of enquiry (Source: based on Sherratt *et al.*, 2000, pp.17–18)

There are four elements in the cycle of enquiry:
1 Psychological research starts with the framing of appropriate, answerable *questions*.
2 The answers to these questions are *claims*. These claims have to be clearly identified so that they can be thoroughly assessed.
3 Assessing claims requires the amassing of information called *data*. The word 'data' is a plural word for the building blocks that make up the *evidence* that is presented in support of a claim.
4 The evidence then has to be interpreted and evaluated. The process of *evaluation* often generates new questions to be addressed as well as providing support for, or disconfirmation of, the original claims.

1.3 The diversity of psychology

Since psychology is concerned with the full range of what makes us human, it is not surprising that the scope of the discipline is extensive. Psychology has always been a diverse, multi-perspective discipline. This partly results from its origins. Psychological questions were asked first by philosophers, then increasingly by biologists, physiologists and medical scientists. The diverse origins of psychology are visible if we consider four 'founders' of psychology – all of whom produced influential work at the end of the nineteenth century and who will be mentioned in later chapters.

Charles Darwin, 1809–1882

Wilhelm Wundt, 1832–1920

William James, 1842–1910

Sigmund Freud, 1856–1939

In 1877, Charles Darwin, the biologist who later put forward the theory of evolution, was doing the first scientific infant-observation study, observing and writing about his son's behaviours and emotions in descriptive psychological terms. Darwin was trying to make inferences about what his baby's internal mental states might be, based on what he could observe 'from the outside'. Darwin went on to become a renowned biological scientist whose methods were essentially the painstaking collection, description, categorization and cataloguing of biological diversity. These were the data that later provided the evidence for his theory of evolution.

Wilhelm Wundt is considered by many to have started psychology as a formal discipline when he opened the first psychological laboratory in 1879 in Leipzig, Germany. He was interested both in philosophical and physiological questions and, as a result, advocated a range of methodological approaches to collecting evidence. His own methods included use of the *scientific experimental method, introspection* (asking people to think about and report on their inner feelings and experiences), and *ethnography* (observations of human culture).

William James, an American professor trained in philosophy, medicine and physiology, who published the influential *Principles of Psychology* in 1890, also advocated a multi-method approach that included introspection and observation. Sigmund Freud, the first psychoanalyst, was a medical doctor and research physiologist who opened his psychology consulting room in Vienna in 1869. Freud, working at the same time as Wundt and James, pioneered a method that involved listening closely to people's personal *accounts* of their symptoms, emotions, and their lives more generally, asking insightful questions and attending to the particulars of language use and unconscious phenomena.

The methods established by Darwin, Wundt, James and Freud – observation and description, experimentation, introspection and a focus on language – provided psychology with the beginnings of its diverse traditions. Some of these continue to be influential, whilst others have lost favour or been substantially developed.

Although psychology has diverse roots, psychologists with different approaches and methods have not always happily coexisted. There have been many heated debates about the scope of the subject matter and methods that can be claimed to be psychological. Many of the clashes have been about what can be thought of as 'real' or 'legitimate' evidence. But it has not just been individuals with their own inspirations and beliefs who have introduced particular ways of doing psychology. Different historical periods, cultures and countries generate their own assumptions about what to study and how knowledge, including psychological knowledge is, therefore, situated in time and place.

A graphic example of this concerns the impact of the Second World War on the development of Western psychology. Many Jewish German psychologists and others from German-occupied territories fled, some to Britain (for example, Freud), but most to the USA. These eminent psychologists brought their substantial influence – their ideas and European way of thinking about psychology – to universities in the USA where psychology was expanding. And then the horror at what had happened in Nazi Germany led some psychologists to direct their research to issues like authoritarianism, conformity, prejudice, leadership, small-group dynamics and attitudes.

It is not only cataclysmic events that have led to change and development in psychology. There have also been gradual cultural shifts in ways of thinking about how knowledge should be gained and evaluated. It is perhaps not surprising that different historical periods can produce dominant trends in psychology that occur almost simultaneously in different countries – no doubt influenced by international contacts between psychologists. It is striking, for example, how *laboratories* devoted to systematic psychological research were initially founded in several Western countries within about 10 years of each other (see Table 1). But the climate of thought can also be very different in different countries and the topics and methods of psychological research, at a given time, may be very different across different countries.

Table 1 Foundation of early psychological laboratories

Germany:	1879 (Wundt opened the first psychological laboratory in Leipzig)
USA:	1883 (American Psychological Association founded in 1892)
Denmark:	1886
Russia:	1886
Japan:	1888
France:	1889
Italy:	1889
Canada:	1890
Belgium:	1891
Switzerland:	1891
United Kingdom:	1891 (British Psychological Society founded in 1901)
Netherlands:	1892

Source: adapted from Zimbardo et al., 1995, p.6

In psychology, different historical times have also been characterized by the dominance of different methods and theories. For example, dissatisfaction with the limitations of introspection as a method of enquiry – resulting from the difficulty of reporting on conscious experience – gradually developed in the early twentieth century. This difficulty with the method of looking inward into the conscious mind and with the kinds of data that can be collected by this means led to the rise of *behaviourism*, which became dominant in the 1940s and 1950s. Behaviourism insists that psychologists should study *only* behaviours that are observable from the outside and should make no inferences at all about mental states and what might be going on inside the head.

Then, in the 1960s, there was a 'cognitive revolution', a rather dramatic phrase which describes what was indeed an important shift in thinking about psychology. Many (although not all) researchers in psychology began to take a greater interest in what goes on in the mind. This change of perspective led to what is known as *cognitive psychology*. The shift began with the study of learning, as you will see in Chapter 3 ('Three approaches to learning'), but became established as the study of information processing associated with mental activities such as attention, perception and memory. Researchers in cognitive psychology did not return to introspective methods but devised other ways of testing their ideas about mental processes. They have, for the most part, continued the tradition of using experimental methods but have adapted them to investigate what goes on in the mind; for example, by finding out how well people remember words presented in lists of related words (e.g. 'Fox' in a list of animals), compared with words presented in lists of unrelated words. A clear behavioural measure (the numbers of words remembered) can be used to make inferences about how the lists have been processed and how memory works. This scientific experimental method continues to be dominant within psychology.

More recently, there has been a second cognitive revolution; this time the shift being a broadening of focus from mental processes to studying how meaning is understood through cultural practices and language. As a result there are a variety of methods available to psychologists who want to study language and culture. And many psychologists who conduct experimental investigations of cognitive or social processes now also attend to participants' own accounts of their experiences.

All areas of psychology are increasingly concerned with investigating issues relevant to people's everyday functioning and their social and cultural contexts. The practical and professional application of psychology is important in many areas of life. Psychologists work as professional advisors, consultants or therapists in a range of settings such as education, the workplace, sport and mental health; and they increasingly research areas of immediate practical concern such as dyslexia, stress, police interviewing of eye-witnesses, and autism. For many people, one of the most salient aspects of mental life is our awareness and experience of our own consciousness. In the last three decades there has been a revival of interest in our awareness of consciousness and the whole mysterious phenomenon of consciousness itself. It is proving to be a topic that can be studied from several different perspectives. For example, some approaches to consciousness are essentially biological, such as neuropsychological investigations of brain processes, some are cognitive, exploring mental processes, some are social, some are from humanistic psychology and some are from psychoanalysis.

So, whilst earlier traditions like psychoanalysis or behaviourism still contribute and produce important innovations, the discipline of psychology has continued to develop in ways which have fostered an ever broader range of perspectives. No one approach is either 'right', or adequate for answering all psychological questions. As a result, psychology is now seen as legitimately multifaceted, with many traditions working in parallel, and also drawing on other disciplines and their methods for inspiration. The chapters that follow in this book demonstrate this psychological diversity by covering identities, evolutionary psychology, learning, biological psychology, personality, perception and attention, experimental social psychology, memory, psychoanalytic psychology and humanistic psychology.

The second book in the course (*Challenging Psychological Issues*) covers a selection of topics in psychology (such as consciousness and language) that present a challenge for psychologists to study and that have been usefully examined from a number of different perspectives. The third book (*Applying Psychology*) presents examples of applied psychological research.

1.4 Exploring psychology: context and history

Since psychology is diverse, and has changed and continues to change, it is helpful for an understanding of the discipline to map these changes over time and illustrate the patterns of influence of people and events. For this reason we have constructed an interactive CD-ROM to accompany the course. We have called this *EPoCH* (i.e. 'Exploring Psychology's Context and History'). *EPoCH* is designed as a resource to give you an indication of the historical period and place in which the psychologists you study were working and provide some details on the individual people concerned. Making use of *EPoCH* should help you gain a sense of their historical location, the cultural influences on their thinking, how they group together in terms of direct contact and influence on each other, and also the impact of traditions of psychology. *EPoCH* is essentially an exploratory resource. You will be able to navigate your own way through, following your own particular interests or researching a specific question. In this way you will be able to develop your understanding of how psychology has come to be what it is today. This resource will be especially useful to you as you read and study the commentary sections – the editorial discussions that follow Chapters 1 to 9 in this book.

Summary Section 1

- In many societies and cultures psychology is now a very visible part of everyday life.
- This book aims to increase your knowledge of psychology and provide you with the tools to think about psychological issues.
- In many countries psychology has an impact on policy, practice and culture in general.
- Psychological research and knowledge may sometimes be developed from common sense, but, as a discipline, psychology is different from common sense in that it is evidence-based and the result of systematic research.
- Psychology has diverse roots – in medicine, philosophy, biology, psychoanalysis and ethnography.
- Psychological knowledge, like all knowledge, is a product of different cultures, historical periods, ways of thinking, developing technologies and the acceptability of different methods and kinds of evidence.
- There is no single 'right' way to answer psychological questions: psychology, at the start of the twenty-first century, is a multifaceted discipline.

2 The breadth of psychological research

We have seen that psychology is an evidence-based enterprise and we have also seen that disputes about what *should* count as evidence have had an important impact on the development of psychology as a discipline. For example, the rise of behaviourism was driven by the idea that only observable behaviour is legitimate data for psychology because only data that can be observed by others, and agreed upon, can be *objective*. Many other disciplines have had less trouble with this issue, partly because they have fewer choices about which methods to use, what kinds of data to collect and what kinds of evidence to accept. Think, for example, of mechanical engineering, chemistry or geology and compare these with psychology. The range of choices open to psychologists arises from the complexity of their subject matter – understanding and explaining humans and, to a lesser extent, other species.

Psychology is unusual because its subject matter (ourselves) is not only extremely complex but also reactive, and because we are inevitably involved in it, personally, socially and politically. This involvement is part of what fuels debates about how to do psychology and what counts as legitimate data.

This section will give some examples of how the unusual nature of psychology as a subject influences the practice of research. We shall look at the impact of our 'involvement' on how research questions are formulated, at the various kinds of evidence that could be used, and at the range of methods that are available to collect the evidence and to evaluate findings.

2.1 Researching ourselves

Psychology aims to provide understandings of us, as humans. At a personal level this closeness to our private concerns draws us in and excites us. However, since psychologists are humans, and hence are researching issues just as relevant to themselves as to their research participants, they can be attracted towards researching certain topics and maybe away from others. This is perhaps more evident for psychological research that is most clearly of social relevance. At a societal level all kinds of social, cultural and political pressures, explicit or subtle, can influence or dictate what kinds of psychology, which topics and which theories, are given priority and funding. Until relatively recently, for example, it was difficult to obtain funding for research that was based on qualitative methods. This was because there was an erroneous belief in psychology, and in the culture more generally, that qualitative research could only help in gaining very specific and idiosyncratic understandings of particular individuals and could not make any useful contribution to broader understandings of people and psychological processes.

At a more personal level, what might psychologists bring to their theorizing and research? Think about Freud. Many writers have speculated on what might have influenced Freud's work. One of his basic propositions was that all small boys, at approximately 5 years of age, are in love with and possessive about their mothers, seeing their fathers as frightening rivals. He called this the 'Oedipus complex'. We don't have to think too hard to realize that there could be a link between Freud's idea that the Oedipus complex is universal (applies to all male children in all cultures) and Freud's own childhood. He was the eldest son of a young and reputedly beautiful second wife to his elderly father. In the next chapter in this book, Chapter 1 ('Identities and diversities'), you will meet another example, where the early personal life of the influential psychologist, Erik Erikson, may have affected his later theorizing about the difficulty of finding an identity during adolescence. This kind of personal basis for theorizing is why we have included biographical information on *EPoCH* and biography boxes in some of the chapters.

Freud and his mother (1872)

It is possible also that our desires, beliefs and ideologies define not only *what* we want to study but also *how we interpret our findings.* Bradley (1989) alerts us to this possibility in relation to the study of children when he argues that different theorists have found support for their own theories from their observations of children. This indicates that personal values and beliefs are important in influencing the ways in which we view the world. Suppose you were engaged in an observational study of the effect on children's aggressive behaviour of viewing aggression on television. If you felt strongly about this issue, your observations of the way that children play after watching aggressive programmes might be biased by what you believe. It would be difficult to be objective because your own feelings, beliefs and values (your *subjectivity*) would have affected the evidence. Personal prejudices, cognitive biases, 'bad days' and unconscious factors can affect what we 'see' when we observe other people. We shall see later in this chapter and throughout the book how the experimental method has endeavoured to minimize this kind of subjectivity, whilst other approaches – those concerned essentially with meanings and with people's inner worlds – have used subjectivity (people's reflections on themselves) itself as a form of data.

2.2 A brief look at different kinds of data

For a long time there has been a very important argument about what are the 'legitimate data' of psychology – what can and should be used as evidence. We have already seen that, from the very beginnings of psychology as a formal discipline, psychologists have used experimental methods, observations and introspection. In one form or another these methods continue to be central to psychology. The experimental method, adapted from traditional science, has most consistently been considered the dominant psychological method, providing data which can be 'seen from the outside' (outsider viewpoint) without recourse to introspection or people's own accounts of their mental states (insider viewpoint). However, as the research questions asked by psychologists have changed over time, research methods have broadened to include a range of different methods that produce different kinds of data. *Outsider viewpoints* gained from experiments and observations and *insider viewpoints* from introspection, interviews and analyses of what people say (and how they say it) all flourish as part of psychology in the twenty-first century. What *are* the legitimate data of a multi-perspective psychology? What can different kinds of data usefully bring to psychology?

A simple scheme can be used that divides the varieties of *data* into four categories.

Behaviour

First, for many decades, 'behaviour' has provided the most dominant kind of evidence – what people and animals can be seen to do. Behaviour can cover a very wide range of activities. Think about examples such as a rat finding its way through a maze to a pellet of food, a participant in a memory experiment writing down words five minutes after having done a memorizing task, a small group of children who are observed whilst they, jointly, use a computer to solve a problem, a teenager admitting to frequent truancy on a questionnaire. Some of these examples are behaviours that are very precisely defined and involve measurements – how fast the rat runs, how many words are remembered. This would be classed as quantitative research (i.e. with measurements and probably a statistical analysis). Other behaviours, such as the children learning to solve a problem using a computer, are less well defined but can be observed and described in detail, qualitatively (i.e. not measured and subjected to statistical analysis), or sometimes quantitatively (for example, when the frequency of particular actions can be counted up). The truancy example involves a *self-report* about behaviour that is not actually seen by the researcher. These particular examples of behaviours as data come from quite different psychological research traditions which you will learn about in the chapters that follow. The important point here is that behaviour is, in principle, observable – and often measurable in relatively objective ways – from the outside.

Inner experiences

A second kind of data is people's inner experiences, including their feelings, beliefs and motives. These cannot be directly seen from the outside; they remain private unless freely spoken about or expressed in some other way. Examples of these inner experiences include feelings, thoughts, images, representations, dreams, fantasies, beliefs and motivations or reasons. These are only accessible to others via verbal or written reports or as inferred from behaviours such as non-verbal communications. Access to this insider viewpoint relies on people's ability and willingness to convey what they are experiencing, and it is always problematic to study. This is because we often do not have the words to say what we experience, or we are not sufficiently aware of what we are experiencing, and/or cannot describe experiences quickly enough or in ways that others would understand. And parts of our inner worlds may be unavailable to consciousness. The psychoanalytic approach (which you will meet in Chapter 9) suggests, for example, that much of what we do is driven by unconscious motives, making it difficult or impossible to give accounts of our motivations. An example of the kind of data that comes from the insider viewpoint is people's answers to the question 'Who am I?', which you will meet in the next chapter as a method for studying identity. Notice, however, that there is a paradox here. Although the data are essentially from the inside, the very process of collecting and interpreting the data inevitably introduces an outsider viewpoint. Sometimes the researcher can focus as far as possible on the subjectivity of the data – its meaning for the individual concerned – in effect, trying to see and think about the data 'through the eyes of the other'. This is what happens most of the time in psychoanalytic sessions. But for other purposes the researcher may stand further back from the individual and impose 'outsider' categories and meanings on the data. This, too, happens in psychoanalytic sessions when the analyst makes an interpretation of the patient's account from an outside, theoretical or 'expert' position.

Material data

A third kind of data is 'material' and provides more direct evidence from bodies and brains. This comes from biological psychology and includes biochemical analyses of hormones, cellular analyses, decoding of the human genome and neuropsychological technologies such as brain-imaging techniques. The data that can be collected from the various forms of brain imaging provide direct evidence about structures in the brain and brain functioning, enabling direct links to be made with behaviours and mental processes. For example, in Chapter 8 ('Memory: structures, processes and skills') you will read about different kinds of failure of remembering, each of which can be shown to be associated with injury to particular locations in the brain. A familiar example of material evidence is the lie-detector technique where the amount of sweat that is excreted under stress changes the electrical conductivity of the skin.

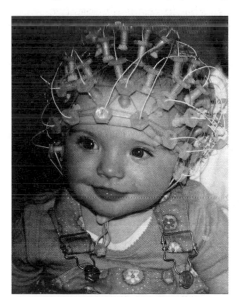

Psychologists at Birkbeck College, University of London, have pioneered a method of studying brain activity in infants as they attend to different pictures

The actual raw data are the measures of the amount of current that passes through the skin, but these data are a direct indication of the amount of sweat produced, which in turn is an indicator of stress and so assumed to be evidence of lying.

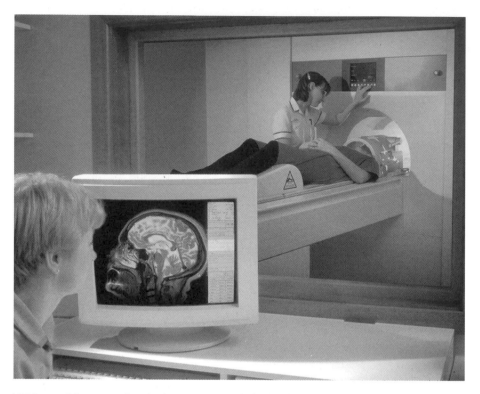

While participants are in a brain scanner, psychologists (or doctors) view their brains on a linked computer

Symbolic data

The fourth kind of data is essentially symbolic – symbolic creations of minds, such as the texts people have written, their art, what they have said (recorded and transcribed), the exact ways they use language and the meanings they have communicated. These *symbolic data* are the products of minds, but once created they can exist and be studied and analysed quite separately from the particular minds that created them. These kinds of data are used to provide evidence of meanings, and the processes that construct and communicate meanings. You will meet an example of this kind of data, and how it is used, at the end of the next chapter where the language – the actual form of words – used to describe an identity is shown to give a specific meaning to that identity. And the aim of the research is to understand the process of meaning-making rather than understand the inner world of the particular person who spoke the words. The point about these approaches is that they see language as constructive – the speakers (or writers), those with the inside viewpoint, are not always aware of what they are constructing. In general we could say that this fourth kind of data is analysed from an outsider viewpoint that attempts to take the insider viewpoint seriously, but does not privilege it.

2.3 A brief look at psychological methods

We have looked briefly at the kinds of data that psychologists use as the basis for their evidence and we now offer an overview of the *methods* used to collect these data. Learning about methods is a skill necessary to building up psychological knowledge and moving beyond the base of common-sense knowledge about people that we all use. This section will outline the fundamentals of research procedures and provide you with a terminology – the beginnings of a research language that will help you to understand psychology as well as to evaluate research findings presented in the media.

You will learn a great deal more about methods as you proceed with this book and the other parts of the course. There will be opportunities to try out methods in some of your assignments, and at the Residential School; and you will put together a 'methods file' of your project work and other material concerned with research methods. The first set of these methods materials will introduce the range of research methods typically used by psychologists, discussed in more detail than we can here. The course 'workbook' will also give you opportunities to consolidate your knowledge of the research process.

The beginning of the research process

What distinguishes psychological research from common sense is that psychologists approach information and knowledge in a systematic and *consciously articulated* way. They use rules and procedures about how to build and apply theories, how to design studies to test hypotheses, how to collect data and use them as evidence, and how to evaluate all forms of knowledge. (See Figure 1, 'The cycle of enquiry' in Box 1.)

The start of the research process requires a gradual narrowing of the field. A topic has to be chosen, concepts have to be defined and the aims of the research have to be clearly specified. The process of choosing a topic or area to research will be influenced by one of several factors that usually interrelate. In practice, researchers come to a field of study already constrained by many factors. They bring with them their personal concerns. They may be part of a research group where the topic is already defined and the project is under way. They are likely to be working with a particular set of theoretical assumptions by virtue of their location – in time and in a culture, a society, a particular university, and a particular interest group. Certain types of research question are fashionable; some attract funding, some don't. Researchers generally already have ideas about what would be an 'appropriate' theory. In other words, they have preconceptions about 'the nature of people', what would be a suitable question, and what would be acceptable evidence. What all this means is that research is done within a context that is made up of assumptions about the subject matter and the ways in which it should be studied. This kind of context is called a *paradigm.*

Researchers have to ensure that research is relevant and establish what research has already been done on the topic by examining the existing literature. This helps to ensure that they do not unintentionally repeat what has previously been done or found to be a dead end.

The research question itself has to be answerable; many questions about human psychology that might seem to make good sense could not usefully be researched. For example, the question 'Why do we remember?' is potentially interesting but it is not sufficiently precise to be the basis of a research project. It does not, for example, distinguish whether we should look for parts of the brain that are associated with memory, or consider the mental strategies that facilitate memory, or investigate the social and emotional motivations that make it more likely that we will remember some things rather than others.

However, we can ask a more specific question, such as 'Are different areas of our brain involved in remembering familiar, compared with unfamiliar, faces?' This question serves to guide us towards using the technique of brain imaging in an experimental setting – recording images of brain activity whilst the research participants try to remember either familiar or unfamiliar faces. It is then possible to formulate a *hypothesis* (a testable claim) about the relationship between brain functioning and memory for faces. We may, for example, hypothesize that more areas of the brain will be involved in remembering familiar compared with unfamiliar faces. Then we have to work out exactly what is going to count as a familiar, as opposed to an unfamiliar, face; for example, close family members in an ongoing relationship as opposed to people never before encountered. We also have to work out how the raw data of the brain images will be interpreted and how they will be used – will it be a comparison of locations of activity or a measurement of the extent of brain activity? This process of defining concepts and making them useable in practice is called *operationalizing* the research problem.

Many areas of psychology require that researchers generate hypotheses before they start the process of research investigation. These are usually the areas of psychology and the traditions where research is already well-established. But in a new area or in a tradition where exploration and detailed description is itself the research goal, research begins without specific hypotheses. Darwin's work of describing, cataloguing and categorizing species is an example of research in what was then a new area, before any theory was devised and therefore without hypotheses. Since that time, his theory of evolution has generated many hypotheses which have been tested; some of these will be discussed in Chapter 2 ('Evolutionary psychology'). On the other hand, in Chapter 1 you will read about research on identities, some of which aims to understand how people think about their identities rather than test hypotheses about identity.

Once the research question has been devised and the problem operationalized, researchers then need to decide on the people they are going to include in their research – the *participants*. For the 'memory for faces' question mentioned above, the possible population for the research could be everyone in the country and it is obviously impossible to study them all. It is, therefore, necessary to work out what the *sample* should be. The researcher may, for example, have negotiated permission to ask for volunteers from a particular company. She may then define the sample as 'one volunteer in every 20', chosen at random. Since the volunteers will be undergoing brain imaging, each participant would be brought into the specialist hospital for access to the imaging technology. For this study, it is clear that brain imaging will be the method used to collect data and the data will be the actual images produced, although these images have to be 'read' and interpreted and converted into evidence.

The example above uses direct imaging which is a neuropsychological technique, but it is used as part of an experiment (i.e. comparing the effect on brain activity of viewing familiar and unfamiliar faces). The most commonly used psychological methods are experiments, questionnaires, interviews, psychological tests, observations, and meaning and language-based methods.

Experiments

Experiments, the most common psychological method, are used to try to discover if there are causal relationships between *variables* (so called because their values can vary). If, for example, the variable we are interested in is the time taken for drivers to react to an emergency, we may devise an experiment where we *manipulate* the noise levels in their cars to see whether this has any impact. In this case, the noise level in the car will be the *independent variable* and the driver's response time (a behaviour which we hypothesize is dependent on in-car noise levels) will be the *dependent variable*. This sort of experiment may take place in a driving simulator in a laboratory or on private roads. In an experiment, there are often two groups of participants: a *control group* that is not subjected to the manipulation of the independent variable and an *experimental group* that is subjected to the manipulation. In the example here, the control group may not be subjected to any in-car noise at all. Findings from experiments are analysed statistically. Psychologists using experimental methods have a number of techniques at their disposal to ensure that they do not simply find what they expect or what they want to find. These include *random allocation* to groups where the researcher does not choose whether a participant goes into the experimental or control group, and '*blind scoring*', where those who score a participant's behaviour do not know which group the participant belongs to.

Questionnaires and interviews

If we are interested in what people think or feel, or in behaviours that are difficult to observe in humans, we need to *ask* people about themselves. This is a variant on introspection, in that researchers are not looking inside themselves but are using the best possible means to obtain other people's introspections. Psychologists do this through both questionnaires and interviews. Many of you will have filled in questionnaires from market researchers on the street or at home. *Questionnaires* are written questions designed to elicit short answers or choices between options. They can be completed whether or not the researcher is there and so can be used with thousands of people in a study. For this reason they are usually tightly structured, with questions asked in an invariant order and often with the range of possible answers worked out in advance so that the data can easily be entered into a computer for statistical analysis.

Interviews are face-to-face conversations between a researcher and an interviewee or group of interviewees. Since they are face-to-face, samples used are usually smaller than for questionnaires. Interviews can be tightly structured (as for questionnaires) or more open-ended. They can, therefore, be analysed either quantitatively and statistically, or qualitatively, where researchers transcribe tape-recordings of the interviews, read them repeatedly and analyse their themes.

Examples of questionnaire and group interviews

Psychological tests

The most commonly used *psychological tests*, such as intelligence tests and personality tests, are highly structured forms of self-report where participants have to solve problems or choose from fixed alternatives on a questionnaire. Researchers then work out a score for each participant that gives information about their intelligence or personality. These tests are different from ordinary questionnaires in the way they are constructed and pre-tested. They are tried out on large numbers of people before being used as research or diagnostic tools. This gives a picture of how the test scores are distributed across the population for which the test is designed. It is, therefore, possible to compare a particular individual's test scores with the average from the population and to make statistical comparisons between different groups. You will learn about these tests in Chapter 5 ('The individual differences approach to personality').

Observations

Observations are the most direct method of getting information about people's behaviour. In everyday life we all frequently observe other people. Psychologists have devised a range of methods for systematically observing other people. These range from participant observation through to highly structured and targeted observations. In *participant observation*, the researcher is part of what is being observed and writes up notes whenever possible. Sometimes these notes include an insider viewpoint account of how the researcher is feeling. A well-known example is that of Rosenhan and seven collaborators in the 1970s who, although not ill, feigned mental illness and managed to get themselves admitted to a psychiatric hospital (Rosenhan, 1973). Once in the hospital they behaved 'normally', i.e. as they would in the outside world. They kept notes of all they observed (outsider viewpoint) and what they experienced (insider viewpoint), including the experience of having their 'normal' behaviour and talk interpreted as evidence of their mental illness. (They had a lot of trouble getting discharged from the hospital.) The data from observations such as these are analysed qualitatively, paying attention to meanings and to the place of the researcher in the observation.

In more *structured observations*, researchers may have clear categories of behaviour on which they know they want to focus. They may choose a specific individual such as a target child in a school, perhaps counting the number of times that child makes a friendly approach to another child and noting down what is said. They may also observe through a one-way mirror so that they are not visible to the people being observed and, hence, do not interfere with whatever is being observed. These kinds of observations can be analysed either quantitatively and statistically, or qualitatively.

Meaning and language-based methods

In recent years many psychologists have become interested in language as an important human 'product' (the symbolic data described in Section 2.2 above). There are various ways in which psychologists analyse conversations, data from interviews and written texts. One of the most popular methods is *content analysis*, which involves counting up the prevalence and sequencing of certain words, sentences, expressions, metaphors, etc. in texts such as newspaper articles or transcripts of interviews. It can also be used to identify the types of explanations people give for their own behaviour or use in order to persuade people to support them or agree with their argument. It is predominantly a quantitative method.

Another popular method is *discourse analysis*. This is a qualitative method that provides detailed analyses of exactly what language is used and how it is used. For example, discourse analysts would try to identify the rhetorical devices by which we all as speakers seek to persuade each other of our arguments, and the functions served by various discourses. Discourse analysts do not aim to find 'the truth' about how people use language. They are more interested in the processes whereby people construct meanings socially and individually. Most discourse analysts are interested in subjectivity – people's own sense making – and often include an analysis of the researcher's own subjective understandings as part of the analysis of data, thus using a mixture of insider and outsider viewpoints. Discourse analysis is an example of a *hermeneutic* approach. Hermeneutic approaches focus on meaning-making; that is, the work of interpretation. People are treated as meaning-producers, with the task of the psychologist being to interpret meanings. Hermeneutic approaches, therefore, tend to use qualitative methods (rather than measuring variables, taking group averages and drawing conclusions with the help of statistics as in experimental and other quantitative methods). The data they produce tend to relate to particular individuals in specific contexts, rather than generalizing to a population as a whole.

Different paradigms and different methods

These different methodologies alert us to the fact that psychology is not just one enterprise, but a series of interlocking enterprises in which psychologists have different views about the best ways to try to understand or explain people and their behaviour and experience. These are arguments about *epistemology*; that is, what questions to ask, what sort of evidence to look for, what sort of criteria to use to evaluate explanations, and what sort of methods to use.

All knowledge and all efforts to gain knowledge operate in a context, a set of connected and compatible assumptions about what exists and the way to gain knowledge of it. And we have already seen that research is done within a paradigm, which is a philosophical framework made up of assumptions about the subject matter and the ways in which it should be studied, including the methods and the kinds of data that are considered to be legitimate. The doing of psychology within a given paradigm will, in this book, be referred to as a *psychological perspective*. The coexistence of different perspectives means that there are debates between psychologists operating in different paradigms, as Peter Barnes explains:

> *By now you will have gathered that there is no one approach to the study of psychology – each approach has its advocates and each has attracted its critics. At any one time some approaches are in the ascendant while others are in the doldrums. Different views exist on what subjects are worthy of investigation – and even on whether it is possible to investigate them – and these, too, have fashions.*
>
> *(Barnes, 1985, p.28)*

The chapters which follow build on this brief review of methods, in that each chapter highlights and discusses particular 'featured methods' that are important to the area of psychology being written about – at the same time as providing detail of studies that have contributed to the area. These featured methods will allow you an opportunity to get to grips with the kinds of methods that are characteristic of different paradigms in psychology.

Research methods will be taught elsewhere in the course, including booklets in your methods materials, on video, in your statistics book (Dancey and Reidy, 2002) and in the workbook. There are research projects so that you can try different methods as part of your assignments and at the Residential School. You should keep your methods materials all in one place in a ring binder.

2.4 Ethical considerations

Since psychological research is mostly done on people and animals, it is often the case that the observations or experimental interventions that a psychologist might want to make have the potential to harm participants and hence raise ethical issues. Furthermore, consequences that might not be directly undesirable for the participants might raise more general ethical principles to do with moral standards and values. Psychologists have increasingly become aware of ethical issues and recognized that psychological research has sometimes been ethically questionable.

An example from the middle of the last century illustrates this. Between 1959 and 1962 Professor Henry Murray, a personality theorist, carried out a series of experiments on 22 undergraduate men at Harvard University in the USA. These were designed to measure how people respond to stressful interpersonal confrontations during mock interrogations. The aim appears to have been to understand which types of men were likely to be able to withstand brainwashing and interrogation in situations of war. Murray had been engaged in work relevant to this issue during the Second World War. Participants were volunteers who were given a small fee and simply asked if they would be willing to contribute to the solution of 'certain psychological problems'. They were placed in brilliantly lit rooms, filmed through a hole in the wall, and were connected to electrodes that recorded their heart and respiratory rates. While the students had been told that they would be debating their views with another undergraduate, they were actually faced with an older, more sophisticated opponent who belittled their values, making the students feel humiliated and helpless, and rousing them to a great deal of anger. After spending approximately 200 hours as research participants, they were still not clear what the research was about. Chase (2000) suggests that even 25 years later some of the participants recalled how unpleasant was the whole experience. More seriously, however, one of the participants in these experiments was Theodore Kaczynski, who became a student at Harvard in the spring of 1958, when he was only 15 years old. He was later to be nicknamed 'the Unabomber' for mailing or delivering 16 parcel bombs to scientists, academics and others over a 17-year period, killing three and injuring 23. Obviously, it is not possible to say what effect, if any, taking part in Murray's study had on Kaczynski. However, one of his major resentments against scientists was because he felt that they were trying to develop techniques for controlling people's behaviour.

It is not clear whether or not Murray's research has been applied to the control of behaviour by any governments. However, in the 1970s, Tim Shallice (an influential British cognitive psychologist) argued that psychological research on sensory deprivation has been used by governments (including the British government in Northern Ireland) to devise successful methods of preparing prisoners for interrogation. In sensory deprivation experiments, psychologists study the effects of depriving people of sensation by, for example, confining them in isolation in a bed or suspended in a warm water tank. Participants may be kept in the dark or in a room with either no sound or constant 'white noise' – which sounds rather like a radio turned on, but not tuned into any station. Most participants become anxious and disoriented after between 3½ and 10 hours in these conditions, with some reporting nightmares afterwards. According to Shallice, such research proliferated because it has been funded by the military. Shallice (1972, p.385) argues that there should be 'more stringent editorial control of papers on sensory deprivation in order to reduce the chances' of their being misused to break the resistance of prisoners. There have, therefore, been areas of psychological research whose application raises difficult ethical issues.

In the Murray study, and arguably in sensory deprivation experiments, the potential psychological benefits of the study are far from clear. However, ethical concerns have been raised about two rather more famous US experiments, the findings of which many psychologists see as invaluable. In the 1970s, Zimbardo set up a mock prison in his psychology department. He then randomly assigned Stanford student volunteers to 'guard' or 'prisoner' status. In an experiment designed to last two weeks, the 'guards' became so harsh and the 'prisoners' so distressed that the

Stanford prison experiment: dejected 'prisoner'

experiment was terminated after six days. This experiment is discussed further in Chapter 5 ('The individual differences approach to personality'). Follow-ups over several years showed no apparent long-term ill effects of the experiment (Zimbardo *et al.*, 1995). Although the experiment is often praised for its dramatic demonstration of how easily people could fall into 'bad gaoler' or 'victim prisoner' roles in socially produced situations, the question of whether it is ethically defensible to put people into such situations is still hotly debated. For example, would it be possible to arrive at these findings in other ways?

Similarly, Milgram's classic 1963 experiment, on the relationship between obedience to authority and aggression, continues to stimulate ethical debate. His study was an attempt to research a complex social behaviour, compliance with orders to be aggressive to another person, by taking it out of a real-life context and bringing it into the psychological laboratory. This is an example of research informed by a concern to understand the atrocities committed during the Second World War. Participants were told that this was an experiment to test the effect of punishment on learning. The person to whom they believed they were administering shocks was actually Milgram's confederate who pretended that he was being shocked. The real participants (who were non-student men) were 'instructed to "move one level higher on the shock generator each time the learner gives a wrong answer"' (Milgram, 1974, pp.20–1). Of the 40 participants, 26 continued obeying the orders of the experimenter to the point where

Stanley Milgram, 1933–1984

they had administered what they believed were potentially fatal shocks (by pushing two switches labelled 'XXX' on the control panel which were beyond the switch labelled 'Danger: Severe Shock'). The participants were told afterwards, in what is known as a *debriefing* session, that they had not inflicted any pain, but many of them, after realizing the implications of what they had been doing, became extremely upset. However, Milgram (1974) sent a follow-up questionnaire to his entire sample and 92 per cent of them returned it. Only 1 per cent of them reported that they were sorry to have participated in the study.

The ethical dilemma raised by this study concerns whether its potential benefit in helping us to understand how human beings can commit atrocities against each other outweighs the stress and pain it may have caused. Milgram believed that the participants in his series of experiments demonstrated a parallel psychological process to Nazi guards' obedience to authority in Germany in the Second World War. He considered that his studies were 'principally concerned with the ordinary and routine destruction carried out by everyday people following orders' (Milgram, 1974, p.178).

The dramatic findings from both Zimbardo's and Milgram's studies suggest that it is all too easy for negative aspects of human behaviour to be demonstrated. However, they also show the force of the experimental setting and the power of authoritative researchers to control the behaviour of participants. The experiments brought to light very important issues about the ethics of psychological studies. They raise the major, and difficult, issue of whether the findings of studies justify the possible ill effects which they produce on participants.

Milgram's study informed decisions by both the American Psychological Association and the British Psychological Society to make ethics central to their prescriptions about research. In Britain there was a further impetus in the late 1970s. A psychology department was prosecuted for allowing a postgraduate student to observe the predatory behaviour of cats on canaries when the department had never had a licence to keep canaries for research purposes. There is no doubt that psychological research can lead to harmful effects on humans and animals. Ethical debates, the explicit consideration of the ethics of each research project and the provision of ethical guidelines are the ways in which psychologists attempt to address these problems. The move in the late 1990s by the British Psychological Society (and a little earlier by the American Psychological Association) to change the term used for those who take part in studies from 'subjects' to 'participants' reflects a greater concern for ethics in terms of respect of individuals.

The British Psychological Society (BPS), along with psychological societies around the world, has produced ethical guidelines for the conduct of research. (You will receive a full copy of the BPS *Code of Conduct, Ethical Principles and Guidelines* to keep in your methods file.) Any psychologist who breaks these guidelines is subject to disciplinary action. Box 2 provides an extract adapted from a recent version of these BPS ethical principles for work with human participants. The British Psychological Society and The Experimental Psychology Society have together agreed guidelines for research with animals. It is usual practice now for all psychological research to require ethical approval from an appropriate group.

2 BPS Ethical Principles for Conducting Research with Human Participants

- The experimenter should consider the ethical implications of their research and the psychological consequences for their participants. In order to do this, they may need to consult people who belong to the group from which their participants are to be drawn (bearing in mind gender, ethnicity and age, etc.). Ethics committees or colleagues used to considering ethical principles should assess the risks and the costs/benefits of research.
- Wherever possible, investigators should inform their participants of their objectives and all aspects of the research that might reasonably be expected to influence their willingness to participate, especially any potentially negative consequences.
- Investigators must ensure that they obtain informed consent and ensure that if anybody cannot give informed consent (because they are too young or learning impaired), their parents or guardians give informed consent. Participants should be told that they can withdraw from the study at any stage and that this includes the right to have their data destroyed after the data are collected.
- The experimenter should consult with experienced and impartial colleagues about any proposed deceptions or encroachments on privacy.
- Deception or withholding information from participants should only be used when other means would damage a study that is likely to produce valuable results. Impartial advisors should assess whether the potential value of the study justifies the deception.
- The experimenter should consider the risks of stress or encroachments on privacy; and should emphasize the participant's right to withdraw from the experiment should they so wish at any point in the study.
- Data obtained from participants must be treated as confidential.
- Studies on non-volunteers (e.g. those who are observed in public places without their knowledge) must respect their privacy and their psychological well being.
- The experimenter should maintain the highest standards of safety. Participants must be protected from physical and mental harm caused by research. The risks to a participant should never be greater than any they would normally encounter in their everyday lives.
- Participants must be able to contact the researcher after they have participated in a study to report any stress they have experienced. In such cases, the researcher must take steps to avoid causing similar stress to other participants.
- Research on children should only be carried out with the informed consent of the children if they are able to give it and with informed parental consent.
- If a participant asks advice on psychological problems, care must be exercised in giving answers and if necessary the participant should be referred to professional advice. Researchers should not exceed their professional

competence (e.g. by giving advice if they are not therapists or experts on the advice needed).

- Participants should be debriefed properly and informed about findings etc.
- Research should not help to produce social inequities. It should, therefore, not stigmatize or patronize people on the basis of age, social class, gender, sexuality, disability status, 'race' or ethnicity.
- The researcher must ensure that all their associates, employers or students comply with these standards.
- Any psychologist who believes that another psychologist is breaking the above rules should try to make the other rethink their ideas and, if necessary, consult other psychologists.

Source: adapted from British Psychological Society, 2000, pp.8–11

Note that the last but one item in the extract above states that *students* must comply with these standards. This includes you. All Open University students, during their project work at home and at Residential School, must comply with the BPS ethical principles.

Psychology has changed since the 1960s and 1970s when Murray, Milgram and Zimbardo conducted their studies. Today, however, psychologists are still faced with ethical issues, many of which are subtle and difficult to foresee.

For example, in a research project on mothering, one of the authors of this chapter conducted an interview where the mother's husband was present. While this was not ideal because the interview was meant to be only with mothers, it was very difficult to obtain interviews in this study and so the researcher felt that every opportunity had to be seized. The session seemed to go very well and the mother appeared frank and forthcoming. However, at the next interview with the mother, a year later, the husband put on his coat as soon as the researcher appeared. When the mother asked where he was going, he explained that he was not going to stay to hear her 'winding him up again'. The previous interview had clearly raised issues for their relationship. With hindsight, it may have been ethically preferable for the researcher not to have done the interview with the father present – even though the mother had been very keen to continue. Or, rather than only concentrating on the mother, it may have been better to include the father in the interview since he was there. However, any interview can raise unanticipated ethical questions since just talking about topics can raise unexpected issues for participants in research.

To take another example, suppose you are doing a non-participant observation of an infant with his/her mother, in a naturalistic setting (the home) where the older sibling is also in the room, playing. What happens if the mother puts the infant in the crib and then goes into the kitchen but the older child immediately comes over and rocks the crib so violently that the baby is in danger of falling out? What do you do? It would be usual to intervene to avoid harm to the baby and probably that is what you would do. But then you would no longer be a non-participant observer – you would have entered the action and would be affecting what you were supposed to be recording. This could constitute an ethical dilemma. Alternatively, what should a researcher observing a family do if, having promised confidentiality to a mother, she sees a child obviously drunk and carrying a vodka bottle? It is normal good practice, in research and therapy, to assure the participants or clients of confidentiality, but with the explicit proviso that the researcher or therapist has a duty of care if the participants or clients are seen to be in danger of serious harm or harming others.

The above examples may seem simple in that they were not directly caused by the psychologist but were problems that arose within the research setting. (Note, however, that the mother in the infant observation example may have left the older child with the infant only because there was another adult in the room, who, the mother presumed, would intervene if necessary.) But these examples also illustrate that psychologists have to consider ethics when they make research choices about what to do, how to do it and how to analyse it. In other words, psychologists face ethical dilemmas in all aspects of how they conduct their research. For example, psychologists' approach to working with animals has changed enormously; when the authors of this chapter were students it was not uncommon for undergraduates to do research with animals. While this has become generally unacceptable, and many psychology departments no longer have animal laboratories, animals are still used for some research on learning and on brain functioning – although advances in neural imaging and computer modelling of brain functioning have made the use of animals in psychological experiments much less necessary. When animals *are* used now, ethical guidelines require that psychologists demonstrate that they could not do the same research without using animals and that the animals used are not subjected to any more pain or discomfort than is absolutely necessary. However, some people undoubtedly find any use of animals in psychological research unacceptable.

The question of deception often raises ethical dilemmas. Yet, it is not always ethically indefensible for psychologists to deceive the participants in their studies (as is clear from the British Psychological Society ethical guidelines). For example, it is common for memory researchers not to tell their participants in advance *what* they will be expected to remember during the tasks they are given or even that they are taking part in a memory experiment. This is because telling participants what they will be asked to remember is likely to change the way they approach tasks and, since this minor deception does not result in harm, psychologists generally consider it acceptable for this form of deception to continue. But memory researchers now consider it ethically important to reveal any deception that has been used to the participants after the study, during a process of debriefing.

Similarly, experimental social psychologists frequently do not tell their participants exactly what is being studied or the basis on which they have been selected. For example, in a well-known experiment (which you will read about in Chapter 1), Henri Tajfel and his colleagues (1971) randomly assigned boys to groups. However, they told the boys that they were being divided on the basis of their liking for the paintings of either Klee or Kandinsky, to make the participants think that amongst them there were 'two sorts of people'. This is not usually considered ethically problematic. However, some social psychological experiments raise potentially more troubling ethical issues. For instance, some psychologists stage minor accidents (such as someone tripping up and falling over in apparent pain) in order to observe helping behaviour. While there may be important benefits from understanding what influences helping behaviour, the psychologists doing the research have to weigh up whether the potential benefits of the study outweigh the distress that may be caused to passers-by. And all psychological research should offer, or be ready to offer, professional support for participants who might become distressed. This also applies to the researchers, who may in some situations require support themselves. It is important that researchers think about, and take care to remain within, their own competence levels, thus not exposing their participants or themselves to situations which they, the researchers, may not be able to deal with.

Activity 3

Look back at the description of the Murray study at the beginning of Section 2.4. Using the ethical guidelines presented in Box 2, note down how the Murray study contravenes current ethical principles. Having done this, consider how the interview described in the mothering study above might fail to fit with the guidelines. The fact that this interview situation is not a clear-cut example should help you to see some of the difficulties involved in making ethical decisions in psychological research.

Psychologists have also become increasingly conscious of ethical issues in professional practice. The importance of ethics has been underlined by the large number of psychologists who now work with patients or clients in the helping professions, business settings, forensic psychology or other roles (see the third course book, *Applying Psychology*). In the consulting room, patients or clients are often in distressed or in dependent states and are particularly vulnerable. Ethical issues around confidentiality, data protection and the legal status of case notes also now contribute to the level of awareness that professional psychologists need in order to work within their professional guidelines and their national codes of conduct. Since ethics are important to psychology, we have highlighted examples of the ethical issues raised by psychological research in the chapters that follow. Try to keep the British Psychological Society's ethical principles in mind as you think about the studies you encounter.

Summary Section 2

- Because the subject matter of psychology (ourselves and non human animals) is complex and reactive, psychologists have to choose from amongst a wide range of methods.
- Psychologists make use of methods that aim to maximize objectivity; they also use methods that focus on and explore subjectivities and meanings.
- Depending on the topic they are researching, psychologists can choose to adopt an outsider viewpoint or an insider viewpoint.
- During the research process, psychologists collect data and use it to arrive at evidence for their claims. Four different types of data are used by psychologists from different paradigms: behavioural data; personal accounts of inner experiences; material data such as biological and neuropsychological data; and symbolic data.
- The research process starts by isolating a sufficiently specific and answerable question. In some studies it then involves choosing an appropriate method(s) which will provide data to test the claim or the hypothesis underlying the research.
- Some research projects do not begin with a specific question or a specific hypothesis but are about understanding meanings.
- The most commonly used psychological methods are experiments, questionnaires, interviews, psychological tests, observations, and meaning and language-based methods.
- Psychological research is conducted within a paradigm – a framework made up of assumptions about the subject matter and ways it should be studied, the methods and data that are considered to be legitimate.
- Contemporary psychologists work in different paradigms: the doing of psychology within a given paradigm will be referred to in this book as a psychological perspective.
- Ethical issues are a major factor in psychological investigations and practice.

3 Mapping psychology

The above sections will already have made clear to you that psychology is a diverse, multifaceted discipline, with numerous sub-disciplines that draw on different traditions and whose boundaries and definitions change over time. And these different areas of psychology are, to varying extents, interconnected. This all adds to the excitement of studying psychology and the experience of gradually seeing the pieces of a jigsaw fall into place. But the first step towards creating a coherent picture may seem a little daunting. Building a jigsaw into a meaningful whole requires a strategy. How can we *start* the process of mapping the discipline of psychology?

This section describes the strategies we have used in this first book as we set out to *map* the discipline. The second book in this course (*Challenging Psychological Issues*) takes five important topics in psychology and examines how different perspectives used in psychology can, each in their own way, contribute to our understanding of these complex issues. The third book (*Applying Psychology*) illustrates the practice of psychology in professional settings and shows how psychology can be used to understand problems such as stress, bullying at work, and detecting lying in legal evidence.

3.1 Navigating your way through the chapters in this book

The first step for us as authors was to choose a set of topic areas. Each of those we have chosen is important in its own right within the discipline of psychology; and as a set they address a range of the complexities of people and how they are studied. The particular topics we have chosen also provide an opportunity to discuss a number of more general themes and issues that are important across psychology. We have selected nine topic areas (such as learning, personality, and memory) for this first book, and each is allocated a chapter (Chapters 1–9). These are not meant to be the sum total of what makes up psychology, but this selection is a substantial and representative sample of the variety of psychological topics. So *the first aim of the book* is to introduce you to the diversity of psychology by presenting, chapter by chapter, the findings – the established knowledge – on a variety of topics central to psychological enquiry.

These particular nine topics taken together also introduce most of the major perspectives in psychology; this is *the second aim of the book*. By the end of this book you will have encountered cognitive psychology, experimental social psychology, biological psychology, evolutionary psychology, behaviourism, sociocultural psychology, personality measurement, psychoanalytic and humanistic psychology. Two other areas of what might be considered the 'core curriculum' of psychology are covered elsewhere: language is one of the topics in our second book; and child development is the subject of another Open University level 2 course, although there is material on development over the lifespan in our second book. Different perspectives, as well as different topics, tend to be associated with different methods, so the set of topics we have chosen for the current book demonstrates a substantial range of methods for obtaining data and evaluating evidence – this is *the third aim of the book*.

Overall, a consideration of the nine topics provides you with the tools for understanding very varied psychological concerns and the methods psychologists use. But chapters have to be presented in sequence, at least in the first instance. So how, as authors, did we set about placing these nine topics into a coherent story? We have set out to present the material in an order that enables you to build up your knowledge gradually. For that reason we have taken care to start from common, everyday experiences and, wherever possible, to illustrate theories with examples you are likely to recognize from your own experience. Since psychology is an evidence-based discipline, it is important that you learn about psychology both as a body of knowledge and as a discipline that constantly changes through research. We therefore want you to understand and appreciate the diversity of questions that psychologists ask and the variety of research methods they use to gain evidence with which to evaluate their questions and answers. The ordering of the chapters is designed to teach you, in manageable steps, not only about current psychological knowledge but also about *how psychologists do psychology*.

In putting the nine topics into a sequence, we have also been careful to keep hold of important strands of psychological thought, old and new. But this is *not* a story driven by history. When a historical approach is used it can mistakenly make it sound as if psychologists are making steady progress from their early, sometimes rather clumsy, attempts at studying particular aspects of people towards a single 'right answer' exemplified by what has been studied most recently. Instead, we weave the topics into a story of how psychologists have tried to understand the complexity of the subject matter. The list of topics and chapter titles is shown in Table 2.

Table 2   **The sequence of chapters in Book 1: Mapping Psychology**

Introduction: Psychology in the 21st century

Chapter 1: Identities and diversities

Chapter 2: Evolutionary psychology

Chapter 3: Three approaches to learning

Chapter 4: Biological processes and psychological explanation

Chapter 5: The individual differences approach to personality

Chapter 6: Perception and attention

Chapter 7: Perceiving and understanding the social world

Chapter 8: Memory: structures, processes and skills

Chapter 9: Person psychology: psychoanalytic and humanistic perspectives

The order we have chosen is an exploration beginning where you as a person already are and asking the fundamental question: 'What is it is that makes you the individual that you are?' This is the study of 'Identities and diversities' (Chapter 1), which is concerned with understanding what makes us uniquely ourselves. The chapter discusses a range of theories and methods social psychologists have used to address this issue. It starts from your understandings of your own identities before presenting the work of identity theorists.

In Chapter 2 we move on to the question of what makes us as humans both different from and similar to non-human animals by focusing on the burgeoning area of evolutionary psychology. This chapter ('Evolutionary psychology') moves from considering how we are unique as individuals to how humans came to be unique as a species. It focuses on how understanding of our evolution as a species, over an enormous period of time, can illuminate current, everyday human behaviour. As a result, some of the methods it uses are rather different from those used in other areas of psychology.

Whilst evolutionary adaptation and change are extremely slow, adaptation and change also happen within each of us in our lifetime – through the process we call learning. In Chapter 3 ('Three approaches to learning') we look at different aspects of learning in humans and animals, and consider how we are similar to and different from animals.

In Chapter 4 ('Biological processes and psychological explanation') we explain and illustrate how a biological perspective is essential to understanding behaviour. New developments in neuropsychology made possible by the development of brain-imaging techniques, as well as more established methods for studying the brain and nervous system, are discussed.

The notion of measuring and mapping differences and similarities between people, in particular their personality traits, is explored in Chapter 5 ('The individual differences approach to personality'), introducing and evaluating the methods used to do this. In Chapter 5 we build on the material in Chapter 4 by considering possible biological origins of personality and by addressing the question of the heritability of personality. And, as in Chapters 2 and 3, the crucial role of environments is explored, in this case the impact of people's environments on the development and expression of their personalities.

The next three chapters (6, 7 and 8) present psychological knowledge that has been gained primarily through the use of experimental methods. In these three chapters the focus is on the processing of information and on cognition. Chapters 6 ('Perception and attention') and 8 ('Memory: structures, processes and skills') present the perspective known as cognitive psychology. Chapter 7 ('Perceiving and understanding the social world') bridges social psychology and cognitive psychology, presenting a topic called social cognition. Chapter 6 helps to build up psychological ideas about how we see the world. It focuses on the structures and processes that underlie our essentially similar (universal) abilities to attend to and perceive (by hearing and seeing) the world. Chapter 7 continues the theme of perception, but, whereas Chapter 6 examines the general processes of perception of the material world, Chapter 7 looks at how these processes operate when we perceive other people. It considers what happens when we try to work out why other people behave as they do, and when we perceive aspects of the world that are emotionally loaded or require complex judgements.

Chapter 8 introduces research on memory structures and processes. It demonstrates how remembering is fundamental to everyday learning, to constructing our identities and making sense of others. This chapter also shows how processes of remembering are dependent on the way the brain works; and that memories are reconstructed and not necessarily accurate or complete. The chapter considers both what we share with other people (the processes of memory) and how our own memories can be unique.

The last chapter of the book, Chapter 9 ('Person psychology: psychoanalytic and humanistic perspectives') is rather different from all the others in the extent to which it places its emphasis on whole individuals and their motivations and experiences of being themselves. It reconsiders aspects of both personality and identity introduced earlier in the book, and looks at the influence of both conscious and unconscious parts of our minds through a discussion of psychoanalytic psychology and humanistic psychology. By doing this it returns to the question 'Who am I?' with which we began in Chapter 1, but from different perspectives and using different methods from the other chapters in the book.

3.2 Issues and debates in psychology: the editorial commentaries

The nine chapters that follow are written either by single authors or by several authors working together. These authors have presented and evaluated their topics, choosing their material and demonstrating the methods that are typically used and the kinds of data that are typically collected. But between the chapters you will find additional, short commentary sections. These editorial 'commentaries' will have three functions, designed to help you to build an overall map of the discipline.

The first function of the commentaries is to highlight a range of theoretical debates arising from the different perspectives and their traditions, as they appear in the chapters. References will be made to the *EPoCH* CD-ROM which you can explore in order to set the historical traditions in their contexts.

The second function of the commentaries is to explore issues around the methods psychologists use in their studies. Three particular method-related issues are discussed as they feature in the chapters:

1   The tensions between holistic approaches to people (as in the study of identity) and a focus on more specific psychological processes (like perception).
2   The uses of insider or outsider viewpoints and the kinds of data that are collected.
3   Issues about which level of analysis to use to explain particular psychological phenomena. For example, the phenomenon of memory can be studied at different levels of analysis. It can be approached from the level of neuropsychology, or cognitive processing, or cultural practices – or perhaps all of these – each giving its own, different insights.

Finally, the commentaries will carry and discuss *themes* that are set up in the early chapters but are relevant to all the chapters of the book, themes that underpin the different ways we explain humanness. One of these is: What makes us distinctively ourselves in comparison with other humans? Another is: What makes us different from other animals? Should we see people (and non-human animals) as relatively fixed or as essentially flexible, with the capacity to adapt to circumstances and to develop and change? Yet another theme is a familiar psychological issue, closely related to that of our adaptability: How – in what ways – are we the product of *nature* (our genetics and biology more generally) *and nurture* (our experiences in environments – physical, social and cultural)?

These three functions of the commentaries help to build up a map of the discipline of psychology in its diversity and its connectedness, showing how the perspectives in each chapter interrelate with those in other chapters.

By the time you have finished this book you should have made a good start on mapping the diversity of psychology and understanding that it is possible to subdivide psychology in a range of ways. We hope that you enjoy the journey.

 # References

Barnes, P. (1985) E206 *Personality, Development and Learning*, Unit 1, *Raising Questions*, Milton Keynes, The Open University.

Bradley, B.S. (1989) *Visions of Infancy*, Cambridge, Polity.

British Psychological Society (2000) *Code of Conduct, Ethical Principles and Guidelines*, Leicester, British Psychological Society.

Chase, A. (2000) 'A lesson in hate', *The Guardian*, 22 June, pp.2–3.

Dancey, C.P. and Reidy, J. (2002) *Statistics Without Maths for Psychology* (2nd edn), Harlow, Pearson Education.

James, W. (1890/1950) *The Principles of Psychology*, 2 vols, New York, Dover Publications.

Milgram, S. (1974) *Obedience to Authority*, London, Tavistock.

Rosenhan, D. (1973) 'On being sane in insane places', *Science*, no.179, pp.250–8.

Shallice, T. (1972) 'The Ulster depth interrogation techniques and their relation to sensory deprivation research', *Cognition*, vol.1, no.4, pp.385–405.

Sherrat, N., Goldblatt, D., Mackintosh, M. and Woodward, K. (2000) DD100 *An Introduction to the Social Sciences: Understanding Social Change*, *Workbook 1*, Milton Keynes, The Open University.

Tajfel, H., Billig, M., Bundy, R.P. and Flament, C. (1971) 'Social categorization and intergroup behaviour', *European Journal of Social Psychology*, vol.1, pp.149–77.

Zimbardo, P., McDermott, M., Jansz, J. and Metaal, N. (1995) *Psychology: A European Text*, London, HarperCollins.

Acknowledgement

All Open University course materials are developed as part of an extended process of team discussion and redrafting based on the comments and suggestions of many people (see the course team list at the front of this book). The editors have received extensive course team comments during the development of this chapter in particular, and wish to thank all members of the team for their valuable contributions. Where similar issues and debates have been discussed in earlier courses, the strengths of these previous formulations are built on, and so we would also like to thank the previous course team (DSE202: *Introduction to Psychology*) and its Chair Ilona Roth for making material, and their reflections on it, available to the current team.

Identities and diversities

Ann Phoenix

Contents

Aims

This chapter aims to:

- consider what is meant in psychology by the concept of identity
- present three types of psychological identity theory
- introduce the concept of embodied identities
- outline the reasons for divisions into 'personal' and 'social' identities in some theories
- indicate why a focus on identities requires a reciprocal focus on diversities
- introduce some of the methods used to study identities.

 # Introduction: identity as an everyday psychological issue

Identity is an area of psychological study that is centrally concerned with understanding people and their everyday lives. An interest in identities and how to understand them is far from new. More than a century ago, William James (1890) produced a psychological theory of identity. However, identity is now a popular topic of discussion in many contemporary societies, in everyday talk, in the media and in several academic disciplines. Yet, since it is used in a range of different ways, it is frequently not entirely clear what it means. Psychological theories of identity aim to define identity and to explain the processes that produce it.

1.1 The scope of the chapter

Identity often seems to be an obvious and everyday issue and there are some simple methods for researching it. Yet, psychologists have found that identity is more complex than it seems to be. As a result, they have devised various theories to help them understand it. This chapter considers some of the main research methods and theories that psychologists use to help them think about identities.

The rest of this section introduces a technique, the Twenty Statements Test, that can easily be used to study identities. Section 2 considers how the fact that we all have a body is likely to affect our identity – sometimes without our being conscious that it does. The chapter then moves on to consider how we can understand identities by discussing three influential psychological theories. Section 3 is concerned with theories that have addressed personal identity in social context, referred to as psychosocial theories. Section 4 presents a theory of social identity: Social Identity Theory. Section 5 examines theories of the social construction of identities, which make no distinction between personal and social identities. The final section (Section 6) considers how well the theories of identity considered in the chapter can help us to understand the identities of people with physical impairments.

1.2 Describing ourselves

It is likely that all of us at some point will think about who we are. Although it can be difficult for us to define ourselves with precision, we each have implicit ideas about the behaviours that typify 'me'.

Activity 1.1

Without thinking about it first, quickly jot down 10 words or phrases you might use to answer the question 'Who am I?' When you have done that, note how you think one of your close friends would describe you and then, if you have time, how a family member and then a distant acquaintance would describe you. Give yourself 10 minutes to do this activity.

Keep your notes, as you will return to these later in the chapter and again in Chapter 5.

Comment

When you compare the different words or phrases you have written, you may notice some similarities between the way you would answer the question about who you are and the ways in which you think others might describe you. You may also notice that you seem to be a different person in different contexts and depending on who you are with. Indeed, you may be struck by contradictions between who you seem to be in one situation and who you seem to be in another. This may have led you to wonder which of the characteristics you put down are the 'real' you, or you may, alternatively, have felt confident that there are clear and consistent answers to the question 'Who am I?' If your answers included 'I am not ...', this links with the arguments of identity theorists who generally agree that an understanding of who we are also requires an understanding of who we are not. When you look at your answers, you may be surprised at the wide range of characteristics you ascribe to yourself. Whether we have one real identity or many and whether or not identity is consistent from situation to situation are both issues which psychologists debate.

This exercise may have raised questions for you about what the difference is between 'self', 'identity' and 'personality'. Psychologists view these terms as interrelated. The process of categorizing the 'self' (which you have just done) can be said to be a building block of identity; for if we consider that we fit into a particular category, that aspect of the self becomes part of our identity. Identity can be understood as our own theory of ourselves, created from many sources. These include what we consider to be our characteristic ways of acting (our personalities) and our relationships with other people who react to us in particular ways and give us indications of how they think of us. Personality is frequently measured without reference to how people actually describe and see themselves, whereas identity requires that psychologists take account of this.

The exercise you have just done employs a similar method to one used by some psychologists to help them gain insights into how people think about themselves (see Box 1.1).

1.1 **FEATURED METHOD**

The Twenty Statements Test: an introspectionist method for studying identity

Nineteenth-century psychologists considered that it was the ability to reason and think that differentiated human from non-human animals. They therefore wanted to study people's minds. Because no-one can read other people's minds, they had to find a way of gaining indirect access to mental processes through their own and other people's verbal reports. This method, called **introspectionism,** was used by both William James and Wilhelm Wundt (two 'founders' of modern psychology). However, introspectionism fell out of favour because it is difficult for any of us to be entirely conscious of all our mental processes, to remember them or to put them into words accurately so that they can be clearly understood by others.

Introspectionism
Method for gaining indirect access to people's mental processes through their verbal reports.

Yet, since it is psychologically informative to understand what goes on in people's minds, many psychologists have continued to devise methods to gain access to what people are thinking. One such method, referred to as the 'Twenty Statements Test', was devised by Kuhn and McPartland (1954). This was a simple pen-and-paper method designed to make explicit people's thinking about their identities. Kuhn and McPartland gave the participants in their study 12 minutes to write down 20 answers to the question 'Who am I?' They then divided the answers into categories based on the most common responses. People doing the Twenty Statements Test often give answers that can be categorized into:

- *characteristics* such as gender or age;

- *social roles* in terms of relationships to other people (e.g. 'I am a father'; 'I am a secretary');

- *personality* (e.g. 'I am a happy person');
- *interests and tastes* (e.g. 'I am a fan of popular music');
- *attitudes* (e.g. 'I am in favour of free health care');
- *current state* (e.g. 'I am tired').

Using this system, Kuhn and McPartland were able to identify the most commonly used self-descriptions that appeared to be important to people's identities. They could also work out the percentage of their sample that answered in a particular way. Since the 1950s, numerous psychologists have refined this method.

The advantage of this method is that it quickly allows insights into how people think of their identities. It is possible to obtain data from a whole roomful of people at the same time and to analyse their answers fairly rapidly. In addition, it allows people to disclose several identities without giving them time to censor their responses by changing what they have written after thinking about it. The disadvantages are that it can reduce the richness of people's thinking about their identities to the categories devised by the researcher; it allows little time for participants to reflect deeply; and it pays little attention to the exact words participants use to describe themselves or the reasoning behind their choices.

Although the Twenty Statements Test is very popular amongst some identity researchers, it has two shortcomings that mean that it cannot be the only method psychologists use to study identity. First, it can only study those identities that people can bring to mind. Yet, there may be many aspects of our identities that we take for granted and never think about except if they go wrong. For example, people who become disabled, either physically or by losing their memories, are often more conscious that their bodies affect their identities than those who do not experience such impairments. Second, the Twenty Statements Test cannot explain why we have the identities we do. We need theories of identity to help us explain this.

Summary Section 1

- Identity is a popular topic that has been studied by psychologists since the discipline began.
- The apparently simple, everyday exercise of making 'I am ...' statements about ourselves forms the basis of a commonly used psychological method of studying identity.

- Kuhn and McPartland (1954) devised the Twenty Statements Test which allows researchers to collect data quickly. Refinements of it have been used continually since then.
- The Twenty Statements Test cannot study identities that people do not think of. Nor can it help us to understand why we have the identities we do.

2 Embodying identities

In recent years, some psychologists and other academics have turned their attention to the importance of **embodiment**. Since our bodies are central to our lives, it would be surprising if they were not important to our identities. However, the term 'embodiment' signals more than simply that we live in our bodies. It suggests that bodies are physical and biological as well as social and psychological. We use our bodies to look at, talk to, touch and avoid other people, and to signal the kinds of people we are and the groups we consider ourselves to belong to. At the same time, our bodies have an impact on our identities. What our faces look like, how tall we are, how well or badly our bodies (including our brains) work – all affect our identities through how we feel, what we can do and how other people treat us.

For centuries, people have attempted to change their bodies to fit with culture, fashion and individual tastes. Clothes, wigs, control of food intake, and decoration (through painting, tattoos, scarification, etc.) have long been used. More recently, the availability of plastic surgery techniques and knowledge about body building have made the body a resource that can be transformed to suit our identities. It is even possible to change height, weight, shape, gender and colour. Bodies, therefore, have been, and continue to be, social symbols of identity. As such, they are often sources of worry and dissatisfaction as well as pleasure for their owners.

It is because bodies are a public presentation of identity, interpreted by other people, and amenable to

Embodiment
Indicates that we live in and through our bodies and that we simultaneously experience our bodies physically and biologically as well as socially and psychologically.

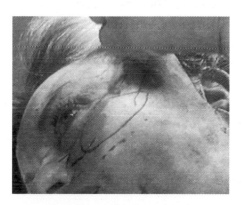

The performance artist Orlan remains conscious during plastic surgery operations as part of her art

limited change that they are often 'projects' which people attempt to mould to suit their identities (Woodward, 2000). This is most evident when groups of people adopt similar styles of dress and hairstyle, forming group identities for themselves. Body projects are part of what Michel Foucault (1988) called 'technologies of self' – the ways in which we use our bodies to produce identities for ourselves. Of course, no body is entirely malleable. Nor are all means of changing the body affordable for everybody. Therefore, body projects can create and reproduce inequalities (Shilling, 1997).

The clothes we wear and the styles of fashion we adopt are part of our 'technologies of self'

It is not only the visible body that affects our identities. **Neuropsychological approaches** have added to our understanding of embodied identities by demonstrating that there are many different ways in which identity can be altered when the brain is damaged. An aspect of brain functioning that is essential to our identities is our memories. Take the following example from a 31-year-old man, Philip Fletcher, who sustained a head injury which resulted in his forgetting everything that had happened to him since he was 17 years old:

> I didn't know my name or my job. I didn't recognize me, my wife, or my children. I had no recollection of ever being married for 12 years or of having a family. I had no identity … I was desperate for a set of younger clothes. I also detested the family car … It felt like I'd walked into someone else's family and taken on a different identity.
>
> (Sims, 2000, pp.91 and 92)

In a rather different way, people with damage to the frontal lobes of their brain sometimes lose their memories about themselves but make up fictional memories that they entirely believe (Conway and Fthenaki, 2000). Such examples show that some aspects of identity can best be understood by studying cases where identity has broken down.

You may have included something about your body in answer to the 'I am …' activity in Section 1. On the Twenty Statements Test, people sometimes mention their body shape, perception of their attractiveness, colouring, fitness or lack of it, dress style, etc. However, it is often easier to be conscious of the importance of our bodies to our identities when our bodies do not work well. Since the 1970s, the campaigns of what has come to be known as the 'disability movement' have provided insights into how embodiment and identities are interlinked. Those who have campaigned to shift views of disability argue that people with physical impairments experience 'individual limitation', but that disability is a 'socially imposed restriction' (Oliver, 1990).

This **social model of disability** argues that the everyday experiences of people with physical impairments are not simply the consequence of biology. Instead, they result mainly from the limitations imposed by other people and by environments (Swain *et al.*, 1993). They thus demonstrate the importance of embodiment (that bodies are simultaneously physical, biological, social and psychological). An example with which many people are familiar concerns access to buildings for those using wheels rather than legs. If there are adequate ramps or flat entry points, sufficient space in which to turn wheelchairs, lifts and suitable lavatory facilities, people with

Neuropsychological approaches
These study brain function by examining damaged brains, the structure of the brain and neural activity.

Social model of disability
A model that considers that people with physical impairments are as disabled by the limitations imposed by society as by their impairments.

disabilities are enabled, rather than disabled, in the negotiation of space. Their disability relates to being unable to negotiate space for themselves in buildings not designed with disability in mind. The argument, therefore, is that people with physical impairments are often made conscious that embodiment affects their identities because their needs are not catered for in society.

Although embodied identities are clearly important and are increasingly being studied in psychology and other disciplines, theories of identity have relatively little to say about them. The final section of this chapter will draw upon the accounts of people with physical disabilities in order to consider how well the theories of identity presented here fit with what they say.

Summary Section 2

- Embodiment is important to our identities because it is simultaneously physical, biological, social and psychological.
- Many people engage in 'body projects' to produce particular identities.
- Identities and brain and body functioning are interlinked.
- The importance of embodiment to identities is most evident when people have physical impairments.

3　How can we understand personal identity?

Psychosocial
Psychosocial identity recognizes the influence of both personal and social factors on identity development.

Core identity
The central identity that individuals have to achieve from different aspects of their identities if they are to be psychologically healthy.

At the heart of many theories of identity is the notion that knowing who we are requires that we know who we are *not*. Kroger (1989/1993) argues that identity represents 'the balance between self and other'. Identity therefore has both individual and social elements. This section considers the contributions to thinking about identity made by Erik Erikson and James Marcia who view identity as **psychosocial** (simultaneously psychological – that is, personal – and social) and as a bridge between the identity that is most central to us (our **core identity**) and the social context.

3.1 Erikson's psychosocial theory of identity

As a psychoanalyst, Erikson developed his theories from clinical and naturalistic observations as well as his analyses of the biographies of great men. Erikson was the first theorist to view identity as psychosocial, meaning that the community in which children and adolescents live helps to shape their identity. Identity for Erikson consisted of 'a conscious sense of individual uniqueness ... an unconscious striving for continuity ... a solidarity with a group's ideals' (1968, p.208). In other words, identity involves the development of a stable, consistent and reliable sense of who we are and what we stand for in the world that makes sense for us and for our community. It is this 'core identity' that gives us a sense of continuity with the past and a direction for the future. Erikson also considered it important for people to feel that their social group views them as the same over time.

Erikson's clinical work with veterans of the Second World War led him to conclude that when life is going well, identity is taken-for-granted and we are unselfconscious. However, the importance of identity is most obvious and definable when it is no longer possible to take for granted that we shall continue to exist and experience ourselves as unique individuals, as is the case for soldiers fighting wars or when people become aware that they will eventually die. In Erikson's view, identity crisis was central to the period in which he lived. This is because he lived through two world wars, which, not surprisingly, led many people to think about their own mortality and so generated identity confusion.

Erikson's focus on continuity did not mean that he considered that, once achieved, identity never changed. Instead, he saw the achievement of identity as a lifelong developmental process involving a progressive resolution of conflicts or normative crises between individual needs and social demands and between positive and negative developmental possibilities. He considered these conflicts to be common to most people and hence typical, rather than abnormal. This is what he meant by 'normative crisis'.

Erikson identified eight stages of identity development in which each stage builds on what has gone before, but goes beyond the previous stage to provide the foundation for the next. These start with the infant's developing sense of time and end in old age. Erikson considered that the final period of human life (stage eight) was one where older people struggled to find integrity against the risk of despair caused by problems with body functioning and the prospect of death (see Table 1.1).

Table 1.1 **The place of identity development in Erikson's eight developmental stages**

Age/Stage	Normative crisis	Possible outcomes
1 Age birth–1 year	Trust vs mistrust	Trust or mistrust of people
2 Age 1–3 years	Autonomy vs doubt	Self-control or self doubt
3 Age 3–6 years	Initiative vs guilt	Sense of purpose or low self-esteem
4 Age 6–11 years	Industry vs inferiority	Competence or helplessness
5 Adolescence	Identity achievement vs role diffusion	Identity achieved or uncertainty
6 Early adulthood	Intimacy vs isolation	Personal relationships or loneliness
7 Middle adulthood	Generativity vs stagnation	Care for others or self-absorption
8 Late adulthood	Integrity vs despair	Fulfilment or disappointment

---

BIOGRAPHY   ***Erik Erikson*** *1902–1994*

Erik Erikson, 1902–1994

Erikson was a psychoanalyst who made major contributions to the field of psychology with his work on child development and on 'identity crisis'. He had a rich and dramatic life and a consideration of some of the events in his personal history provides an insight into how the interests and interpretations of scholars are often interlinked with the theories to which they become attached.

Born in Frankfurt, Germany, to Danish parents who were not married and separated before he was born, he was raised by his Jewish mother and Jewish-German stepfather. He was brought up as Erik Homburger – the name of his stepfather. One biographer has suggested that it is possible that some of his later interest in identity came from his feelings of puzzlement at being raised by two dark-haired Jewish parents when he himself was blond and blue-eyed.

Erikson's adolescence was turbulent. Later, he came to conceptualize adolescence itself as necessarily a time of 'crisis'. He spent seven years travelling through Europe trying to establish himself as an artist and later acknowledged that he had been deeply neurotic (and close to psychosis) in his adolescence. Throughout his life, he wanted to know who his birth father was and he spent a long time in unsuccessful searching.

In 1927 Erikson met Freud's daughter, the Austrian psychoanalyst Anna Freud, in Vienna and was psychoanalysed daily by her for six years. With her encouragement he began studying at the Vienna Psychoanalytic Institute, where he specialized in child psychoanalysis. In 1933 he left Austria because of the Nazi threat and went to the USA, where he became interested in the influence of culture and society on child development. He was a pioneering child psychoanalyst in Boston. He made up the Danish and Christian (as opposed to Jewish) name Erikson after becoming a US citizen in 1939.

Erikson considered that what happened to individuals depended on what was happening in society during the historical period in which they lived. His studies of Native American children led him to relate personality growth to parental and societal values. As he continued his clinical work, Erikson developed the concept of 'identity crisis'. This he saw as an inevitable conflict that accompanies the development of identity in late adolescence.

Sources: Microsoft Corporation, 1996; Gardner, 1999; Kroger, 1989/1993; Stevens, 1983

Although Erikson viewed the development of identity as a lifelong process, he considered it to be particularly important during the fifth psychosocial stage, adolescence, in which the achievement of identity was the major developmental task. For Erikson, adolescence is a period in which several life decisions have to be faced and, by the end of which, **ego identity** (a secure feeling of who and what one is) has to be achieved. For example, sexual relationships, employment and independence from parents all have to be negotiated (even if they are not embarked upon). As a result, commitments and beliefs that have hitherto been taken for granted are questioned as young people consider not only who they are, but also who they can be in the future.

Erikson saw adolescence as a period of **psychosocial moratorium**, because young people could postpone making definitive social choices while working out the various elements of their identity. In this period, young people can, for a while, try out various identities without commitment before finding their own niche in society. The word 'moratorium' means an officially approved period of delay. Erikson used it to indicate that, in this period, it was socially approved for adolescents to delay taking on adult responsibilities so that they can be helped to make the difficult transition to adulthood. However, by the end of adolescence, Erikson considered that healthy development required a clear sense of who we are and what we stand for. For Erikson the term 'ego identity'

Ego identity
Erikson's term for a secure feeling of who and what one is. It suggests the psychosocial nature of identity.

Psychosocial moratorium
A socially approved period in which young people can try out different social roles and so find their own niche in society.

indicated the coherent whole that results from this process of integrating perceptions of the self into a central identity which is both psychological and social (i.e. psychosocial).

Erikson observed that some young people find it impossible to make commitments to adult roles and that many experience some difficulty. This, he argued, was because they were at war with themselves. Hence, it is a period characterized by **identity crisis**. The nature of the 'identity crisis' to be faced depends on the society and historical period in which young people grow up. In Western societies, this often takes the form of drifting between different social roles and occupations or, more extremely, drug taking and suicide. Erikson called the failure to achieve a secure ego identity **role diffusion**. He was probably influenced partly by his own turbulent youth and by his friend and analyst Anna Freud's (1958) belief that it was 'abnormal' to be 'normal' during adolescence.

Erikson's theory explains why young people are often very involved with their social groups. He considered that solidarity with a group's ideals is important in the development of identity. Since adolescent identity crisis is potentially frightening, Erikson argued that young people might temporarily over-identify with cliques and crowds. As a defence against feelings of loss of identity, they are sometimes particularly nasty to those they consider outsiders. They may be 'remarkably clannish, intolerant, and cruel in their exclusion of others who are "different", in skin color or cultural background, in tastes and gifts, and often in entirely petty aspects of dress and gesture arbitrarily selected as the signs of an in-grouper or out-grouper' (Erikson, 1968, pp.132–3). Erikson also argued that people whom we consider to be very different from ourselves can threaten our sense of identity and that this can lead to aggression. This issue was, not surprisingly, one with which he was concerned since the fact that he was born Jewish put him at considerable risk in Austria prior to the Second World War.

Erikson's ideas about young people's 'clannishness' can help to explain current social issues such as the prevalence of bullying in schools. However, the notion of 'identity crisis' in adolescence has not received widespread support. Studies on adolescents who are not in clinical treatment generally find that they do not experience the period of crisis Erikson suggested. Instead, many studies find that there is a tendency for the self-esteem of young people to increase steadily over the adolescent years (Coleman and Hendry, 1990). In his biography of Erikson, Lawrence Friedman (1999) argues that only a person with a troubled identity could see identity crisis as universal.

Identity crisis
A period in which some young people find it impossible to make commitments to adult roles and many experience some difficulty.

Role diffusion
The failure to achieve a secure ego identity.

Activity 1.2

Erikson's theory suggests that the development of identity involves conflict. Does it seem to you that you have ever been caught up in what Erikson would define as an 'identity crisis'?

- If so, was this during adolescence, earlier or later?

- Would you say that it was caused by your life stage or by a specific event?

- Did you 'achieve' your identity in that period or has your identity achievement been more continuous over the course of your life?

- If you currently know anybody who has recently been an 'adolescent', do they appear to have experienced an 'identity crisis'?

Comment

Many people now suggest that Erikson overemphasized both the importance of adolescence as the period when identity is achieved and the idea that adolescence is a time of crisis. For example, the notion of a 'mid-life crisis' is now in common currency. Although your own experiences (as a sample of only one) cannot provide confirmation of a theory, consideration of your experiences may help you to understand how you feel about Erikson's theory. It can also give you further insight into the place of introspection in psychological theory development. Psychologists have frequently used different people's hunches and feelings as the basis for theory generation and evaluation. Remember also how Erikson's own identity (see biography box) appears to have been important to the theory he developed, and note that psychologists often work on issues that are important to them.

3.2 The identity status model

Erikson was a visionary thinker whose work has influenced a whole genre of research that continues today. The work of the US clinical psychologist and psychotherapist James Marcia (pronounced 'Marshia') has been particularly influential because it has provided a method that allows Erikson's ideas on identity to be measured. Marcia (1966, 1980, 1994) focused on Erikson's fifth stage (adolescence) and proposed a variant on Erikson's theory which could be used to assess how adolescents' identity changed over the long period of adolescence – which many people consider lasts from 13 to 25 years of age. Marcia developed the Identity Status Interview to study development in 18 to 25-year-old college students (using only male samples until 1970). This **semi-structured interview** (see Box 1.2) has been used in hundreds of studies and is probably the most popular instrument for studying identity in adolescence (Kroger, 2000). It has also been adapted to questionnaire formats.

Semi-structured interviews
Interviews designed to cover particular themes that allow flexibility in how questions are asked.

1.2 **FEATURED METHOD**

The semi-structured interview

Semi-structured interviews are designed to cover particular themes and to do so they include relevant questions. However, they allow the researcher to ask questions in a different order and to use participants' own words rather than those written on the interview guide. This enables researchers immediately to follow up participants' ideas and stories using unscripted and probing questions. Also, semi-structured interviews do not constrain the range of possible answers respondents can give. Researchers are therefore able to cover all the issues they consider important to their study with every participant, but to explore these in different ways with each person. The interview has the feel of a conversation between the researcher and the participant. This is not the case when participants have to respond to a questionnaire with questions presented in an invariant order with preset choices for how they can respond.

Semi-structured interviews are often tape-recorded so that researchers can listen to what participants say rather than writing down what is being said. Tape-recording also allows researchers to refer back to the transcript or tape when doing their analysis. These interviews can be analysed quantitatively and/or qualitatively. For quantitative analysis, researchers often code what the participants say into categories and then look at the percentage of the sample who give particular types of answers. They can also do statistical analyses to see if there are systematic differences between the types of answers given to different kinds of question or by different participants. Also, because participants have been allowed to talk fairly freely, it is possible to analyse their accounts qualitatively by identifying themes, concepts and ideas in each participant's account.

A major advantage of using semi-structured interviews is that they allow researchers to collect a great deal of rich data from a range of participants and to analyse it in different ways. However, it is more time-consuming to do each interview than it would be to give participants questionnaires to fill out. For this reason, samples can never be as large as they could be for questionnaire studies. Analysis can also be very time-consuming since tapes either have to be transcribed or listened to several times, and much care and perseverance are needed to interpret the data.

Marcia's semi-structured Identity Status Interview explores the extent of commitments or crises for 18 to 25-year-old US college students in relation to occupation, religion, politics, sexual behaviour, friendship and, in later versions, female identity. It takes approximately 30 minutes for researchers to get answers to all the questions. To explore commitment to particular roles, Marcia asks questions such as: 'How willing do you think you would

James Marcia

be to give up going into [career or job X] if something better came along?'; 'Have you ever had any doubts about your religious beliefs?'

Marcia wanted to examine the extent to which young people make active choices between possible alternatives before making commitments to particular roles. For Marcia, active choice involved making efforts to learn about the opportunities open to them – that is, by engaging in exploration. Commitment and exploration are the two dimensions on which he categorizes young people (as high or low). From the combination of their position on exploration and on commitment Marcia categorizes young people into one of four possible identity statuses (see Box 1.3). For any particular sample of young people studied, it is possible to see how many fit into which identity statuses. These statuses are related to personality, in that each young person will have a specific way in which they usually experience and deal with the world. For Marcia, identity status at adolescence has an impact on later identity and how young people will go through future life stages.

1.3 Marcia's four identity statuses

In **identity diffusion** (low commitment and low exploration), young people have not yet experienced an identity crisis and are not committed to a consistent set of values and goals. They tend either to have carefree, uncommitted lifestyles or to give the appearance of being rather empty and dissatisfied. Because they do not have a firmly established sense of identity, they are very impressionable and very easily change opinions about themselves in response to feedback from others. For Marcia, this is the least developmentally advanced status, although it can be adaptive if it is difficult for young people to explore their identities because they are in difficult circumstances. A young person in identity diffusion may answer many of the questions on the Identity Status Interview with 'Well, I don't know, it doesn't make much difference to me. I can take it or leave it'.

Identity foreclosure (high commitment and low exploration) happens when young people commit themselves to identities without having explored other options. Foreclosed young people are often self-satisfied, have authoritarian, fixed views about what is right, and consider their identity coherent. Some young

Identity diffusion
Period in which young people are neither exploring social roles nor committed to a consistent set of values and goals.

Identity foreclosure
Period in which young people commit themselves to identities without having explored other options.

people will explore other identities later, but others reach identity resolution with a single set of values and goals that often come from their parents. Muuss provides the following example: 'When a young man is asked what he wants to become, he may answer, "I want to be a dentist," and when asked why, he may respond, "Because my father is a dentist"' (1988, p.71). Marcia sees this as a less developed stage of identity development than the next two identity statuses.

Moratorium
An active process in which young people search for the identity to which they want to be committed.

Moratorium (low commitment and high exploration) is an active process in which young people search for the identity to which they want to be committed. (Marcia used almost the same term as Erikson – who used 'psychosocial moratorium' – to indicate the same process.) It can last for several years. Those in moratorium are preoccupied with exploring options (occupational, ideological and interpersonal) and with working towards commitment. They are often uncertain of themselves, but overcritical of others and institutions. They are active, but ambivalent and anxious about their struggles for identity. They do not make commitments in intimate relationships, although they may recognize what commitments would be like. Marcia considered moratorium an essential prerequisite for identity achievement. The response (to a question about religious commitment) 'I'm not at the point where I'm ready to commit myself to one thing – I'm more open-minded in everything at the moment' is indicative of moratorium (Kroger, 1989/1993, p.180).

Identity achievement
Young people have experienced and resolved their adolescent identity crisis by going through a period of moratorium.

Identity achievement (high commitment and high exploration) is Marcia's most developmentally advanced status. Young people who have achieved identity have experienced and resolved their adolescent identity crisis through a period of moratorium. It is a status in which they have strong, coherent identities. As a result, they are more independent, flexible, self-confident and intellectually creative than are young people in the other statuses. Those in this status are thoughtful, introspective, function well under stress and can manage interpersonal relationships. Allen gives the following example:

Interviewer: Thinking back to the time you decided on a career, what information did you have about what kinds of occupations were options?

Young woman: At that time, I didn't know a lot … I had to do a lot of research. I had to question, ask a lot of people. All I knew then [was] that I wanted to be in the business field. What part, I didn't know until I started talking with people.

(Allen, 1999)

Numerous pieces of research using Marcia's research method suggest that we should not view identity statuses as permanent qualities because some young people change between statuses before they achieve their identity. Some studies have also found that young people can have different identity statuses for different aspects of life such as employment and sexual relationships.

Although Erikson and Marcia view identity as psychosocial, they have concentrated more on the individual, personal aspects of identity than on group identities. The next section discusses a theory of social identities that focuses on group, rather than personal, identities.

Summary Section 3

- Erikson developed the psychosocial theory of identity from clinical work, naturalistic observations and probably his own experiences.
- Social and personal identities are interlinked. This is partly because we all need other people to show that they view us as the same over time, and partly because, for Erikson, identity requires that we feel solidarity with a group's ideals.
- Different identities are produced in different historical periods and different cultures.
- A sense of continuity, uniqueness and worth is important for a positive sense of identity.
- We all have a variety of sources of identities, but integrate them into a coherent whole.
- The development of identity is related to how people see both their past and their future.
- The achievement of identity is the central task of adolescence (Erikson's fifth psychosocial stage of development) and is necessarily accompanied by normative 'crisis'.
- Threats to identity lead to over-identification with cliques and/or aggression.
- Marcia adapted Erikson's theory and devised the Identity Status Interview as a method of studying the four identity statuses he identified: identity diffusion; identity foreclosure; moratorium and identity achievement. For Marcia, the ideal trajectory is from moratorium to identity achievement.

4 A focus on group identities

Social Identity Theory (SIT) addresses two sets of issues identified as problems with psychosocial identity theory. First, although Erikson thought of personal and social identities as interlinked, he and Marcia treated them as separate systems. As a result, large-scale social identities (e.g. of 'race', gender, disability and social class) were neglected until recently in this approach. Second, Social Identity Theory is designed to address the social processes by which people come to identify with particular groups and separate themselves from others. Erikson's theory dealt with this by focusing on how we achieve our individual identities, rather than how we develop group identities. Social Identity Theory focuses on identities associated with 'we' and 'us' rather than those associated with 'I' and 'me' as in psychosocial theory.

4.1 Social Identity Theory

As a result of the Second World War and the Holocaust, more psychologists than previously wanted to understand relationships between groups and the causes and effects of prejudice (Hogg and Abrams, 1999). Henri Tajfel was a European Jew who had managed to survive Nazi persecution and was interested in understanding its possible causes and effects. He devised a theory of social identities and intergroup relations, which was specifically designed to produce a social, rather than an individualistic, theory of identity. This theory was termed Social Identity Theory (SIT) by two of Tajfel's students (Turner and Brown, 1978).

Tajfel divided identity into two relatively separate sub-systems: personal identity (related to personal relationships such as a friend, parent, child, etc.) and social identity (related to wider social relations such as English, a man, white etc.). Central to SIT is the notion that social identity is largely composed of self-descriptions which derive from the characteristics that we believe define the social groups to which we belong. A social group for Tajfel was two or more individuals who shared a common identification or who saw themselves as members of the same social category. A category is only a category in comparison with another

Henri Tajfel, 1919–1982

category or categories (e.g. black/white; man/woman; working class/ middle class). So in this theory, as in Erikson's, knowing who we are requires knowing who we are not and, hence, recognizing difference and diversity. The act of self-categorization provides us with labels for ourselves and with a set of appropriate attitudes and behaviours that can guide our actions. If a particular social identity is important to us, then we will express that identity in our attitudes and behaviours through a process of self-stereotyping and acting in accordance with that stereotype. It is the subjective feeling of belonging to a group which is important in SIT rather than membership as defined by outsiders or simply sharing some characteristics with other group members (Turner, 1987).

Tajfel used a quite different research method from those used by Erikson and Marcia – the **experimental method** (see Box 1.4). With his colleagues he conducted a range of laboratory studies on artificially created 'minimal groups' which addressed the question of whether being a member of a group is enough *in itself* to promote identity with the ingroup and hostility against the outgroup.

Experimental method
The most commonly used psychological method. It examines causal relationships between variables by controlling factors that may affect the results.

1.4 The classic 'minimal group' experiment

The classic study by Tajfel et al. (1971) was done on 14- and 15-year-old schoolboys in Bristol. The boys were divided randomly into two groups, but told that they had been divided according to whether they preferred paintings by the artists Klee or Kandinsky. Each boy then worked alone in a cubicle and was asked to allocate points (which they were told could be converted to money after the study) to a member of their own group and to a member of the other group (but not to themselves). They had to choose one of three strategies for allocating the points. They could give the member of their own group as many points as possible provided that they also gave fairly high points to the member of the other group. Or they could give equally high rewards to boys from both groups. Alternatively, they could choose a strategy that favoured their group (the **ingroup**) and gave the maximum difference between the ingroup and the other group (the **outgroup**), even though this would result in the member of their group actually getting fewer points than if they had chosen one of the other strategies.

The task was therefore arranged so that a strategy of equal sharing would be most advantageous (in monetary terms) to the boys' own group. However, boys consistently maximized the difference between the groups to their own group's advantage. They chose to maintain as large as possible a gap between the points available to their group and to the other group.

In later experiments, participants were told that they had been randomly assigned to groups but this produced the same results. Since membership of

Ingroup
People who belong to the group to which we consider we belong.

Outgroup
People who do not belong to our group.

Minimal groups
Groups set up in Social Identity Theory research to identify the minimum conditions necessary for group identities to form.

these groups was arbitrary (hence they were **minimal groups**), participants had no practical purpose or reason for being in a group and there was no 'real' conflict of interest between the groups. Yet, membership of such groups still seemed to generate intergroup discrimination, in that, when faced with the task of allocating rewards to members of their own group and of the other group, people repeatedly gave preferential treatment to members of their own group.

Tajfel interpreted the findings from the minimal group experiments as indicating that simply categorizing individuals into groups is sufficient to generate prejudice between the groups. This was a dramatic but robust finding (meaning that the findings are the same when this experiment is repeated). The creation of artificial social groups by experimenters appeared to be enough to induce discrimination in favour of the ingroup and against the outgroup. It provided the minimum conditions necessary for social differentiation to take place and for people to consider that they were similar to members of their own group and different from non-members. But what is the point of discrimination in this context since individuals do not gain from denying benefits to the outgroup?

Tajfel (1978, 1981) explained these findings in terms of subjective, psychological benefits. He argued that people build social identities from their group membership and have basic psychological needs for satisfying social identities. In order to create satisfactory social identities, we need to have a sense of belonging to groups that have a positive image and high status in comparison with other groups. This leads individuals to attempt to maximize the differences between their ingroup and outgroups on those dimensions that favour the ingroup. They therefore try to maintain positive social identities in comparison with members of other groups.

Although the minimal groups experiment is based on trivial differences between groups, SIT applies the findings to large-scale social differences. It argues that society is composed of **social categories** that have different amounts of power and status in comparison with one another. Social categories refer to the division of people on the basis of gender, 'race', nationality, class, occupation, religion, etc. According to SIT, the drive towards a fulfilling social identity is at the root of prejudice and discrimination. Prejudice bolsters self-esteem because it allows outgroups to be conceptualized as inferior. It is, therefore, inevitable. The converse of this is that minority groups that experience prejudice and discrimination will always try to improve their position. So, while prejudice is inevitable, so is resistance to it.

Social categories
The division of people on the basis of characteristics, such as gender, 'race', nationality, class, occupation, religion, etc., that have differential power and status.

Unlike psychosocial theories, SIT explicitly discusses how social differences in power affect identity. It allows for change in social identities by explaining how socially subordinate groups may seek to improve their social position, and so make their social identity more positive, in relation to dominant groups. According to SIT some members of subordinate groups use **social mobility** (e.g. through promotion in employment) to improve their position by leaving behind their (previous) social group. Alternatively, people can work for social change. This is particularly relevant if social group boundaries are not easily permeable (e.g. gender or 'race').

Social change occurs in two ways – through **social creativity** and/or **social competition**. An oft-cited example of social creativity is the 'Black is Beautiful' slogan produced by the US Black Power movement of the 1960s and 1970s. This promoted a positive redefinition of the social identity of black people (the subordinate group). Social creativity can also involve promoting positive views of one's own devalued group through comparison with another devalued group. Examples of this include homophobia expressed by some working-class people. Social creativity differs from social competition because it does not attempt to change existing social relations. For example, the 'Black is Beautiful' slogan promotes a positive view of black people but does not demand racial equality. However, social competition advances social change through strategies that demand alternative social arrangements based on new ways of thinking about social groups (i.e. cognitive strategies). Examples of this include Mahatma Gandhi's passive resistance to colonialism, Black Power; civil wars and revolutions.

Social mobility
Process by which members of groups improve their status by leaving behind their (previous) social group.

Social creativity
A process of positive redefinition of a devalued social group in order to improve the social identity of its members.

Social competion
Strategies that advance social change by demanding alternative social arrangements based on new ways of thinking about social groups

Some psychologists criticize SIT on the grounds that it treats groups as if they were individuals and so is not as social a theory as Tajfel intended. This is because, in SIT research, participants are generally asked to react to individuals. They are then assumed to be reacting to the groups to which individuals belong (rather than to the individual they can see or have been told about). Their reactions are also assumed to result from their own group membership. Yet, their reactions may have nothing to do with the group identities the researcher is investigating.

This problem arises partly because SIT has been developed from laboratory-based studies that have to simplify complex social processes and so are not like everyday contexts. As a result, some people argue that SIT trivializes important social differences, such as those of (dis)ability, gender and 'race', by treating them as equivalent to the differences found between groups set up on the basis of minimal differences instead of as major inequalities of power (Henriques, 1998).

4.2 An intergroup 'natural experiment': blue eyes against brown eyes

In 1968, Martin Luther King (a prominent black civil rights leader) was assassinated. The television discussion of this event led Jane Elliot (a teacher of 7-year-olds in Riceville, Iowa, USA) to put into practice an exercise that she had frequently contemplated. Elliot wanted the children to learn the meaning of the Native American maxim: 'Oh Great Spirit, keep me from ever judging a man until I have walked in his moccasins.' Since all the children in Riceville were white, she decided to divide them according to eye colour. On the first day of her exercise she introduced segregation against the blue-eyed children (easily identified by the wearing of collars). She told the class that blue-eyed people were stupid and badly behaved and denied them privileges. Within a day, the blue-eyed children became depressed, sullen and angry and their schoolwork suffered. In contrast, the brown-eyed children's school performance improved, but they discriminated against their former friends in ways that very much surprised Elliot, calling them 'dirty blue-eyes', refusing to play with them and (for the boys) also fighting them. On the second day, Elliot explained that she had lied and that the blue-eyed children were better than the brown-eyed children who now had to wear the collars. The effects on school performance and behaviour switched round. After debriefing the children, all their school performance improved and,

When children in the 'class divided' exercise wore the collars and were discriminated against, they were unhappy, but they enjoyed not wearing the collars and being in the privileged group

years later, they claimed that this exercise had made them closer friends and better people who, unlike their parents, were not racially prejudiced.

Elliot repeated this exercise for several years and did variants of it with workers in the Iowa penal system and other adults. The exercise was filmed and several television programmes as well as a book (*A Class Divided*, Peters, 1987) were produced.

There are similarities between Jane Elliot's exercise and the minimal group experiment. For example, the intervention is a trivial and arbitrary categorization into discrete groups based on eye colour. The results demonstrated ingroup solidarity and hatred of 'outgroups' shown in viciousness and name-calling that disrupted friendships. There are, however, also important differences from SIT. For example, in her intervention, Elliot, an authority figure, imposed notions of dominance and subordination on the children. She introduced what may be seen as 'realistic conflict' since racism continues to be prevalent in US society. Unlike SIT, this intervention aimed to change the children's attitudes. The results were also different from those generally reported in SIT in that, when debriefed, the children in Jane Elliot's intervention focused upon the emotional effects of the exercise (e.g. saying they felt like a 'dog on a leash', a 'prisoner in chains', or 'like dumb people'). However, participants in SIT research do not generally report that they have been upset by the procedure. At best then, this 'natural experiment' provides qualified support for the minimal group experiments, but equally it lends support to other psychological theories.

Jane Elliot's intervention is not what psychologists generally think of as an experiment, in that it was not possible to control for all the factors that might influence the results. For example, we cannot be sure whether the results she obtained were because of prejudice, because the children felt themselves to be in competition for privileges, or because Jane Elliot – an authority figure – dictated how each group was to be treated.

All research raises ethical issues. Do you think that this intervention would fit with BPS ethical principles? Jane Elliot is not a psychologist and so is not bound by psychologists' ethical codes. However, her exercise raises a number of difficult questions. It can be seen from the TV programmes that the children were clearly hurt and angry. Is this acceptable even if Jane Elliot's social policy aim of reducing discrimination was realized? Is it likely that the lesson of the exercise will transfer from colour of eyes to colour of skin? Could the children learn something unintended such as that anything to do with 'race' is necessarily unpleasant and should be avoided?

Summary Section 4

- SIT developed from the work of Henri Tajfel, a Holocaust survivor who wanted to understand the processes that led to prejudice.
- Tajfel studied intergroup relations in order to understand social identity, which he differentiated from personal identity.
- A major feature of SIT is the finding that if people categorize themselves as belonging to a group, they will be prepared to discriminate in favour of their group (the ingroup) and against others (the outgroups).
- Tajfel and his colleagues found that intergroup discrimination occurred even if differences between groups were minimal.
- SIT suggests that the status of the groups to which we belong affects our feelings about our personal identity. Therefore, social identity has emotional consequences for self-esteem.
- According to SIT, intergroup discrimination occurs because we all need to belong to groups that are distinctive from other groups and have high status.
- Individuals and groups can use strategies of social mobility, social creativity and social competition to improve their social status in relation to other groups.
- The 'class divided' exercise can be seen as providing limited support for SIT in a natural setting. However, it raises ethical questions.

5   The social construction of identities

A third, burgeoning field of work on identity within psychology has a rather shorter history than both the Eriksonian psychosocial tradition and SIT. It can broadly be defined as 'social constructionist'. Unlike the previous theories discussed in this chapter, there is no one originator of social constructionist theories. This is partly because social constructionists consider that ideas are socially produced and, hence, not originated by a single person. It is also because social constructionist ideas have diverse origins in a number of disciplines and there are many social constructionist perspectives.

Social construction
Theory that the ways in which we understand the world are not just 'natural', but are 'constructed' between people in everyday social interactions.

5.1 The meaning of 'social construction'

The term **social construction** itself gives a good pointer to the most important ideas in social constructionism, so it is helpful to begin by focusing on each of the component words. If we take 'construction' first, this suggests that the ways in which we understand the world and the things we consider true are not just 'natural' ways of understanding reality. Instead, they are 'constructed' between people as they go about their everyday lives and interact with each other. This may sound unlikely. However, if we think about a concrete example, it becomes clearer. For a long time in Western societies, many people thought that it was 'natural' for women, rather than men, to do all the housework. It was not surprising that it seemed 'natural' because it was what usually happened and had happened for as long as people remembered. Yet, once feminists argued for equality with men, it became clearer that it was not 'natural' for women to do all the housework. It was an example of a construction that was taken for granted as 'natural' because it was the accepted pattern for a long time. The idea that it is not 'natural' is itself a more recent construction.

What about the 'social' part of social construction? This tells us that construction is a social process. Everything that we know is constructed in and through social relations, including the language available to us, our interactions with other people and the ways in which our society treats particular groups of people. Even the information we get from the books we read and the television programmes we view is social because they are produced by people for other people. How we understand them is influenced by our histories and the histories of the cultures in which we live.

5.2 Everyday identities are constructed through language and social relations

The same thing can be understood in different ways

The implication of the idea that we socially construct our worlds is that there are many different ways of understanding the same issue. An often-used example (e.g. in Potter and Wetherell, 1987) that illustrates this is whether we call someone a 'freedom fighter' or a 'terrorist'. Although these two terms can refer to the same person, each constructs a different way of viewing that person and the world. It follows from this that the language we use justifies particular responses to people and to situations. It also constructs what are called 'power relations' between people because how we treat people depends on how we view them. Nelson Mandela, the first president of post-apartheid South Africa, provides a famous example of this. When he was defined as a terrorist by the white South African state under apartheid he was imprisoned. However, as the anti-apartheid movement grew throughout the world, he was increasingly defined as a hero and a symbol of freedom. Eventually, those who continued to construct him as a terrorist did not have sufficient power to make enough people accept their construction and had to give way to those who constructed Mandela as a freedom fighter. In 1990, he was released from gaol, greeted as a hero and became the president of South Africa and a greatly respected world statesperson.

We actively construct identities through everyday social relations

Kenneth Gergen

If constructing the same person differently by calling them either a terrorist or a freedom fighter has implications for how we view the world, it follows that language is fundamental to the processes of social construction. We use language to talk with others, to think, and to communicate generally. The ideas that we take for granted, how we treat each other and are treated, and power relations in society are all constructed through language. It provides the categories and concepts from which we create and maintain our ideas and beliefs and is crucial to our interactions. This means that, according to social constructionists, when we talk or write, we actively construct ways of understanding things.

Social constructionist theories of identity are based on the idea that our identities do not simply unfold. Instead, people actively construct their identities through social relations. The US psychologist Kenneth Gergen, who has been a major social constructionist theorist since the 1970s, gives an everyday example which helps to make clearer what this means:

> *I grew up with fountain pens. As a child they were as 'natural' to me as my family. My father's pen seemed to produce an endless stream of mathematical scribbles that somehow transformed themselves into papers in journals. Meanwhile, my mother's musings gave way to bursts of inspirational writing – short stories, travelogues, and the best letters a boy away from home could ever receive. The pen was destined to become my life. And so it did, as I slowly worked my way toward a professorship in psychology. I loved to ponder and to write; the sound of the pen on paper, the flowing of the ink, the mounting columns of 'my thoughts' – all*

produced a special thrill. And wonder of wonders, I could be paid for it! But now the pen is gone. Some years ago I was informed there would be no more secretaries to transform my handiwork into solid print. I was to write by computer. I loathed the idea. Writing was a craft, not a technology; I needed to touch the paper physically; feel the words flowing from fingers to shaft and shaft to 'my being made visible.' The act of writing was very close to physical contact with the reader. In contrast, the computer was a wedge between us – a piece of brutish machinery separating our humanity. I refused to purchase a computer. Finally, in frustration, the college administration delivered one as a gift. A goose quill now sits nearby on the desk to remind me of my roots. I use my pen only for signing letters.

This machine has virtually transformed my life. It's not simply the ease of writing; there are possibilities for endless experimenting, storing of random ideas, and the like. It also delivers electronic mail and opens the vast horizons of the World Wide Web ... Dozens of times daily I receive messages ... from around the world.

(Gergen, 1999, p.1)

How is Gergen's account relevant to the social construction of his identity? Well, for as long as he could remember, Gergen's identity had been associated with 'the pen' and writing. Asked to fill in the Twenty Statements Test, he may well have included 'I am a writer by pen' among his answers. Yet this identity cannot be said to have unfolded 'naturally' over the course of his life. Rather, Gergen had constructed for himself an identity as an academic whose writing with a pen was central to his identity.

Furthermore, it is clear that Gergen constructed his identity from his social relations. His apparent admiration of his parents led him to value writing by pen. But his identity as someone who wrote by pen was not simply copied from his parents although his statement that 'The pen was destined to become my life' might suggest this. Instead, the pen became important to his identity because he valued what his parents did, saw that they gained social status through publishing their writing, worked to become like them and found that he could become a successful published academic. Other social relations facilitated his identity as a writer by pen. His university provided him with secretarial support to type up his handwriting. Gergen's identity as a writer by pen may well have seemed natural and 'destined' to him. However, he actively constructed for himself this beloved identity through social processes. He clung on to it even when his university administration removed his access to a secretary to type up his writing. This changed the social relations that supported his identity as a pen writer so that it required more effort than previously to sustain such an identity.

Identities change over time and as society and our relationships change

It is clear that Gergen's identity underwent a marked and fairly sudden change. Having been given a computer by the university administration, he says 'This machine has virtually transformed my life'. His identity, therefore, changed dramatically in response to social and technological changes. This illustrates another aspect of the way in which social constructionists theorize identities: the identities available to us and that we take up are affected by our social histories, social positions, relationships and experiences, as well as by social and technological changes (Connell, 1995; Hollway and Jefferson, 2000). As in Erikson's theory, the historical period and culture in which people live are considered to affect the identities they can construct. Identities are, therefore, said to be historically and culturally specific.

We reflect on our own identities and choose particular ways to tell our stories

There is another way in which the example from Gergen helps to illustrate social constructionist theories of identity. It is Gergen himself who tells us about his identity and how it changed. In social constructionist terms, his interpretation of who he is and how that changes is central to the construction of his identity. In order to see why this matters, it is helpful to recognize that Gergen could have told his story in a way that constructed his identity differently. He could have told us that he took pen use for granted in his life – treating it as a utilitarian tool that he rarely thought about until new technology and cuts in university funding made it almost redundant. We would still have got a sense of the importance of pen writing to Gergen's identity, but we would have thought of it as an implicit identity that he was not conscious of until it had to change. Alternatively, he could have told us that, despite his newfound competence on the computer, he would always remain a pen writer at heart – his identity had not changed although he was now forced to use computers.

So while Gergen may not have been aware that there are many ways in which he could tell his story, the story that he has told about himself nevertheless constructs his identity in a particular way. This is what social constructionist theorists mean when they argue that language is central to the construction of our identities. Bruner (1990) suggests that we 'make ourselves' and our identities through the stories about ourselves that we tell others and ourselves (our autobiographical narratives).

Activity 1.3

For this activity you should make brief notes, but you should try not to spend more than 10 minutes doing it. Think about an important event in your life that happened some time ago. Have the stories you tell about it changed over time?

- If so, can you pinpoint how?

- Do you tell different versions of this story to different people? If so, what changes do you make for different audiences?

- Whether or not you have told different versions of the story, do you think that the telling of your story constructed your identity?

On the basis of your answers, consider whether you feel convinced by social constructionist ideas that identities are fluid, changing over time and from situation to situation.

Identities are constructed differently in different cultures

The way in which we talk about things includes not only the vocabulary we use and our actual words, but also our tone, sentence construction and non-verbal signals. All of these carry meanings and sometimes contradict each other. The conventions of how to express ourselves and the ways of talking about things are different in different cultures. It follows from this that how we construct our identities depends on the ways of thinking and talking (**discourses**) about identities currently available in our society. This idea is supported by the fact that various researchers have found differences between countries in the way that people respond on the Twenty Statements Test, according to whether their society is rated as more individualist or more collectivist (Smith and Bond, 1998). People living in Japan and China (which are considered predominantly collectivist) are more likely to respond in terms of their relationships to other people, their place in society and a specific context (e.g. 'I am a student at Beijing University'). By way of contrast, people living in the USA (which is considered predominantly individualist) are more likely to respond in more personally meaningful ways without mentioning the contexts in which their identities occur (e.g. 'I am a student').

Discourses
The ways of thinking and talking about issues currently available in our culture – that is, the processes by which people construct meanings.

Identities can be changed and so are provisional and dynamic

Since there are always different ways of talking about the same thing (as in the terrorist/freedom fighter example at the beginning of Section 5.2), we can change the ways in which we construct our identities. Social constructionist theories view identities as always in the process of being formed and so as provisional and dynamic, rather than achieved and fixed. The same people can produce different narratives of the same episodes as

Michael Jackson

Katharine Hepburn

Liv Ullman

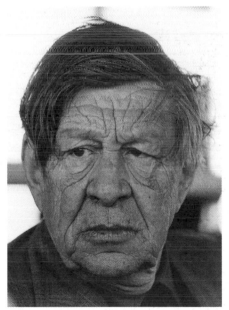

W.H. Auden

People's appearance changes a great deal over their lifetimes. Psychologists disagree about whether their identities also change or mostly stay the same after adolescence

their identities change. But since identities are socially produced, we can all produce different versions of the same story for different audiences. This may partly explain why you may have found that you appear different to different people in Activity 1.1.

There is no distinction between personal and social identities

All the theories discussed in this chapter assume that consideration of who we are requires consideration of who we are not. This idea is crucial to social constructionist theorists, however, because they argue that identities can never be produced in isolation from social relations and that we have different identities when we interact with different groups or individuals. This means that, unlike other theories, no distinction is made between personal and social identities – all identities are social.

Identities are resources we use to negotiate everyday interactions

Just as the ways in which we construct other people affect how we treat them, so our construction of our own identities affects the ways in which we view ourselves and act in the world. Sue Widdicombe (1998) suggests that identities are resources that we all use and negotiate in everyday interactions. If we think back to the Gergen quotation above, we can see that he used his identity as a pen user as a resource to help him to resist using a computer. At a relatively simple level, we are all more or less skilled at negotiating and shifting identities as speakers and listeners. Knowing consciously what we need to do to be effective speakers and listeners, and temporarily taking on those identities in conversation are crucial to being able to converse with others.

We may not even consider that we are negotiating shifting identities in conversations (although being 'a good listener' or an 'amusing conversationalist' may be part of our identities). However, we also regularly negotiate more complex identities in interactions. For example, Derek Edwards (1998) points out that if we construct ourselves as 'married-with-kids', we take up a different identity position from married parents who do not explicitly construct themselves in this way. We can, for example, use it to signal that we are comfortably settled in relationships with responsibilities or, instead, that we are weighed down with responsibilities and need light relief. Identity is not, therefore, just an achievement (as in psychosocial theories), it is also a resource that we can use in interactions.

5.3 Differences between people who apparently have the same identities

SIT proposes that people have a range of identities, which become salient in different contexts. However, social constructionist theorists of identity argue that there are also differences *within* social categories. This way of understanding identities has been much influenced by feminist debates which have had to grapple with the fact that the category 'woman' is not characterized by any single essence: women are not all the same but differ in many ways. Many feminist theorists have written a great deal about how women are differentiated by 'race', ethnicity, sexuality and social class as well as more personal characteristics (Brah, 1996). This means that generalizations about women (or any other category) can never be entirely true because women (and all other social groups) differ. The following concrete example helps to clarify these somewhat abstract points:

> In 1991, President Bush, anxious to restore a conservative majority to the US Supreme Court, nominated Clarence Thomas, a black judge of conservative political views. In Bush's judgement, white voters (who may have been prejudiced about a black judge) were likely to support Thomas because he was conservative on equal-rights legislation, and black voters (who support liberal policies on race) would support Thomas because he was black. In short, the President was 'playing the identities game'.
>
> During the Senate 'hearings' on the appointment, Judge Thomas was accused of sexual harassment by a black woman, Anita Hill, a former junior colleague of Thomas's. The hearings caused a public scandal and polarized American society. Some blacks supported Thomas on racial grounds; others opposed him on sexual grounds. Black women were divided, depending on whether their 'identities' as blacks or as women prevailed. Black men were also divided, depending on whether their sexism overrode their liberalism. White men were divided, depending, not only on their politics, but on how they identified themselves with respect to racism and sexism. White conservative women supported Thomas, not only on political grounds, but because of their opposition to feminism. White feminists, often liberal on race, opposed Thomas on sexual grounds. And because Judge Thomas is a member of the judicial elite and Anita Hill, at the time of the alleged incident, a junior employee, there were issues of social class position at work in these arguments too.
>
> (Hall, 1992, pp.279–80)

Social constructionist methods focus on the everyday

As we have seen, key principles of social constructionism are that identities are part of our everyday practices, produce particular ways of acting on the world and are constructed as we go about our daily life. They can therefore be studied in all aspects of what people do and say and are best studied in 'natural' settings rather than in laboratories. Kenneth Gergen's and Stuart Hall's accounts are therefore good ways with which to gain access to an understanding of the ordinary social construction of identities.

Multiple, de-centred identities

Hall's example illustrates something that has come up in all the theories discussed above – that understanding identity requires that we understand diversity and difference. However, it presents a good illustration of the social constructionist idea that different identities can be constructed in response to the same event in everyday life. In this case, news reports led people to take sides for or against Anita Hill or Clarence Thomas on the basis of how they identified with what they saw as important characteristics of each.

Hall analyses some ways in which 'race', gender and social class affected people's construction of their identities in relation to the Hill–Thomas incident. He suggests that people who are often considered to belong to the same groups, in terms of 'race' and gender (e.g. white women; black women; black men; and white men), differed in the identities they constructed. Others, who are usually considered to belong to different groups, shared identities in terms of support for, or opposition to, Hill and Thomas. This fits with social constructionist identity theorists since they argue that there is nothing fundamental (i.e. essential) to being black, white, a woman, a man, or from any particular social class. Instead, people construct for themselves the meanings of any groups to which they consider themselves to belong.

Unlike psychosocial theories, social constructionist theories reject the notion that people have one, core identity that is at the centre of who they are. Instead, they suggest that people have many different identities that are de-centred because they always operate in relation to other identities. This means that, however important any particular identity may be, it cannot completely occupy the 'centre' of our identities, since there are always other identities in evidence. In the quotation above, Hall talks of some identities prevailing over others for particular people with respect to Hill and Thomas. This allows us to think about another aspect of social constructionist theory – that people's different identities are potentially contradictory. For example, some black women's identities as black people may have contradicted the identities they held as women.

You may feel unconvinced about social constructionist theories of identities because they suggest that everybody has multiple, de-centred and changeable identities while you might feel that you have a core, centred identity that has been stable for as long as you can remember. Social constructionists would respond by suggesting that we can acquire and maintain a distinctive and continuous identity by constructing an autobiographical narrative of ourselves as having one core, centred identity. They would argue that, in order to maintain a life story that fits with this, we reconstruct the past in ways that help us to understand the past, present and where we expect to be in the future (Hall, 1996).

The argument that our identities are multiple, de-centred and changing but that we construct unified autobiographical narratives is difficult to disprove. It is possible to see this either as a strength or as a shortcoming of social constructionist theories of identities.

Identities involve power relations

Social constructionist theories suggest that all identities involve power relations because they are constructed in relation to other people within social contexts that involve relationships of power. In the Hall example, if a black, working-class woman identified as black, she may have been more likely to support Clarence Thomas than if she identified as working-class. This is because particular identities produce different power relations and hence different ways of viewing social issues and other people. This demonstrates a further social constructionist idea – that power is relational. In other words, power is produced as people relate to each other and nobody has absolute power over anybody else. In the Hill–Thomas dispute, for example, white, middle-class people (who are powerful in many ways) were divided about how to respond and had little power over how other people responded.

Activity 1.4

Look again at the 10 'I am ...' statements you noted down at the beginning of this chapter for Activity 1.1.

- Would you say that the statements suggest that you have multiple identities or that you have one core identity?

- Take one identity and try to think of the power relations that are associated with it. For example, if you wrote 'I am tall', there is an implicit comparison with people who are shorter. Is being tall more or less powerful than being short? Is this the same in every situation and for all people?

Summary Section 5

- Identities are socially constructed (as opposed to occurring naturally) as we go about our everyday lives.
- We all construct our identities within networks of social relations. They are, therefore, relational and necessarily social.
- No distinction is made between personal and social identities in social constructionist theories.
- We construct our identities in language and they are affected by the discourses available within society.
- Identities can be viewed as resources for interaction.
- Identities shift over time and from context to context. They are, therefore, provisional, dynamic and historically and culturally specific, rather than fixed.
- There are similarities as well as differences in the identities of people who are constructed as belonging to different groups. Likewise, there are differences as well as similarities in the identities of people constructed as belonging to the same groups.
- Identities are multiple, de-centred and changeable rather than singular, centred and stable.
- Identity positions involve power relations.
- A variety of identity positions are available to everybody. These can be contradictory.

1.5 Similarities and differences between the theories of identity

Identity is a commonly used term whose meaning can be studied quickly and simply using the introspectionist test of identity called the Twenty Statements Test. However, identity is a complicated concept that includes embodiment as well as how we evaluate ourselves. This chapter has considered three types of psychological theory of identity: psychosocial identity theory originated by Erikson and developed by Marcia; a theory of group social identity introduced by Tajfel; and social constructionist theories which have no single author. Each uses different research methods.

There are several shared features of the theories presented in this chapter:
- All are influential and vibrant, with research and theoretical work helping to address criticisms.
- All consider that identities are historically and geographically located and produced through social relations.
- To some extent, all agree that people are active in the construction of their identities.
- All recognize that diversity is important to identity and that there are several aspects to our identities.

The theories differ, however, in the degree to which they consider identity should be viewed as:
- singular or multiple
- achieved and fixed or provisional and dynamic
- particularly formed in adolescence and part of a developmental process
- influenced by our biographies or achieved in current social relations and contexts
- a resource for negotiating interactions
- constructed through language
- related to power relations
- involving intragroup and intergroup differences.

Activity 1.5

Look at the ways in which the theories of identity differ (in Box 1.5). Note which of the three theories discussed in the chapter fits which features of the theories discussed in Box 1.5. This activity will help you to revise the theories so do look back over the chapter.

6   Can the theories help to explain the identities of people with physical disabilities?

6.1   All the theories are relevant to a consideration of embodiment

All the theories discussed in this chapter continue to generate studies that help to refine the original theories. However, theories are only useful if the abstract ideas they propose make sense when applied to concrete issues. This section will consider how the different theories we have examined might help us to understand the embodied identities of those with physical impairments. Since the theories focus on different aspects of identity, there is no suggestion that any one theory provides all the answers.

Theories are generally tested in two sorts of ways: by applying them to real-life issues or by using them to predict what is likely to happen and then seeing if the predictions are correct. In this section they are applied to accounts provided by people who have physical impairments

The theories all treat embodiment as important to identity. They do this, however, in very different ways. For SIT, the importance of embodiment is implicit in its concern with intergroup discrimination which allows it to consider, for example, identities associated with people who have physical impairments. Some social constructionist theories are concerned with how embodiment allows the construction of particular identity positions and how people negotiate embodied identities. The psychosocial theories of Erikson and Marcia are explicitly concerned with bodily aspects of identity since the body affects the psychosocial issues we face (e.g. in old age when the body does not work as well as it did).

In recent years, many have campaigned for those who are 'non-disabled' to stop thinking of people with physical impairments as 'the disabled'. Allan Sutherland explains the reasons for this in the introduction to his book on the issues raised by disability:

Throughout this book I shall be using the phrase 'people with disabilities' rather than talking about 'The Disabled'. That is a phrase which many people with disabilities, including myself, find extremely objectionable, because it both depersonalizes us and writes us off as individuals by implying that our disabilities are our identity.

(Sutherland, 1981, p.13)

Sutherland is making the point that the term 'the disabled' treats people with disabilities as less than human. In the decades since Sutherland wrote this, many of those who themselves have disabilities have chosen to use the term 'disabled people' as a positive, collectively agreed, term.

The implicit assumption that disability is the only identity possible for people with impairments has been challenged by theorists of disability and by groups for people with impairments. They argue that the wide variation between types of impairment and within groups of people who have the same impairments mean that they are not a single group, but have multiple, diverse identities (Keith, 1994). There is, therefore, no such thing as a 'disabled identity' or any one identity shared by people with physical impairments. A 14-year-old boy argues: 'I am not my disability, I'm me. I have dyslexia and I've had polio, but I'm not a "dyslexic" or "a cripple", I'm me' (Swan, 1981, p.84).

A drawing by a child (Wong Sai Ming) with physical impairments indicating that those with and without disabilities are equal

Since many people with disabilities have campaigned to change how others refer to them, this seems to support the common theme in psychological theories that identities require positive recognition from others. It also highlights the importance of diversity to identities, in that differences between groups as well as differences between people who are

If the social environment is suitable, people with physical impairments are able fully to participate in a range of activities

within the same group all affect identities. In addition, the concern to alter the ways in which language is used to exclude or define people with physical impairments provides support for the social constructionist notion that the discourses available help to construct identity positions (see Box 1.6).

1.6 *Tomorrow I'm Going to Rewrite the English Language*

The following poem, by disabled writer Lois Keith, takes an ironic look at the power of language:

Tomorrow I am going to rewrite the English Language.
I will discard all those striving ambulist metaphors
Of power and success
And construct new ways to describe my strength.
My new, different strength.

Then I won't have to feel dependent
Because I can't stand on my own two feet.
And I'll refuse to feel a failure
When I don't stay one step ahead.
I won't feel inadequate if I can't
Stand up for myself
Or illogical when I don't
Take it one step at a time.

> I will make them understand that it is a very male way
> To describe the world.
> All this walking tall
> And making great strides.
>
> Yes, tomorrow I am going to rewrite the English Language
> Creating the world in my own image.
> Mine will be a gentler, more womanly way
> To describe my progress.
> I will wheel, cover and encircle.
> Somehow I will learn to say it all.
>
> *(Keith, 1994, p.57)*

6.2 The importance of continuity, 'crisis' and adolescence to identity

Erikson argued that a sense of continuity is important to identity. Those who face threats to their lives would, therefore, be particularly conscious of identity. This may help to explain why people who suddenly become physically impaired often report profound consciousness of their embodied identities (e.g. Dandeker, 1994; Morris, 1993). To some extent this fits with social constructionist theories, which argue that our identities are multiple and change throughout our lives but that we often construct an illusory sense of continuity through our autobiographical narratives. SIT provides a rather different, but equally plausible, explanation of the consciousness of identity for those who became physically impaired in adulthood. It would suggest that it is the change of belonging to a group of lower social status (and hence to being treated as a member of a devalued category), rather than just change in itself, that leads to consciousness of identity.

Erikson and Marcia are the only theorists discussed in this chapter who argue that the development of identity is accompanied by normative 'crisis' and that the achievement of identity is particularly the task of adolescence. This view is supported by the following quotation from a woman, Micheline Mason, who describes a period of 'identity crisis' in early adolescence when she really understands for the first time that her physical impairments are permanent:

> *The first time the doubt that I belonged to this particular planet struck me, was a glorious, calm, blue-skied day when I was twelve years old.*
> *... I was thinking about growing up. Until that moment I think I had somehow believed that when I grew up I would become 'normal', i.e. without a disability. 'Normal' then meant to me, 'like my big sister',*

*pretty, rebellious, going out with boys, doing wonderful, naughty things
with them, leaving school and getting a job, leaving home, getting
married and having children. That momentous day I suddenly realized
that my life was not going to be like that at all. I was going to be just the
same as I had always been – very small, funnily shaped, unable to walk.
It seemed at that moment that the sky cracked ...*

*The next two years seemed like a dark roller-coaster ride, sometimes
happy, often plunging into despair. My main preoccupation seemed to
be desperately trying to deny the awareness of my difference which had
started on that day.*

(Micheline Mason, in Campling, 1981, pp.23–4)

It seems that embodied identities can also become crucially important in
adolescence for young people without physical impairments. It is in that
period, for example, that youth subcultural styles are most prominent and
that eating disorders are most likely to occur.

However, Erikson and Marcia's emphasis on identity achievement as
central to adolescence somewhat limits the fluidity of identities since, if a
crucial part should ideally be achieved early in the life course, this makes
later change less possible. Yet, most of those who have campaigned for
shifts in social perceptions of people with physical impairments are adults
– some of whom became physically impaired in adulthood. Both SIT and
social constructionist theories allow more possibilities for changes to
identities throughout the life course than do psychosocial theories.

6.3 Do we choose core identities or construct and use flexible identities?

All the theories allow some agency over choice of identities. However,
both Erikson's and Marcia's theories can be criticized for suggesting that
we have more choice over our identities than most of us do. For example,
Grotevant (1992) argues that there is a contradiction between the
assumption that it is possible to have choices between our 'identity
options' and the fact that some identities (such as the identity of an
adopted child) are not open to choice. It would not, for example, make
sense to think of Micheline Mason (quoted above) as going through an
extended period of moratorium in which she could explore and choose
possibilities associated with able-bodiedness.

Erikson and Marcia argue that identity has to be achieved in different
areas of people's lives (e.g. sexuality, education, and relationships with
parents). However, they consider that people develop one central identity
from these different domains. This issue of whether people have one core

identity or several equally important identities continues to be debated by identity theorists. A consideration of how 'race', gender and disability intersect demonstrates that people can simultaneously have several equally important identities – although it cannot prove that no-one has one core identity:

> *I don't remember race being an issue in the hospital where I spent a lot of my childhood and there were so many Asian people where I lived that I did not stand out as being black. It took me a long time to understand why people who did not know me in my neighbourhood called me 'spastic', 'bandy legs' or 'Ironside' and why people with disabilities called me 'paki' or 'nigger'. Eventually I learned that wherever I went I would probably stand out as being different from the majority and I had to be prepared to accept being called either paki or bandy legs, and sometimes both.*
>
> *... But I've come a long way ... I've reclaimed my identity by refusing to accept a concept of 'normality' which tells me I must walk, have fair skin and try to blend in by wearing Western clothes.*
>
> *(Begum, 1994, pp.50–1)*

The woman, Nasa Begum, quoted above seems to see her identity as part of an active process in which she has learned to resist other people's constructions of her as 'abnormal' because of her impairment, skin colour or clothes. Clearly, group identities are important in her account (as SIT suggests). Her identities are continually 'achieved' within her social context (as psychosocial theories suggest) and they are actively constructed and negotiated (as social constructionist theories suggest) as her understanding (and society) changes. Her identities are, therefore, culturally and historically specific, as all the theories suggest.

As we have seen, one of the claims made by social constructionist theorists is that identities are not merely achieved, but are available to be used as resources in everyday interactions. Furthermore, they argue, identities are fluid, rather than fixed, changing from setting to setting as well as over time. The following quotation from a study of 'life as a disabled child' illustrates both these themes:

> *Children displayed fluidity in claiming disability as an identity. They described how they were not always disabled. One girl talked about how wheelchair basketball equalized social relationships and, as she put it, 'in some situations I'm not, we're not, always disabled'. ... For some of the children in special schools, disability was normalized, and hence disappeared as an identity in that setting. Even when children refused to occupy the disability category, there could be a strategic claim of*

privilege and exemption in certain school situations ('can we go early, Miss, 'cos we're disabled'.) In these examples, the difference could become a benefit.

The children's own sense of identity also became apparent through their resistance to dominant discourses about them. The ... children adopted strategies through which they attempted to assert their own agency ... In some cases this agency was read by adults as bad behaviour, and the children were labelled as having difficulty coming to terms with their impairment.

(Watson et al., 2000, p.19)

Social constructionist theories are able to explain the children's strategic, flexible and ironic employment of identities for their own advantage. However, the other theories we have examined can also explain this, albeit in a more limited fashion. According to SIT, for example, people use their identities in order to improve low social status or to maintain high social status by discriminating against other groups. While it is less clear how SIT would account for the flexible, situational use of identity indicated in the example above, it can account for the children's use of their group identity as 'disabled' to improve their social status.

In psychosocial theories, the use and the categorizing of identities are interlinked. For example, psychosocial researchers categorize young people's identity status according to how they act in their everyday lives. Yet, their identity status helps to *produce* particular ways of interacting with the world. This is, arguably, a circularity which makes it unclear how this theory would help in the analysis of the quotation above. However, social constructionist theories have also been criticized for suggesting that we have numerous, flexible identities, particularly since people who experience themselves as fragmented are often considered to have mental illnesses.

Summary Section 6

- Although the theories we have considered in this chapter pay relatively little attention to embodiment, all are relevant to a consideration of embodied identities as expressed in accounts written by people who have physical impairments.
- Different aspects of each theory are relevant to a consideration of the identities of people with physical impairments.

Further reading

You are not expected to read the books and chapters that are listed below. However, no chapter can present a complete picture of the work done in an area. The further reading is intended to give you an idea of how the theories presented in the chapter have been developed and applied. It describes work not mentioned in the chapter that is relevant to a wider understanding of identity. A brief look at this section will help you to get a clearer view of the psychology of identity and, if you have time and are interested – whether during the course or later – you could read any of the publications that interest you.

Archer, S. (1992) 'A feminist's approach to identity research', in Adams, G., Gullotta, T. and Montemayor, R. (eds) *Adolescent Identity Formation*, London, Sage

Sally Archer is a feminist psychosocial identity researcher who points out that Erikson largely ignored women's identities and that his theory was Eurocentric. In this chapter she argues that identity researchers need to do more complex work on gender differences and to study the impact of relationships on identities.

Ashmore, R. and Jussim, L. (eds) (1997) *Self and Identity: Fundamental Issues*, Oxford, Oxford University Press.

This book brings together a collection of chapters from eminent identity theorists working in psychology, sociology and anthropology. It addresses two of the questions that have been explored in this chapter: Do we have one identity or many?; Is identity personal or social? It also considers the ways in which history, culture and society affect identity. In doing so, it considers some major theories of identity and discusses the authors' research.

Billig, M. (1995) *Banal Nationalism*, London, Sage.

Michael Billig was a student of Tajfel's and worked with Tajfel on the early minimal group experiments. However, he has moved away from Social Identity Theory and is now one of the foremost social constructionist identity theorists. In this book, Billig was not interested in extreme expressions of nationalism, but in more everyday forms of nationalism, which are so common that they are generally taken-for-granted as 'natural' and 'innocent'. These regularly occur in media reports including of news, sports coverage and the weather forecast; postage stamps; currency; and the symbolism of national flags and the occasions when they are used. Billig argues that for there to be a notion of who 'we' are and who 'they' are, there has to be a constant 'flagging' of the national identity through such everyday forms of 'banal nationalism'.

Billig, M., Condor, S., Edwards, D., Gane, M., Middleton, D. and Radley, A. (1988) *Ideological Dilemmas: A Social Psychology of Everyday Thinking*, London, Sage.

This book deals with research on the social construction of identities. The authors argue that, in everyday life, we all constantly face dilemmas and, hence, have to make decisions. An examination of the everyday dilemmas that people face is important to the understanding of how people negotiate the identity positions they take up.

Bosma, H. (1992) 'Identity in adolescence; managing commitments', in Adams, G., Gullotta, T. and Montemayor, R. (eds) *Adolescent Identity Formation*, London, Sage.

This chapter demonstrates how Erikson and Marcia's work on identity has influenced the construction of specially developed scales to measure identity. Harke Bosma, a Dutch developmental psychologist at Groningen University, developed one such scale – the Groningen Identity Development Scale – in order to study the process of identity development. This scale is designed to measure developmental changes in identity by asking about the content and strength of young people's identity commitments and the amount of exploration and change involved in their identity achievement.

Burr, V. (1995) *An Introduction to Social Constructionism*, London, Routledge.

This book aims to present the central tenets of social constructionism in an accessible way, by using everyday examples and recent research.

Hutnik, N. (1991) *Ethnic Minority Identity: A Social Psychological Perspective*, Oxford, Clarendon Press.

This book focuses on the identities of British young people from minority ethnic groups and assesses the relevance of various psychological theories (including Erikson's and Tajfel's) to a consideration of this. It then presents the findings of Hutnik's own study of ethnic minority identity in young British people – a major part of which involves using the Twenty Statements Test. Hutnik concludes that ethnic minority identity is not necessarily fixed and singular, but may be hyphenated (e.g. British-Asian).

Kelly, C. and Breinlinger, S. (1996) *The Social Psychology of Collective Action: Identity, Injustice and Gender*, London, Taylor and Francis.

This book reports research which takes forward the ideas proposed in Social Identity Theory by studying naturally occurring, rather than laboratory imposed, groups and by interviewing group members, rather than doing experiments on them. It investigates the relationship between attitudes, identities and collective action amongst trade unionists and members of various women's groups. The researchers found that memberships of groups could have positive effects (unlike the mainly negative effects reported in this chapter). Their findings also indicate that people have views about their group membership and identities, and so talking to them helps to inform analyses of social identities.

Marcia, J. (1998) 'Peer Gynt's life cycle', in Skoe, E. and von der Lippe, A. (eds) *Personality Development in Adolescence: A Cross National and Life Span Perspective*, London, Routledge.

Although James Marcia has influenced hundreds of studies using questionnaires and interviews to study his four identity statuses, he himself has extended the methodology suitable for studying his statuses to an analysis of fiction. In this chapter, Marcia applied Eriksonian theory together with his own measures of identity status to an analysis of Henrik Ibsen's verse play *Peer Gynt* (based on a folk tale from Ibsen's Norway). This demonstrates how even a mythic character demonstrates the identity statuses that would be expected from Marcia's theory. The analysis of *Peer Gynt* leads Marcia to invent a new verb 'adolescing' in recognition of the fact that identity is reformulated throughout life. Thus, while he maintains the notion that adolescence is the period for major identity development, he does address criticism of his overemphasis on the achievement of identity in adolescence by making it a more lifelong possibility.

Mead, G.H. (1934) *Mind, Self and Society*, Chicago, IL, University of Chicago Press.

George Herbert Mead has been variously called a social philosopher, social psychologist and sociologist. In his posthumously published lecture notes (1934), he, like William James (a founder of psychology), divided the self into the active 'I' and the passive 'me' on whom others act, and identity into the personal and the social (as in psychosocial identity theory). Mead focused on language as the supreme symbolic system for communicating and for negotiating interactions. He argued that it allows people to carry on 'internal conversations' with themselves and anticipate other's responses. This allows people to assume social roles and to internalize other's attitudes in forming their identities. This focus on language as a symbolic system central to interaction means that Mead's ideas can be said to have anticipated social constructionist theory.

Robinson, W.P. (ed.) (1996) *Social Groups and Identities: Developing the Legacy of Henri Tajfel*, Boston, MA, Butterworth-Heinemann.

This book discusses the major contribution made by Henri Tajfel to social psychology in Europe. Many researchers who worked with Tajfel in Bristol discuss how they have been influenced by his theory and taken forward his theory and methods in various ways, including by developing Social Identity Theory.

References

Allen, A. (1999) 'Placing the school-to-work transition in the context of adolescent development', in Crain, R.L., Allen, A., Thaler, R., Sullivan, D., Zellman, G., Little, J.W. and Quigley, D.D. (eds) *The Effects of Academic Career Magnet Education on High Schools and Their Graduates* (MDS-779), Berkeley, CA, University of California, National Center for Research in Vocational Education. [on line] http://ncrve.berkeley.edu/abstracts/MDS-779/ [accessed 22 February 2001]

Antaki, C. and Widdicombe, S. (eds) (1998) *Identities in Talk*, London, Sage.

Begum, N. (1994) 'Snow White', in Keith, L. (ed.).

Brah, A. (1996) *Cartographies of Diaspora: Contesting Identities*, London, Routledge.

Bruner, J. (1990) *Acts of Meaning*, Cambridge, MA, Harvard University Press.

Campling, J. (ed.) (1981) *Images of Ourselves: Women with Disabilities Talking*, London, Routledge and Kegan Paul.

Coleman, J. and Hendry, L. (1990) *The Nature of Adolescence* (2nd edn), London, Routledge.

Connell, R. (1995) *Masculinities*, Cambridge, Polity.

Conway, M. and Fthenaki, A. (2000) 'Disruption and loss of autobiographical memory', in Boller, F. and Grafman, J. (eds) *Handbook of Neuropsychology* (2nd edn), Vol. 2, Amsterdam and New York, Elsevier.

Dandeker, C. (1994) 'Different dances', in Keith, L. (ed.).

Edwards, D. (1998) 'The relevant thing about her: social identity categories in use', in Antaki, C. and Widdicombe, S. (eds).

Erikson, E. (1968) *Identity, Youth and Crisis*, New York, W.W. Norton & Co.

Foucault, M. (1988) *Technologies of the Self*, Boston, MA, University of Massachussetts Press.

Friedman, L.J. (1999) *Identity's Architect: A Biography of Erik Erikson*, New York, Scribner.

Freud, A. (1958) 'Adolescence', *Psychoanalytic Study of the Child*, vol.13, pp.255–78.

Gardner, H. (1999) 'The enigma of Erik Erikson', *New York Review of Books*, 24 June, pp.52–6.

Gergen, K. (1999) *An Invitation to Social Construction*, London, Sage.

Grotevant, H. (1992) 'Assigned and chosen identity components: a process perspective on their integration', in Adams, G., Gullotta, T. and Montemayor, R. (eds) *Adolescent Identity Formation*, London, Sage.

Hall, S. (1992) 'The question of cultural identity', in Hall, S., Held, D. and McGrew, T. (eds) *Modernity and Its Futures*, Cambridge, Polity/The Open University.

Hall, S. (1996) 'Introduction', in Hall, S. and Du Gay, P. (eds) *Questions of Cultural Identity*, London, Sage.

Henriques, J. (1998) 'Social psychology and the politics of racism', in Henriques, J., Hollway, W., Urwin, C., Venn, C. and Walkerdine, V. (eds) *Changing the Subject: Psychology, Social Regulation and Subjectivity* (2nd edn), London, Routledge.

Hogg, M. and Abrams, D. (1999) 'Social identity and social cognition: historical background and current trends', in Abrams, D. and Hogg, M. (eds) *Social Identity and Social Cognition*, Oxford, Blackwell.

Hollway, W. and Jefferson, T. (2000) *Doing Qualitative Research Differently: Free Association, Narrative and the Interview Method*, London, Sage.

James, W. (1890) *Principles of Psychology*, New York, Holt.

Keith, L. (ed.) (1994) *Mustn't Grumble: Writing by Disabled Women*, London, Women's Press.

Kroger, J. (1989/1993) *Identity in Adolescence: The Balance Between Self and Other* (2nd edn), London, Routledge.

Kroger, J. (2000) 'Ego identity status research in the new millennium', *International Journal for the Study of Behavioral Development*, vol.24, no.2, pp.145–8.

Kuhn, M.K. and McPartland, S. (1954) 'An empirical investigation of self-attitudes', *American Sociological Review*, vol.19, pp.68–76.

Marcia, J.E. (1966) 'Development and validation of ego-identity status', *Journal of Personality and Social Psychology*, vol.3, pp.551–8.

Marcia, J. (1980) 'Identity in adolescence', in Adelson, J. (ed.) *Handbook of Adolescent Psychology*, New York, John Wiley.

Marcia, J. (1994) 'The empirical study of ego identity', in Bosma, H., Graafsma, T., Grotevant , H. and de Levita, D. (eds) *Identity and Development: An Interdisciplinary Approach*, London, Sage.

Microsoft Corporation (1996) *Encarta 96 Encyclopaedia* [CD-ROM].

Morris, J. (1993) *Independent Lives: Community Care and Disabled People*, Basingstoke, Macmillan.

Muuss, R. (1988) *Theories of Adolescence*, New York, Random House.

Oliver, M. (1990) *The Politics of Disablement*, Basingstoke, Macmillan.

Peters, W. (1987) *A Class Divided: Then and Now*, New Haven, CT, Yale University Press.

Potter, J. and Wetherell, M. (1987) *Discourse and Social Psychology*, London, Sage.

Shilling, C. (1997) 'The body and difference', in Woodward, K. (ed.) *Identity and Difference*, London, Sage/The Open University.

Sims, S. (2000) 'Nowhere man', *The Times*, 11 March, pp.91–2.

Smith, P.B. and Bond, M.H. (1998) *Social Psychology Across Cultures* (2nd edn), London, Prentice Hall Europe.

Stevens, R. (1983) *Erik Erikson: An Introduction*, Milton Keynes, Open University Press.

Sutherland, A. (1981) *Disabled We Stand,* London, Souvenir Press.

Swain, J., Finkelstein, V., French, S. and Oliver, M. (eds) (1993) *Disabling Barriers – Enabling Environments,* London, Sage/The Open University.

Swan, J. (1981) Statement in Exley, H. (ed.) *What It's Like To Be Me*, Watford, Exley Publications.

Tajfel, H. (ed.) (1978) *Differentiation Between Social Groups: Studies in the Social Psychology of Intergroup Relations,* London, Academic Press.

Tajfel, H. (1981) *Human Groups and Social Categories: Studies in Social Psychology,* Cambridge, Cambridge University Press.

Tajfel, H., Billig, M., Bundy, R.P. and Flament, C. (1971) 'Social categorization and intergroup behaviour', *European Journal of Social Psychology*, vol.1, pp.149–77.

Turner, J. (1987) 'Introducing the problem: individual and group', in Turner, J., Hogg, M., Oakes, P., Reicher, S. and Wetherell, M. *Rediscovering the Social Group: A Self-Categorization Theory*, Oxford, Basil Blackwell.

Turner, J. and Brown, R. (1978) 'Social status, cognitive alternatives and intergroup relations', in Tajfel, H. (ed.).

Watson, N., Shakespeare, T., Cunningham-Burley, S., Barnes, C., Corker, M., Davis, J. and Priestley, M. (2000) 'Life as a disabled child: a qualitative study of young people's experiences and perspectives', *Report for the ESRC Research Programme, Children 5–16: Growing into the Twenty-First Century*. [on line] http://www.mailbase.ac.uk/lists/disability-research/files/children.rtf [accessed 21 February 2001]

Widdicombe, S. (1993) 'Autobiography and change: rhetoric and authenticity of "gothic style"', in Burman, E. and Parker, I. (eds) *Discourse Analytic Research: Repertoires and Readings of Texts in Action*, London, Routledge.

Widdicombe, S. (1998) 'Identity as an analysts' and a participants' resource', in Antaki C. and Widdicombe, S. (eds).

Woodward, K. (2000) 'Questions of identity', in Woodward, K. (ed.) *Questioning Identity: Gender, Class, Nation*, London, Routledge/The Open University.

How to use the commentaries

The commentaries appear at the end of each chapter and are presented at two levels of detail. After a short introduction, each commentary provides a list of six important points, in a box. This is followed by a more detailed discussion of issues. You can use the six points as a guide to the detailed discussion, as a memory aid and as a summary.

Read the commentaries when you reach the end of each chapter and then return to them when you need to. We suggest that the commentaries will be useful when you are preparing assignments. The commentaries as a set will be especially helpful when you reach the end of the book and also when you are revising at the end of the course. Use the commentaries to help you to:

1   see how each chapter contributes to building up an understanding of the discipline of psychology and its historical traditions
2   understand different kinds of psychological theory
3   understand different psychological methods
4   widen your understanding of some of the themes and debates important to psychology as a whole.

■ Commentary 1: Identities and diversities

In Chapter 1 we have started to build up a picture of the discipline of psychology, fleshing out the map which was drawn in the Introduction. For example, in the Introduction we wrote that psychology is of relevance to thinking about everyday issues, but we also stressed that gaining psychological understanding of such issues is not a simple matter. Chapter 1 demonstrated this by discussing three influential psychological theories about identities and applying them to an everyday issue – the identities of people with physical impairments.

Theory

1 Psychologists take different perspectives on psychological issues, which means that they ask different questions, use different methods and data, and produce different theories.

2 There is no one answer to a psychological question. Instead of telling us the 'truth', theories provide ways of thinking about an issue and about how to test ideas. Psychology is a discipline that makes progress through debate and the putting forward of alternative viewpoints, as well as through building on ideas and research within each perspective.

Methods

3 Some psychological theories are built up from a consideration of people's beliefs, experiences and what they say – taking an insider viewpoint – whilst others make sense of human psychology from an outsider viewpoint.

4 Psychological research on identity is primarily holistic – that is, concerned with the person as a whole rather than with isolated aspects of people's behaviour or particular processes like memory or perception.

Themes

5 The area of identities is concerned with the theme of what it is that makes us unique as individuals and as humans, and so different from other animals.

6 Identity is a topic that raises questions about whether we are relatively 'fixed', staying the same all through our lives, or whether we change over time.

■ Thinking about theory

Not just one answer - different perspectives and different theories

Chapter 1 showed how psychologists have had to devise complex theories in order to study the apparently simple topic of identity. By the very fact that we have set out *three* theories and evaluated them, we have already underlined the idea that no single theory provides the one 'correct' psychological view of identity.

At the same time, we have highlighted another crucial issue for students of psychology. Psychology progresses not only through devising, applying, testing and evaluating theories and building on previous research, but also through debate about how best to understand psychological concepts such as identity. It is because psychologists take different perspectives on psychological issues that they produce different theories and methods. It is this debate that has made psychology a vibrant, dynamic discipline.

By raising this point about the diversity of perspectives and theories, we have also provided an opportunity to think about what theories can do, what they cannot do and where they come from. In themselves, theories cannot tell us 'the truth' about the world or about a particular idea. Instead, they provide us with ways of thinking about an issue and about how to test the theory, both formally and by seeing if it makes sense when applied to everyday life. As you know from considering the three theories of identity (psychosocial theory, Social Identity Theory and social constructionism) discussed in Chapter 1, those who develop theories often focus on different aspects of a particular topic and different issues. And they are motivated by different psychological concerns. For example, psychosocial theorists are concerned with how the achievement of identity fits into other aspects of development over the life course. Social Identity Theory tries to explain why it is that prejudice is produced through group identities; and social constructionist theories focus on how identities are constructed in everyday life. So here we have an illustration of one topic that has been viewed from different perspectives, and an illustration of what we mean by the term *perspective*. Each perspective has a different focus, a different set of methods and data and produces different theories.

Tracing traditions

The perspectives of the three theories presented here have histories tha we can trace, and we are calling these histories the *traditions*. For example, the psychosocial identity theory could be said to originate in at least two traditions: that of William James's introspectionist concern with identities; and that of psychoanalysis, since Erikson's work draws heavily on Freud's psychoanalytic ideas. The SIT theorists work in a tradition that can be traced back to the experimental work of Wundt. SIT research is also part of a general perspective called *experimental social psychology*, which you will meet again in this book in Chapter 7 ('Perceiving and understanding the social world'). Social constructionist theories of identity are part of a different psychological perspective. They are a central part of the 'second cognitive revolution' within psychology that we mentioned in the Introduction, in historical terms a relatively new tradition. This 'revolution' involved a broadening of focus in psychology from the study of universal mental processes like perception and memory to include the study of how we all understand *meaning*. Social constructionism is part of this 'second cognitive revolution' in that it focuses on the study of language and culture within psychology. It has become an important perspective in modern social psychology.

Traditions, history and context

James, Wundt and Freud started working in the nineteenth century. They have influenced many other psychologists and their influence will appear in several of the chapters of this book. Each of them was initially influenced by his own contemporary culture; and the psychologists who followed have also tackled questions generated by the ideas of their own time, place and experience. For example, we saw that Erikson considered that his period of history was characterized by identity crisis. Tajfel's work was much influenced by his experience of being a European Jew who had escaped from the concentration camps of the Second World War, and, as we saw in the chapter, Gergen's identity was affected by the social changes that followed the widespread introduction of computer technologies. You can find out more about how particular psychologists, traditions, times, places and people interconnect by looking at *EPoCH* (CD-ROM).

■ Thinking about methods

As we saw in Chapter 1, different theories *require* different methods to test them and therefore tend to be associated with different methods. This is the case even in an area such as identity where it is generally agreed that, to understand people's identities, we need to use insider accounts: that is, people's accounts of their experience of their own identities. But you will have seen that the outsider viewpoint has also been used, in research that tests SIT. If we are to understand identity, the main focus is usually going to be on the whole person, but again SIT is different: it looks at psychological processes that happen in groups without particular reference to individual 'whole people' and their experiences.

Insider or outsider viewpoints?

Psychosocial theories have developed through clinical and naturalistic observations, ethnography and biographical work. They have progressed through tests and questionnaires that tap beliefs and experiences about identity, through semi-structured interviews, as well as through analyses of real biographies and fiction. These methods aim to gain access to individual identities in their social and historical contexts. You will remember that the two featured methods in Chapter 1 were the Twenty Statements Test and semi-structured interviews. If you look back to the Introduction, Section 2.2 ('A brief look at different kinds of data') you will recognize that these two featured methods produce the kind of data we have categorized as inner experiences. In identity research these inner experiences can be analysed very much with the intent of understanding the viewpoints of particular individuals. But they can also be analysed so as to look for commonalities that are chosen by the researcher, from an outsider viewpoint. For example, Kuhn and McPartland categorized individuals' responses to the Twenty Statements Test into categories based on the most frequently given answers. And Marcia used individuals' responses from semi-structured interviews to make generalizations about Identity Statuses. In other words, Marcia used an outsider viewpoint to analyse young people's insider accounts, in order to convert his data into evidence.

In contrast, Social Identity Theory, which was concerned with finding out what are the minimum conditions that will produce intergroup discrimination, used an entirely outsider viewpoint. It is difficult to see how asking people about their inner experiences or beliefs would provide data or evidence for this theory since it is highly unlikely that anyone would 'know' why they made prejudiced decisions. For that reason, Tajfel and his colleagues devised an experimental method that would allow them to test this by looking at behaviour (see 'Behavioural data' in the Introduction, Section 2.2) from an outsider viewpoint.

The third theory examined in Chapter 1 makes no distinction between social and personal identities and considers everyday life and language important to the construction of identities. Not surprisingly, then, it uses methods that allow the study of people in everyday life and focuses particularly on language, partly from an outsider viewpoint (see 'Symbolic data', in the Introduction, Section 2.2), but also from an insider viewpoint.

■ Thinking about themes

At the end of the Introduction we highlighted some themes that are important in psychology. In the commentaries we will pick up these themes as they appear in the chapters and use them to make explicit some of the underlying stories that psychology has to tell.

Explaining ourselves as human

Identity, the topic of Chapter 1, is clearly a particularly human issue – a preoccupation with thinking about *who we are*. A concern with our identities focuses both on what it is that makes us individuals, unique amongst other humans, and also on what separates us from other animals.

All the theories we considered in Chapter 1 are concerned with differences between people in relation to identities. They therefore address the question of what makes us distinctively ourselves in comparison with other humans.

By way of contrast, the next chapter (Chapter 2, 'Evolutionary psychology') addresses a different question. Whilst Chapter 1 deals with diversity and individuality, Chapter 2 considers the ways in which all humans are the same – what are the universal features common to all people but that, for the most part, separate us from non-human animals?

Fixity and change

Perhaps one of the main features of humanness is the sense of continuity that enables us to be conscious of 'being ourselves'. But are we conscious of ourselves as relatively fixed or can we maintain a sense of who we are whilst also experiencing changes in our bodies, our relationships and our lives in general? Chapter 1 indicated that people are active in creating identities for themselves. However, the theories differed in terms of whether they allow for changes in identity throughout the life course (e.g. social constructionist approaches) or assume that, once achieved, identity is relatively fixed (e.g. Erikson's psychosocial approach).

Some areas of psychology generally view people (and other animals) as relatively fixed, while other areas consider that they are essentially flexible, with a large capacity for adaptation to circumstances and consequent development and change. Questions around fixity and possibilities for change can be found throughout this book and we will return to this theme as the chapters progress. But remember that it is a theme that appears in several different guises and you need to keep track of these. There are issues concerning the extent to which we actively seek change and growth. For example, there are the kinds of change that we hope we can consciously promote in ourselves, perhaps through learning and broadening our education by studying a course or learning a new language. Or these could be changes of the kind motivated by a wish to 'have better relationships with people' or perhaps even thinking about having some therapy. But a great deal of change is something that happens to us relatively passively and unconsciously. To what extent are we born with genetic endowments that unfold and fix or seriously constrain who we can become? To what extent are we changed as we interact with and adapt to our environments? To what extent do we develop and grow because we are able to choose and/or modify our environments – physically, socially or culturally? As you work through this book you will see that the story of psychology is very much a story about humans, and other animals, *in their environments*.

Avoiding dichotomies in psychological thinking

Another theme that appears in many areas of psychology, and one that is related to questions about change and human adaptability, is the influence of nature *and* nurture. This shorthand phrase is in common use, very often as an unhelpful dichotomy: 'Are we the product of our genes or of our environments – physical, social and cultural?' It is important to note here that, whilst psychological debates are often presented as dichotomies (fixity *versus* change; nature *versus* nurture), these debates should *not* be seen as requiring either/or choices. The behaviour of people and other animals cannot be understood without taking account of the influence of their environments as well as their biology. You saw in Chapter 1 that identity has a basis in biology and the body, but that social and cultural environments, and each person's experiences in those environments, are also crucial.

In the next chapter (Chapter 2, 'Evolutionary psychology'), the impact of environments on what we have become as a species is approached in a very different way.

Evolutionary psychology

Brenda Smith and Richard Stevens

Contents

Aims

This chapter aims to:

- present the approach of evolutionary psychology
- outline the processes involved in evolution, such as natural and sexual selection
- sketch the evolutionary origins of the human species
- explore the evolutionary bases of the human mind
- discuss what insights an evolutionary approach might offer for understanding the social behaviour and experience of contemporary humans
- introduce some of the methodology used in evolutionary psychology
- briefly review the contribution made by evolutionary psychology.

1   Introduction

In the previous chapter, as part of the exploration of the topic of identity, some of the influences that might make us similar to some people but different from others were examined. This chapter again deals with similarities and differences, but not between individuals or groups of people. Here we are interested in what distinguishes us as a *species,* i.e. what makes humans similar to and different from other animals. The reason we look for similarities is that our basic biological structure is similar to that of other animals and, like all living things, we are subject to evolutionary forces. But, although we may share many attributes with other animals, we are clearly different. Only humans have organized the world to suit ourselves and developed the multiplicity of complex physical and social structures across the planet. So, what kind of animal are we? Evolutionary psychology focuses on how human beings came to be the apparently special animal we are today. What were the forces or influences that supported us in developing our particular abilities?

Activity 2.1

Have you ever watched chimpanzees at a zoo? If so, no doubt you were impressed by how uncannily like us they can be. Write down some of the things that you think make us similar to chimpanzees. Now consider and write down some of the key things that you think differentiate us from them.

Functional explanation
An explanation that focuses on origins, e.g. *why* a particular behaviour or characteristic has evolved.

Tooby and Cosmides (1992) define evolutionary psychology as psychology informed by the fact that the inherited structure of the human mind is the product of evolutionary processes. In other words, evolutionary psychologists assume that human abilities are the product of a long period of evolution and are interested in understanding how and why our abilities have developed as they have. They argue that this approach may enable us to enhance understanding of our contemporary behaviour. In this way it differs from other approaches that you will encounter in this book since it seeks what is called a **functional explanation** of human behaviour.

Uniquely human

Functional explanations are often contrasted with **causal explanations**. The latter are explanations that look for the immediate precursors or causes of behaviour. For example, earlier you noted some of the differences between chimpanzee and human behaviour. You may have noted spoken language as among the factors that differentiate us from chimpanzees. A causal explanation for the existence of spoken language might point (among other factors) to differences in the structure of the throat and larynx between humans and chimpanzees – so, causal explanations help us to answer questions about *how* species are similar or different.

Functional approaches, however, add an additional question: *why* did these differences between human beings and chimpanzees arise in the first place? In this case, why, when so many other aspects of our physiology are similar, are we different in this respect? What were the evolutionary pressures that supported the development of spoken language in humans but not in chimpanzees? Functional explanations attempt to understand the *origins* of

Causal explanation
An explanation that focuses on the immediate precursors or causes of behaviour (e.g. physiological processes).

behaviour in our evolutionary past, and for this we need to look to our ancestors. The argument is that if we can understand the kind of problems our ancestors had to solve in everyday life, then we should gain insight into the psychological processes that evolved to solve those problems.

As you can imagine this is not an easy task. A major difficulty, for example, is that our ancestors aren't around for us to study them! What evolutionary psychologists essentially do is to use reason and inference to draw conclusions about the evolutionary bases of behaviour, working from a knowledge of the principles of evolution and a range of different kinds of evidence. These include the study of the behaviour of other animals, especially those close to ourselves such as apes, and relevant information from paleoanthropology (the study of physical and psychological characteristics of ancient, prehistoric humans and cultures) as well as observations of contemporary peoples who still live in hunter–gatherer fashion. You will see examples of this methodological approach in the pages to come and it will be briefly reviewed in the final section.

The attempt to tease out the evolutionary origins of animal and human behaviour began in the last century with the work of Darwin (see Biography Box on Charles Darwin, p.114). Then, after a period of relative neglect, interest in the subject was rekindled in the 1970s by a subdiscipline known as sociobiology (e.g. Wilson, 1975). Evolutionary psychology is the most recent and vigorous expression of the approach, attempting to understand the human mind in this way and, in doing so, stimulating much debate. Those involved include not only psychologists, but also philosophers, ethologists (those who study animal behaviour in the wild) and biologists.

2.1 Reverse engineering

Reverse-engineering
The process of inferring the function of an object or an adaptation from the way it is structured.

Evolutionary psychology has been described as a kind of **reverse engineering** (Tooby and Cosmides 1992). In other words, it is rather like using knowledge of mechanical principles and observations of the way a car operates to deduce how and why it was designed in that particular way. So we can use our knowledge of evolutionary principles and about past environmental conditions to identify the kind of cognitive and social capacities that would have been most effective for survival and reproduction in human prehistory.

This approach is sometimes called functional analysis and has been criticized as being overly speculative. However, empirical testing of hypotheses and the use of well established principles of evolution help overcome this reservation. (See Featured Method Box 2.4.)

Section 2 of this chapter outlines the processes of evolution that underpin evolutionary psychology. Section 3 will then describe how researchers have applied some of these principles to the explanation of the human mind and contemporary human behaviour. Section 4 explores the insights an evolutionary approach might offer into the complex social and technological skills we display in contemporary times. The concluding section then reflects on the perspective's contribution to contemporary psychology.

2 What is evolution and how does it work?

Essentially, **evolution** is a theory of change. It argues that over long periods of time, all species change in small but important ways so that the various species we see today are not the same as those that were living a million or so years ago. Furthermore, evolution is still occurring, so how we are now is not necessarily the same as we are likely to be in the future. So, how does evolutionary change come about and why? The basic elements involved in the process of evolution are *time*, *genetic transmission and diversity*, and *natural and sexual selection* over many generations.

Evolution
The process by which species develop from earlier forms.

2.1 The elements of evolution

Time

Time is a crucial element of evolution. The species we see today are the descendants of different species that lived in former times. The age of the earth and our solar system is about 5,000 million years (which is well over halfway to the point where it will become uninhabitable, according to recent estimates). Evidence of primitive life forms has been dated to as far back as 3,300 million years. Not though until relatively recently (on that time scale!) did life evolve to the complexity of the first shell-fish. They emerged roughly 600 million years ago, about one-eighth of the time from the earth's creation to the present. Only in the last 70 million years, after the great reptiles died out following a 135 million-year reign, did mammals begin to evolve rapidly. Anthropoid apes, or great apes (the species most closely related to humans and which includes chimpanzees, gorillas and orangutans), do not come into the picture until very recently – about 15 million years ago. Because these time scales are so enormous by the standards of our life experience, they are not easy to fully appreciate.

Genetic transmission and diversity

Genes
Sequences of DNA which serve as coding instructions for making proteins.

DNA
Deoxyribose nucleic acid, a chemical sequence in which genetic information is encoded.

Genetic transmission refers to the fact that structures called **genes** provide the basis for passing on physical characteristics from one generation to another. You will learn more about the details of genetics in Chapter 4, but for now, the main thing to grasp is that genes are made up of particular sequences of a complex chemical called *deoxyribose nucleic acid* (i.e. **DNA**).

Genes are coding instructions for making proteins – the molecules that provide the building blocks of the body. Such building blocks help to shape both our physiology and thereby certain aspects of our behaviour (for details of this see Chapter 4). An individual's

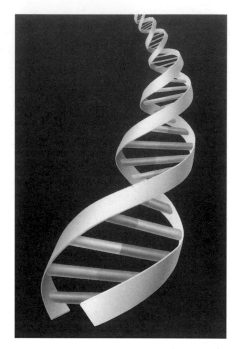

DNA double helix

particular pattern of genes is repeated identically in the nucleus or core of every cell in his or her body. Genes are strung along thread-like structures called chromosomes. In almost all cells of the body there are 46 chromosomes arranged as 23 pairs. The exceptions are sperms and eggs (both known as *gametes*, see Chapter 4). The pairs of chromosomes separate when gametes are formed so each gamete contains only one of each pair; 23 chromosomes in all. When a sperm cell fertilizes an egg cell to form a *zygote* (a fertilized egg, see Chapter 4), the 23 chromosomes in the mother's egg and the 23 in the father's sperm join up to make pairs. The zygote now has a full complement of 46 chromosomes, organised as pairs, each of which is made up of a mixture of genes from both parents.

This mixing of our mother's and father's genes means that, while we have similarities to each of our parents, we are also different from them. In this way, genetic transmission underpins diversity and this diversity allows change to occur and hence is the basis of the evolutionary process. (It is worth being aware of the enormous potential for diversity that can result from such admixture. Even with just the same two parents the different possible genetic patterns that could result number more than 70 billion!).

Another way in which diversity may be introduced into a species is through mutation. Mutations may occur due to faulty chromosome duplication, or due to the effects of environmental influences like radiation or certain chemicals such as mustard gas. When a mutation occurs, the DNA is altered and this leads to a change in the genetic instructions coded for by the gene. This mutant gene may well be capable of reproducing itself (provided the organism is not rendered unable to reproduce as a result of the gene). Some gene mutations appear to arise spontaneously in unrelated individuals. For example, the mutant gene for haemophilia (a disease where the bloodclotting necessary to stop cuts bleeding is defective) has occurred independently a number of times. Most mutations are harmful because, over many generations, the genes best suited to the environment tend to get passed on to the next generation. However, where there is a change in the environment, a high incidence of mutations may result in variations better adapted to this new environment than the original type.

Through the process of sexual reproduction, then, genes are passed on to the next generation. But, because the mother and father's genes are mixed up in new and unique ways, the offspring are different from both parents while at the same time sharing genes with them. Thus there is a process of change underlying evolution, but also a process of stability. Change is also introduced through occasional mutations but many mutations are harmful and are not reproduced, so again there is the dual tension of stability and change. The next important question to ask then is when are changes likely to occur and are certain kinds of change favoured over others? This brings us to the next element of the evolutionary process:

Natural and sexual selection

The theory of evolution derives mainly from the work of Charles Darwin. Although he was by no means entirely the innovator of the idea of evolution, nor yet of selection, what he did do was to assemble the pieces and come up with a workable theory. His breakthrough (see Biography Box on Charles Darwin) was to realize that some forms of diversity are more **adaptive** than others. The term adaptive means that the characteristics and behaviour coded for by its genes help the animal to survive and reproduce, and therefore pass those genes onto its offspring. But not all individuals survive to reproductive age. Of those who do survive to reproduce, some are more successful than others. What is involved is a process of selection? Darwin distinguished two kinds:

Natural selection refers to the fact that an animal that inherits bodily structures or behavioural patterns that are well adapted to its particular environment is more likely to survive and pass those genes on to the next generation. Those individuals that are less well adapted may die and so their genes will gradually reduce in the population.

Adaptive
Likely to promote survival and/or reproduction.

Natural selection
The process whereby physical and behavioural characteristics which enable survival (and the genes which code for these) are passed on to descendants.

Sexual selection
The process whereby physical and behavioural characteristics which promote reproductive success (and the genes which code for these) are passed on to descendants.

Sexual selection, like natural selection, involves differential success, but here it is differences between individuals' reproductive capacity that are crucial. The extent to which an individual's genes are passed on to future generations depends on how many offspring are produced that in turn grow to sexual maturity and reproduce. In most species, there is considerable variation in the reproductive success of different individuals. So, any genetically inherited attribute that ensures reproductive success (e.g. which makes an individual attractive to a potential mate or helps them to win where there is competition with rivals) would be adaptive.

Thus, diversity supports the selection of a genetic make-up that is more adaptive to the environment and that facilitates reproduction. Gradually, over many generations, these changes may accumulate in groups of animals and new species might evolve, each displaying subtle and highly effective adaptation to their natural habitats.

BIOGRAPHY   *Charles Darwin* 1809–1882

Charles Darwin was born on 12 February 1809. In spite of coming from a distinguished family (his grandfather Erasmus Darwin had been an eminent physician and naturalist and he was related to both the Wedgwood and Galton families), he did not shine either at school or university. His passion, even before he went to school was collecting. '... I collected all sorts of things, shells, seals, franks and minerals.' Later, Darwin was particularly proud of his study of the barnacles *Cirripedia* on which he worked for eight years, eventually publishing two thick volumes describing all the known living species.

After considering and rejecting his father's suggestions of careers in medicine or the Church, Darwin made the journey that was to provide the basis for his later work. For five years he travelled as an unpaid naturalist on board HMS *Beagle* in a survey expedition to South America and the Pacific. Darwin's job was to make detailed observations, often based on long excursions inland, of geological formations, flora and fauna, and of the customs and ways of life of the inhabitants he encountered. A contemporary review described the journal that Darwin later published (1845) of his findings as recording 'the observations of a mind singularly candid and unprejudiced – fixing upon nature a gaze, keen, penetrating, reflective and almost reverent'.

The most significant phase of Darwin's voyage came when the *Beagle* sailed out along the Equator 600 miles west of the coast of Ecuador for a four-week visit to the Galapagos Archipelago. Here, Darwin was overwhelmed by the number of species of birds, shells, insects and animals he had never before encountered. He recorded 26 species of landbirds, only one of which had been seen elsewhere. He noted that the varied species about him often shared many characteristics in common and differed only by gradations. Among the landbirds he discovered

Darwin

there were 13 different kinds of finch. In his journal he wrote: 'Seeing this gradation and diversity of structure in one small intimately related group of birds, one might really fancy that, from an original paucity of birds in the Archipelago, one species had been taken and modified for different ends!' He noted also that each of the closely related species of plants and animals tended to be identified with one island in particular; 'different islands to a considerable extent are inhabited by a different set of beings'.

In 1836 at the age of 27, Darwin returned home and began a series of notebooks to develop his ideas. He reasoned that the range of characteristics displayed by the various species of Galapagos finch had evolved due to a particular kind of survival advantage conferred by a chance hereditary variation. He noted how the beaks of some finches were appropriate for feeding on insects, those of other species for feeding on seeds. Given time and aided by separation on different islands, the accumulation of such chance differences had led to the evolution of different species of finch, each with its own characteristic habits and each filling its own individual 'ecological niche'. Soon he had developed the position that species were not fixed at creation but could change over time, with different isolated populations gradually evolving away from common

The Beagle

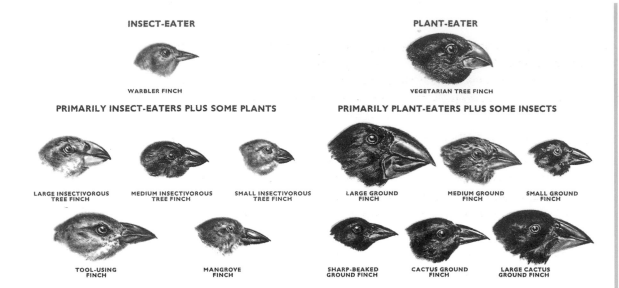

Varieties of Finch from the Galapagos

ancestors, and he began exploring possible processes through which this evolutionary change could have come about. He observed among other things, the importance of sexual reproduction for creating variation so that the environment could act as a selective force, and of isolation and separation as a way of maintaining and increasing differentiation between species.

It was not until 1858, when it became clear that another naturalist Alfred Wallace had come up with similar ideas, that he eventually published *On the Origin of Species* (1859). Enthusiastic supporters included Thomas Huxley and Karl Marx. (Marx later requested that he be allowed to dedicate the English translation of *Das Kapital* to Darwin – Darwin refused). It also generated much controversy especially among those who considered (correctly) that the theory contradicted the biblical account of the fixed creation of each species. The ensuing controversy culminated in a stormy public debate between the Bishop of Oxford and Darwin's supporter Huxley.

Subsequently, Darwin published *The Expression of the Emotions in Man and Animals* (1872) and *The Descent of Man* (1874) in both of which he attempted to apply his theory more directly to human behaviours.

2.2 Human evolution

Now we know a little about the general principles of evolution. As psychologists, though, we are particularly interested in our own species, so what is the story of human evolution?

Activity 2.2

Imagine that the period between the beginning of life on this planet and the present were represented as 24 hours running from midnight to midnight. At what time do you think that the earliest humans, our direct ancestors, initially appeared? Note your estimate here, then check it against the answer which appears later in this section.

Biologists have classified all living things into groups based on how different species, both contemporary and ancestral, are related to each other. Human beings (*Homo sapiens*) belong to the Primate order, which also includes all monkeys and apes and the extinct ancestors of human beings.

When life first appeared on earth, the structure of DNA was pretty common to all forms of life. Over long periods of time however, as different species began to emerge, so the structure of DNA underwent subtle changes. The shorter the time lapse since one species has split in two, the closer in structure will be their DNA. Since the structure of DNA evolves at a fairly constant rate, we can work out mathematically when two species diverged. As you can see from Figure 2.1, our common ancestor with new and old world monkeys was a considerable time back, but we shared a common ancestor with the great apes (i.e. chimpanzees, bonobos, gorillas and orangutans) until much more recently and only diverged from a common ancestor with the chimpanzees and bonobos around 5 million years ago.

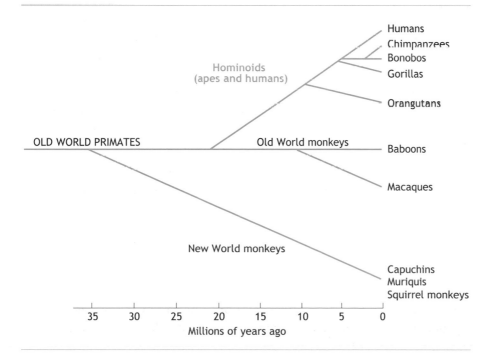

Figure 2.1   Showing branching of monkeys, apes and humans

Common chimpanzee

Hominid
The term 'hominid'
refers to all members
of the human group,
including humans
themselves and our
fossil ancestors.

DNA analysis reveals that human and chimpanzee DNA is remarkably similar and supports the fossil evidence of a split around 5 million years ago. Note though that the ape-like creature who was the ancestor to both humans and chimpanzees is not the same as modern-day apes. Since the two species diverged, chimpanzees, like humans, have changed and evolved along their own path. For example, if you look closely at Figure 2.1, you will see that the chimpanzees themselves diverged around 3 million years ago into two species known as the common chimpanzee and the bonobo (Waddell and Penny, 1996). In terms of DNA structure, we are closer to chimpanzees than they are to gorillas (Sibley and Ahlquist, 1987). The extremely close DNA relationship between both species of chimpanzees and humans led Diamond (1991) to call our species 'the third chimpanzee'.

Since around 5 million years ago, human beings have been on their own individual evolutionary path. However, there were several sub-branches along the way and different forms of early human have been discovered in the fossil record.

The oldest **hominid** fossils suggest that by about 4 million years ago our ancestors were bipedal (i.e. walked on two legs) and were living a hunter–gatherer existence on the African savannah. At that time, their brains had not increased much in size from those of earlier primates (the brains of the adults were about 450 mls in volume). The brains of our ancestors did not begin to increase much in size until the genus *Homo* appeared around 2 million years ago. By about one million years ago, the fossil record indicates that brain size had increased extraordinarily rapidly to reach three times its earlier size (i.e. 1,350 mls), much the same as in modern humans. The appearance of our own particular species, *Homo sapiens* only emerged some 100–150,000 years ago, eventually supplanting (or possibly merging with) other forms such as Neanderthals. This is extremely recent in evolutionary

Bonobo

terms. We are really 'new kids on the block' but evolutionary psychologists argue that the kind of behaviour patterns we display today will have been considerably influenced by the kind of environments that early humans lived in, perhaps even before we existed as a separate species.

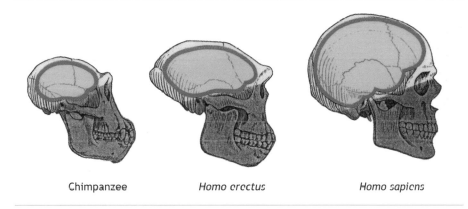

Chimpanzee   Homo erectus   Homo sapiens

Figure 2.2   Relative cranial size of chimpanzee, early hominids and *Homo sapiens*

Answer to Activity 2.2

If life on earth is conceived of as a 24 hour clock, our early hominid ancestors appeared about 50 seconds before midnight (2 million years ago) and our own species of **Homo sapiens** emerged around 4 seconds before midnight (150,000 years ago)! This gives you some sense of the time scale involved and how recent in relation to life on earth is the appearance of the human species.

Although 150,000 years may sound a long time, it does not represent that many generations. If you imagine your ancestors strung out in a line (the first being your mother, the next her mother, etc.) it would only take some 6,000 people before, through a series of gradual, imperceptible changes, you had shifted from a modern human to a prehuman being.

So, how far back should we look in order to understand our biological adaptations? The emergence of *Homo sapiens* seems to be a critical event since this species succeeded in removing all other hominid species. The genus *Homo* is generally associated with an enlargement of the brain, the beginnings of culture, a more advanced bipedal gait and less emphasis on mastication in the preparation and consumption of food (Corballis, 1999). Evidence strongly suggests that humans were primarily hunter–gatherers until about 10,000 years ago. The first cities were only established then, and much of the world's population lived in conditions that were untouched by what we call civilization until only a few generations ago.

Of course, tremendous developments in technology and culture have occurred in more recent times and there is some debate as to whether any significant biological adaptations may have occurred during this time. However, in evolutionary terms, this is a very short period of time and most evolutionary psychologists make the assumption that the distinctive aspects of human brains and minds probably owe their origins to the lengthy period of adaptation (i.e. over the last 150,000 years at least) to the hunter–gatherer way of life (Tooby and Cosmides, 1989; Cosmides and Tooby, 1992).

2.3 Implications of evolutionary understanding

In thinking about evolution, it is very important to bear in mind that the critical issue is to identify factors in the distant past of each species that may have favoured some inheritable, physical and/or behavioural predispositions over others. It is *not* implied that animals (even humans) have evolved in this way because they realized a particular way of behaving would lead to reproductive success. No intention or purpose is presumed on the part of the animals involved (even though in discussing examples it may sometimes seem to come over in that way). In broad principle, it is just that some characteristics would have been adaptive in promoting survival and reproduction and others would have not. (It is a little more complicated than that, in that some behaviours, which may not in themselves be adaptive, may be related to, and therefore 'carried by', adaptive ones.) Genes that coded for adaptive characteristics would thus have been propagated in a way that the others would not. As the biologist Richard Dawkins puts it, 'natural selection is the blind watchmaker, blind because it does not see ahead, does not plan consequences, has no purpose in view. Yet the living results of natural selection overwhelmingly impress us with the appearance of design as if by a master watchmaker, impress us with the illusion of design and planning' (Dawkins, 1986, p.21).

An example that illustrates this is a famous study of peppered moths (Kettlewell, 1971). Kettlewell found a much higher density of dark-coloured moths in industrial compared with rural areas. These survived more effectively than light-coloured moths because of the greater camouflage, their dark colouring provided against soot-coated trees and walls. A follow-up study after laws on smoke emission had reduced pollution, found light-coloured ones came to dominate. The moths did not, of course, purposefully change their colouring. Rather, those that happened to be darker were more likely to survive predators and live long enough to produce dark offspring in their darkened industrial environment

Dark and light peppered moths camouflaged (or not) against different backgrounds

until eventually they dominated the population. Then, once the industrial area had been cleaned up, the environment favoured the survival of light-coloured moths and in turn the survival of their offspring.

Although it is clear that we have had a long evolutionary history, human civilisation has occurred only very recently, in the last 10,000 years. Therefore, it is very likely that at least some of the effects of the pressures we evolved under during the last million years or so are still operational today. Indeed, this is why the anthropologist John Tooby and the psychologist Leda Cosmides (Tooby and Cosmides, 1989; 1992) say that the distinctive aspects of human minds and brains probably owe their origins to the lengthy period of adaptation to the hunter–gatherer way of life. An examination of the problems our ancestors would have had to solve provides a window on the way our modern minds may still operate. In the next section, we will look at how our evolutionary past may have led to the attributes and abilities we observe today.

Activity 2.3

Note that not all characteristics that were adaptive in our hunter–gatherer past are necessarily adaptive today. For example, in our evolutionary past, a taste for sugar was likely to have been advantageous when berries were nutritious but scarce. Thus, when berries were available our ancestors would have made a considerable effort to find them. However, in a world where sugar is freely available, this preference now leads to obesity, tooth decay and so on.

Can you think of one or two other examples of adaptations to our hunter–gatherer lifestyle that may not be adaptive today?

Summary Section 2

- Causal explanations look for the immediate causes of behaviour.
- Functional explanations attempt to explain *why* particular behaviours have evolved.
- The elements of evolution are a) time b) genetic transmission and the diversity that results from the shuffling of genes in sexual reproduction and mutations c) natural and sexual selection.
- Darwin developed ideas based on initial observations in the Galapagos islands into his influential theory of evolution.
- The emergence of the human species occurred very recently – around 150,000 years ago.
- Evolutionary psychologists argue that we need to look in particular at the way of life of our hunter–gatherer ancestors (a lifestyle that predominated until around 10,000 years ago) to understand many aspects of the modern mind.

3 The evolutionary origins of the human mind

There is no doubt that human beings regard themselves as the most intelligent and complex species on the planet today. We produce all kinds of technological wonders from the simple pencil to the computer linked to the Internet. We have considerable social complexity – think of all the different cultures, ideas and ways of life in your own country, let alone world-wide. Unlike other animals, we also have language that allows us to communicate not only about aspects of our world but about our inner feelings and emotions as well.

Our range of skills seems so removed from that of other animals that, over the years, researchers have sought to identify 'the' factor that defined humans in comparison to all other animals. Many critical features have been put forward as this definitive criterion. For example, in the middle of the twentieth century, our technical expertise impressed many researchers and Oakley proposed that 'when the immediate forerunners of man [sic] acquired the ability to walk upright habitually, their hands became free to make and manipulate tools' (Oakley, 1949, p.1). 'Man (sic) the Tool Maker' came to symbolize what marked us off from other species and came to be seen as the precursor to all our varied abilities. However, in the late 1960s information began to emerge from Jane Goodall's work (1971). She had gone to live among and study chimpanzees in the Gombe Stream area of Tanzania. She found that they too used tools and over the years it became apparent that not only do they *use* tools, but they also *make* them (see the *fOCUS* CD-ROM). So like all hypotheses that call on a *single* factor to explain the development from clever ape to even more clever human being, the idea of humans being the only technological species was found wanting.

More recently, a rather broader approach has begun to develop within evolutionary psychology. This posits (on the basis of rational inference, evolutionary principles and observations of related species like chimps) that there are a variety of factors working together to produce complexity of various kinds.

3.1 The Machiavellian hypothesis

In 1988 Richard Byrne and Andrew Whiten (both psychologists with a particular interest in primate behaviour) published a book called *Machiavellian Intelligence: Social Expertise and the Evolution of Intellect in Monkeys, Apes and Humans.* This book signalled the gathering together of various strands of thought that focus on the complexities of the social life of our ancestors as a possible route to understanding the development of our distinctive abilities. By 1997 they published an extension and evaluation of this approach, which had become known as the **Machiavellian hypothesis**. As they indicate in their opening chapter, this had come to be recognized as a group of hypotheses that supported the notion that intelligence began in 'social manipulation, deceit and cunning cooperation' (Whiten and Byrne, 1997, p.1).

A primary stimulus for this approach was a seminal paper entitled 'The social function of intellect' published several years earlier by Nicholas Humphrey (1976), one of the first British psychologists to champion evolutionary psychology. Humphrey's view of how social complexity arose started a flurry of research and re-thinking about the nature of human intellect and why it came about. Humphrey began by noting that every animal's world is full of problems and asked himself what exactly are those problems, how do they differ from animal to animal and what benefits accrue to an individual who can solve them? He also defined his terms carefully. For instance, the term intelligence has modern day connotations associated with passing examinations, IQ tests and so on. But Humphrey defined intelligence in a more general way as the ability to modify behaviour on the basis of valid inference from evidence. From this definition he argues that there is what might be called 'low-level' intelligence, which he defines as the ability to infer that something is likely to happen merely because similar things have happened in comparable circumstances in the past. For example, your cat or dog may present

Machiavellian hypothesis
The idea that the evolutionary origins of high-level intelligence lie in the adaptive value for social animals of 'social manipulation, deceit and cunning cooperation'.

themselves for dinner when they hear the sound of the tin opener. Many instances of their dinner appearing after this sound lead them to 'expect' food. This kind of intelligence Humphrey thinks is widespread in the animal kingdom (see Section 2 on learning as conditioning in Chapter 3 of this book). In contrast, **high-level intelligence** is the ability to infer that something is likely to happen because it is implied by a novel conjunction of events (Humphrey, 1976). He sees this kind of 'creative' intelligence as more rare and characteristic of higher primates (i.e. chimpanzees, gorillas, orangutans and humans).

High-level intelligence (or creative intelligence)
The ability to infer in novel situations that something is likely to happen because it is implied by a particular combination of events.

Humphrey argues that most of the practical problems of subsistence life such as that lived by our hunter–gatherer ancestors (and by most higher primates today) are solved by imitation and trial and error learning and low-level intelligence. He cites evidence from studies of gorillas, chimpanzees and living hunter–gatherers. By definition, evolution does not directly support abilities that do not have adaptive value, so there must have been an adaptive value to the existence of high-level, or creative, intelligence. Humphrey then sought out the problem that creative intelligence had evolved to solve.

Note how Humphrey used the 'reverse engineering' approach mentioned in Section 1. He begins by asking why *human intellect came about – why was it adaptive? He then uses his knowledge of the environments and ways of life of other animals to hypothesize that all animals need to solve problems. Partly from knowledge of animal behaviour and partly from logical thinking, he then hypothesises that while some problems arise regularly and may require intelligence, dealing with new problems requires a different order of intellect that is only demonstrated in higher primates. As we see below, this then leads to further hypotheses and further use of the 'reverse engineering' approach.*

In brief, Humphrey proposed that the reason for the existence of creative intelligence was that effective hunter–gatherer lifestyles rely on the community having a wide factual knowledge of practical techniques and the habitat. This knowledge can only be acquired within a *social* community, one that allows cultural transmission of knowledge and a safe environment in which the individual can learn. But, individuals live in a world populated by other individuals. In complex societies like those of all higher primates, there are benefits to be gained for each individual from preserving the overall structure of the group, while at the same time there are also benefits to be obtained by exploiting and out-manoeuvring other individuals within it. Thus, Humphrey reasoned, social primates are required by the very nature of their society to be calculating beings, inclined both to compete and cooperate. To decide which option is best, they must be able to calculate the consequences of their own behaviour, to calculate the likely behaviour of others and the balance of advantage and loss. Furthermore, they must do this in a situation where their calculations are based on ambiguous cues, which are also likely to change. Such social skills require intellectual qualities of the highest order. Thus, Humphrey argues that creative intelligence was the solution to the problem of holding society together.

This is why Whiten and Byrne named their approach 'Machiavellian'. It refers to these complicated calculations in the social environment – negotiating what is of best advantage to you at least cost, while the individual you are interacting with is making exactly the same calculation. Thus, cooperation becomes not a naive 'trusting' of others, but rather a calculated option. As an individual, the ability to cheat others would clearly increase one's chances of maximizing individual benefit, but again, since this process does not occur in isolation, the individual you are attempting to cheat will maximize his or her benefit by being able to predict when you are cheating. So begins a series of elaborate and complex calculations!

Let's take an example. If we are interacting with you and want to persuade you to give us that very tasty bar of chocolate you have and which you want to keep, then we wish by our behaviour, to change your behaviour. But you are also a player in this game. You may detect our intentions and may begin thinking up strategies to prevent us getting the chocolate or ways in which you could give us the chocolate but gain something else that you want in return. We do not have immediate access to your thoughts or plans: nor you to ours. Rather, we must each try and estimate how we think the other is feeling and will react in certain circumstances. Once this pattern of calculation had emerged, there would have been selective pressures for it to increase in complexity because each individual will try to increase their ability to out-manoeuvre others and to detect cheating.

3.2 Theory of mind

For Humphrey, humans are 'natural psychologists' in that they don't make these kinds of calculation purely on the basis of external behaviour. Rather, a crucial aspect of human society, he argued, was the ability to understand or 'read' the mind of another individual. In other words, individuals develop the ability to 'put themselves in the place of' the other – to reflect on how they would react/behave in a similar situation and to make predictions based on this empathic understanding as well as the external markers of behaviour. This process entails attributing beliefs and motivations to others.

The idea of social complexity being based on mutual understandings of intentional systems prompted Premack and Woodruff (1978) to examine the apparently 'human-like' understanding of each other that chimpanzees display. They described animals who have the ability to understand the mind of another as possessing a **theory of mind** (i.e. a theory of 'the other') and this term has subsequently been taken up by developmental psychologists. Essentially, having a theory of mind or being able to mind-read concerns the ability of an individual to respond to assumptions about the beliefs and desires of another individual, rather than in direct response to the other's overt behaviour (Whiten and Byrne, 1997, p.8).

Detecting that a child or an animal has a theory of mind is not a simple matter (see Box 2.2). Since no-one is able to look directly into another's mind, we have to be careful to ensure that what we observe is not simply an individual reading another's *behaviour* but reading another's *mind*. Clearly, however, what we think, feel and intend is related to our behaviour so there is an interaction between the two. So how do we try to identify the more complex skill of mind-reading from the simpler skill of directly interpreting behaviour? Whiten (1996) suggested four forms or aspects of mind-reading.

- *Implicit mind-reading:* where an individual appears to understand that another person's actions are related to the experience and perceptions of the person acting. For example, if I see you eating a sandwich I may infer that you feel hungry.
- *Counter-deception:* where an individual is able to discriminate between the actual intentions of another individual and the form his/her behaviour may take on the surface. This is much like the earlier example where you might detect that despite our apparent behaviour what we were really trying to do was to get you to give us the bar of chocolate.
- *Recognition of intervening variables:* this aspect of mind-reading refers to the awareness that certain circumstances generate states in other individuals that in turn allow us to predict their behaviour. For example a threat situation such as a fire is likely to cause a person to feel afraid and we can predict that they are likely to run away.
- *Experience projection:* where an individual can make predictions based on his or her own experience as to how another will behave in similar circumstances. For example, one's own experience of having a bad day at work making you tetchy at home might allow you to predict that if your partner had a difficult day then s/he too might be a little more argumentative in the evening.

Theory of mind
The ability to understand or 'read' the mind of another individual; the ability to 'put oneself in the place of another'.

Whiten sees the last two as the most important ways of distinguishing more complex 'mind reading' from simpler 'behaviour reading'.

2.2 A theory of mind experiment

In a study by Premack (1988) an adult chimpanzee called Sarah was shown videotapes of a human actor experiencing 'problems' of different kinds. For example, an actor was shown in a situation in which he was having difficulty in getting bananas that were overhead and out of reach. Sarah was then shown two or three photographs that depicted alternative actions, only one of which provided an effective solution to the problem (e.g. stepping on a chair). Sarah chose the correct 'solution' often enough for the rate of her correct answers to be well above the level of chance, which Premack interpreted as showing she understood what the actor's intentions were.

Other studies indicate that children at age 3, however, when tested with the same video and other similar ones, are not able to select the appropriate solution. Not until they reach approximately the age of 4 do they have the same ability demonstrated by Sarah.

Developmental psychologists have tried to trace the emergence of mind-reading abilities in children. At each age there appear to be limitations in the extent to which children really demonstrate an 'empathic' rather than a more direct reading of actions and situations. So, human children appear to develop a full theory of mind only gradually during the first few years of life. On the basis of both studying children's development and thinking through carefully what is meant by the phrase 'theory of mind', Simon Baron-Cohen (1999) has distinguished eight ways in which it might be manifested. These are:

- intentionally communicating with others;
- repairing failed communication with others;
- teaching others;
- intentionally persuading others;
- intentionally deceiving others;
- building shared plans and goals;
- intentionally sharing a focus or topic of attention;
- pretending.

Baron-Cohen (1990) has undertaken much stimulating and innovative research with children with autism and suggests that this condition demonstrates to us what human life would be like without a theory of mind. You will learn more about autism later in the course. For now, you can understand it as an inability to read others' minds (Baron-Cohen, 1990). The child's abilities to socialize, communicate and use imagination are affected. Children with autism are unable to understand a speaker's communicative intentions, are unable to 'read between the lines', fail to understand jokes, and cannot amend their speech to fit the listener's context such as their knowledge, interest, expectations and so on. The close relationship between the development of theory of mind and the development of language is supported by the finding that children with autism invariably show language delay (Baron-Cohen, 1999, p.267). If Baron-Cohen is correct, these studies indicate the crucial role that having a theory of mind plays for an effective social life.

There is no evidence that monkeys possess a theory of mind. Although non-human apes do show some of the simpler features of theory of mind (and this suggests that the basic elements were most likely present in our common ancestor) the evidence indicates that their ability is limited. The degree to which chimps possess a theory of mind is a matter of considerable debate (see Vines, 2000). Although they can infer emotional states and intentions in others and do engage in deception and counter-deception, observations of chimps in the wild suggest they are limited in their ability to imagine novel entities or situations that do not have a clear relation to their lived circumstances. In contrast, the archaeological record indicates that around 30,000 years ago, early humans were painting and creating 'impossible' entities such as the half-man/half-lion ivory statuette from Southern Germany (Mithen, 1996).

It is not the existence of works of art itself that indicates the probability of a theory of mind (since children with autism are sometimes able artists). Rather, it is evidence that the artist was representing his/her own thoughts rather than simply what they saw. The lion–man statuette is a fiction: no such beings ever existed. The statue is, therefore, indirect evidence for the ability to pretend, to use symbolic representations. Similarly, around the same time we see evidence of burial rituals with the dead person being adorned with jewellery and other accoutrements. This suggests that the people of this time wanted others to appreciate that the dead person was beautiful, of high status or whatever.

So, it would seem that we are beginning to see the development of an evolutionary line in relation to social expertise. Our common ancestor with modern monkeys had complex social structures but these must have worked on the basis of reading off the *behaviour* of others. In contrast the common ape ancestor appeared to develop the rudiments of a theory of mind, whereby not just the behaviour but the *intentions* of others is taken into account when deciding whether to cooperate or deceive. Only

An early creation of the human mind

humans, however, have the full constituents of theory of mind, marking the differentiation between ourselves and our nearest relatives, chimpanzees.

3.3 Interplay between social and cognitive skills

In this section so far we have looked at the role of social factors in an attempt to understand human intelligence. But, as we noted at the beginning of this section, it is unlikely that any *one single* pressure resulted in the range of intelligence we display today.

By 1997, the Machiavellian hypothesis had become somewhat more refined, and theorists and researchers working under its banner began looking at the relationship between social skills and the ability to deal with technical problems in the physical world by using cognitive skills. Whiten and Byrne (1997), for example, suggest that the skills that developed in the early ancestors of both apes *and* monkeys were geared towards the social arena. Only later did the ancestors of apes develop an enhanced intelligence that applies to both social *and* technical domains.

Byrne (1999) argues that explaining the emergence of the high level of human intelligence as a result of the need for social skills created by social complexity is also plausible because it allows for 'positive feedback'. What this means is that if some members of a group have the ability to acquire some useful new social skill then others in the group may be at a disadvantage in survival or reproductive terms. The scene is then set for the rapid evolution of increasing levels of sophistication. However, on what are such social skills based? Is it just a question of theory of mind, or is it also dependent on a significant increase in cognitive abilities such as memory and learning? We have already seen in the previous section that while apes demonstrate 'theory of mind', monkeys do not. Yet, monkey societies demonstrate similar levels of social complexity so could it be cognitive skills that provide the basis for this difference?

In the past, those arguments that focused on social influences on the development of high-level intelligence were often set in opposition to arguments that focused on cognitive pressures. Byrne (1999) argues that rather than being alternatives, both factors may be required for effective understanding of the divide between monkeys and apes, and, therefore, the origins of human intelligence. Successful use of Machiavellian intelligence also requires a good memory and rapid learning of socially relevant information.

Byrne supports his argument by pointing out that it is not just in social circumstances that apes and humans excel. In the area of tool use, for example, we see a divide between monkeys and apes. Under laboratory conditions, monkeys can learn to use an object as a tool. But if the tool is removed, they do not select replacements on the basis of its properties nor do they seem to understand basic principles of causality or how they produce the effects they do (Visalberghi and Trinca, 1987; Visalberghi and Limongelli, 1994). In contrast, even in the wild, chimpanzees select appropriate objects for tools, sometimes away from the site where they will be used, and they modify natural materials to make them more efficient as tools (see *fOCUS* CD-ROM). Byrne argues that these skills are based on the ability to form mental representations of information that is not physically present at the time, not yet in existence or even observable in principle (Byrne, 1995).

Another striking way in which monkeys differ from apes is in their imitative capacity. Byrne's (1999) review of available evidence suggests that monkeys have difficulty in imitating whereas there is increasing evidence for imitation in great apes. This leads him to suggest that great apes operate at 'programme level'. Rather than simply noticing the details of the behaviour they observe, great apes appear to understand how actions are related to one another and how they relate to the overall function of that behaviour. Another way of describing this ability is to say

Ant dipping

Using a stone to open nuts

that great apes have the capacity to represent abstract problems. Once the ability to represent problems, 'simulate' possible actions and compute the possible outcomes becomes established, then this can be applied to any sort of problem. It can be applied to hypothesizing how a rival will behave *or* how to modify an aspect of the physical environment to perform a task.

So, now we have a reasonable explanation of the ways in which we are similar to apes and why both humans and apes differ from monkeys. But humans have gone much further than chimpanzees – why? Whiten (1999) suggests that the crucial factor is the move of early humans away from the forests into the more open savannah-like habitats (i.e. grasslands dotted with bushes and trees). The other apes remained in the forests – an environment to which they were well adapted. But in the savannah, new pressures came into play – not least of which was the presence of other large mammals, especially the large cats – who both competed with early humans for food and posed a considerable threat as predators.

Analysis of the !Kung San people of the Kalahari desert in Africa, until recently a hunter–gatherer people and extensively studied by Lee (1979), provides an example of how hunting can be a very complex cognitive enterprise. First, unlike other animals, hunter–gatherers do not usually have direct contact with their prey – e.g. they don't bite or sting them. The San shoot poisoned arrows and when an arrow hits the prey and it gallops off, they often make no attempt to immediately pursue it. Rather they go to the place where the arrow hit the animal and read the signs – for instance how much poison was taken in and how much blood might have been lost. They then track the animal's progress but usually return to camp and wait for the next day before they track the animal to the point where it died. Only then do they butcher it. This is very different from chimpanzee hunting behaviour, which relies on sensory contact with the prey and more or less immediate consumption.

!Kung San bushmen on a hunt

Whiten (1999) argues that the San's hunting behaviour indicates complex cognitive skills. It requires the ability to plan (not to chase now but return later), the representation and mental manipulation of objects in their absence (the arrow signs), understanding of technology (how to construct the arrows) and the ability to reason (about signs such as animal tracks). This argument does not set itself against the social argument outlined in the previous section because Whiten notes that all of these cognitive processes take place within a social environment. For instance, hunts are planned and discussed in advance, often based on information given by members of the group who have travelled recently and noted signs of good locations. After the hunt, what happened, how and why, will be discussed and lessons learned for the future. Thus cognitive skills develop alongside social skills so that the two become interdependent and each encourages a refinement of the other.

Whiten calls this the development of 'deep social mind'. He argues that what differentiates human society from chimpanzee society is the level of cognitive sophistication at which the social integration operates. This form of cognition in our ancestors developed in such a way that it provided social support for dealing with the non-social, technological aspects of the environment, in particular the new pressures posed by the savannah habitat. However, it also developed to handle the complexities of the social structure itself.

3.4 The evolution of a modular mind?

In the previous section we saw how recent theorists have begun to reject arguments that point exclusively to *either* cognitive *or* social pressures as the key to understanding the development of humans from something rather like a clever chimpanzee. Rather, both seem to be inextricably linked and related to environmental pressures. So how might these different factors demonstrate themselves in the human mind?

One way of viewing the evolution of the human mind is to view it as based on a set of functionally differentiated modules each serving a particular and restricted function (i.e. as a '**modular mind**'). Thus, Cosmides (1998) has proposed that the multi-modular nature of the mind is rather like a Swiss-army knife that has lots of different functional features like scissors and tweezers, rather than one single-purpose blade.

Gigerenzer (1997) argues that such modules serve to solve specific problems of adaptive significance and to do this quickly. Although such problems may be varied, they have features in common that enable us to react to them in a similar way. Let us imagine, for example, that there is a module designed for handling social contracts in a hunter–gatherer society. Initially, this may have involved negotiations over the exchange of food or for making alliances. Later, as currency came into being this module would have been extended to enable an individual to negotiate the possible benefits and costs of monetary transactions. Later still, as economic systems developed, the module would have to represent and work with abstract notions such as shares and futures. Gigerenzer's argument is that although the details of how the social contract is negotiated have changed dramatically, the actual mechanisms of the module haven't – it still works out the possible benefits and costs to oneself (and/or one's kin).

Modular mind
The notion that the human mind is constituted in part by a set of usually diffused modules that serve specific cognitive-emotional functions.

Think of the exchange of gifts at Christmas or other celebratory occasions. In what ways, might this be considered as a form of social contract? To what extent, for example, do givers gauge the value and nature of their gifts in the context of the relationship? What would be your emotional reaction, for example, if someone gave you a gift incommensurate with your relationship, perhaps in excess of what you might have anticipated and of the present you might have given to them?

Social contract module
The particular set of inter-related cognitive, emotional, behavioural and emotional processes that govern the human ability for handling social contracts.

In each module, Gigerenzer argues, various cognitive, emotional, behavioural and motivational processes are connected together in the brain. Each module is therefore complex. For instance, a **social contract module** might include the following:

- the ability to recognize different individuals
- a long-term memory of past exchanges with other individuals in order to know when to cooperate and when to defect
- knowledge about what constitutes a benefit and a cost to oneself
- emotional reactions such as anger that signal to others that one will pursue cheaters (Cosmides and Tooby, 1992).

2.3 *Specialized inference procedures for detecting cheating*

Cosmides and Tooby (1992) reasoned that if humans do have inference procedures for engaging in social contracts, then for this to be adaptive, it would need to involve specific skills to detect cheaters. This would be part of the modular basis for our ability to engage in social contracts. An alternative to this, however, is that any skill in detecting cheating simply reflects our ability to make logical inferences. The following experiment describes one of many studies designed to distinguish between these two hypotheses.

Gigerenzer and Hug, for example, devised the following scenario:

> *Two Germans are hiking in the Swiss Alps and the local Alpine Club has cabins in the mountains to serve as overnight shelters for hikers. Because no trees grow at this height, the following rule applies. 'If one stays overnight in the cabin, then one must bring a load of firewood up from the valley'. There are rumours that the rule is not always followed.*
>
> *(cited in Cosmides and Tooby, 1992, p.195)*

Participants were given a series of sample situations (framed as selection tests). In one version participants are asked to take the perspective of a guard whose job it is to check on violations of the rule and infer from hikers' behaviour whether or not they are cheating. In another version participants are asked to take the perspective of visitors from the German Alpine Association who want to know how the Swiss clubs run their cabins. They are required only to work out what the rules are on the basis of hikers' behaviour. If social contract problems are simply a matter of thinking clearly and logically, then it shouldn't matter whether the reasoning was framed as detecting cheating or not. We should be able to solve both problems equally well. However, the results indicated that 83 per cent of participants correctly solved the version that framed the problem as one of detecting cheating, compared with only 44 per cent on the version that did not refer to cheating.

One problem with this study is that there may be alternative interpretations of the results found. For example, it may be that the first version (taking the guard's perspective) is easier to solve because it frames the problem in a more concrete way rather than because it relates to a possible 'social contract module'.

On the basis of the study in Box 2.3 and from similar experiments of their own, Cosmides and Tooby (1992, p.222) consistently found that people are particularly adept at strategies for detecting cheating in social contract type situations. They argue that for humans, in whose evolutionary development social relations have been so crucial, a module of complex cognitive skills for cheater detection has been selected. Such skills would have been crucial to our ancestors if altruistic relations with non-related individuals were to be of adaptive value. They conclude that their results support the idea that 'the evolved ... human mind contains functionally specialized, content-dependent cognitive adaptations for social exchange' (Cosmides and Tooby, 1992, p.222). As with the Machiavellian hypothesis, this idea of a modular concept of social intelligence rejects the notion of looking for whether social or cognitive influences are most important. Rather it suggests that the two are integrally related.

In line with their analogy of the Swiss army knife, Tooby and Cosmides (1992) envisage the mind as rather like a set of organs, each one designed to deal with a different adaptive pressure faced by our ancestors. Each one of these would have evolved because of the role it played in our early survival or reproductive success, and the logic of its operation is therefore largely specified by genetic programming. These mental 'organs' or modules are not conceptualized as discrete areas of the brain but are quite likely to be diffused and reflect the way in which the brain is organized and 'wired'. Given their complex basis, they are also likely to be programmed by the information from multiple genes. Note that the idea of modules does not imply that learning is unimportant. Rather, the modules facilitate learning by sensitising individuals to particular patterns of stimuli and making certain kinds of response both possible and more likely. Learning is thus not just the outcome of what we are exposed to but is also shaped by the design logic of the modules themselves.

Different ways of processing information have evolved in different species (rather as variations in their sensory receptors have also evolved). While there is considerable overlap among species in the ways that these work, there are certain cognitive adaptations that are particular to each one. Other animals' brains may be equally effective, if not more effective than ours in processing information that is adaptively relevant to them.

Some birds, for example, have been found to be able to remember thousands of hiding places in which they have placed caches of food (Sherry and Schachter, 1987).

In addition to a module for social contract exchange, what modules might we expect specifically to feature in humans? As the preceding sections have shown, the ability to mind-read would be a good candidate. So also would the capacity to understand particular kinds of cause-effect relationship. For example, monkeys (in contrast to chimps) are unable to use a set of sticks to retrieve an out-of-range fruit – although they use the sticks, they tend to push the fruit away as often as they manage to pull it towards them. In contrast, young children (around 1 year old) seem quite able to solve this problem (Leslie in Plotkin, 1997, p.189). Plotkin argues that the understanding of causal relations may be one reason why we have become such good tool-makers.

One of the best candidates for an adaptive module is language. This appears to be a complex of interrelated subdomains such as the skills for acquiring vocabulary, hearing spoken words, understanding their meaning, and being able to generate meaningful statements. Language is clearly a capacity that not only distinguishes humans from other species, but must have been both crucial to our evolutionary development and also the basis for the complexity and development of human cultures. The importance of language will be looked at specifically in Book 2.

According to Tooby and deVore (1987), another distinctive and important capacity that has been selected in human cognition is relational and abstract thinking – the ability to understand the principles of how things work and to generalize from these. Thus human knowledge is not tied to specific instances but can be easily put to use in novel situations.

Summary Section 3

- Evolutionary psychologists claim that their evidence and interpretations help us to understand why and how we have developed our distinctive human abilities.
- No single factor provides sufficient explanation of why humans differ from chimpanzees and other primates.
- Taking a 'reverse engineering' approach, Humphrey has argued that the creative intelligence that is characteristic of higher primates, evolved because of its value in enhancing the capacity of social individuals to both compete and cooperate.
- Such skills depend on having a 'theory of mind' – the ability to infer the thoughts and feelings of others. Monkeys do not have this ability, chimps only to some extent, young children take time to develop it fully.

- Later versions of the Machiavellian hypothesis assert that humans acquired particularly high-level intelligence because social relations skills developed in conjunction with the high-level cognitive abilities required by hunting in the novel environment of the savannah.
- Evolutionary psychologists argue that the development of modules in our minds (e.g. a social contract module), which allowed us successfully to solve problems in our ancestral environment, underpins our thinking, feelings and behaviour today.

4   Evolutionary understanding of social behaviour

In the previous section we explored the significance of the complexity of the social life of our ancestors in helping to shape the evolution of the human mind and have seen how cognitive and social functions are intrinsically interlinked. What can evolutionary psychology tell us about other aspects of social life and what light does this shed on the ways in which we feel and respond to others today?

4.1   The expression and interpretation of emotional states

Given the importance of social life, and alliance and conflicts in early human groups, the ability to recognize and remember others would have been crucial. There is certainly good evidence in contemporary humans of highly evolved skills in face recognition for both humans and primates (e.g. Roth and Bruce, 1995; Bruce, 1988). The fact of **prosopagnosia**, i.e. that specific forms of brain damage can disrupt *just* our ability to recognize faces (Etcoff *et al.*, 1991), may give some plausibility to the claim that it operates as a specific functional module.

Prosopagnosia
The inability to recognize faces, caused by damage to a particular area of the brain.

The human ability to 'mind-read' depends on abilities both to interpret and to express emotional states. There is evidence that much emotional expression in humans is in many respects 'universal', in the sense that it is common across cultures. Darwin's book *The Expression of the Emotions in Man and Animals* (1872) provides many examples of this, as have subsequent researchers. The cross-cultural psychologist Paul Ekman (1999), for instance, has found that people from a variety of cultures (including those with little contact with western societies such as people

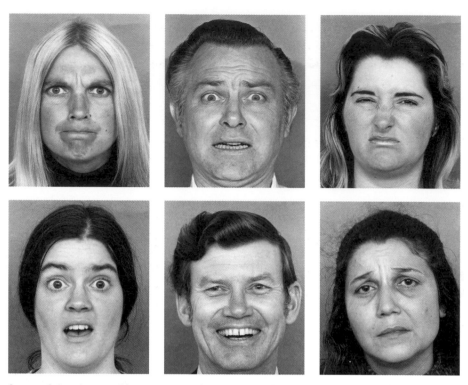

Some of the photos of human expressions used by Ekman

from Papua New Guinea) could recognize fear and disgust, as well as happiness, sadness, anger, and surprise when shown photographs of European actors depicting these emotions. Likewise, people from Western societies have no difficulty in interpreting the emotions expressed by a Papuan. However, while major forms of emotional expression appear to be common across cultures, Ekman emphasizes that the situations that elicit them and the interpretation placed on them may be open to considerable variability both culturally and historically. So, for example, while the expression of weeping may be universal, whether or not it will be

Can you recognize the emotions this Papuan man is expressing?

considered appropriate to do this at a public funeral will be culturally variable. Thus, like the social contract module discussed in the last section, while all humans share the adaptive ability to recognize particular forms of emotional expression, the precise operation of this ability varies between different groups. Another related observation of Darwin, which has also been confirmed subsequently, is that children who are born blind and deaf are able to show facial expressions consistent with their feelings and that are recognizable by others. This again suggests the inherited modular basis of the ways in which we express emotions.

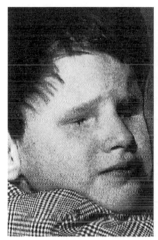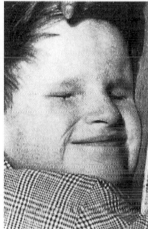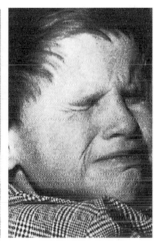

Photos of child born blind and deaf, with neutral expression, then smiling and crying

4.2 Altruism and reciprocity

Primate social life consists not just of competition but cooperation as well. But how might cooperative, caring and altruistic behaviours have evolved?

Some biologists (e.g. Dawkins in his book *The Selfish Gene,* 1989) have argued that we should really think of evolutionary development in terms of populations of successful (in terms of propagation) genes rather than individuals. With this notion, it is not difficult to understand why we should care for and support our kin at least. A parent has 50 per cent of genes in common with his or her offspring. Therefore, ensuring that children grow to sexual maturity and maximizing *their* chance of producing further offspring would be an adaptive strategy for parents in ensuring the propagation of genes identical to their own. Parental care would thus have been selected for in the course of evolution. But we also share *some* proportion of our genes with all our relatives, so promoting the welfare of all those related to us would also be a useful reproductive strategy. Our early human ancestors lived in small groups with many genetically related members. On the basis of observations of modern hunter–gatherer societies and population growth patterns, it has been estimated that infant mortality alone was probably in the order of about 65 per cent (Symons, 1979). If this was the case, the benefits of helping behaviours could have been substantial in maximizing the transmission of genes. It is interesting in this context that giving relations special status and consideration (for example giving them money or resources, or helping them in time of difficulty) seems to be a feature of almost all human societies. Such support is often roughly allocated in relation to genetic affinity: children and siblings, for example, are usually the primary beneficiaries in a will.

However, humans do not only care for kin, they quite often care for others who are unrelated to them. For example, people give money to charities. As Robert Trivers (1971) has pointed out, in our ancestral past, altruistic behaviour may have had reproductive fitness value even when relatives are not involved. Supporting someone in your group may well encourage them to reciprocate by helping you or your children on some future occasion. However, there would also be benefits for an individual in cheating – in accepting favours and then not returning these. Therefore, the evolution of **reciprocal altruism** crucially depends not just on the ability to communicate but on being able to compute benefits and, in particular, to detect non-reciprocation or cheating. This is precisely the kind of social contract or reciprocity module for which Cosmides appears to have found evidence (see Section 3.4). Given that reciprocal altruism depends on the ability to monitor trustworthiness and detect cheating, Crook (1980) has argued that this reciprocal altruism may itself have played a critical role in the evolution of both theory of mind and self-awareness. For it is on these particular skills that cheater-detection would depend. We might also suppose that the capacity for empathy (or the ability to think and feel as another person does, which is made possible by possessing a theory of mind) would have strengthened the human tendency for altruism by adding an emotional dimension. So, not only may we want to help other people but we may *feel* for them as if their concerns were our own.

More generally, Trivers (1985) has proposed that emotions could have played an important role in regulating both reciprocity and 'cheating' (i.e. where favours given are not returned). Feelings such as gratitude, sympathy, and liking would have encouraged the person feeling these to be good to those who elicited these feelings, whereas guilt and shame (as well as the indignation of the cheated) would serve to inhibit cheating.

Reciprocal altruism
A term used in evolutionary psychology to explain the evolution of behaviour benefiting others who are not kin in terms of the adaptive value for our ancestors of mutual help.

Stop for a moment and consider the following questions on the basis of what you have just read. How might an evolutionary psychologist explain why a) so many people tend to leave money to their children b) so many people give to charities?

4.3 Evolutionary origins of morality

We often tend to think of morality as a feature of more advanced and recent human societies. However, the anthropological evidence is that moral behaviours and prescriptions seem to be present in almost all known human societies. Even certain behaviours of primates have on occasion been interpreted in this way (de Waal, 1996).

What does morality and moral behaviour mean to you? What sorts of behaviours are involved? Given what you now know of our likely early human origins and the nature of evolutionary processes, can you think of any reasons why such behaviours might have evolved?

Morality may be regarded as constituted by an amalgam of several attitudes and styles of behaviour. Krebs (1998), for example, distinguishes *concern for others*, *respect for rules of justice* and *respect for authority* as being key components.

1 One aspect of all moral systems is that they advocate some form of *concern for others as well as ourselves.* As we have seen in the last section, evolutionary psychologists argue there are good reasons why altruism should have evolved, not just in respect of our kin but of unrelated individuals as well.

2 Another feature of moral systems is that they advocate certain *principles of justice* or behaviours that are perceived as fair. Evolutionary psychologists regard the evolution of mechanisms of social exchange and the implicit rules governing reciprocity and what is perceived as 'fairness' as providing the prototype for these. Krebs argues that it was the evolution of exchange strategies involving reciprocity and the detecting of cheating that provided the psychological basis for the subsequent development in human societies of notions and systems of justice. As we noted above, Trivers also suggests that moral systems and notions of justice and reciprocity would not only have been subject to external rewards and punishments but would also have been regulated by emotions such as shame and guilt.

3 Krebs also argues that moral systems are often sustained by *deference to authority.* In the case of religious moral systems, this may take the form of deference to the authority of the voice of God as represented by holy scriptures (e.g. the Bible or the Koran) or by an institutional leader (e.g. the Pope). In the case of secular and political ideologies, it may express itself in the influence and power of charismatic leaders (e.g. Lenin, Mao-Tse-tung, J.F. Kennedy). Such behaviours are usually sustained 'internally' by emotions such as empathy, awe and fear.

'Krebs argues that moral systems are often sustained by deference to authority'; this deference can be, for example, to the voice of God or to a charismatic leader

Dominance hierarchies, involving status and power, and demanding subservience from subordinates, are common among primate groups. This type of social network would have value for a particular group in promoting social stability among its members, making it more effective in competition with other groups and in dealing with the needs of survival. By acknowledging the dominance of a more powerful member of the group lower ranking members may also forge an alliance that may give them greater security (and perhaps even some share of power).

Krebs asserts that human societies are also characterized by dominance, status, and power hierarchies. He points out that several classic social psychological studies show the strength of tendency in humans to conformity and obedience (e.g. Asch, 1955). You may remember one of these studies from the Introduction to the book (Section 2.4) where Milgram (1974) found that, under certain experimental conditions, the majority of his participants were prepared to give electric shocks to another person when instructed to do so. In extreme cases, followers of

Jonestown, Guyana, 1978. Members of this cult had accepted their leader's order to drink cyanide

charismatic leaders have even been known to take their own lives when they have been ordered to do so.

Krebs' argument is then that tendencies to conformity and deference for authority, which forms an ingredient of human social and moral orders, would have been selected for their value in promoting cohesiveness and social stability and hence the survival of the group and the members who comprise it.

Reflect for a few moments on the society in which you live. What evidence and examples do you see of dominance hierarchies in work, politics, and particular social areas with which you may have some experience? In this context, think of the deference paid to celebrities, actors and public figures. Try to imagine your feelings if you had occasion to meet your Head of State. Can you see any other kinds of explanation that might explain deferential and conformist behaviours where they do occur?

Think about some of the strengths and weaknesses in Krebs' explanation of moral behaviours. On the one hand, for example, it may be useful in providing a fresh, and you may think plausible, analysis of why humans behave in moral ways. On the other, you may feel that this argument is partial in that it takes insufficient account of other possible factors, such as the influence of particular cultural and religious beliefs and socialization.

4.4 Ingroup cohesion and outgroup hostility

Human social behaviour is characterized not only by altruism and concerns for morality and justice but also by hostility and hate. One way of understanding this paradoxical conjunction of opposite social attitudes is to view it in the context of *ingroup* and *outgroup* differences. In other words, there is a strong tendency in human behaviour to favour members of one's own group and be indifferent or overtly hostile to outsiders. This pattern of bias may operate even in the case of groups formed in the most casual way, for example as in the 'minimal group' experiments of Tajfel *et al.* (1971) and the blue/brown eye studies discussed in the last chapter (see Chapter 1, Section 4.1). As you saw there, Tajfel's explanation of his results was in terms of social identity - that favouring the ingroup served to enhance the self-esteem of its members. While this might seem a reasonable account on a 'surface' level, evolutionary psychologists would argue that it is necessary to dig deeper to explain *why* such processes have evolved. An explanation in evolutionary terms for this pattern is that if, as we assume, our ancestors lived in small tribal groups, such ingroup/outgroup differentiation would have had adaptive value in the past. For group members who supported and cooperated with others within their group, but who were prepared to compete with outsiders for resources, would have been more likely to survive and reproduce. As with the modular basis for social exchange (see discussion of Gigerenzer in Section 3.4), however, while ingroup behaviour involves common underlying patterns of response, these also come in very different forms. So in contemporary life, we see ingroup/outgroup behaviour expressed not only in tribal hostilities and nationalism but also in political and religious rivalries. It could be argued that it is the driving force in team sports and may well be one of the factors that has led to the popularity of football all over the world.

Activity 2.4

Talk to any people you know who are football fans and try to gauge how much of their motivation in watching football, especially at national level, is the delight in the skills of the game and how much is the pleasure of supporting their particular team.

Football is a relatively benign example. But there are far more terrible expressions of this ingroup tendency in the modern world, for example the conflicts that have scarred the former Yugoslavia, Northern Ireland and Rwanda, to name but a few. Group aggression has produced some of the most savage atrocities in human history. In such situations both ingroup conformity and outgroup hostility can come into play. Particularly when others are regarded so much as outsiders as to be less than human, violence may get out of hand.

Football supporters displaying ingroup cohesion

4.5 Some other applications of the evolutionary approach

Evolutionary psychologists take the view that, as powerful motivators of, and controls on human behaviour, feelings of liking and dislike evolved because of the adaptive or reproductive function they served in the lives of our ancestors. So, they argue, we enjoy sweet and not bitter flavours because these, on the whole, are likely to be the taste of nutritious and safe foods. And we respond to sexual stimulation because this is linked to responses and actions that, at least in the pre-contraceptive past, would have been more likely to produce offspring. Some evolutionary psychologists have even claimed that our preference for particular landscapes is explicable in evolutionary terms.

Activity 2.5

Reflect for a moment on what kind of landscape you find most attractive. In what kind of setting could you imagine, for example, building a house when you retire? Note some of the features that such a landscape would have and try to explain why you have made the choices you have.

As Tooby and Cosmides point out, a key criterion of survival for hunter–gatherers is the place where they choose to live. They relate this to the experience of camping:

> *Having to carry water from a stream and firewood from the trees, one quickly learns to appreciate the advantages of some camp-sites over others. Dealing with exposure on a daily basis, quickly gives one an appreciation for sheltered sites, out of the wind, snow, or rain. For hunter–gatherers, there is no escape from this way of life: no opportunities to pick up food at the grocery store, no telephones, no emergency services, no artificial water supplies, no fuel deliveries, no cages, guns, or animal control officers to protect one from the predatory animals. In these circumstances, one's life depends on the operation of mechanisms that cause one to prefer habitats that provide sufficient food, water, shelter, information and safety to support human life, and cause one to avoid those that do not.*
>
> *(Tooby and Cosmides, 1992, pp.551–2)*

On the basis of such reasoning, Orians and Heerwagen (1992) have proposed the 'savannah hypothesis'. By savannah they mean grassy areas with occasional trees and bushes and ideally some glint of water. They argue that humans display an innate preference for this kind of landscape. This is just the kind of environment, they argue, in which our early ancestors evolved and one that offered many advantages. The grassland attracts large animals, which can be hunted for food. Bushes and trees yield accessible fruits. The open views meant dangerous intruders can be easily spotted, and the trees offer both shade and a safe resting place from predators.

Orians and Heerwagen followed these ideas up by seeking the advice of a variety of photographers, painters and landscape gardeners about what kinds of landscape people find beautiful. Across cultures, key features seem to be semi-open space, with water, large trees, slightly hilly, with paths leading into the distance and views to the horizon. In other words a landscape that offers prospect and refuge, or seeing without being seen (Appleton, 1990). Kaplan and Kaplan (1982) have proposed a further ingredient of natural beauty – although humans like environments that are easy to read they also like a hint of mystery. Particularly enjoyable are scenes where paths wander round hills, with meandering streams or greenery that partially obscures the view while stimulating a sense that there may be interesting resources out there to be discovered.

An idyllic landscape?

How convincing do you find the arguments and evidence that our preference for particular landscapes may have, at least in part, an evolutionary basis?

There are numerous other examples of attempts to view contemporary human behaviours and characteristics in the light of their likely evolutionary origins. We will be picking up on some of these in later chapters. In the second book of the course, for example, we will consider how and why both language and consciousness might have evolved, and the ways in which men and women relate to each other and the implications of their different reproductive potentials.

It should be noted that evolutionary psychologists make no claim that all human social behaviours are explicable in terms of evolution. To make a claim that the origins of a particular behaviour lie in our evolutionary past, the behaviour should appear to be pretty universal across cultures and it should be possible to establish a reasoned argument that it is linked to some survival or reproductive advantage in the past. Only a limited selection of social behaviours would meet these criteria. Having established such an argument, evolutionary psychologists try to check how far the contemporary evidence is consistent with their explanations, in some cases designing experiments to try to test these out.

Explanations provided in this way inevitably remain open to question and should not be regarded as fact. Rather they are interesting ways of looking at and stimulating our thinking about the behaviours in question. Each explanation needs to be evaluated in terms of the plausibility of the account offered and its consistency with the evidence available. In each case, it is worth asking what, if any, other kinds of explanation, might do the job as well.

In conclusion, it is worth noting that explanations of human social behaviour in terms of evolutionary origins do not, in themselves, *justify* any of the behaviours in question by suggesting that they are 'natural' and therefore 'good' (making this false assumption is known as the **naturalistic fallacy**). The kinds of social behavioural patterns discussed above evolved because they happened to have adaptive and reproductive value under the particular conditions of early human existence. In no way do such origins provide moral justification for these behaviours. On the contrary, it may be argued that many behaviours that have evolved in this way are no longer even functionally relevant or adaptive in the contemporary world. Ecological conditions change and the adaptations shaped by the totally different situations of the past may no longer work. They may even become a liability. So, for example, while ingroup/outgroup tendencies are likely to have promoted the survival of humans in our ancestral past, now in an age of atomic weapons they can pose a serious threat for the continuation of our species. Such a situation, where a characteristic that was once adaptive becomes a liability because of changing circumstances, is a major reason why more than 99 per cent of all species that have ever lived are now extinct, and why we may well now need to be wary of at least some of the predispositions shaped by our evolutionary past.

Naturalistic fallacy
The false assumption that because behaviours have evolved that they are therefore morally justified.

Summary Section 4

- Arguments have been put forward proposing that several kinds of human social behaviour can be accounted for in terms of evolutionary development. These include the expression and interpretation of emotions, altruism and reciprocity, conformity and deference to authority, concern for morality and justice, ingroup cohesion and outgroup hostility. The human preference for particular kinds of landscape has also been explained in this way.

● Other human attributes explicable in these terms (and that we will examine later in the course) include language, consciousness and relations between the sexes.

5 Using evolutionary psychology

Let us recap for a moment before we conclude by considering the advantages and limitations of taking an evolutionary psychology approach. Evolutionary psychologists argue that, as biological beings, we are subject to evolutionary forces. Contemporary civilization is very recent, representing only a small proportion of the time that humans have been in existence. Thus, many of the specific human adaptations derive from pre-history – especially from the long period of hunter–gatherer society that began around 500,000 years ago (before the advent of *Homo sapiens*) and lasted until around 10,000 years ago. Since our ancestors no longer exist we need to look to other sources of evidence. As we have seen, we can gain some information from fossil and archaeological records (see, for example, the lion–man discussed in Section 3.2), some from analysis of the ecological and social environments that hunter–gatherers lived in, and some information from species to which we are closely related. We can also consider, as we have done, the possible evolutionary origins of some of our species-typical abilities and social behaviours.

Bear in mind here that not all physical or behavioural processes are a direct result of evolutionary adaptations. For example, no one claims that blood is coloured red because this is of particular adaptive or reproductive value. It just happens to be the colour of the molecule that was selected for because of its capacity to carry oxygen in the blood. Likewise, many behavioural characteristics may take this 'by-product form'. Evolutionary psychology only purports to account for behaviours that have in the past been directly related to survival or reproduction. These encompass, as we have seen, some key human attributes, including mind-reading, the perception of causality, predispositions to altruism, conformity and ingroup cohesion, and our preference for fair exchange and justice.

5.1 Methods

A variety of methods are used by the researchers and theorists whose ideas have featured in this chapter. First do the activity below, then see Box 2.4.

Activity 2.6

Look back over the account of Darwin given in the biography box in Section 2.1. How did Darwin develop his theory of evolution?

Look back over the chapter. List some of the varied kinds of evidence that have been drawn on. What do you think of as the primary method used by evolutionary psychologists? For answers to these questions, read Box 2.4 below.

2.4   FEATURED METHOD

Some specific methods used by Darwin and by evolutionary psychologists

Evolutionary psychology has developed within the systematic and empirical approach of natural science (i.e. involving reference to observations from the 'real-world'). However, it uses a range of methods that are not always easy to disentangle.

Observation, classification and induction (the methods of natural history)

Induction
Rationally inferring and developing general laws on the basis of observing many specific instances.

Darwin's approach was to be insatiably curious, to collect an enormous range of samples and observations of plant and animal life, order or classify these and then to try to develop theoretical concepts (e.g. like natural and sexual selection) to make sense of his data. He observed how some varieties of finches in the Galapagos were found on some islands and not on others, and tried to find reasons why this might be so. In doing this, he was helped of course by his knowledge of other related ideas current in the intellectual climate of the times. This approach of inferring and developing general laws on the basis of observing many specific instances is known as **induction**.

Deduction
Rationally inferring implications and consequences on the basis of knowledge of established principles and facts.

Darwin also used **deduction** – drawing out the implications and consequences of established principles and facts. Thus he reasoned that, if animals produce many offspring and yet the population remains stable, then it follows that many must die. Thinking about which ones would be eliminated led him to the idea of selection.

Hypothetico-deductive reasoning and testing

Hypothetico-deductive reasoning
Formulating specific hypotheses or predictions on the basis of principles and established knowledge and then testing these.

Once the evolutionary principles have been established, they can then be used to formulate hypotheses or predictions in relation to specific instances – **Hypothetico-deductive reasoning**. Hence we can predict as in the Kettlewell study (see Section 2.3) that with reduced pollution following restrictions on smoke emission, lighter coloured moths would begin to come into their own. Testing of evolutionary hypotheses and concepts has not only been done by observing animal behaviour and changing populations, but also by mathematical and computer modelling. By working from certain assumptions based on the theory, the researcher can explore what consequences are likely to result (e.g. Dawkins, 1986).

Much of the research and ideas in this area is based on a mixture of approaches. For example, the research into the Machiavellian hypothesis (discussed earlier in this chapter) took evolutionary principles, coupled them with the assumption that early human societies were socially complex, supplemented it with observations of primate and human societies, and explored what might be the likely effects.

'Reverse engineering' or functional analysis (see Box 2.1)

This approach takes examples of seemingly universal human (or other) behaviours and asks, in the light of evolutionary theory, what conditions would have been necessary for these to have evolved (i.e. what would have been their adaptive or reproductive value)? We saw examples of such reasoning in the last section. While such analyses can be criticized for being inevitably inferential, the best examples are well grounded in firmly established evolutionary principles and observations and supported by empirical tests (e.g. Cosmides' experiments on cheater detection – see Section 3.4). With the method of reverse engineering, however, evaluation inevitably rests on the coherence and plausibility of the analysis in making sense of the data, criteria which are not easy to establish or get agreement on.

Logical inference supported by evidence

Overall, the most common method used by evolutionary psychologists is a process of logical inference about the origins of human behaviour and mind on the basis of knowledge of evolutionary principles. Such reasoning is supported by evidence from a wide range of disciplines including ethology (studies of animals in the wild), controlled experiments with animals and humans, clinical studies (such as the effects of brain damage on perception of faces, see Section 4.1), paleoanthropology (e.g. ancient artefacts like the lion–man statue) and anthropological and cross-cultural observations and experiments on contemporary societies (see, for example, the work of Ekman discussed in Section 4.1).

Activity 2.7

In your response to Activity 2.6, check and see how far you have included examples of the kinds of methods noted above. If you have missed any, look back over the chapter and try to locate examples of these.

5.2 The contribution of evolutionary psychology

There are a number of ways in which evolutionary psychology can be seen as highly relevant and valuable to contemporary psychology:

1   The Machiavellian hypothesis and the modularity hypothesis both propose that our brains are structured in such a way as to 'solve' the adaptive problems our ancestors had to face and to do so quickly. The modularity of the mind is a topic to which you will return in the later chapters on cognition in this book, but it is a notion that relies on an evolutionary psychological analysis to provide a rationale for the kind of modules there might be.

2   Evolutionary psychology suggests that any straightforward separation between cognitive and social capacities is likely to be unsatisfactory. The unprecedented complexity of human minds, as compared to those of monkeys and apes, has come about precisely because these two domains are integrated in mutually reinforcing ways. This integrative approach is not unique to evolutionary psychology but is characteristic of it. (In similar fashion, throughout this book you will find that 'social' and 'cognitive' aspects are taken as interrelated, in contrast to many traditional introductory textbooks in psychology where they may be more or less treated as separate domains.)

3   We share many things in common with other animals and in particular with chimpanzees with whom we shared a common ancestor. Evolutionary psychologists believe therefore that we can learn many things about our own evolution by looking at the behaviour of other animals. For instance, we may detect the possible beginnings of important human capacities such as tool use, theory of mind and culture in chimpanzee societies. However, there is an important caveat: human beings (like chimpanzees) have continued to evolve in ways that are different from the common ancestor. Therefore we cannot simply 'read off' implications for human behaviour from observations of other animals.

4   Throughout this chapter you have read about evolutionary psychologists drawing on research that has come from a variety of disciplines – ethology, sociobiology, primatology, philosophy, anthropology, archaeology as well as psychology. Evolutionary psychology encourages an interdisciplinary approach, arguing that because human beings are so complex and have a long evolutionary history, then evidence from several disciplines is required for a satisfactory explanation of human behaviour and existence.

5   By asking functional questions, evolutionary psychology can generate new investigations and new understanding. For example, for many years empirical evidence consistently demonstrated a male advantage in

spatial ability on tasks such as mental rotation of objects, mentally constructing figures from patterns, map reading and estimating the speed of a moving object. In 1992, Silverman and Eals used the 'reverse engineering' approach to investigate this phenomenon. They proposed that many of the measures that demonstrated male superiority in spatial ability correspond to attributes that would enable successful hunting. They hypothesized that it was likely that an array of spatial abilities related to foraging would also have emerged since they would have adaptive advantage for females. Thus, they devised different kinds of spatial tests corresponding to spatial abilities conducive to successful foraging, for example, memory for the location of objects. These tests reliably demonstrated a female advantage. Males do not therefore have an advantage over females in terms of spatial ability – rather the two genders have *differing* spatial abilities that may well be closely related to the kind of problems they had to solve in our ancestral past.

5.3 Criticisms of evolutionary psychology

Two general criticisms often levelled against evolutionary psychology are as follows:

1 The apparently deterministic aspect of evolutionary explanations. In other words, evolutionary psychology seems to suggest that humans are compelled to behave in certain ways. But there is considerable diversity in human culture and societies.
2 The impact of change in the ways in which humans live. Contemporary lifestyles, it is argued, differ so very dramatically from the lifestyles of hunter–gatherers that evolutionary explanations can be of only limited value.

Evolutionary psychologists would respond to these criticisms by making the following kinds of points:

1 Evolutionary psychology does assert that there is a common structure to all human minds and that this structure is closely related to the kinds of problems our ancestors had to solve. However, the core argument of the Machiavellian hypothesis is that the key feature of the structure of the human mind, in contrast to that of other animals, is the human capacity for creative intelligence. This necessarily entails the idea that there are several ways of solving the same problem. Thus, evolutionary psychology would *predict* cultural diversity and would suggest that its origins lie deep in the ancestral past that we share with chimpanzees. Support for this hypothesis comes from an extensive literature detailing how different communities of chimpanzees have different cultures,

which kind of tools they habitually use and the way in which they use them (McGrew, 1992). Note though that while evolutionary psychology points to the aspects of behaviour that were adaptive in our ancestral past, it does not deny the human facility for choice in behaviour. What evolutionary psychology does highlight are the structures that have been adaptive over a long period of time and thus may be more resistant to change.

2   There is little doubt that contemporary human life differs dramatically from that of hunter–gatherers. However, as Sections 3.4 and 4 demonstrated, many of the modules and predispositions of the human mind that must have developed during the long period we spent as hunter–gatherers are still relevant today. For instance, while the content informing the social contract module may have changed, the logic of its operation has not. However, the causal factors that support the continuance of a particular behaviour may be different in contemporary society. For example, while gaining expertise in hunting was adaptive for our ancestors by producing high quality food, obtaining a well-paid job today serves a similar purpose. Nevertheless, humans, like other animals are still evolving and adapting to their environment. Aspects of behaviour that were adaptive in our ancestral past may not be adaptive today – the example of our preference for sugar was mentioned earlier, also the changing adaptive value of the human ingroup/outgroup tendency. While there have not been sufficient generations to allow significant biological change to have occurred (the period of hunting and gathering still represents 99 per cent of human existence), this is not to deny that such changes are taking place and at some time in the rather distant future new adaptations may supercede the adaptations of hunter–gatherer society.

5.4 Conclusion

We have tried to show how the kinds of explanation that evolutionary psychology offers, while not providing a complete understanding of human behaviour, can enrich our understanding of it. As Stephen Pinker puts it: 'The mind is an exquisitely organized system that accomplishes remarkable feats no engineer can duplicate. How could the forces that shaped that system and the purposes for which it was designed be irrelevant to understanding it?' (Pinker, 1998, pp.22–3). A satisfactory psychology must not only ask *causal* questions but also *functional* ones.

Further reading

Pinker, S. (1998) *How the Mind Works*, London, Penguin.
An excellent overview of the modularity hypothesis and a fascinating account of the application of evolutionary principles to understanding the mind. Highly recommended for understanding both evolutionary and cognitive psychology.

Plotkin, H. (1997) *Evolution in Mind*, London, Allen Lane
An accessible account of how evolutionary explanations have been viewed within contemporary psychology and why they are relevant.

Goodall, J. (1971) *In the Shadow of Man*, London, Collins.
Goodall, J. (1991) *Through a Window: Thirty Years with the Chimpanzees of Gombe*, Harmondsworth, Penguin.
Both these provide interesting descriptions and discussion of chimpanzee behaviour in the wild.

 References

Appleton, J. (1990) *The Symbolism of Habitat*, Seattle, Washington, University of Washington Press.

Asch, S.E. (1955) 'Opinions and social pressures', *Scientific American*, vol. 193, November, pp.31–55.

Barkow, J.H., Cosmides, L. and Tooby, J. (eds) (1992) *The Adapted Mind: Evolutionary Psychology and the Generation of Culture*, Oxford, Oxford University Press.

Baron-Cohen, S. (1990) *Mindblindness: An Essay on Autism and Theory of Mind*, Cambridge, MA, MIT Press.

Baron-Cohen, S. (1999) 'The evolution of a theory of mind', in Corballis, M.C. and Lea, S.E.G. (eds).

Bruce, V. (1988) *Recognising Faces*, Hillsdale, NJ, Erlbaum.

Byrne, R.W. and Whiten A. (eds) (1988) *Machiavellian Intelligence: Social Expertise and the Evolution of Intellect in Monkeys, Apes and Humans*, Oxford, Clarendon Press.

Byrne, R.W. (1995) *The Thinking Ape: Evolutionary Origins of Intelligence*, Oxford, Oxford University Press.

Byrne, R.W. (1999) 'Human cognitive evolution', in Corballis, M.C. and Lea, S.E.G. (eds).

Corballis, M.C. (1999) 'Phylogeny from apes to humans' in Corballis, M.C. and Lea, S.E.G. (eds).

Corballis, M.C. and Lea, S.E.G. (eds) (1999) *The Descent of Mind: Psychological Perspectives on Hominid Evolution*, Oxford, Oxford University Press.

Cosmides, L. and Tooby J. (1992) 'Cognitive adaptations for social exchange', in Barkow, J.H. *et. al.* (eds).

Cosmides, L, (1998) Invited address to Annual Conference of British Psychological Society, Edinburgh.

Crook J. (1980) *The Evolution of Human Consciousness*, Oxford, Oxford University Press.

Darwin, C. (1845) *Journal of Researches into the Geology and Natural History of the Various Countries visited by HMS Beagle*, London, Henry Colburn.

Darwin, C. (1859) *On the Origin of Species,* London, Murray.

Darwin, C. (1872) *The Expression of the Emotions in Man and Animals,* London, Murray.

Darwin C. (1874) *The Descent of Man, and Selection in Relation to Sex*, London, Murray.

Dawkins, R. (1976/1989) *The Selfish Gene*, New Edition, Oxford, Oxford University Press.

Dawkins, R. (1986) *The Blind Watchmaker: Why the Evidence of Evolution Reveals a Universe Without Design*, London, Penguin.

de Waal, F.B.M. (1996) *Good Natured: The Origins of Right and Wrong in Humans and Other Animals*, Cambridge MA/London, Harvard University Press.

Diamond, J. (1991) *The Rise and Fall of the Third Chimpanzee*, London, Vintage.

Ekman, P. (1999) 'Afterword', in C. Darwin, *The Expression of Emotions in Man and Animals*, (3rd edn), London, HarperCollins.

Etcoff, N.L., Freeman, R. and Cave, K.R. (1991) 'Can we lose memories of faces? Content specificity and awareness in a prosopagnosic', *Journal of Cognitive Neuroscience*, vol.3, pp.25–41.

Gigerenzer, G. (1997) 'The modularity of social intelligence', in Whiten, A. and Byrne, R.W. (eds).

Goodall, J. (1971) *In the Shadow of Man*, London, Collins.

Goodall, J. (1991) *Through a Window: Thirty Years with the Chimpanzees of Gombe*, Harmondsworth, Penguin.

Humphrey, N.K. (1976) 'The social function of intellect', in Bateson, P.P.G. and Hinde, R.A. (eds) *Growing Points in Ethology*, Cambridge, Cambridge University Press.

Kaplan, S. and Kaplan, R. (1982) *Cognition and Environment: Functioning in an Uncertain World*, New York, Praeger.

Kettlewell, H.B.D. (1971) 'Darwin's missing evidence', in Srb, A.M., Owen, R.D. and Edgar, R.S. (1971) *Facets of Genetics: Readings from the Scientific American*, San Francisco, CA, W.H. Freeman.

Krebs, D.L. (1998) 'The evolution of moral behaviors' in Krebs, D.L. and Crawford, C. (eds) *Handbook of Evolutionary Psychology: Ideas, Issues and Applications,* Mahwah, NJ, Lawrence Erlbaum.

Lee, R.B. (1979) *The !Kung San: Men, Women and Work in a Foraging Society*, Cambridge, Cambridge University Press.

McGrew, W.C. (1992) *Chimpanzee Material Culture*, Cambridge, Cambridge University Press.

Milgram, S. (1974) *Obedience to Authority*, London, Tavistock.

Mithen, S, (1996) *The Prehistory of the Mind*, London, Penguin.

Oakley, K.P. (1949) *Man the Tool Maker*, Trustees of the British Museum, London.

Orians, G.H. and Heerwagen, J.H (1992) 'Evolved responses to landscapes', in Barkow, J.H. *et al.* (eds).

Pinker, S. (1998) *How the Mind Works*, London, Penguin.

Plotkin, H. (1997) *Evolution in Mind*, London, Allen Lane

Premack, D. and Woodruff, G. (1978) 'Does the chimpanzee have a theory of mind?', *The Behavioral and Brain Sciences,* vol.1, pp.515–26.

Premack, D. (1988) 'Does the chimpanzee have a theory of mind? Revisited', in Byrne, R.W. and Whiten, A. (eds).

Roth, I. and Bruce, V. (1995) *Perception and Representation: Current Issues*, Buckingham, Open University Press.

Sherry, D.F. and Schachter, D.L. (1987) 'The evolution of multiple memory systems', *Psychological Review*, vol.94, pp.439–54.

Sibley, G.C. and Ahlquist, J.E. (1987) 'DNA hybridization evidence of hominoid phylogeny: results from an expanded data set', *Journal of Molecular Evolution*, vol.26, pp.99–121.

Silverman, I. and Eals, M. (1992) 'Sex differences in spatial abilities: evolutionary theory and data', in Barkow, J.H. *et al.* (eds).

Symons, D. (1979) *The Evolution of Human Sexuality*, Oxford, Oxford University Press.

Tajfel, H., Billig M.G. and Bundy, R.P. (1971) 'Social categorization and intergroup behaviour', *European Journal of Social Psychology,* vol.1, no.2, pp.149–78.

Tooby, J. and Cosmides, L. (1989) 'Evolutionary psychology and the generation of culture, Part 1. Theoretical considerations', *Ethology and Sociobiology*, vol.10, pp.29–49.

Tooby, J. and Cosmides, L. (1992) 'The psychological foundations of culture', in Barkow, J.H. *et al.* (eds).

Tooby, J. and DeVore, I. (1987) 'The reconstruction of hominid behavioral evolution through strategic modelling', in Kinzey, W.G. (ed.) *The Evolution of Human Primate Behavior: Primate Models*, New York, SUNY Press.

Trivers, R. (1971) 'The evolution of reciprocal altruism', *Quarterly Review of Biology*, vol.46, pp.35–57.

Trivers, R. (1985) *Social Evolution*, Reading, MA, Benjamin/Cummings.

Vines, G. (2000) 'Are chimps chimps?', *New Scientist*, October, no.2260.

Visalberghi, E. and Trinca, L. (1987) 'Tool use in capuchin monkeys: distinguishing between performing and understanding', *Primates*, vol.30, pp.511–21.

Visalberghi, E. and Limongelli, L. (1994) 'Lack of comprehension of cause-effect relationships in tool-using capuchin monkeys (Cebus *apella*)', *The Journal of Comparative Psychology*, vol.103, pp.15–20.

Waddell, P.J. and Penny, D. (1996) 'Evolutionary trees of apes and humans from DNA sequences', in Lock, A.J. and Peters, C.R. (eds) *Handbook of Symbolic Evolution*, Oxford, Clarendon Press.

Whiten, A. (1996) 'When does smart behaviour reading become mind-reading?', in Carruthers, P. and Smith, P.K. (eds) *Theories of Theories of Mind*, Cambridge, Cambridge University Press.

Whiten, A. (1999) 'The evolution of deep social mind in humans', in Corballis, M.C. and Lea, S.E.G. (eds).

Whiten, A. and Byrne, R.W. (eds) (1997) *Machiavellian Intelligence II: Extensions and Evaluations*, Cambridge, Cambridge University Press.

Wilson, E. (1975) *Sociobiology: The New Synthesis*, Cambridge, MA, Harvard University Press.

Yee, M.S. and Layton, T.N. (1981) *In my Father's House: The Story of the Layton Family and the Reverend Jim Jones*, New York, Holt, Rinehart and Winston.

Commentary 2: Evolutionary psychology

Chapter 2 has focused on an area of psychology that is relatively new but fast developing. Evolutionary psychology makes use of a mixture of existing data, evidence and methods from other domains of psychology like neuropsychology, psychometrics, cognitive psychology and group behaviour, as well as other disciplines such as genetics, paleoanthropology and primatology. However, it can still claim to be a specific perspective within psychology.

Theory

1   Although psychologists work within different perspectives and advance different theories, their approaches to research produce coherent bodies of knowledge which develop over time. Evolutionary psychology is a relatively new perspective.

2   Evolutionary psychologists do not look for causes of behaviour, but for understanding in terms of how behaviours evolved and the evolutionary functions they must have served (i.e. functional explanations).

3   Psychologists often find it invaluable to use metaphors that help them to see issues in new ways. Evolutionary psychologists use the metaphor of 'reverse engineering' to guide their questioning.

Methods

4   Because evolutionary psychologists draw on other areas of psychology and other disciplines, they make use of a variety of methods and data to arrive at their evidence. They use material data, behavioural data and occasionally symbolic data, such as early art.

Themes

5   Two central themes addressed in evolutionary psychology are 'What makes humans as a species different from non-human animals?' and 'How have humans changed over long periods of time?'

6   In evolutionary psychology, change is never thought of as 'having a purpose' (i.e. as being purposive).

Thinking about theory

Evolutionary psychology as a perspective

Evolutionary psychology is a perspective because it is a coherent way of thinking about psychology. It is a body of knowledge and a process of investigation that is driven by specific ideas about the nature of human and non-human species, and about the processes of evolution that underpin Darwin's evolutionary theory. What holds evolutionary psychology together as a perspective is its overarching claim that modern humans have brain structures and tend to exhibit behaviours and motivations that evolved a long time ago but are sustained as genetically transmitted, biologically-based predispositions passed down the generations.

By placing a chapter on 'Evolutionary psychology' immediately after one on 'Identities and diversities' we are drawing your attention to the existence of dramatic contrasts within psychology. Evolutionary psychologists aim to understand people in very different ways from identity theorists. This is because of both timescale and focus. In contrast to theories of identity (Chapter 1), or theories of learning (Chapter 3), evolutionary psychologists are not looking for the immediate causes of behaviour (i.e. causal explanations), but for *functional* explanations. Evolutionary psychologists try to find out how the mind operates (and thus how human societies work) by understanding *how* this might have come about (through evolutionary processes), and *why*. Other aspects of this endeavour are to question the extent to which these functions are still applicable; and also to question to what extent these functions and behaviours have been modified by generations of cultural influence and cultural transmission.

The use of metaphor to extend understanding

In evolutionary psychology the basic search for the functions of the human mind has been described using a compelling metaphor – that of reverse engineering. You may remember that Tooby and Cosmides compared reverse engineering to using knowledge of what a car can do, plus knowledge of basic mechanical principles, to deduce how and why a car is the way it is. This metaphor allows psychologists to use their knowledge of evolutionary principles and past environmental conditions to guide their questioning and to work out which cognitive and social abilities would have been most effective for human survival thousands of years ago. You will find that metaphors are used throughout psychology, and you should try to watch out for them as you read.

The use of functional explanations will be illustrated again in this book, for example in Chapter 4 ('Biological processes and psychological explanation'), but the centrality of 'reverse engineering' is unique to evolutionary psychology.

Traditions, history and context

Although Darwin was not a psychologist, his work is clearly central to evolutionary psychology. Yet, even work as original as his was 'of its time'.

Darwin was not the only person to generate ideas of evolution and natural selection: he was driven to complete his major book only when Alfred Wallace developed similar ideas. This is a clear example of similar ideas arising within the same social context and historical period. The intellectual climate in which naturalists were working in Europe in the middle of the nineteenth century, together with the painstaking and time-consuming methods of the natural history approach to data collection, were fostered by self-supporting, wealthy individuals who were passionately interested in this endeavour. The conjunction of time, money and a climate of curiosity and advancement was a feature of the early industrial society in parts of Europe but has also happened in other cultures at other times: for example, the art, architecture and engineering of the Minoans in Crete around 3000 BC; the art and science of the Renaissance which started in Italy in the 1400s AD; and the sculpture and metal work in the kingdom of Benin, west Africa in 1400–1600 AD.

It would probably not have been possible for Darwin to develop his theory without the progress that was being made in biology at the time he was working. Similarly, evolutionary psychology would not have been possible without later developments in genetics, biology, ethology, and even more recent technical developments in archaeology, neuropsychology and psychology, which could be combined with Darwin's original insights.

Thinking about methods

A multi-method enterprise

Because evolutionary psychology draws on other areas of psychology and other disciplines, it advances by using a variety of data. This is not unusual since psychology is a multi-method enterprise. Evolutionary psychology uses behavioural data, material data (biological and archaeological) and symbolic data (prehistoric cave pictures and other art).

The featured methods in Chapter 2 concerned the *higher level* of methodology, closer to the cycle of enquiry you met in the Introduction, (i.e. the cyclical process of *arriving* at theory and *testing* hypotheses). The inductive part of this process, in evolutionary psychology, is illustrated by paleoanthropology – the collecting and documenting of ancient artefacts and tools, the observation methods of primatology (the study of the primates) and the detailed social anthropological observations made of people who still live in hunter–gatherer groups in modern times. The hypothetico-deductive part of the cycle, for evolutionary psychologists, involves devising hypotheses that will test their basic theory and the piecing together of a variety of evidence – where the data are often pre-existing but need to be assembled. It is obviously not possible to study the behaviour and social organization of humans who lived thousands of years ago other than through paleoanthropological evidence and, very indirectly, by observing modern day hunter–gatherers. Evolutionary psychologists also test their theory by formulating hypotheses about group behaviour, about the possible development of cognitive modules that continue to affect our thinking and feelings today, and by using primatology, ethology and genetics to see if the theory of evolutionary psychology can be supported by the new data.

■ Thinking about themes

By reading the Introduction and Chapters 1 and 2 in this book, you have probably already seen that there are themes that are common across psychology. But you will also be beginning to appreciate that these themes can be approached in very different ways in different areas of psychology.

Explaining ourselves as human

Evolutionary psychology seeks an understanding of humanness by addressing the question 'What makes humans *as a species* different from non-human animals?' It is, therefore, not concerned with what makes each of us a unique human being (the focus of Chapter 1). Instead, it is concerned with what makes us the same as each other, and similar in some ways to other primates (with whom we share a high percentage of our genes) but different from all other animals.

Chapter 2 contributes an understanding of how our evolution as a species might help to illuminate current, everyday human behaviour. An important point raised by evolutionary psychology is that the ways in which we think (cognition), our social organization and our biology were *simultaneously* all centrally important to evolutionary processes and adaptation, and affected each other. According to evolutionary psychologists, our current biology and psychology still reflect the crucial *interplay* of social and cognitive adaptations to environments on an evolutionary timescale.

Fixity and change

The notion of change is at the centre of evolutionary psychology. But it is change in a very different sense from Chapter 1. We have already seen in Chapter 1 that some theories of identity are concerned with changes in identity over the life course of an individual. The next chapter (Chapter 3, 'Three approaches to learning') is about learning – another kind of change that also occurs during one person's lifetime. Evolutionary psychology is the only area within psychology that is concerned with change over immensely long timescales.

In Commentary 1 we pointed out that the dimension of fixity and change should not be treated as a dichotomy. Evolutionary psychology contains both these themes and they are not in opposition. Evolutionary psychology considers that we are products of our evolutionary history and genes and so are relatively fixed by our natures (although it recognizes that evolution is a process that continues today). However, it also sees evolution as a process of change by means of social and biological adaptation to environments over a very long timescale.

Also in Commentary 1, we noted that in psychology the concept of change is used in different ways. In Chapter 1, you saw that there was a sense that changes in identity were either developmental, unfolding in interaction with environments and life events, and/or consciously and actively pursued. In evolutionary psychology, changes in species are in no sense consciously pursued changes or purposive adaptations. There is no choice, purpose, or planning in evolution.

However, in thinking or writing about evolutionary change, it is very difficult to avoid ideas and words that suggest some kind of purpose. When it is suggested, intentionally or inadvertently, that there is a purpose or preconceived design underlying evolutionary change, this is called *teleology*. In evolutionary psychology it is very important to try to avoid teleological explanations or wordings that sound as if they imply purposive change. Evolutionary changes are due to random genetic events that lead to biological and behavioural changes that can only be sustained if, *by chance*, they happen to give some sort of reproductive or survival advantage. Over a long period of time these lead to changes in the genetic pool at a species level.

In direct contrast, the next chapter (Chapter 3, 'Three approaches to learning') considers how humans and animals change over their life course – sometimes very quickly – as a result of what they learn.

CHAPTER **3**

Three approaches to learning

Karen Littleton, Frederick Toates and Nick Braisby

Contents

Aims

This chapter aims to:

- outline and discuss three different approaches to understanding learning
- illustrate different methods psychologists use to study learning
- consider the practical implications of psychological theories and research on learning.

1 Introduction

What do we mean by the term 'learning'? This chapter is designed to show some of the ways in which psychologists think about this question.

Activity 3.1

Stop and think of some instances when you use the term 'learning'. You might come up with some examples such as learning to ride a bicycle, learning French or learning psychology. What have these all got in common? Try to generate a statement of their common features. Are there any clear similarities and differences between these examples of learning? Could you put them into categories?

Comment

Learning
The acquisition of new knowledge or skills.

You will no doubt have thought of many different situations in which the word **learning** is applied, and in the present chapter we hope to convey some of this variety. What you might also have arrived at is a statement that all instances of learning involve acquisition of new knowledge or skills. They all involve experience and change of some kind. The essence of learning is that a learner is changed as a result of experience. The change is one that opens up new possibilities. For example, your performance at riding a bicycle might be disastrous at first and you crash to the ground. However, persistence pays and after a few hours you are able to maintain balance and negotiate your environment effortlessly. Similarly, when you first started studying psychology you might have had only a vague notion of what it was about but, with persistence of study, your ideas will become structured and you will be able to present a coherent account of what psychology is.

Were you able to categorize different types of learning? One possible distinction that you might have formulated is that between skills and knowledge. This is not a perfectly clear-cut dichotomy but psychologists find it useful and it will be reflected in this chapter. Learning to ride a bicycle consists of acquiring a skill, which can only be revealed in behaviour. You learn how to ride a bicycle. Learning that Bucharest is the capital of Romania is somewhat different from this. It represents the acquisition of knowledge that in principle might never be revealed in behaviour. Rather than learning *how*, it is learning *what*.

If we define learning as a process of change that opens up new possibilities, let us consider this in the context of another process of change – that of evolution, described in Chapter 2.

From a biological perspective, both evolution and learning are processes of change that permit better coping with the environment. However, a fundamental and uncontroversial difference between evolution and learning is that evolution is a very slow process whose effects are only felt over generations, whereas learning occurs within the lifetime of a given individual. Evolution is a process by means of which changes are inherited from one generation to another; thus, over long periods of time, a better adaptation is seen. Learning is a process whereby individual animals, human and others, are able to acquire knowledge or skills that equip them to cope better with the environment; for example, learning to walk, to hunt prey, or to predict the consequences of planting seeds. Another difference is that evolution appears to be the result of chance (e.g. random mutations) as described in Chapter 2, whereas learning appears to be more intentional and conscious (e.g. learning to read). However, some influential approaches suggest learning is an ongoing and emergent process that happens without conscious intention.

This chapter will concentrate on how human and non-human animals 'acquire information' as a result of experience in the environment. However, the process of learning must depend to some extent upon 'what is there already', whether we are thinking of learning later in life or learning from the moment of birth. Therefore, a complete picture depends upon understanding learning in the context of the whole person or animal, its evolutionary past, its genes and its life history. These might be such as to make some things easier to learn than others.

All psychologists would probably agree with the idea of learning being a change in response to experience in the environment. But there are differences of emphasis concerning what is important in learning and there are differences between perspectives within psychology as to what is the best way to study learning. For example, should we look at what happens 'inside the head' of a learner? Or should we look simply at the behaviour of the learner? If we take the first approach and ask what happens 'inside the head' when learning takes place, this could lead us to adopt a biological perspective and study the brain itself. Some researchers do this. But, although in principle we could try to observe the biological changes in the brain during the course of learning, it would be difficult from this information alone to find out exactly what learning had taken place. On the other hand, consideration of 'what happens inside the head' could sidestep biology altogether and focus on hypothetical processes 'in the head' – information processing, representations of information and memory. As will be shown in this chapter, psychologists do make inferences about the events underlying learning and they do this by confining themselves to examining behaviour during and after learning. They speculate on the kinds of process involved and then see how far the speculation will take them.

The chapter is designed with three main sections that give you some feel for the diversity of approaches to learning. In each section a different psychological approach to learning is illustrated, ranging from rats learning how to press a lever to earn food, to the formation of concepts by humans. The perspectives introduced discuss very different examples of what is learned and how learning occurs. However, they are not rival claims to the truth, rather they look at *different aspects* of learning and are best understood as offering *different kinds* of insight into learning processes.

We start with an approach to learning that is based largely on the behaviour of non-human animals. We then move on to consider types of learning that are more peculiarly human.

Summary Section 1

- Learning is a process of change as a result of experience.
- In contrast to evolution, which leads to change over generations, learning in individuals can be seen as adaptation to the environment over a lifetime.
- Psychologists study some very different types of learning in different contexts.

2   A comparative approach

2.1   Introduction

Comparative approach
The study of different species of animal in order to establish general and specific features of behaviour.

Psychologists have gained insight into learning by studying non-human animals and considering human learning in the light of this. The term **comparative approach** refers to this process of looking at and comparing different species. There is not just one such approach. Some psychologists have played down the significance of differences between species, suggesting that there are important common principles. Others have argued that each species is adapted to a particular environment by evolutionary processes, and that this will be reflected in different methods of learning.

The tradition in psychology known as **behaviourism** has emphasized common features amongst species, studying, in particular, rats and pigeons with an eye to extrapolation to humans. Behaviourism was essentially a revolt against the then prevailing ways of doing psychology. The revolt was staged in the early part of the twentieth century and was initially most closely associated with the American psychologist John Watson. (You can explore behaviourism and the researchers who worked within, or were influenced by it, on the *EPoCH* CD-ROM.) In Watson's hands, there were two prongs to the attack on established psychology. First, there was a conviction that the methods then being used by psychologists were the wrong ones. One of Watson's principal targets for attack was the idea that we can usefully gain insight by introspecting on our mental states. To Watson, this was an unscientific way of approaching the subject.

Watson wished to make psychology a science comparable to biology, physics or chemistry. He believed that the hallmarks of a scientific psychology should consist of objective observation and measurement. Other sciences dispassionately observed, recorded and measured the world 'out there' as Darwin had done (see Chapter 2) and Watson wished psychology to do the same. In the case of psychology, what is 'out there' to be observed is behaviour, hence the name 'behaviourism'. Mental states are not 'out there', they are not public data to be observed by detached scientists and so, according to Watson, they should have no place in the subject.

The second prong of Watson's radical critique of established psychology was directed at the weight given to so-called 'innate' or 'instinctive' factors. These terms refer to that with which an animal is equipped at birth and does not need to learn by experience. Watson did not deny the existence of such factors and indeed he researched them. He suggested that learning builds on innate factors. However, he argued that innate factors had been given unreasonable emphasis in psychology, which he claimed had underestimated the role of environmental factors. To Watson, human behaviour was largely at the mercy of the environment. For example, to him, saints and sinners were largely formed by early environmental influences.

As far as both prongs of the attack were concerned, ammunition was obtained from some highly significant experiments being carried out in Russia during the late years of the nineteenth century and early part of the twentieth century.

Behaviourism
The tradition that advocates that psychology should be a science of behaviour, without reference to mental states that cannot be observed.

2.2 Classical conditioning

Background

The experiments of Ivan Pavlov on conditioning have entered the popular imagination. We commonly hear expressions of the kind 'They have just been conditioned to do it – that's all.' What exactly is conditioning and what is the root of the term?

Pavlov was not a psychologist and somewhat unwittingly got himself attached to the discipline of psychology. He was a **physiologist**, a type of biologist who studies the structure and function of the body. His research concerned the secretion of juices by the body in connection with the ingestion and digestion of food. At the most basic level, the process underlying such secretions is what is termed a **reflex**. A reflex yields a relatively stereotyped reaction to a particular stimulus. Thus, for example, meat juice (the stimulus) placed in the mouth of a dog triggers salivation (the response), the process linking stimulus and response being termed the salivation reflex (see Figure 3.1(a)). Similarly, as part of another reflex, when food arrives in the stomach, it triggers the secretion of digestive juices that serve to break the food down into simpler chemical components. Up to this point, much of the story is unambiguously the business of the biological sciences, but there was a complication.

Pavlov had established what the triggers were that reliably stimulated the secretion of such juices, but sometimes the dogs were observed to behave in ways that did not fit Pavlov's physiological science. He observed that sometimes juices would be secreted in advance of the presentation of stimuli such as food in the mouth. For example, just the appearance of a particular scientist at the apparatus might in itself be sufficient to trigger the secretion of saliva. Pavlov termed such reactions 'psychic secretions' and at first regarded them as something of a nuisance, contaminating the 'proper' scientific study of reflexes. However, in time, Pavlov came to study 'psychic secretions' as a phenomenon in their own right. This is where the interests of psychologists enter the picture.

To formalize and control his study of 'psychic secretions', Pavlov presented a **neutral stimulus (NS)** just before stimuli that were known to trigger reflexes. For example, a bell or a light constitutes a neutral stimulus since neither has any intrinsic capacity to elicit the secretion of juices. Pavlov investigated the effect of *pairing* such a neutral stimulus with a 'natural physiological stimulus', such as food in the mouth (see Figure 3.1(a)). The arrangement of stimuli in a learning experiment is termed a contingency; in this case the **contingency** is between two stimuli (see Figure 3.1(b)). On first pairing with the presentation of food, the neutral stimulus did not acquire any capacity to trigger a reaction. However, after

Physiologist
A scientist who studies the structure and function of the body.

Reflex
An automatic response to a stimulus.

Neutral stimulus (NS)
A stimulus that evokes no particular response.

Contingency
An arrangement between two events.

a number of pairings the neutral stimulus on its own was able to cause the secretion of saliva. It was no longer neutral. How should we describe it?

The power of the bell or light to evoke salivation is conditional upon its earlier pairing with the food. Hence, we term such a stimulus a **conditional stimulus (CS)** (see Figure 3.1(c)). Often the term 'conditioned stimulus' is used, but 'conditioned' reflects an inaccurate translation from Russian. The procedure is termed conditioning. More specifically, since this was the first kind of conditioning to be studied scientifically, it is termed **classical conditioning** (or 'Pavlovian conditioning'). It arises from the presentation of a classical contingency.

Conditional stimulus (CS)
A stimulus, the power of which depends upon its pairing with an unconditional stimulus.

Classical conditioning
Learning arising from a pairing of two events outside the control of the animal.

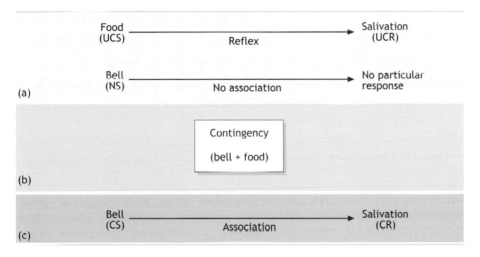

Figure 3.1 The stages in classical (Pavlovian) conditioning: (a) prior to, (b) during, and (c) following conditioning

The response of salivation that the bell evokes is termed the **conditional response (CR)** and the reflex that links the bell and the salivation response is termed the **conditional reflex**.

In relation to the notion of conditioning, the original stimulus that triggers the salivation response in the mouth also acquires a description. Food is termed the **unconditional stimulus (UCS)**. The reason for this term is that food does not need to go through a process of conditioning in order to acquire a capacity to trigger salivation. It is seen as an example of innate behaviour upon which learning can build. The salivation triggered by the food is termed the **unconditional response (UCR)**.

Link with Watson

The experimental demonstration of classical conditioning was a godsend to Watson, incorporating everything that he felt the subject of psychology should embrace. On the one hand, the whole process was measurable. Drops of saliva could be observed and reliably measured. The intensity of

Conditional response (CR)
A response that is triggered by a conditional stimulus.

Conditional reflex
A reflex triggered by a conditional stimulus.

Unconditional stimulus (UCS)
A stimulus that evokes a response without the necessity for a history of conditioning.

Unconditional response (UCR)
A response that does not require learning.

lights and tones could be quantified. One did not need mental terms such as mind and consciousness in order to account for the behaviour of the dog. If we wanted to probe what went on inside the dog, then the biology of the brain was the appropriate language to use. On the other hand, conditioning clearly embodied a change of behaviour. The previously neutral stimulus of the bell or light was transformed into a conditional stimulus having a new power. This appealed to the radical within Watson who saw human behaviour as largely the product of each person's history of conditioning.

Watson often boasted of the power of the technique of conditioning to change behaviour. The most famous example of this is with the infant called 'little Albert'. The case serves well to illustrate the meanings of the terminology that you have just met. Albert had a pet rat of which he was not at all afraid. In this regard it was a neutral stimulus. That was, until little Albert met Watson. On observing little Albert reaching for the rat, Watson banged a piece of metal behind little Albert. Subsequently little Albert reacted to the rat with fear.

Activity 3.2

In the context of little Albert, try to see whether you can define the terms neutral stimulus, conditional stimulus, conditional response, unconditional stimulus and unconditional response. Consider also what are some of the ethical issues involved in this form of experimentation. Watson would have difficulty doing such an experiment these days, as you will realize if you look back at the guidelines for ethical research included in the introductory chapter of this book.

Comment

The rat, prior to conditioning, was the neutral stimulus. The loud sound had an unconditional capacity to elicit fear in small children and so was the unconditional stimulus. The startle and withdrawal reaction triggered by the noise was the unconditional response. The pet rat became a conditional stimulus and the withdrawal reaction that it triggered was the conditional response. Again, conditioning built on something innate, in this case little Albert's fear of sudden loud noises.

Interpretation and applications

Classical conditioning is widely recognized as a fundamental process that contributes to human, as well as non-human, animals' adaptation to an environment (as described in Chapter 2). How might the process revealed by Pavlov achieve this? An animal salivates and produces digestive juices in response to stimuli that accompany the delivery of food. This means that the food arrives in a gut that is already prepared to handle it. Similarly, by showing fear to a neutral stimulus once it has been associated with a danger signal we are prepared for the arrival of danger and can take pre-emptive action.

Phenomena that might otherwise be inexplicable can be understood in terms of classical conditioning. For example, why do drug addicts often die from drugs when they are taken in an unfamiliar environment? One theory is as follows (Siegel, 1984). Injection of a drug such as heroin not only has psychological effects but affects a wide variety of bodily systems. It represents a massive challenge to the physiology of the body and can easily halt respiration. The body responds automatically with countermeasures to the challenge of the presence of a drug in the body. These countermeasures serve, amongst other things, to protect the respiratory system. Let us call the drug an unconditional stimulus and the physiological countermeasures an unconditional response. The drug arrives in the body within an environmental context (e.g. the syringe and needle, fellow drug-users and a familiar room). These become conditional stimuli, able to evoke some of the physiological countermeasures slightly prior to the drug's arrival. However, if the drug is taken in a new context, some of these stimuli will be absent and hence the conditional countermeasures will be less strong. Objectively, the amount of drug may not be excessive by the criteria of a regular user but the effect is excessive since the body has not been forewarned by the usual cues, or conditional stimuli.

Types of classical conditioning

In the 100 years or so during which classical conditioning has been researched scientifically, the number of examples of the effect that have been studied has increased greatly.

How can we best account for the change that is encapsulated by the term 'conditioning'? What kinds of processes underlie conditioning? Consideration of these questions raises a fundamental issue. We can all agree on the reality of the phenomenon of conditioning. Conditioning entered psychology largely within the context of the behaviourist revolution, with its emphasis on observable behaviour. However, do we still need to study it only from this behaviourist perspective? After all, these days most psychologists would not subscribe to the idea that the only way to do psychology is to study behaviour itself. The study of such things as cognition and states of consciousness have a place in today's psychology. So if we broaden the psychological base, what does this say about the nature of conditioning?

Psychologists have assembled evidence that, when an animal undergoes conditioning, *there can be more than one type of change involved* (Hirsh, 1974; Mishkin *et al.*, 1984; Toates, 1998). In a given learning situation, different processes can be involved simultaneously.

In such terms, exactly *what* did Pavlov's dog learn? Was it simply a change of behaviour? Did learning involve simply forming a new reflex of the kind stimulus–response (bell–salivation); that is, learning *how*? Such a **stimulus–response association** is usually referred to using the abbreviation **S–R**. Alternatively, or in addition to such learning, did the dog learn something about the world (i.e. learning *what*); in this case, that one event (bell) predicts another event (food) (i.e. bell → food). The evidence is that, depending on the circumstances, animals can learn either of these or can learn a combination of both.

Suppose one of Pavlov's dogs was hungry and in another room, and then the bell was sounded. How would the dog be expected to react? Anyone who has ever kept a pet dog will be able to extrapolate an answer to this. Such things as the sound of a can-opener appear to create an **expectancy**: that is, the sound of the can-opener predicts food (sound of can-opener → food) and this guides the dog's behaviour. The dog has not simply formed a reflex, to salivate to the sound of the can-opener, though such a reflex is formed in parallel with the expectancy. The notion of expectancy (i.e. that the animal has acquired knowledge) is not something that can be directly observed but is an inference made by psychologists and based on the available evidence.

Stimulus-response association
The link assumed to be formed by an animal whereby a stimulus triggers a response.

S–R
An abbreviation for stimulus–response.

Expectancy
Knowledge about a sequence of events (anticipation).

Don't be drawn into thinking that this kind of language (i.e. 'learning how' and 'learning what' and forming 'expectancies') means that conscious awareness is necessarily involved. A great deal of learning – perhaps most – happens without awareness. It also happens without a conscious intention to learn something. This applies to human learning as well as animal learning.

We now turn to another form of conditioning and find that a similar set of considerations applies.

2.3 Instrumental conditioning

Background

Another form of conditioning is termed **instrumental conditioning**. It can be exemplified by the behaviour of an animal (e.g. a rat) in a maze (see Figure 3.2). If the animal negotiates the maze successfully it receives a reward at the goal box. The animal's behaviour is instrumental in the outcome, hence the name for this kind of conditioning. The contingency is arranged between behaviour and an outcome – an instrumental contingency (see Figure 3.3).

> **Instrumental conditioning**
> A form of conditioning in which the outcome depends on the animal's behaviour.

A version of instrumental conditioning was pioneered by the American behaviourist, Burrhus Frederick Skinner. In honour of him, the apparatus involved became known as a Skinner box (see Figure 3.4). In this case a rat is rewarded with small pellets of food for pressing a lever. In a form designed for pigeons, a peck on a key delivers a pellet of food. This version of instrumental conditioning is known as **operant conditioning**, since it is said that the animal 'emits' **operants**, behaviours that have some effect on the environment. If the frequency of pressing the lever is seen to increase

> **Operant conditioning**
> A variety of instrumental conditioning that traditionally has been studied in a Skinner box.

> **Operant**
> A behaviour freely emitted by an animal which can be reinforced (e.g. lever-pressing).

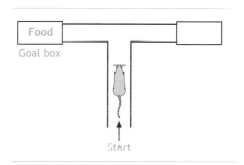

Figure 3.2   A simple maze. Food is found to the left, whereas to the right the goal box is empty

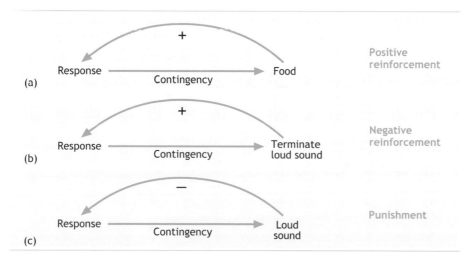

Figure 3.3   Instrumental conditioning: (a) positive reinforcement, (b) negative reinforcement, (c) punishment

as a result of the consequence of pressing (gain of food), then food is said to be (defined as) **positive reinforcement** for the animal (see Figure 3.3(a)).

To use the language of behaviourism, in an operant situation an animal freely emits behaviour (meaning that it is spontaneous). For example, all rats spontaneously sniff, investigate and manipulate their environment in a seemingly random way. The environment is such that it automatically 'provides' consequences for behaviours. In an experiment on operant conditioning, these 'consequences' are controlled and manipulated by the experimenter (see Box 3.1). The term 'reinforcement' conveys the idea that behaviour is strengthened – in other words is more likely to happen again. The adjective 'positive' denotes that the 'something' that is obtained as a result of behaviour is the strengthening agent.

How is an animal persuaded to press a lever or peck a key in the first place, such that it can be reinforced with food for doing so? Let us consider the case of a rat. The experimenter watches the rat and controls when the pellet is given. At first a pellet is given for the rat's head simply being near to the lever. Then it is given only when the animal physically

contacts the lever. The criterion is made still more stringent by only reinforcing when the lever is actually lowered. Finally, the rat then has to lower fully the lever, at which point the rat triggers pellet delivery automatically. This procedure is termed **shaping**.

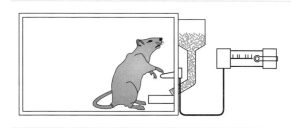

Figure 3.4 Skinner box showing lever, food dispenser and, outside box, chart with pen recording lever-presses

---

3.1 FEATURED METHOD

Experiments I: The importance of control and manipulation

What exactly is an experiment? An experiment is an artificial set-up designed to investigate cause and effect. The experimenter aims to control all possible variables and keep all but one of them constant. This one variable (the independent variable) is then manipulated in a controlled way and its effect on behaviour is measured (the dependent variable). So the major features of experimentation are (a) the control of all variables except one, (b) the controlled manipulation of this one variable, and (c) accurate and objective measurement of the effect. These features are clearly demonstrated by the research methods of the behaviourist perspective.

Consider the example of the Skinner Box (Figure 3.4). This apparatus is designed to control as many variables as possible. The same rat is used in the same physical environment. In a typical experiment, the diet and times of feeding of the rat are kept constant. The position of the lever and the pressure required to press it often remain exactly the same. The variable that is manipulated is the delivery of the food pellets: usually whether a pellet is delivered at all or when — that is, after how many lever-presses. This is the independent variable (the putative cause). The dependent variable (the effect) is the pattern of lever-pressing by the rat. There is no possibility of ambiguity — either the lever is pressed sufficiently to trigger delivery of a pellet or it is not; and the number and speed of presses can be automatically recorded to measure the dependent variable.

This kind of use of a rigorous experimental setting has permitted behaviourist psychologists to arrive at a general rule — a clear statement of cause and effect that links learning and reward. The **law of effect** states that a response that is followed by satisfaction to the animal will tend to increase in frequency, whereas one followed by discomfort will tend to be less likely to occur.

Law of effect
A law that states that responses having favourable consequences will be learned.

Operant conditioning occurs in a context and researchers have investigated the role of context. For example, one might train a pigeon that a peck delivers food when the Skinner box is illuminated by green light. It does not receive food if a red light is on. Under these conditions the pigeon will come to form a **discrimination** between red and green, such that it only responds in the presence of the green light. In a sense, such learning is context dependent, in this case on the colour of the light. Human learning can also be said to be context dependent, but in a much more complex way. This will be discussed in Section 4.

Discrimination
A response made in the presence of one stimulus and a lack of response made in the presence of another.

Aversive events

Suppose that something unpleasant, such as a loud sound, is terminated as a result of behaviour. For instance, a rat might be exposed to a loud sound that is switched off in response to a lever-press by the rat. If the frequency of lever-pressing increases under these conditions, then by definition the consequence is reinforcing. Since it is arranged that a stimulus (loud sound) is terminated by behaviour, the stimulus is serving as **negative reinforcement** (see Figure 3.3(b)).

Another term in the behaviourist vocabulary is **punishment** (see Figure 3.3(c)). To define this, consider something such as a loud sound that has been proven to work as a negative reinforcer. Suppose that the arrangement is altered so that the loud sound is now presented as a consequence of behaviour. Such an arrangement is one of punishment.

Negative reinforcement
Something that is terminated by behaviour and where the frequency of this behaviour increases.

Punishment
Something normally described as aversive which follows a behaviour and lowers the probability that the behaviour will occur again.

Negative reinforcement and punishment are often confused, even in the psychology literature, but there should be no reason for this to happen. Negative reinforcement involves an *escape from* something normally described as aversive, whereas punishment involves the *presentation of* something normally described as aversive. There is symmetry here. In punishment, the thing presented (e.g. a loud sound) would typically also be able to serve as negative reinforcement if an (escape) contingency were to be arranged.

One's expectation might be that behaviour would invariably be suppressed as a result of the presentation of electric shock or something similar that is described as aversive by humans. Although the naive assumption of suppression often fits reality, it is violated in a number of cases. For instance, one might suppose that, in rats, if electric shock follows lever-pressing, it would inevitably lower the frequency of responding. In reality, and as something of a puzzle, lever-pressing sometimes increases in frequency under these conditions. Thus rats occasionally seem to switch into an automatic mode of behaving which cannot at present be understood in terms of its immediate consequences. Rather than this being an embarrassment to behaviourists, they use such evidence in favour of their argument. They suggest that one must observe behaviour and the subtle interplay of factors that determine it, rather than speculating on how things should be, based on intuition or rationality: nature is always right but theories can be wrong.

The use of even loud noise or mild electric shocks raises ethical issues. Is it justified to inflict painful stimuli on captive animals?

Comparison with evolution

Skinner drew an analogy between the process of evolution and that of operant conditioning. You should recall from Chapter 2 that, in evolutionary terms, some mutations are adaptive and are 'favoured' by the environment. They increase in frequency over generations. Conversely, some mutations are maladaptive and thereby reduce in frequency in the population over time. According to Skinner, what occurs over evolutionary time for a species is closely comparable to what happens within the lifetime of an individual. In each case what occurs in the first place is the outcome of chance. The animal comes into the world with a tendency to emit behaviour freely. The environment will (not usually by design) provide positive reinforcement for some behaviour and that behaviour will increase in frequency. For example, it is often argued that parents reinforce disruptive behaviour by paying attention to it. This will strengthen the tendency to repeat this behaviour in future. Conversely, some behaviour will tend to (and only 'tend to') decline in frequency as a result of what is described as punishment. In both evolutionary and operant conditioning terms, Skinner argues that the natural world is such as to permit better adaptation to the environment.

Applications of the instrumental contingency

The methods of Skinner have proven their worth in changing problem behaviours, a technique termed **behaviour modification**. For example, in a study dealing with children having learning difficulties and showing classroom disruption, teachers identified acceptable behaviour (e.g. concentrating on the task in hand) and unacceptable behaviour (e.g. running around the classroom) (Jones and Kazdin, 1975). At regular intervals the children's behaviour was observed and, if it fitted the acceptable category, reward was given. This consisted of praise and a token (e.g. a plastic chip). The tokens were collected and later exchanged for other rewards, such as the opportunity to listen to music. The assumption was that desirable behaviour was reinforced in this way and thereby would increase in frequency. Indeed, using this method, an increase of desirable behaviour and a decrease of undesirable behaviour was found.

> **Behaviour modification**
> A technique of changing behaviour by means of positive reinforcement.

What about the effect of punishment? Does punishment work to modify behaviour? Skinner was a passionate advocate of the position that punishment is both (a) unethical and (b) relatively ineffective as a means of changing behaviour. Only in a life-threatening situation would a devotee of Skinner argue that arranging a punishment contingency is justified. Punishment and aversive contingencies cannot be used to target behaviours because they arouse anxieties which can easily have an unpredictable 'spreading influence', much of which will lead to unwanted behaviours. Suppose a school child emits a particular behaviour judged to be unacceptable to others. If an aversive event is made contingent upon showing this behaviour then that behaviour might (and only might) decline in frequency. But other behaviours might also be expected to be affected. For example, punishment in school might create a general fear of teachers and lead to truancy. Positive reinforcement is a much less gross procedure and can be more finely tuned. Skinner's message was that the ills of society such as violence, vandalism and alienation arise because of society's failure to adopt a technology of *positive* reinforcement. Skinner wrote a Utopian novel *Walden Two* about a society based upon such principles (Skinner, 1948/1990). Interestingly, although written in 1945, the book was also a plea for a more ecologically viable society in which waste was eliminated. Not surprisingly, the Skinnerian message evokes passion both for and against.

Critique of Skinnerian perspective

Skinner has proven to be one of the most controversial of psychologists, triggering both unqualified admiration as an enlightened humanist and social reformer, and bitter opposition as a scientific dinosaur and narrowly focused scientist. To some extent the critique of Skinner is part of a broader one directed at the whole behaviourist enterprise.

What evokes the least controversy is perhaps the argument that behaviour can be altered by certain contingencies of reinforcement. Critics might argue that this would seem to be common sense. Nor are Skinner's humanitarian ideals the target for criticism. Rather, it is what Skinner ignores or denies that evokes the most scorn. To portray humans as little more than glorified banks of available responses to be selected by the environment is seen as not only degrading but also scientifically inaccurate. Thus, it might be argued that a capacity to respond to contingencies of reinforcement is only one amongst many different processes underlying behaviour. Humans have some conscious insight into their condition and may be the active agents of change based on this. They are very much more than a complex series of emitted responses shaped by the environment.

Skinner's research has also evoked criticism for retreating into a 'ghetto' of behaviourism and operant equipment, somewhat cut off from the animals (human and otherwise) that live in a natural environment. However, none of this criticism detracts from the fact that behaviour can be changed by operant techniques.

Types of instrumental conditioning

All might agree on the efficacy of contingencies in changing behaviour. However, unlike Skinner, a number of other psychologists were, and are, keen to make inferences about events in the animal's head during learning, and they often use distinctly non-behaviouristic language to do so. For example, Tolman (1932) observed rats running to the goal box in the maze apparatus shown in Figure 3.5(a), in which a morsel of food was placed at the goal box. During training, the hungry rats were placed at the start point (A) and had one fixed route A, B, C, D, E and F to follow in order to get to the food. Following training, the rats were transferred to the apparatus shown in Figure 3.5(b). This provided a number of possible routes for getting to the 'expected' location of the goal box (i.e. a choice of 18 routes/arms, with the way ahead blocked). Which route would they choose? What had they learned? If they had simply learned *how* to get food and they repeated the behaviour shown earlier, they would take the choice nearest to straight-ahead (i.e. arm 9 or 10). If, however, they had learned something about the location of the goal box (i.e. learned *what*), they might tend to extrapolate to its location and thereby tend to choose arms 5, 6 or 7. This was indeed what they did tend to do, suggesting that animals can make inferences and that learning involves 'something in the head' as well as a change in behaviour.

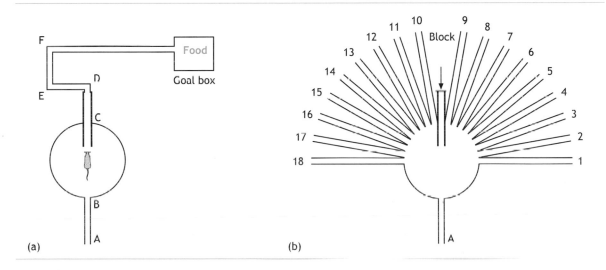

Figure 3.5   Apparatus used by Tolman: (a) learning phase, and (b) testing phase

As was described for classical conditioning, there appear to be different types of learning that can occur during instrumental conditioning. These can occur in parallel. In a given situation, one of them might dominate and account for behaviour.

Take, for example, the experiment illustrated in Figure 3.6. The rat is released from the south end (Figure 3.6(a)) and runs north. At the T-junction it is confronted with a choice of turning left or right. If it turns left it obtains a reward of food, but a right turn is not rewarded. After a number of trials it is reliably turning left each time. Has the rat learned to perform a simple turn to the left, a stimulus–response association (S–R association), or has it learned something more abstract about the situation, such as that food is near the window of the room (a so-called 'extra-maze cue')? One way of finding out is to try, as shown in Figure 3.6(b), to run the maze experiment from a north start.

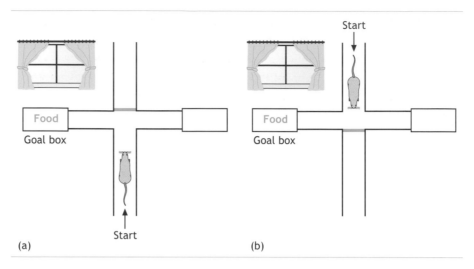

Figure 3.6　Rat negotiating a T-maze: (a) training phase, (b) testing response after a new start point

Activity 3.3

Work out what behaviour on the part of the rat is predicted on the basis of learning understood in terms of: (i) forming a stimulus–response association, or (ii) acquiring knowledge about the maze and room.

A stimulus–response link will take the rat left (i.e. east), whereas exploiting knowledge about the room will take it right (i.e. west). In practice, animals tend to learn both things in parallel. Which level of learning dominates depends upon such things as the length of experience and the nature of the maze and the room.

Similarly, in a Skinner box, rats sometimes appear to learn a rather straightforward stimulus (i.e. lever)–response (i.e. press) association. In this regard they act something like automatons, triggered into activity by the physical stimulus of the lever. At other times they also appear to acquire an expectation (or 'expectancy') of the form (behaviour) →(outcome); for example, (lever-press) → (food) (Bolles, 1972). They sometimes start out by forming an expectancy and with extended experience move into a more automatic mode of control (Adams, 1982; Dickinson, 1985).

Why do we infer that a rat has formed an expectancy? Could we try to create an expectancy and then see what happens when it is violated? We can, for example, change the size of reward earned and look at the rat's behaviour. Suppose that a rat has been used to earning two small pellets of food in response to a lever-press. Then the reward is changed so that it earns only one pellet. Finding such a reduced size of reward is followed by an increased secretion of hormones normally associated with stress (Goldman *et al.*, 1973). Conversely, if the rat obtains four pellets, this is associated with a suppression of the secretion of such hormones relative to the background rate. The original two pellets were associated with no change in secretion of such hormones. It appears that the rat has formed an expectancy of the consequences of its behaviour. If these are less good than expectation, a negative ('stress') reaction is triggered. If they are better, it seems that a positive emotion is triggered.

Does the description of rats forming expectancies of the outcome of their behaviour imply that they do this at a conscious level? Does the term 'expectancy' necessarily suggest this?

Theorists do not imply that a description in terms of expectancies means that the animal necessarily forms a *conscious* representation of the outcome of its actions, though we know that humans are able to do this. So, used in this context, maybe the term 'expectancy' should be put in inverted commas in order to suggest that it is being used cautiously, somewhat as a metaphor. Whether metaphor or not, it is a useful term. Expectancy distinguishes processes that are immediately sensitive to the consequences of an action (as with the case of reward size in the example just described) from processes that involve an automatic stimulus–response link. Only by considering the history of the animal in terms of earning reward can we understand the effect of shifting reward. The term 'expectancy' conveys the sense that the animal does not always react in a way that can be explained by a simple stimulus–response connection between food received and behavioural and physiological reaction.

Assessment of the comparative approach

So, what has the study of different species contributed to our understanding of learning? Although only a limited range of learning phenomena can be captured in such a simple apparatus as the Skinner box, the principles of conditioning that emerge apply across species, and are of fundamental importance and broad application. However, although many psychologists might acknowledge this, they might view the mind and its conscious aspect as being central to any understanding of the *human* condition. They would regard the temporary dominance of behaviourism as a retrograde step in the development of psychology.

Nevertheless, the behaviourist perspective has endowed us with some insights into the laws of behaviour and some practical tools of psychology that are still in very wide use. For example, within instrumental approaches, many psychoactive drugs (e.g. those to combat anxiety or depression) are tested on rats pressing levers in Skinner boxes. The rat is made anxious and the reduction in lever-pressing for food observed. The effect of anti-anxiety drugs on restoring lever-pressing is then measured.

Ethical decisions always need to be made about the possible value of gains from such studies, weighed against any potential harm to the animals involved.

The use of the principles of behaviour modification derived from instrumental conditioning has already been illustrated by the study of the effects of giving reward tokens in reducing disruptive classroom behaviour.

General principles of classical conditioning also provide the basis for practical applications, although therapeutic treatments usually involve both classical and instrumental conditioning. The example of little Albert in Section 2.2 demonstrated how classical conditioning principles are involved in the *acquisition* of fear as a response to specific stimuli. But phobias are *maintained* by instrumental conditioning. For example, whenever someone with a spider phobia runs away from a spider, the 'spider–fear' association is strengthened because the escape is negatively reinforcing. Therapeutic treatment of such phobias often uses a technique known as 'in vivo' (in life) exposure whereby the phobic person is gradually exposed to the feared stimulus. Clients initially experience an increase in anxiety, but so long as they do not *avoid* the exposure, their anxiety responses diminish considerably as they habituate to (get used to) the spider. In habituation it is almost as if the nervous system 'becomes bored with' the aversive stimulus. In this procedure the individual reverses the stimulus–response association.

A classical conditioning technique known as counter-conditioning is also used to treat phobias. It involves training the client to substitute a relaxation response for the fear response in the presence of the feared stimulus. The treatment is called systematic desensitization. The therapist gradually increases the level of exposure to the feared object. There are three basic steps: (1) training the client to relax; (2) establishing a hierarchy of the feared stimuli; and (3) counter-conditioning relaxation as a response to each feared stimulus, beginning with the least feared and moving up the hierarchy until all levels have been counter-conditioned.

This classical conditioning approach is usually combined with a cognitive intervention (cognitive behavioural therapy). This involves the therapist helping the client to think differently about spiders; for example, that they are a useful and necessary part of the ecological system, that they have not evolved to hunt or intentionally attack humans, and that their bites are rarely fatal.

Behaviourism emphasized a search for universal principles of learning that apply across situations and species; and some of these, such as the law of effect, do indeed apply. But it is sometimes necessary to state where the generalization is applicable and where it isn't. For example, researchers have established that under some conditions animals are good at learning some things and bad at learning others. For example, an animal such as a rat readily learns that a particular food is followed by gastrointestinal upset (Garcia, 1989). It forms an association between the food and the upset, such that it avoids food of this flavour in the future. By contrast, it learns with great difficulty that a visual stimulus is associated with gastrointestinal upset. To some theorists, this suggests that animals come into the world already equipped with a *bias* in favour of certain types of learning and with constraints against learning other things.

In addition to its use within the behaviourist tradition, the Skinner box has been employed as a *tool* within other theoretical orientations. Data arising from the tradition of behaviourism have enabled psychologists to formulate other models of learning. These are summarized in such terms as (event 1 → event 2), meaning that an animal comes to expect event 2 as a result of experiencing event 1. Observing rats in a Skinner box has led to the formulation of the expectancy model, summarized by (behaviour) →(outcome). Although the architects of such models employ the techniques of behaviourism, the explanations that they derive appeal to events in the head of the rat, such as knowledge about an expectancy. Clearly these cannot be directly observed but are inferred, and so the basis of such an approach is very different from the original guiding principles of behaviourism.

Consider another example. Suppose one wanted to know whether and how pigeons categorize the world? How could this be researched in a species that cannot speak? The answer is: with the help of a Skinner box. The pigeon is kept hungry and trained to earn food by pecking at a key. If it pecks when 'the scene contains a person', it earns reward, while pecking at a 'non-person scene' does not earn reward. In this way it is taught a discrimination between scenes containing a person and the scenes without a person. Using this procedure, it can be shown that pigeons are good at performing this (and other) discrimination tasks. They *seem* to extract features to form an internal representation and build a concept of 'person' which they apply to 'persons' of different shapes and sizes in various settings. And they seem to be quite good at forming these discriminations. This capacity in pigeons which is revealed using a learning technique (pecking a key for food) leads to several important questions that apply to people as well as animals. In the next section we begin to explore concept formation in humans.

Summary Section 2

- Behaviourist psychology is a perspective which advances the view that psychology should confine itself to the study of observable events.
- Pavlov pioneered an experimental approach termed 'classical conditioning'.
- In classical conditioning, a contingency between stimuli is arranged, a neutral stimulus is paired with an unconditional stimulus and it becomes a conditional stimulus.
- In instrumental conditioning, a contingency is arranged between behaviour and an outcome, e.g. gaining food.
- The type of instrumental conditioning studied in a Skinner box is known as operant conditioning.
- In both classical and instrumental conditioning, learning can take more than one form.

3   The cognitive perspective: category learning

So far we have seen how complex behavioural responses to stimuli can be learned. An important claim has been that animals can acquire expectancies through learning. However, suppose that, rather than learn the specific relationship concerning just the actual events an animal has experienced (lever-pressing and release of food pellets, for example), animals may learn a general relationship, one that also includes stimuli and events that have not yet been experienced. Different kinds of animal have been shown to learn such general relationships. Mercado *et al.* (2000) found that bottlenosed dolphins taught to classify pairs of shapes as either the same or different could *generalize* this ability – that is, they could apply this ability to pairs of shapes they had not seen before. Sappington and Goldman (1994), having tested the abilities of Arabian horses to learn to discriminate patterns, claimed that some could acquire concepts such as 'triangularity' as opposed to specific patterns to which they had been exposed.

But if animals acquire expectancies or even **concepts** which are 'in the head', then these are not publicly observable. So how can we make sense of the idea that animals have expectancies? How do we reconcile talk of things that we cannot directly observe with a scientific approach to psychology? In this section, we consider the cognitive perspective on learning, an approach that attempts exactly this kind of reconciliation. Whereas section 2 focused on how relationships between stimuli and responses lead to learning, this section focuses on what intervenes between stimuli and responses – what happens 'in the head'.

Concepts
Ideas that are structured in terms of attributes and refer to categories in the world.

3.1 The cognitive perspective

The cognitive approach to psychology arose partly from dissatisfaction with behaviourism. It was felt that the more complex functions of the mind such as language and thinking could not really be explained in terms of stimulus–response relationships. However, cognitive psychology also developed from a series of technological and theoretical advances in computing and mathematics that suggested some deep connections between people and complex machines such as computers – notably that both could be understood in terms of **information processing**.

Information processing
Information is assumed to be received via the senses, further processed or transformed, and then used to guide action and behaviour.

Cognitive psychology has its roots in work that sees important relationships between people and machines, despite their superficial differences. Some researchers believe that the machine therefore provides a convenient metaphor, according to which an understanding of machines, such as computers, may shed light on the workings of the mind. Others, however, believe that the connection is much closer, and that people literally are machines of a certain sort.

Cognitive psychologists believe that it is possible to describe what is 'in the head' (i.e. what is called the mind) at a *functional* level (in terms of what the mind does) and a *process* level (how the mind does what it does) without having to specify in detail how those functions and processes are physically instantiated in the brain (Marr, 1982). Cognitive psychologists might, for example, describe memory in terms of what gets remembered (and what doesn't) and the factors that influence this. Perception might be described in terms of, among other factors, what people perceive, when they perceive it, and, perhaps, how prior knowledge influences perception.

Much of our understanding of everyday complex systems – such as computers and cars – typically resides at these levels of function and process. Although we may understand how to format and prepare a document on a computer, most of us have no understanding of how the electronic hardware of the computer gives rise to these functions. Similarly, we might understand that a starter motor plays a role in the process of starting a car's engine, but have little understanding of how this function is physically achieved.

Cognitive psychology's strategy of trying to understand the mind in terms of its functions and processes is therefore not very far removed from our everyday understanding of other complex systems. Cognitive psychologists typically assume that a mature psychology will integrate this functional understanding with knowledge about the brain's physical basis, and there are growing signs that our understanding of some of the mind's activities is approaching this level of maturity. Increasingly, cognitive psychologists are studying neuropsychological disorders and using scanning techniques that provide images of brain activity, in order to inform their views of the mind.

Our vehicle for outlining the cognitive perspective on learning is **category learning**. Although cognitive psychologists have investigated many different kinds of learning, category learning provides a clear example of what the cognitive perspective involves. As adults we typically take categories for granted, yet at some point in our lives we come to understand that things belong together in categories. For example, we recognize that all our disparate experiences of other people have a common element – they are all experiences of *members of the same category, 'people'*. Categories therefore provide a means for organizing our experience, and making sense of the world. They also allow us to extrapolate from past experiences, to plan and make predictions, abilities that would have bestowed an evolutionary advantage. Indeed, it is likely that without concepts our world would strike us, as William James put it, as a 'great blooming and buzzing confusion' (1890/1950, p.488).

So the focus of this section will be on how we come to organize our experiences into categories; how, for example, we come to recognize that spiders, birds, and people, all belong to the category of 'animals', while things like houses, cars, clouds, and ideas do not. We shall consider to what extent we can explain the *learning* of categories such as these. However, we shall also see that some researchers consider that at least part of our understanding of categories is innate or inborn. In considering these issues, we will try to answer the following questions.

Category learning
The learning that occurs when people come to understand that certain objects or entities belong together in particular categories.

- How is it that people come to possess the information that they have about categories?
- To what extent might some of this information be innate as opposed to learned?

3.2 How might we acquire new categories?

Cognitive psychologists interested in learning have focused on the information people gain during learning, and on the mechanisms or principles that enable people to acquire that information. Essentially, the question they are concerned with is 'What are the things in the head that give rise to and arise from learning?' Perhaps the most consistent answer to this question involves the notion of a **hypothesis** and its successful testing.

Hypothesis
A suggested explanation for a set of observations that may or may not turn out to be supported.

The study of category learning by cognitive psychologists began some time ago. In a pioneering account, Bruner *et al.* (1956) explained category learning in terms of hypothesis testing. Although much research has been conducted since, their work still frames some fundamental aspects of psychologists' thinking about category learning. To illustrate category learning, try Activity 3.4 that uses an example from Bruner *et al.*

Activity 3.4

Suppose you travel to another country and a friend introduces you to many new people. After introducing each one she tells you either 'This person is influential' or 'This person is not influential'. After a while, your friend leaves you, and you decide that you should try to work out for yourself who is influential and who is not. How would you do this?

Comment

One way in which you might approach this task is to try to recall particular attributes of those people who have been identified as influential, and which did not apply to those identified as not influential. Perhaps all the influential people were expensively dressed. This might allow you to generate a hypothesis about 'influential people' that you could go on to test.

To see how hypothesis testing might work in practice, consider some of the stimuli that Bruner *et al.* used in their studies, shown in Figure 3.7.

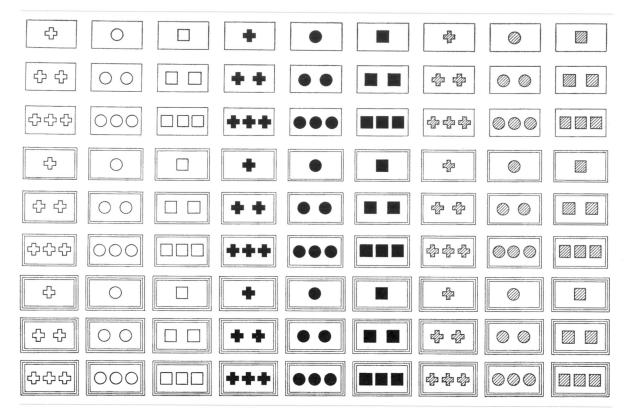

Figure 3.7   An array of 81 rectangular stimulus cards used in Bruner *et al.*'s study of category learning. Each card
is printed with a varying combinations of the following four properties: shape (square, circle or cross);
number of each shape (1, 2 or 3 instances); shading of the shapes (plain, black or striped); and number
of borders round the card (1, 2 or 3) (Source: Bruner *et al.*, 1956, Figure 1, p.42)

Bruner *et al.* began by pointing to one of the cards shown in Figure 3.7,
and telling their participants that it belonged in a particular category. They
described the categories in terms of nonsense labels. Nonsense labels are
'made up' words – let us imagine that Bruner *et al.* called their category
'fep'. So the participants might be told that the card third down from the
top in the leftmost column 'is a fep'. Their task was to learn the category
'fep' by pointing to other cards and asking whether or not they were also
in the category.

Activity 3.5

Imagine that you are a participant in Bruner *et al.*'s study, and have been told that the
third card down from the top in the leftmost column is a 'fep'. What hypotheses
would you have about the nature of 'feps'? Which card would you point to next?
Why?

After being given the answer for each instance they pointed to, the participants would write down their hypothesis, pick the next instance, and continue in this way until they settled on the right hypothesis. By asking participants to write down their hypotheses, Bruner *et al.* only considered hypotheses of which their participants were conscious. But the important question is whether this kind of hypothesis testing might explain category learning in general, even when the hypotheses are not conscious. Chapter 4 of the second course book (*Challenging Psychological Issues*) considers consciousness in more detail.

Among other measures, Bruner *et al.* recorded the number and nature of the instances their participants asked about before settling on the right hypothesis. Based on this evidence, Bruner *et al.* claimed their participants used particular strategies to learn the category. In the strategy they called 'successive scanning', participants entertained one hypothesis at a time, and continually tested the hypothesis until it was shown to be in error. They then considered the next plausible hypothesis. If, in the example above, you hypothesize that 'All feps contain three crosses', then you might ask whether the card in the top right-hand corner is a 'fep'. If the answer is yes, then you will have to choose another hypothesis. If the answer is no, you might continue testing. The difficulty with successive scanning is that each choice carries relatively little information. A positive answer does not mean the hypothesis is true – there may be other hypotheses compatible with the evidence accumulated. And a negative answer gives relatively few clues as to what the right hypothesis will be.

In the other popularly used strategy, 'conservative focusing', participants sought to eliminate *classes* of hypotheses by choosing instances that differed in only one way from the previous ones. In the above example, knowing that a card with a single border and three plain crosses is a 'fep', a participant would seek to determine the relevance of these attributes to membership in the category. The relevance of the single border can be determined by choosing an instance that differs from the first only in this respect – perhaps asking about the card in the bottom left-hand corner, as this contains three plain crosses, but has a triple border. If this card is a 'fep', then the single border is not relevant; if the card is not a 'fep', however, then the single border must be relevant. In this way, through successive choices of instances, the relevance of each of the original card's attributes to category membership can be determined. Since each new piece of information rules in or out whole classes of hypotheses, conservative focusing is in general a much more useful strategy.

Bruner *et al.* found that participants using conservative focusing could learn these categories more quickly than those using successive scanning. When Bruner *et al.*'s stimulus materials were devised using cards displaying meaningful attributes (e.g. boy or girl, frowning or smiling), as in Figure 3.8,

Figure 3.8   Four examples from a 'thematic array' of test materials used by Bruner *et al.* (Source: Bruner *et al.*, 1956, Figure 2, p.107)

participants took longer to learn the category. The researchers suggested that, because of their participants' prior knowledge about the relevance of certain attributes, they tended to ignore logically possible categories that involved combinations of attributes that would be implausible in everyday life. For example, participants might not associate an adult giving a present to a child with the child simultaneously standing as if being rebuked. Because these attributes are meaningful, participants may use this prior knowledge to consider only those categories that would normally make sense.

Developing Bruner's work: meaningful categories

Artificial stimuli
Stimuli devised by the experimenter in order to have no intrinsic meaning.

Ecological validity
The extent to which a study reflects naturally occurring or everyday situations.

Natural categories
Categories that occur naturally and are not invented or devised by the experimenter.

Attributes
Properties of things that are reflected in the structure of concepts.

Bruner *et al.* used **artificial stimuli** because these are largely devoid of prior associations, and so they hoped their findings would better reflect the underlying processes of category learning. Their use of more meaningful attributes showed how these could interfere with their underlying processes, by making it difficult for people to consider all logically possible combinations of attributes. Nonetheless, their studies lack **ecological validity**, and one may question how well their results generalize to more natural learning situations. Unlike the stimuli in Figure 3.7, which can be defined in terms of number of borders, number of objects with a particular shape, and so on, **natural categories** tend not to be definable in terms of combinations of independent attributes. Natural categories seem to cohere, in that their **attributes** belong together for certain reasons – there are connections between them. Birds are not just things that are typically feathered, winged, and able to fly – rather, their being winged and feathered typically *enables* birds to fly, though, of course, there are exceptions. Murphy and Medin (1985) considered this coherence to be critical to explaining the categories we have. To them, the importance of connections between attributes suggests it may be fruitless to try to list all of the attributes of particular categories (as you would be led to do for the categories of Bruner *et al.*). Murphy and Medin believe that our categories have coherence because our prior knowledge explains the connections between their attributes. Following Murphy and Medin, researchers have tended to focus more on the learning of natural, everyday categories, and have looked for evidence that category learning is supported by prior knowledge.

Murphy and Allopenna (1994) showed the importance of background knowledge in category learning. They asked their participants to learn meaningful categories where the category members had a high proportion of attributes in common. Murphy and Allopenna were interested in how quickly their participants would learn that all the members of the category belonged together. They used meaningful attributes that could all be *linked together* by certain themes. For one category, the relevant theme was 'underwater building' – that is, each of the items in this category possessed attributes that could be inferred to be appropriate for underwater buildings. Murphy and Allopenna reasoned that if their participants could use the fact that the different members of the category were all linked to the same theme, then they would learn the category more quickly. This is what they found. The participants did not try to learn the different attributes of each category member, but used their background knowledge to infer a common theme to link the attributes together.

Kaplan and Murphy (2000) extended our understanding of the influence of prior knowledge. They used categories where each category member possessed only one attribute that was relevant to a theme – the remaining attributes were unrelated to the theme. For example, for the category of 'vehicle', one of the themes used was 'arctic use'. Each category member had six attributes – five unrelated to the theme (e.g. has automatic seat belts, has four doors) and just one theme-related attribute (e.g. made in Norway). Their participants were asked to learn two categories – they had to learn to judge which instances belonged to which category, and were given feedback about their accuracy. This process was repeated for all category members until participants answered all questions correctly. Kaplan and Murphy were interested in how long it would take before their participants had learned the categories. They reasoned that if prior knowledge only *weakly* influenced category learning, then the fact that only one attribute was related to the theme might mean that it would not significantly assist category learning. However, their participants still learned the theme-related category more quickly – approximately twice as quickly as those participants who learned categories with attributes that could not be related to a theme. It is worth stressing that participants in these experiments were not told the relevant theme, or even that there was a theme to which the category could be linked.

How can these findings be explained? According to Kaplan and Murphy, people quickly infer that the attributes of category members can be linked by a theme, and they then use this knowledge to guide their learning. For example, their participants might have tried to discover how the attributes of an instance (e.g. has automatic seat belts) *could* fit with the theme (e.g. for use in the arctic), in spite of there being no prior association. Trying to discover connections between attributes thus appears to be an important way in which prior knowledge can influence category learning.

Murphy and colleagues have shown that many of the factors Bruner *et al.* tended to exclude from their studies (such as the meaningfulness of attributes, categories, and category labels), actually play a very important role in category learning. This is not to say that the earlier work was in error – it is just that the primary research questions have shifted. Whereas Bruner *et al.* were interested in how we test hypotheses in category learning, more recent work has focused on how background knowledge can help us focus on some hypotheses rather than others. However, a question has been raised as to whether hypothesis testing, guided by background knowledge or not, can ever properly explain category learning. Indeed, it has been suggested that categories simply *cannot* be learned. Yet if categories cannot be learned, what sense are we to make of the studies that appear to show category learning? As we shall see, how we respond to this suggestion that categories cannot be learned has important consequences for how we are to understand the phenomenon we have called category learning.

3.3 Can categories be learned?

The question as to whether categories are learned or innate has a long history. The Greek philosopher Plato argued that our ideas are innate or inborn. He believed that what appears to be learning is actually the 'recollection' of innately specified ideas. He attempted to show this by constructing an imaginary dialogue in which an uneducated person, when appropriately questioned, showed knowledge of complex ideas such as the principles of geometry.

Nativism
The belief that knowledge is mainly or exclusively innate.

Empiricism
The belief that knowledge is mainly or exclusively acquired from empirical evidence – evidence about the world received via our senses.

Plato's position is a prime example of **nativism** – the belief that knowledge is mainly or exclusively innate. Nativism stands in contrast to **empiricism**, the view that knowledge is mainly or exclusively acquired from empirical evidence – that is, evidence about the world that we receive via our senses.

The nativism–empiricism debate about the nature of knowledge is still played out today. For Bruner *et al.*, people *learn* concepts via a process of generating and then refining hypotheses in the light of further evidence. In contrast, the philosopher Jerry Fodor and the linguist Noam Chomsky suggest that categories *cannot be learned*, and that our concepts – our ideas of categories – must be innate. The arguments of Fodor and Chomsky are critical to our understanding of category learning. How we treat these arguments will influence how we interpret empirical studies of category learning such as those of Bruner and Murphy. As we shall see, the arguments have implications for how we understand learning as a process of change.

You may wonder why psychologists should consider the arguments of philosophers and linguists. After all, you may feel that the methods and techniques of cognitive psychology are sufficient to yield a complete understanding of learning. However, cognitive psychology has a long history of looking to other disciplines in order to gain insight into the workings of the mind. An example is the machine metaphor we considered in Section 3.1. Here, foundational research conducted by logicians and early computer scientists gave psychologists an important new means for understanding the mind. And, as indicated above, learning is a topic that has attracted the interest of philosophers over thousands of years. These other disciplines often provide additional argumentation that can contribute to a psychological understanding.

The arguments of Fodor and Chomsky centre on what has become known as the **induction problem**. For all we know, the very next set of experiences we have may throw into confusion the generalizations we have so far relied upon. So although we may generate hypotheses that generalize on the basis of past experiences, these hypotheses cannot be guaranteed to be correct. Consider the discovery of the platypus, which changed fundamentally our beliefs about mammals (Eco, 1999). Previously, people believed that mammals suckled their young, and did not lay eggs. These beliefs were based on observations of mammals. Discovering the platypus revealed how these observations did not serve as a guarantee of future observations of mammals. When platypuses were observed to lay eggs, people ultimately came to modify their earlier beliefs. If it can happen with mammals, then who is to say it cannot happen with more mundane categories such as dogs, cats, and clouds, let alone complex categories such as 'influential people'? Chomsky and Fodor (1980) argue that this **induction problem** presents real difficulties for the argument of

Induction problem
The problem that arises because our past experiences do not serve as a totally reliable guide to our future experiences.

Bruner *et al.* that category learning is based on hypothesis testing. The problem shows that hypotheses that are compatible with empirical evidence at one time may later turn out to be wrong. The implication of this is that when we first generate and then settle on a hypothesis – like the hypothesis that mammals do not lay eggs – there are actually a number of different hypotheses all of which are compatible with the evidence. Usually it is only when the first hypothesis turns out to be wrong that we come to realize there were other hypotheses we had rejected or ignored.

The critical issue raised by the induction problem is this: if several hypotheses are equally compatible with the empirical evidence, how and why do people settle on just one? Chomsky and Fodor (1980) and Fodor (1980) argue that, because the problem of induction indicates that category learning cannot take place by means of hypothesis testing, the only alternative is that category knowledge must be innate. These arguments present a major challenge to the interpretations that cognitive psychologists have offered of category learning. Their suggestion is that what we have taken to be learning is not *learning* at all!

Fodor and Chomsky's position is extreme. Their view is that knowledge of all categories is innate, from simple categories, such as 'red' and 'cold', to complicated ones such as 'subatomic particles'. How plausible is it that our knowledge of subatomic particles is innate? As future science uncovers new categories, ones of which we are currently unaware, how plausible would it be to claim that these 'new' categories were innate? The developmental psychologist Jean Piaget has argued that the absurdity of Fodor and Chomsky's conclusion shows that their argument is in error (see Piattelli-Palmarini, 1980). However, it is one thing to assert that their arguments are wrong; it is quite another to show it. In spite of the controversy of the their position, there have been few convincing counter-arguments since it was first articulated.

If Fodor and Chomsky are right, we will need to reject the idea that categories are learned. But how can we make sense of this when Bruner and Murphy and others claim to have empirical evidence of people learning categories? How might we resolve this tension?

One possibility is that Fodor and Chomsky are talking about somewhat different aspects of learning from psychologists such as Bruner and Murphy. In characterizing categories as being innate, Fodor and Chomsky are claiming that nothing fundamental alters when someone appears to learn a category. In their view, the difference between someone who appears not to have learned a category and someone who does is not that great. Both have innate knowledge of the category, for example. Both have the ability to settle on the right hypothesis for this particular category, as opposed to the countless competing ones compatible with their empirical evidence. The person who appears to have learned the category has merely succeeded in drawing out their innate knowledge, and has put it to use. The person who appears not to have learned the category possesses the same innate abilities – it is just that they have not drawn out their category knowledge, nor have they put it to use.

Contrast this with the work of Murphy and Bruner. Their studies show considerable differences between those that have and have not learned particular categories. The former reliably identify instances as members of the category. They link their knowledge of the category to their wider knowledge of the world. They reason about the attributes associated with the category, and identify relationships between them and themes that link them together. In terms of information processing, a lot more happens inside the head of someone who appears to have learned a category than that of someone who has not.

At the beginning of this chapter we considered learning in terms of an organism adapting or changing in response to its environment. But we did not consider whether *all* changes could be linked to learning in this way. The tension between the empirical work on category learning and the arguments of Fodor and Chomsky suggests that we may have to consider carefully what kinds of change we can call learning. One way of responding to the arguments of Fodor and Chomsky is to concede that they show that a person's fundamental conceptual resources do not change when they appear to learn a category. If learning is defined as involving fundamental changes in conceptual abilities, then perhaps there is no such thing as category learning. However, if learning involves changes in information processing and behaviour, then perhaps categories are learned after all. So the contrast between the empirical studies, on the one hand, and the arguments of Fodor and Chomsky, on the other, may not be as stark as first it seems. Perhaps the fairest conclusion is that learning is multifaceted, and that the tension arises because researchers are really talking about slightly different aspects of learning.

However, even if we were to define category learning as involving fundamental conceptual change, it is not clear that Fodor's arguments are right. Cowie (1999) suggests problems with Fodor's arguments (though Fodor rejects her analysis), and Fodor himself hints that there may be something wrong: 'What I think it [the argument] shows is really not so much an *a priori* argument for nativism as that there must be some notion of learning that is so incredibly different from the one we have imagined that we don't even know what it would be like as things now stand' (Fodor, 1980, p.269). Fodor suggests that it may be wrong to think of learning as involving hypothesis testing. If he is right then psychologists may need to look for an alternative conceptualization of learning. Where might one look? You may think that Section 4 offers one possibility. It outlines a sociocultural approach to learning, in which learning is seen as involving more than just an individual learner. However we conceptualize learning, the goal of cognitive psychologists will be to explain the information processing that goes on in individuals when 'learning' occurs.

Summary Section 3

- Learning depends not just on the kind of experiences we have, but also on our own abilities to *process the information* we receive, and *relate it to previous knowledge.*
- Bruner *et al.* argued that categories are learned through hypothesis testing. They showed that people differ in the strategies by which they choose to test their hypotheses.
- Murphy and colleagues have shown that people learn categories by seeking to integrate the attributes of new categories with themes suggested by their existing background knowledge.
- Fodor and Chomsky present a serious challenge to theories of category learning by arguing that categories cannot be learned by means of hypothesis testing. The argument relies on the induction problem, according to which there are always many hypotheses compatible with the empirical evidence available to us.
- A response to the arguments of Fodor and Chomsky is to suggest that there are different aspects to learning. Their arguments are pitched in terms of fundamental conceptual abilities, while the empirical evidence examines behaviour and information processing. Another response is to suggest that people may learn categories by means other than hypothesis testing.

4   The sociocultural perspective

The cognitive perspective on learning described in the previous section typically studies how individuals confront and actively make sense of particular learning tasks – the essential challenge being to understand what it is that is going on inside one person's head. In this section, however, we will be asking how mental functioning is related to the interpersonal, cultural, historical and institutional settings in which it occurs. The emphasis will thus shift away from cognitive psychologists' attempts to characterize and understand things 'in the head' – that is, mental representations. Instead, we will be considering how particular contexts and situations either offer or constrain opportunities for learning. The approach discussed in this section represents what has been described as a **sociocultural perspective** on learning. This view of human learning deliberately attempts to avoid seeing learning as either a purely mental or a purely physical activity and, as the name suggests, the idea of 'culture' is of central importance.

In explaining the significance of culture, Charles Crook (1999) draws upon a biological analogy. In biology, a 'culture' is a chemical medium which supports some form of life (bacteria or perhaps tissue cells), and it makes little sense to characterize an organism without reference to the culture which sustains it. Similarly, seen from a sociocultural perspective, if we want to understand and characterize human learning we have to make reference to the culture that supports and sustains such activity. Thus we need to understand learners' use of cultural tools and technologies and we also need to examine the interpersonal and institutional contexts of learning.

> **Sociocultural perspective**
> A perspective on learning which stresses that learning involves the use of tools and artefacts and is embedded within the context of interpersonal relationships, which in turn are embedded in social and cultural systems.

4.1 Learning and the use of tools

In Section 3 of Chapter 2 the technological complexity of human society was discussed with respect to the evolutionary origins of the human mind. In this section we will be considering the significance of technologies and tools for learning. However, as a means of introducing the idea that the use of tools has important consequences for cognition (mental processes), we would like you to consider the impact that different tools and technologies have on mathematical problem solving.

Imagine that we asked you to divide 37,629 by 7.431. How would you approach this task? You might settle down with a paper and pencil and attempt the long division sum by hand, or you might rely on a pocket calculator. Alternatively, you may decide to select the calculator option from the menu bar of your computer. This example illustrates how the actual nature of the cognitive activity involved in producing the answer is significantly affected by whether you use paper and pencil, a calculator or a computer to solve the problem. If you chose to use paper and pencil you would have to lay out the figures on the page, use mental arithmetic, the appropriate calculation conventions and so on. Using a calculator involves knowing the sequence in which to enter the figures and when to use the divide and equals sign. Opting to use a computer would mean that you need to select the appropriate option on the menu bar and know how to enter the figures etc. Your problem-solving activity would have changed depending on your choice of tool.

Whilst the example above clearly relates to solving a problem, rather than learning, the idea that cognitive activity is fundamentally affected by the use of tools and technologies is a key feature of a sociocultural approach to learning. The term 'technologies' may conjure up images of modern 'gadgets' like calculators, computers and so on. However, throughout history people have developed technologies to help them solve practical and intellectual problems and have also used such resources to learn. For example, whilst most of us don't think twice about the act of writing, the technologies of writing (such as the alphabetic symbol system and the associated physical devices such as pens, pencils and paper) are extremely powerful in their effects – culturally, socially and psychologically. You may remember the example in Chapter 1 of how a shift from pen to computer influenced identity for Gergen.

Stop for one moment and consider what life would be like without access to books, newspapers, documents and teaching texts such as DSE212 course materials. What about life minus phone books, address books, diaries and shopping lists? Roger Säljö (1999) claims that it is by pausing to consider such issues that you can begin to see how the ways in which humans learn – retain, reproduce and produce information, knowledge and skills – have changed dramatically since writing became established as a means of documentation and communication.

The key point to note is that human history is characterized by technological change and that human learning involves the mastery of diverse tools and technologies. As Säljö (1999) explains, a fundamental assumption in a sociocultural understanding of learning is that human learning is always learning to do something with tools. But the notion of tools and technologies does not only refer to physical objects such as pens, calculators, computers and so on, it can also be extended to so-called psychological or symbolic tools elaborated within a culture. This means that a mathematical algorithm (a process or set of rules to be followed in calculations or other problem-solving operations) which allows you to do mental arithmetic is just as much a tool as is a pocket calculator. And, perhaps most important of all, language itself (including particular languages elaborated for any particular set of purposes) can also be considered as a psychological tool. In this way of thinking, virtually all intelligent activity involves interacting with a range of tools and technologies, and competence in the use of such tools is central both to intellectual development and to becoming an effective member of society.

Researchers working from a sociocultural perspective thus claim that learning is mediated. In this context, 'mediated' refers to the idea that in between us and the physical and social world are various tools and technologies which affect intelligent activity. The concept of mediation is important as it emphasizes that humans have access to the world around them only indirectly and that *learning is a process that occurs in the interplay between the learner and tools or technologies s/he is using.*

Säljö (1999) has explained how the concept of mediation carries with it important implications for how we conceptualize and study learning: '[The] learning is not only inside the person, but in his or her ability to use a particular set of tools in particular ways and for particular purposes' (Säljö, 1999, p.147). This is why sociocultural researchers often claim that they are interested in understanding what they call 'mediated action'.

James Wertsch (1997, 1998), a leading sociocultural theorist, has explained the properties of mediated action by using the example of pole-vaulting. Here both the pole (a culturally given tool) and the pole-vaulter are intrinsic to the activity. The pole both lends itself to being used in various kinds of ways and at the same time imposes various kinds of constraints. The advent of a new type of pole can make new records possible. Some pole-vaulters will adopt the new pole with enthusiasm and 'make it their own', while others will stick resolutely with the old technology (Light and Littleton, 1999).

This notion of 'making something your own' is referred to as **appropriation**. It is a term specifically used to indicate that tools are not just picked up and put down as and when they are needed, but they become part of how we construe the world, how we approach problems and even how we relate to one another (Light and Littleton, 1999). Appropriation involves more than simply having access to tools and technologies, it involves taking something for one's own use.

Appropriation
To make something one's own.

A crucial additional point is that tools in general are associated in complex ways with the distribution of power and authority within a culture. In the case of computers, for example, powerful vested interests shape the resources that become available to learners, and issues of access and equity arise (Light, 1997; Light and Littleton, 1999). The issue of power, authority and vested interest in relation to computer technology reminds us that tools and technologies are never experienced in isolation, but only within a contextual whole. According to sociocultural theorists, the tools and technologies around us embody a history of human activity (Crook, 1999), which is why they are often referred to as 'cultural tools'. It is also the case, however, that we are able to utilize their design to engage in distinctive new forms of action. Let's explore this idea a little further by considering a practical example relating to computer technology.

At the time of writing this chapter, governments across Europe are investing significant sums of money in the provision of new computing equipment for schools. Therefore, one of the questions we might want to know the answer to is 'Does using computers make a difference to children's learning experience?'

Activity 3.6

How might you design a research study or studies to address the question posed above? Make a note of your ideas. You should spend about 5 minutes on this activity.

Comment

You could have set about answering this question in lots of ways. For example, you may have thought about designing an experimental study where you investigated whether children's performance on a formal academic test was affected by the nature of the learning resources used – were the results better when the children used a computer-package as opposed to traditional text-based materials? Large *et al.* (1994) designed a study broadly along these lines. They compared children's test results when they had used an encyclopaedia in traditional book format or an encyclopaedia on CD-ROM. They found no significant differences.

This kind of study is perfectly acceptable, and the results are interesting. However, this is not the approach a sociocultural researcher would use to investigate the impact of the CD-ROM technology on children's learning. Given the emphasis on mediated activity in sociocultural theory, a researcher working within this perspective would be interested in the *processes of teaching and learning*, not just the learning outcome as assessed by performance on an academic test. The issue would be how the introduction of the CD-ROM made a difference to the children's learning activity. Here the key question would be 'How is the children's activity re-mediated – that is, distinctively changed – by the introduction of the CD-ROM resource?' Getting answers to this research question would mean adopting a very different approach from that adopted in the Large *et al.* study referred to above. Learning would have to be studied as it happens. This would involve the researcher making detailed observations of the children as they went about their work.

Many sociocultural researchers, however, would not stop there. Recognizing that the work with either the CD-ROM or text-based resource would be part of a broader classroom agenda, many researchers would be keen to avoid de-coupling their observations from the ongoing classroom activity. Thus, a sociocultural researcher might also examine the ways in which the teachers integrated the children's experiences of working with the different technologies into ongoing tutorial dialogues and classroom discussions. As Crook (1999) speculates: 'Perhaps it is this contextualizing work that determines much of a new media's cognitive impact' (p.371).

To give you some idea of the potential insights afforded by a detailed analysis of ongoing learning activity, let's take a look at a small-scale research study conducted by a team of researchers at the Open University. Teresa Keogh and her colleagues (Keogh *et al.*, 2000) examined the nature of talk and joint activity observed in same- or mixed-sex pairs of children engaged in a language task. This task required the assembly of two poems from two jumbled assemblages of lines of the poems presented either on the computer screen or on paper. The findings highlighted the impact that the presence of the computer had on the activity of mixed-sex pairs. When the task was presented on the computer, the boys dominated the activity, both in terms of the physical manipulation of the lines and suggestions for ordering the poems. However, when the task was presented on paper, the activity was distributed pretty much equally between the pair members. Should such findings be replicated, they would clearly carry implications for the organization of classroom computer-based language activities.

Children engaged in a computer-based language task

This concern with practical application and educational intervention is a preoccupation for many sociocultural researchers. Their research is often designed not only to inform theory, but also to make a difference for learners. By understanding the activity of learning, they hope to improve the learning experience for students of all ages. This issue of intervention and application is one that will feature again in the next section, where we discuss people learning together.

4.2 Learning as the joint construction of knowledge: the role of talk

A sociocultural understanding of learning recognizes that social interaction is a central part of human experience, and emphasizes that language is the prime cultural tool for mediating our experience of the world. Knowledge and learning are said to 'circulate amongst us' when we communicate with each other on learning tasks. It is not just that opportunities for discussion prompt individual change, but through discussion and joint activity new forms of understanding emerge. Meaning is thus jointly created by learners working together. Given this, there have been a number of detailed studies addressing the issue of how learning occurs within talk. Some of these have focused on analysing the interaction between parents and their children, and some have studied the ongoing classroom talk between teachers and pupils. More recently, work undertaken in higher education settings has begun to appear. For the purposes of the discussion here, however, we will highlight some recent observational work investigating how children learn and solve problems together (see Box 3.3). Underpinning this research is the notion that a learner's interactions and talk with other people mediate between the learner and the world-to-be-learned-about. So, seen in these terms, understanding learning depends upon understanding the particular types of interactions that serve to foster it.

3.3 FEATURED METHOD
Observational studies

Observational studies involve systematically watching, listening to and recording in some way what people do and say. This may include looking at the kinds of activities they engage in, how they talk, their gestures and their facial expressions. Some researchers use an observational method in naturally occurring settings such as in schools or on the street. Others set up the situations in which they observe participants and then record the naturally occurring behaviour, as is the case in the so-called 'strange situation' procedure where infants are observed in a laboratory made to look like a waiting room. Yet other researchers undertake observations as part of an experimental study. For instance, the Introduction, Section 2.4 discussed the example of Milgram's study of obedience to authority, in which researchers observed the emotional reactions of the male participants as they administered shocks to a 'learner'. Researchers also have to decide whether they want to observe behaviours that are readily categorized or those that involve very fine-grained analysis of behaviour. For example, in classroom settings some researchers observe easily visible and definable non-verbal behaviour, such as a child moving from one group to another, while others study behaviours that occur for less than a second at a time and that can only be identified by slowing down a videotaped recording. Whatever the particular research context, the key aim is to produce an accurate record of behaviour, and sometimes talk, for analysis and interpretation. Deciding on exactly what to observe and how to observe it is a crucial part of the research process and typically reflects the researcher's theoretical orientation and research interests.

For example, classroom researchers might have a coding scheme already devised on the basis of earlier (or pilot) research and might target the behaviour of certain pupils, recording how often they speak to their teacher, their peers, who they talk to and how animatedly they converse. The coding scheme would explicitly define each category of behaviour or utterance that was to be recorded, such as 'moving from one group to another' or 'asking a question of the teacher'. The researchers would use this coding scheme from the start of the observation. Using the observational method in this way will enable researchers to capture the frequency of different categories of behaviour and then undertake simple quantitative analyses of their data by counting up the occurrence of the different coded behaviours. This requires a very different coding scheme from studies that, for example, want to see *anything* that children do in their classroom over the course of a morning.

There are difficulties in collecting observational data. For example, behaviours and, even more so, utterances are often ambiguous in meaning and this can make coding difficult. One utterance may have multiple functions which cannot be recorded by most coding schemes. As we have seen, some behaviours are difficult to spot and, for this reason, observational studies often require that two observers agree about how they would code behaviours by getting inter-observer agreement. In addition, meanings change and are renegotiated over time. This may be missed in observations done over a short period.

For some researchers, the goal of observational research is to produce detailed qualitative descriptions (rather than the frequencies with which categories occur) and then analyse dynamic processes, themes and meanings. This kind of observational research is illustrated by the work of Neil Mercer and his colleagues (Mercer, 1995; Mercer, 2000). The data that were collected in these observations were both behavioural (what the children did) and symbolic in that the transcripts of what the children *said* were analysed in terms of meanings in order to understand how children jointly construct understanding together in their talk.

Mercer and his colleagues undertook a naturalistic observation study to investigate the nature of primary school children's talk when small groups were working together on computer tasks in classroom contexts. This involved the research team making video-recordings of approximately 50 hours of classroom talk in 10 English primary schools, which they later transcribed and analysed qualitatively.

When the observations of children's sessions of joint work were analysed it was revealed that the children used three distinctively different kinds of talk, which were described as disputational, cumulative and exploratory talk. *Disputational talk* was effectively unproductive disagreement. Such talk was characterized by an initiation (e.g. suggestion or hypothesis or instruction) followed by a challenge (e.g. rejection or a counter-proposition/hypothesis). Initiations were typically accepted either without discussion or with only superficial amendments, and challenges typically lacked clear resolution or else were resolved in ways that meant children accepted that they disagreed. *Cumulative talk* simply added uncritically to what had gone before so that it was part of an accumulation of ideas. In contrast, so called *exploratory talk* demonstrated the active joint engagement of the children with one another's ideas. In this category of talk, initiations of ideas may have been challenged and counter-challenged, but appropriate justifications for challenge were articulated and alternative hypotheses offered. Where alternative accounts were offered they took note of what had previously been said. Progress was thus the result of the joint discussion and acceptance of suggestions.

Mercer and his colleagues acknowledge that all three types of talk are appropriate in certain circumstances, but consider that exploratory talk offers a potential for learning over and above that offered by the other two types of talk. To illustrate exploratory talk and Mercer's qualitative analysis, let us take a closer look at some of the research team's data. The following transcribed extract of talk taken from the research team's recorded observations is followed by the team's brief comments on this material. The sequence shows a group of three 9 to 10-year-old children working on a computer program called Viking England, a historical simulation package, and engaging in exploratory talk:

Planning a raid

Diana: Let's discuss it. Which one shall we go for?

All: (*inaudible – reading from instructions*)

Peter: 1, 2, 3 or 4 (*reading out the number of options available*). Well we've got no other chance of getting more money because …

Adrian: And there's a monastery.

Diana: And if we take number 2 there's that (*inaudible*) …

Peter: Yeh but because the huts will be guarded.

All: Yeh.

Adrian: And that will probably be guarded.

Diana: It's surrounded by trees.

Peter: Yeh.

Adrian: And there's a rock guarding us there.

Peter: Yes there's some rocks there. So I think, I think it should be 1.

Adrian: Because the monastery might be unguarded.

Diana: Yes 1.

Adrian: 1 Yeh.

Peter: Yeh but what about 2? That, it might be not guarded. Just because there's huts there it doesn't mean it's not guarded, does it? What do you think?

Diana: Yes, it doesn't mean it's not. It doesn't mean to say it's not guarded does it. It may well be guarded. I think we should go for number 1 because I'm pretty sure it's not guarded.

Adrian: Yeh.

Peter: OK, yes, number 1 (*he keys in 1 on keyboard*). No (*computer responds inappropriately*).

Adrian: You have to use them numbers (*he points to the number keys on right of board, and Peter uses them to obtain the right result. Adrian begins to read from screen display*). 'You have chosen to raid area 1.'

Mercer's commentary

'In this sequence we [...] see some children on task, asking each other questions, commenting and making suggestions. They discuss the various options, and also remind each other of relevant information. They are using talk to share information and plan together. They discuss and evaluate possible courses of action and make joint decisions. There is a lot of explicit reasoning in the talk. What is more, this reasoning is essentially *interactive* – not really reducible to the form and content of individual statements, but more to do with how the discourse as a whole represents a social, shared thought process. There was a lot of this kind of talk in the Viking England activity, in which the children seemed to be reasoning together and building up shared knowledge and understanding to a new level through their talk.'

Source: transcript and commentary from Mercer, 1995, pp.101–4

The notion of ideas and concepts being literally built up in talk and constituted in interactive discourse is an important one for sociocultural theorists and it is an idea which emphasizes how 'personal meanings and understandings are created, negotiated and enriched within interpersonal exchanges' (Crook, 1999, p.369). Learning is seen as a creative process of meaning making and 'although meanings are "in the mind" they have their origins and their significance in the culture in which they are created' (Bruner, 1996, p.3). Murphy (2000) and Grossen and Bachmann (2000) emphasize the need to study the *processes* involved in the joint creation of meaning and understanding, especially since our understanding of these processes has important implications for educational intervention. For example, having recognized the potential value of exploratory talk, Mercer and colleagues set about designing and implementing a programme of intervention to encourage children's use of this type of talk. For these researchers, learning how to use particular forms of 'educated discourse' is as important as learning the specifics of the subject matter in hand. This is because, according to sociocultural theorists, 'an important ingredient in the development of knowledge in society is the creation of specialized forms of discursive practices that allow for precise communication about the world in specific settings' (Säljö, 1999, p.150).

What this means is that, for example, learning psychology is not just about learning psychological concepts, it is also about being able to talk the language of psychology – to appropriate the discourses of psychology and engage in the practices of psychology. Thus the learner gradually takes on the forms as well as the substance of this particular intellectual community – and thereby becomes a member of a community of practice. So, as you study DSE212 you are not simply learning abstract psychological terms and concepts, rather you are learning how and when it is appropriate to use these. In effect you are an apprentice psychologist, learning how to 'do' psychology by engaging in, for example, the practices associated with conducting, analysing and reporting research within recognized conventions.

At this point, it is appropriate to return to an idea which was introduced at the beginning of the chapter – namely, the distinction between 'learning what' and 'learning how'. From a sociocultural perspective, there is no clear separation between what is learned and how knowledge is learned and used.

4.3 Learning as enculturation

The idea that there is no clear demarcation between 'learning what' and 'learning how' leads us on to another central tenet of a sociocultural approach to learning. As Crook and Light (1999) explain, if we want to

understand learning we need to understand it in the particular institutional
and cultural contexts in which it occurs. This is because, according to
sociocultural theorists, particular contexts either constrain or afford
particular opportunities for learning. For example, the particular
educational practices we see today in schools and universities are the
result of a long period of historical development, and the activities of
today's students are largely circumscribed by existing practices and
established materials (Crook and Light, 1999). Learners' interactions need
to be understood with specific reference to the broader social and
historical contexts within which they are positioned, and learning itself is
seen as a process of **enculturation**. The following extract, from Seely
Brown *et al.* (1989), explains this process:

Enculturation
A process through
which people adopt
specific cultural
practices and act in
accordance with cultural
norms.

> *Enculturating may, at first, appear to have little to do with learning. But*
> *it is, in fact, what people do in learning to speak, read and write, or*
> *becoming school children, office workers, researchers and so on. From*
> *a very early age and throughout their lives, people, consciously or*
> *unconsciously, adopt the behaviour and belief systems of new social*
> *groups. Given the chance to observe and practice in situ the behavior of*
> *members of a culture, people pick up relevant jargon, imitate behavior,*
> *and gradually start to act in accordance with its norms. These cultural*
> *practices are often extremely complex. Nonetheless, given the opportunity*
> *to observe and practice them, people adopt them with great success.*
> *Students, for instance, can quickly get an implicit sense of what is*
> *suitable diction, what makes a relevant question, what is legitimate or*
> *illegitimate behavior in a particular activity. The ease and success with*
> *which people do this [...] belie the immense importance of the process.*

(*Seely Brown, 1989, pp.33–4*)

These ideas suggest that in some important sense learners have to 'learn
how to learn'. Consider the example of young children starting school.
They actually have to 'make sense of school' in order to take advantage
of the associated opportunities for learning. As Margaret Jackson (1987)
explains:

> *'Making sense of school' involves an increasing awareness of the social*
> *environment and an increasing ability to participate effectively in that social*
> *environment. Children as active learners, bring to bear their past experiences*
> *and their own understandings and perceptions of the situation. These*
> *perceptions may not necessarily match the perceptions of the teacher, for*
> *learning in school can be very different from learning at home.*

(*Jackson, 1987, p.86*)

Jackson argues that children's academic performance in school is closely
related to their competence within the social organization of the classroom

and clearly highlights the problems encountered by children who fail to make sense of school. Just as children have to make sense of school as a learning environment, so too do you have to make sense of the constraints imposed and opportunities afforded by studying psychology as a student within the Open University. You need to make sense of the rituals and routines, and the demands and expectations created by studying in a supported distance education environment. Seen from a sociocultural perspective, then, the clear boundary which is often drawn between the subject matter of cognitive psychology and social psychology is inappropriate. Consider, for example, the relationship between identity formation and meaning. Seen from a sociocultural perspective, processes of learning and identity formation go hand in hand. This suggests the need for work which integrates our understanding of the processes of identity formation (see Chapter 1) with our understanding of learning. Patricia Murphy (2000) studied children working in primary science classrooms. She illustrated, through detailed qualitative analyses of children's talk and joint activity and responses to questionnaires and interviews, the need for 'identity work' to be an integral part of analyses of learning interactions. Her work includes a striking example of a young boy attempting to reconcile his position as a member of a community of boys with his desire for academic success:

> Science mattered to Lee, and doing well also mattered, which the other boys were aware of. He therefore had to deal with the possibility of being labelled as a 'nerd', a 'keener', a 'boffin'; titles that diminish a boy in the peer culture in schools. The boys, when talking about the [learning] activity, referred to Lee's 'Mega stress telling us all what to do'; 'Lee organized it all'. Organizing activity is typically associated with girls' behaviour, hence this was another threat to Lee's identity in this situation.

> (Murphy, 2000, p.150)

Such research throws into stark relief the limitations of approaches to learning which focus solely on the behaviour or cognitive skills of individuals and illustrates that sociocultural theorists are keen to develop an integrated socioemotional approach to the study of learning.

Summary Section 4

- A sociocultural understanding of learning involves a consideration of learners' use of cultural tools and technologies.
- Sociocultural theorists are interested in the interpersonal and institutional contexts of learning.

- Learning is seen as being mediated by physical tools, such as computers, and psychological tools, such as language.
- Learning is characterized as a process of enculturation.
- From a sociocultural perspective on learning, the boundaries which are often drawn between the subject matter of cognitive psychology and social psychology are inappropriate.

5   Final word

We have seen how an understanding of learning is important to many different kinds of situation. Understanding how animals change their behaviour in response to relationships between events, how humans change the ways in which they think about the world as composed of categories, and how children and adults use their social and physical environments to acquire new understandings, all involve an analysis of learning. Examining these different situations has led us to consider different ways of viewing learning. One question that remains for researchers is to decide to what extent learning is a unitary phenomenon, and to what extent different learning situations call for different kinds of explanation.

This chapter has looked at different types of learning and different perspectives on learning: the comparative approach, and the cognitive and sociocultural perspectives. So which of them is right? To pose such a question is to play devil's advocate since we would argue against the idea that one perspective is right and the others, by exclusion, are wrong. Different approaches set different tasks and tap different features of a complex system of learning. Some look at behaviour only and others make inferences such as 'The animal has formed an expectancy' or 'The person has formed a category.' There is not necessarily one learning process that is applicable to each situation.

Teaching a dog to salivate to the sound of a bell might concern fundamentally different processes from those involved in teaching a child to recognize a species of bird. In the comparative approach, it was found useful to draw a distinction between learning 'what' and 'how', but this distinction is played down by those who take a sociocultural perspective.

To return to our initial discussion of what constitutes learning, have we found any evidence that each instance of learning corresponds to a change such that an animal, human or otherwise, can behave in a more adaptive way in its environment? It is surely clear that this is so when looking at a comparative approach. Learning to earn food or avoid aversive stimuli such as thorns clearly enables an animal to fit its environment. Is this also true of the other perspectives?

Successfully acquiring categories represents an economical way of operating in the world. It means that each new instance of experience can be located within an organizing framework. We bring a certain wisdom to a problem and solve it with some economy. Similarly, when looking at a sociocultural perspective, it can be seen that exploiting tools and collaborating with others are ways of equipping a person to survive better in their environment.

Learning takes place within the context of 'what is there already' and predispositions that facilitate some forms of learning rather than others. Animals learn some things with greater ease than others; for example, rats readily associate nausea with the taste of a particular food rather than with a specific visual stimulus. In Section 3, the possibility was raised that some forms of knowledge are innate, perhaps providing the starting point for further elaboration of learning – in the environment. This raises a crucial question about learning. If the appropriate structures and/or some form of innate knowledge are *not* there already, how does learning ever get started?

Another important question for the study of learning is whether an account of learning which focuses on conscious, cognitive processes is sufficient since much learning seems to be dependent upon environmental contingencies and happens without awareness. Moreover, might our understanding of learning be enhanced by the consideration of socioemotional processes such as identity formation? These and other questions continue to stimulate research and debate on the complex topic of learning.

 Further reading

For general introductions to the principles of a comparative approach to learning see:

Domjan, M. (1988) *The Principles of Learning and Behaviour*, Pacific Grove, CA, Brooks/Cole.

Hergenhahn, B.R. and Olson, M.H. (2000) *An Introduction to Theories of Learning*, Harlow, Prentice Hall.

Matute, H. (1998) 'Learning and conditioning', in Eysenck, M. (ed.) *Psychology: An Integrated Approach*, Harlow, Longman.

For a good exposition of the Skinnerian position and its relevance to
ethical and social issues see:
Skinner, B.F. (1971) *Beyond Freedom and Dignity,* Harmondsworth,
Penguin.

For a discussion of the innateness debate see:
Piattelli-Palmarini, M. (ed.) (1980) *Language and Learning: The Debate
Between Jean Piaget and Noam Chomsky,* London, Routledge & Kegan
Paul.

For wide-ranging introduction to sociocultural theory and research see:
Cole, M. (1996) *Cultural Psychology: A Once and Future Discipline,*
Cambridge, MA, Harvard University Press.

For a detailed analysis of the role of talk in creating meaning and
understanding see:
Mercer, N. (1995) *The Guided Construction of Knowledge,* Clevedon, Avon,
Multilingual Matters.

Mercer, N. (2000) *Words and Minds: How We Use Language to Think
Together,* London, Routledge.

References

Adams, C.D. (1982) 'Variations in the sensitivity of instrumental responding
to reinforcer devaluation', *Quarterly Journal of Experiential Psychology,*
vol.34B, pp.77–98.

Bolles, R.C. (1972) 'Reinforcement, expectancy and learning', *Psychological
Review,* vol.79, pp.394–409.

Bruner, J. (1996) *The Culture of Education,* Cambridge, MA, Harvard
University Press.

Bruner, J.S., Goodnow, J.J., and Austin, G.A. (1956) *A Study of Thinking,*
New York, John Wiley & Sons.

Chomsky, N. and Fodor, J.A. (1980) 'Statement of the paradox', in Piattelli-
Palmarini, M. (ed.).

Cowie, F. (1999) *What's Within? Nativism Reconsidered,* Oxford, Oxford
University Press.

Crook, C. (1999) 'The uses and significance of electronic media during
development', in Messer, D. and Miller, S. (eds) *Exploring Developmental
Psychology: From Infancy to Adolescence,* London, Arnold.

Crook, C. and Light, P. (1999) 'Information technology and the culture of
student learning', in Bliss, J., Light, P. and Säljö, R. (eds) *Learning Sites:
Social and Technological Contexts for Learning,* Oxford, Pergamon.

Dickinson, A. (1985) 'Actions and habits: the development of behavioural autonomy', *Philosophical Transactions of the Royal Society of London,* (B) 308, pp.67–78.

Eco, U. (1999) *Kant and the Platypus: Essays on Language and Cognition*, London, Secker & Warburg.

Fodor, J.A. (1980) Fixation of belief and concept acquisition', in Piattelli-Palmarini, M. (ed.).

Garcia, J. (1989) 'Food for Tolman: cognition and cathexis in concert', in Archer, T. and Nilsson, L.G. (eds) *Aversion, Avoidance and Anxiety – Perspectives on Aversively Motivated Behaviour*, Hillsdale, NJ, Lawrence Erlbaum.

Goldman, L., Coover, G.D. and Levine, S. (1973) 'Bi-directional effects of reinforcement shifts on pituitary adrenal activity', *Physiology and Behaviour,* vol.10, pp.209–14.

Grossen, M. and Bachmann, K. (2000) 'Learning to collaborate in a peer-tutoring situation: Who learns? What is learned?', *European Journal of Psychology of Education,* vol.XV, no.4, pp.497–514.

Hirsh, R. (1974) 'The hippocampus and contextual retrieval of information from memory: a theory', *Behavioural Biology*, 12, pp.421–44.

Jackson, M. (1987) 'Making sense of school', in Pollard, A. (ed.) *Children and Their Primary Schools: A New Perspective*, London, The Falmer Press.

James, W. (1890/1950) *The Principles of Psychology*, Vol.1, New York, Dover.

Jones, R.T. and Kazdin, A.E. (1975) 'Programming response maintenance after withdrawing token reinforcement', *Behaviour Therapy*, 6, pp.153–64.

Kaplan, A.S. and Murphy, G.L. (2000) 'Category learning with minimal prior knowledge', *Journal of Experimental Psychology. Learning, Memory and Cognition*, vol.26, no.4, pp.829–46.

Keogh, T., Barnes, P., Joiner, R. and Littleton, K. (2000) 'Computers, verses, paper – girls versus boys: gender and task presentation effects', *Educational Psychology*, vol.20, no.1, pp.33–44.

Large, A., Behesti, J., Breuleux, A. and Renaud, A. (1994) 'Multi-media and comprehension – a cognitive study', J*ournal of the American Society for Information Science*, 45, pp.515–28.

Light, P. (1997) 'Computers for learning: psychological perspectives', *Journal of Child Psychology and Psychiatry*, vol.38, no.5, pp.497–504.

Light, P. and Littleton, K. (1999) *Social Processes in Children's Learning*, Cambridge, Cambridge University Press.

Marr, D. (1982) *Vision: A Computational Investigation into the Human Representation and Processing of Visual Information*, San Francisco, CA, W.H.Freeman.

Mercado, E., Killebrew, D.A., Pack, A.A., Macha, I.V.B. and Herman, L.M. (2000) 'Generalization of "same–different" classification abilities in bottlenosed dolphins', *Behavioural Processes*, vol.50, nos.2–3, pp.79–94.

Mercer, N. (1995) *The Guided Construction of Knowledge*, Clevedon, Avon, Multilingual Matters.

Mercer, N. (2000) *Words and Minds: How We Use Language to Think Together*, London, Routledge.

Mishkin, M., Malamut, B. and Bachevalier, J. (1984) 'Memories and habits: two neural systems', in Lynch, G., McGaugh, J.L. and Weinberger, N.M. (eds) *Neurobiology of Learning and Memory*, New York, The Guilford Press.

Murphy, G.L. and Allopenna, P.D. (1994) 'The locus of knowledge effects in concept-learning', *Journal of Experimental Psychology. Learning, Memory and Cognition*, vol.20, no.4, pp.904–19.

Murphy, G.L. and Medin, D.L. (1985) 'The role of theories in conceptual coherence', *Psychological Review*, vol.92, pp.289–316.

Murphy, P. (2000) 'Understanding the process of negotiation in social interaction', in Joiner, R., Littleton, K., Faulkner D. and Miell, D.(eds) *Rethinking Collaborative Learning*, London, Free Association Press.

Piattelli-Palmarini, M. (ed.) (1980) *Language and Learning: The Debate Between Jean Piaget and Noam Chomsky*, London, Routledge & Kegan Paul.

Seely Brown, J., Collins, A. and Duguid, P. (1989) 'Situated cognition and the culture of student learning', *Educational Researcher*, January/February, pp.32–42.

Säljö, R. (1999) 'Learning as the use of tools', in Littleton, K. and Light, P. (eds) *Learning With Computers: Analysing Productive Interaction*, London, Routledge.

Sappington, B.F. and Goldman, L. (1994) 'Discrimination-learning and concept-formation in the Arabian horse', *Journal of Animal Science*, vol.72, no.12, pp.3080–7.

Siegel, S. (1984) 'Pavlovian conditioning and heroin overdose: reports by overdose victims', *Bulletin of the Psychonomic Society*, vol.22, pp.428–30.

Skinner, B.F. (1948/1990) *Walden Two*, London, Collier Macmillan.

Toates, F. (1998) 'The interaction of cognitive and stimulus–response processes in the control of behaviour', *Neuroscience and Biobehavioural Reviews*, vol.22, pp.59–83.

Tolman, E.C. (1932) *Purposive Behaviour in Animals and Men*, New York, The Century Co.

Wertsch, J. (1997) *The Socio-cultural Approach to Learning*, paper presented to a Inaugural Conference of the Centre for Learning in Organizations, School of Education, University of Bristol, January.

Wertsch, J. (1998) *Mind as Action*, Oxford, Oxford University Press.

■ Commentary 3: Three approaches to learning

Learning is a vital, everyday activity. But, as we saw when considering the issue of identities in Chapter 1, everyday and apparently simple psychological issues are far from simple to study and understand. Because there are many different ways in which psychologists have chosen to define and study learning, the authors of Chapter 3 have introduced (1) the comparative approach, which uses research based in the behaviourist perspective, (2) the cognitive perspective on learning, and (3) the sociocultural perspective on learning. So, in this one chapter, you have met three psychological perspectives: behaviourism, cognitive psychology and sociocultural psychology.

Theory

1 Different perspectives can lead to different theories that allow different insights into an issue. This is because they have a different focus and ask different questions.

2 Different perspectives, and different theories, can be *complementary*, *conflicting* or *co-existing*. In the case of learning, the perspectives may be understood as co-existing and therefore as offering different insights into the diverse processes of learning.

3 Different psychological perspectives and theories can provide a variety of ways of applying their findings to everyday psychological problems.

Methods

4 Both the behaviourist and the cognitive perspectives rely primarily on the most common psychological method – experiments. But behaviourists use experiments to explain *behaviour*, whereas cognitive psychologists use experiments and their findings to make *inferences about mental processes*.

5 The comparative approach in psychology depends on the assumption that humans share characteristics with other animals. The behaviourist perspective on learning assumes that research on learning will generalize, at least across vertebrates, and sometimes to other creatures as well.

Themes

6 The theme of change is central to learning. Unlike change as studied in evolutionary psychology, in learning it is confined to change within the lifetime of each human being or non-human animal. Learning in humans may occur below the level of consciousness or may be the result of conscious effort.

■ Thinking about theory

Choosing and using perspectives and theories

Just three chapters into the book we have already made a good start on illustrating the diversity of psychology. The authors in this last chapter have presented three different perspectives that have been used to examine the topic of learning. In this respect the chapter is similar to Chapter 1 ('Identities and diversities'). In Chapter 1 the aspects of identity on which the different perspectives focused were *somewhat* different. But in Chapter 3 the aspects of learning examined within each perspective are *so* different that we might wonder whether the 'learning' of the behaviourist, cognitive and sociocultural psychologists is in fact the same phenomenon.

The authors of the chapter make clear that it is no easy task to decide how best to study learning and that it requires some ingenuity even to *define* learning in ways that help psychologists to investigate it. One way to think about perspectives is to say that each will tend to focus on different aspects of a phenomenon, define it differently and ask different questions. This has certainly been illustrated in the chapter on learning. Turning that around, another way to look at it is to say that psychological phenomena are so complex that they can be defined in a range of ways, with each definition of the subject matter *demanding* a different perspective for investigation and understanding.

Different perspectives lead to different theories. And different theories can provide different insights into the same issue. So what happens when different theories seem to explain the same topic? Some theories may be discarded because they are not supported by evidence. But sometimes, after substantial research, what remains are very different theories, often from very different perspectives, that *are* supported by their own particular kinds of evidence. So how can we view these different theories? In some instances they can be thought of as *complementary*, each enriching understanding of the issue in its own way. Very occasionally there is a possibility of synthesis, i.e. combining the ideas they produce into a unified whole. Theories can, however, be *conflicting*, and in the chapters that follow you will find that there are examples of theories which introduce serious conflict within psychology. Or theories might just *co-exist* – with little or no communication between those who subscribe to them and minimal consideration of how the theories might or might not relate.

You may remember that the three theories considered in Chapter 1 ('Identities and diversities') shared some common features but also produced different and sometimes contradictory ways of thinking about identities (e.g. as 'core' and 'singular' in psychosocial theories or as 'de-centred' and 'plural' in social constructionist theories). For this reason, the three theories of identities could be said to conflicting, at least in some respects. In the case of learning, the theories, and the perspectives from which they derive, can be understood as co-existing, i.e. as offering different, but not necessarily conflicting, insights into the diverse processes of learning. What we learn from observing animal learning can be put alongside what we know about how people *think* when learning; and the sociocultural conditions that facilitate learning can be thought of as providing a fuller picture of learning as a broad topic. So, whilst psychologists differ in what they believe is most important in the study of learning, such differences between perspectives could be viewed as potentially mutually enriching.

But, on the other hand, and as is often the case, we could claim that the theories simply co-exist because there is virtually no communication between those who subscribe to the different underlying perspectives. In other respects the perspectives themselves could be said to be conflicting. Most clearly, the behaviourist perspective conflicts with the cognitive perspective on the issue of mental processes and whether the focus should be on just behaviour or behaviour that is essentially used to make inferences about what goes on 'in the head'.

As with all theories, the question of whether particular theories are 'correct' cannot be conclusively answered. The more research is done, however, the more we can be certain which theories *do not work*. It is through this process of continual testing, challenging and refining of theories that psychology progresses.

Applying psychological knowledge

There is sometimes another way to think about complementary, conflicting and co-existing theories, and the perspectives from which they derive. We can consider the usefulness of their particular findings – their practical applications. In Chapter 1, the three theories of identity were compared to see how well they could be applied to the everyday identities of people with physical impairments. This 'usefulness' can be one way to evaluate the different theories.

Chapter 3 illustrates this important potential of theories – that they can be *applied* in order to change the world in ways that we hope will be beneficial. (See also the second course book and particularly the third book, *Applying Psychology*). The principles established by the behaviourist perspective on learning, such as the law of effect (one of the most robust laws we have in psychology) certainly have practical value. Applications of behaviourist learning theory based on Skinner's operant conditioning include behaviour modification (for problematic behaviour) and the treatment of patients in some clinical settings. Research using classical conditioning has produced methods of desensitizing people with phobias. In a very different way, the sociocultural perspective provides many insights into how children's learning at school may best be facilitated; for example, Mercer's suggestion regarding the teaching of explicit ground rules for exploratory talk in collaborative work.

Mapping traditions

Contemporary perspectives in psychology have their roots in different historical traditions. The chapter you have just read is helpful in presenting three important traditions in psychology. You can track these traditions and their variants by using *EPoCH*. You can either enter the names of influential psychologists or the names of the perspectives themselves – behaviourism, cognitive psychology and sociocultural psychology.

There was a time when behaviourism was the dominant perspective in psychology; it has a long tradition and continues to be influential. In this tradition the use of an outsider viewpoint and behavioural data were considered to be the only legitimate way to understand psychology. Some psychologists still take this strong position. But many others, although continuing to use mainly behavioural data, would not think of themselves as being part of the strictly behaviourist tradition.

The second perspective on learning introduced in Chapter 3 is cognitive psychology. This broad perspective on psychology could be said to have begun with the 'cognitive revolution' of the 1960s that brought back into psychology a primary interest in what goes on in the mind. But, historically, the cognitive tradition began much earlier than this. In Chapter 3 you saw that a concern with mental processes, such as *purposes* (e.g. the work of Tolman, as early as 1932) and *representations* that exist in some form in the mind (e.g. 'expectancies'), has long been present in the study of learning. This concern came to be thought of as a move away from behaviourism (which was particularly concerned with learning) towards cognitive psychology. But the cognitive tradition was also influencing other areas of psychology and, in fact, its roots *predate* behaviourism.

Interest in thinking, concepts, language and consciousness all came before the focus on overt behaviour. The shift in focus to behaviour – the radical innovation of behaviourism – began as a reaction against the methodological difficulties of studying abstract mental processes. In Wundt's laboratory (opened in 1879), there were attempts to study thinking. As early as 1885, Ebbinghaus, a psychologist who began the empirical work on memory, tried to find out about the mental processes of memory by systematically recording his own capacity to recall nonsense words that he had set out to learn. You will meet this work in Chapter 8, 'Memory: structures, processes and skills'. In the chapter on memory you will also read about a different strand of the cognitive tradition, the work of Bartlett. Bartlett, who published his work as early as 1932, was interested in our memory for meaningful materials (like stories) and schemata – the ways in which knowledge seems to represented in the mind. Yet another strand of the cognitive tradition is the information-processing approach to attention which will feature in Chapter 6 ('Perception and attention'). All these strands, together with other more recent influences like cognitive neuropsychology, philosophy and computer science, make up the contemporary perspective of cognitive psychology.

The sociocultural perspective, the third perspective discussed in the learning chapter, is a relatively new tradition and can be seen as part of what was identified in the Introduction as the 'second cognitive revolution'. This move in psychology emphasized the importance of investigating cognition by studying how meaning is created through participation in cultural practices and through language. According to the sociocultural approach, learning is always affected by the culture in which it takes place and is simultaneously cognitive, social, emotional, and part of a developmental process.

■ Thinking about methods

Diversity of methods

Because different perspectives are presented in the learning chapter, different methods are also described. However, there are also some similarities in method between the different perspectives. For example, behaviourist theories *and* cognitive theories of learning both rely on experiments. The first featured method box in the chapter illustrates the basic principles of experimental method with a behaviourist example, using animals. The cognitive psychology approach to learning concentrates on experiments where *humans* are the participants – because the cognitive perspective is concerned with the human mind. Thus, Bruner and his colleagues' experiments are designed to understand what is going on inside people's heads as they learn to categorize – how they respond to particular learning tasks. In Section 4 on the sociocultural perspective, observation is seen as its favoured method, and the second featured method box discusses different kinds of observational study. However, some researchers in this tradition do use experiments in their work.

Comparative method

Behaviourism uses what is known as the comparative method, taking for granted the idea that we share characteristics with a variety of animals, not just primates as in the chapter on evolutionary psychology, and that this can be usefully exploited in research. The experiments used by behaviourist researchers are designed to study the behaviour that is observable as non-human animals learn. Studies of classical and operant conditioning have used rats, pigeons and other animals as experimental subjects. This is because the behaviourist perspective assumes that research on learning will generalize, for the most part, across vertebrates (and sometimes other creatures). As in Chapter 2 ('Evolutionary psychology'), the authors bring together an understanding of what research on human and non-human animals can contribute to an understanding of human psychology.

■ Thinking about themes

Fixity and change

Learning is about change, but change of a very different kind from that discussed in Chapter 2 ('Evolutionary psychology'). Evolution, as we have seen, is about change over extremely long periods of time. Learning, on the other hand, is the process by which humans and other animals acquire skills and information over the course of their lifetimes.

Learning can be viewed as change that occurs in response to what animals and humans experience in their environments; it is often a form of adaptation. In one sense, all the theories discussed in Chapter 3 are about how animals (human and non-human) are able to adapt to their environments within a generation. Therefore, one important focus is on the ways in which animals can be flexible in response to environmental influences. But this doesn't necessarily mean that the adaptation and learning are purposive. For the most part, as in classical conditioning, instrumental learning and a great deal of category formation, the adaptation and learning are below the level of consciousness. This is a different kind of change from that associated with the curiosity and goal-oriented learning activities in the classroom, as described in Section 4 of the chapter.

In the chapter that follows (Chapter 4, 'Biological processes and psychological explanation'), the author carries forward the themes of fixity and change, examining the ways in which animals adapt to their environments *and* how they maintain internal equilibrium (i.e. stability or fixity) through the process of homeostasis.

CHAPTER **4**

Biological processes and psychological explanation

Frederick Toates

Contents

Aims

This chapter aims to:

- introduce enough of the basics of biology so that you can appreciate the relevance of the subject to the study of psychology
- present the argument that the relationship between biology and psychology is a reciprocal one, in that each discipline can call upon the other for insight
- encourage a critical stance towards the use of biological processes in psychological explanation.

1   Introduction

This chapter is about the insights into psychology that can be gained by looking at biological processes. Many of the chapters in this course consider aspects of psychology that can be illuminated with the help of biological understandings and explanations. For example, in Chapter 3 you considered processes such as forming new associations between stimuli and responses, and developing and using categories. You will have learnt that cognitive approaches could be developed without looking at what might be happening 'inside the brain'. However, knowledge of the brain can enhance such psychological explanation.

Popular and scientific literature contains frequent references to psychology and the brain. For example, it looks at how the structure and activity of the brain can illuminate differences between the sexes or reveal what has 'gone wrong' in the case of violent criminals. There are even claims for the existence of particular parts of the brain that underlie religious experience (Albright, 2000). Religious belief involves complex ideas, goals and feelings; and from a biological view, it could be argued that religious ecstasy, as experienced by saints and mystics, is associated with overactivity of certain brain regions. In terms of the discussion of evolutionary psychology in Chapter 2, it might even be argued that these brain regions have evolved to serve a particular function, since a belief in a God might confer an evolutionary advantage, such as helping to consolidate group action. This chapter will encourage a critical look at such claims.

So, what is biology? It is the science of living things. It looks at animals and plants and concerns their bodily structure and lifestyle. Among other

Physiology
The study of the structure and function of the body.

things, it looks at the components that make-up the body of an animal, such as the brain, heart and lungs, and it examines how animals (including humans) coordinate their actions. This field of biology is termed **physiology**. Biology also looks at the whole animal in its environment, considering such things as how it defends itself, obtains and digests food, and how it mates. Of course, only a limited part of biology is of direct relevance to psychology and that is the part that will occupy this chapter.

We start life as a single fertilized egg in our mother's womb. From this, the adult develops. Our adult form is the outcome of the complex interdependence between biological structures and the environment. First, there is the environment of the egg in the womb, developing into a foetus that is sensitive to taste, smell, sound and movement. Later, there is the environment outside the womb. The environment has both physical and social dimensions, for example that of the mother–infant interaction of suckling. To understand psychological development, we need some knowledge of biology and how the biological being is locked into interaction with its environment.

We are a biological species with bodies that are comparable, in some respects, to those of apes, cats and rats. But in other respects, we are a special species, with the unique capacity to utilize a complex symbolic language and to reflect upon our conscious awareness (as we have seen in Chapters 1 and 3 in this book, and will return to in other places throughout the course). Nonetheless, we are part of the biological world and viewing us in this light can give psychological insights. Our principal interest in this chapter is with the physiology of the human body, especially the brain, and how a study of it can enhance our understanding of behaviour and mental processes. Among other things, we shall ask – what is the relationship between the mind, with its conscious and unconscious aspects, and the physical body?

There are a number of ways in which a study of the brain can illuminate psychology. For example, brain damage can disrupt normal psychological function, such as memory. What happens when a patient with damage to a part of the brain involved in a particular form of memory is set the task of learning to perform a difficult mechanical skill by hand? An example of such a task is to trace a figure while viewing the hand in a mirror that reverses everything left to right. Typically, the patient gets better at the task with practice (Milner, 1966). However, despite repeated experience of the task, the patient fails to remember having done it before and even fails to recognize the psychologist organizing the investigation. This points to a disruption of certain types of memory (e.g. for people), while other types (e.g. a mechanical skill) remain intact. A psychological classification of learning and memory, for example into 'what' and 'how' (see Chapter 3), might therefore draw upon evidence from a biological perspective in this way.

A person's brain can be scanned with special equipment to observe the activity of different regions. Low activity in a region may suggest malfunction, which can often be linked to psychological malfunction in such things as memory. In some cases of brain damage, a patient can react appropriately to the appearance of an object in their visual field but has no conscious awareness of seeing it (Weiskrantz, 1976). In effect the patient says, 'The object, which I did not see, was moving to the left'. This evidence from the analysis of biological damage suggests a dissociation between conscious and unconscious determinants of behaviour, something of central concern to psychologists.

Psychologists like to theorize about behaviour and the mind. Given two rival theories, one might logically favour that which fits a contemporary, biological understanding of the brain. The aim of the present chapter is to show how to relate phenomena of interest to psychologists to underlying biological processes.

Summary Section 1

- A biological psychology perspective encompasses different areas of study such as development, evolution, genetics and physiology.
- Physiology looks at the components of the body, how they interact and how they are involved in the control of behaviour.
- Studying the brain can provide insights into psychological processes and the determinants of behaviour.

2 The role of biology in psychological explanation

What is the exact role and status of biology in terms of providing insights into behaviour and the mind? How should biology be used in psychology? Authors in both the popular media and scientific literature sometimes suggest that explanations for even complex psychological phenomena can *only* be found by looking at genes and brain structure. This approach is exemplified by the influential biologist Francis Crick. In his outspoken work entitled *The Astonishing Hypothesis – The Scientific Search for the Soul*, Crick suggests:

> ... *that "You", your joys and your sorrows, your memories and your ambitions, your sense of personal identity and free will, are in fact no more than the behaviour of a vast assembly of nerve cells and their associated molecules.*

(Crick, 1994, p.3)

Reductionism
An approach to scientific explanation that seeks insight by reducing to a smaller scale of explanation.

Here, Crick articulates a belief in **reductionism**: that potentially all psychological events and experiences can be fully and only explained in terms of the activity within the components of the brain. Since brain science is considered to be both necessary and sufficient to explain psychological phenomena, such phenomena are 'reduced' to a lower level of analysis. In this context, 'lower' means smaller scale and Crick, for example, would argue that complex social phenomena might be explained in terms of genes and the biology of the brain.

The approach underlying the present chapter is different from that of Crick and is based on a number of assumptions (Bolton and Hill, 1996; Stevens, 1996; Toates, 2001):

1   No single discipline (e.g. psychology or biology) has a monopoly on the truth or a superior perspective. We can gain an insight by drawing on knowledge from various disciplines.
2   There are particular laws and principles applicable at a psychological level and these cannot be reduced to the laws of biology, chemistry and physics.
3   The laws and principles of biology apply to both non-humans and humans.
4   Our task is to relate the laws and principles of psychology to those of biology and vice versa.
5   The biologically orientated psychologist (like myself) sits at the frontier of the biological and social sciences, familiar enough with both approaches to see the indispensable role of each.

The relationship between biology and psychology is reciprocal. For example, in one study non-human primates were injected with a standard dose of the drug amphetamine, which influenced their behaviour, but not in any consistent way (Cacioppo and Berntson, 1992). However, sense could be made of the data once the issue of social hierarchy was considered. For animals high in the social hierarchy, amphetamine increased their tendency to dominance, whereas for those that were low in the hierarchy, it increased their tendency to show submissive behaviour in the face of a more dominant animal. An analysis of events within the body on a purely biological level might well have missed an important determining factor in the behaviour of the animals: the influence of social context (Cacioppo and Berntson, 1992).

Another illustration of the relationship between biology and psychology is the link between psychological states and the well-being of the heart and circulation (Allan and Scheidt, 1996). A negative psychological state, such as hostility, has a number of effects in the body including an increased release of fatty substances that can block blood vessels. This effect is less likely when the person is in a positive psychological state.

This chapter takes as a given that biological and psychological factors interact in important ways and adopts what can be termed a 'biological psychology perspective'.

2.1 A biological psychology perspective

Consider the following case. A person goes to their doctor complaining of depression. The doctor might consider some kind of psychological intervention, such as counselling or therapy, to investigate the patient's thought processes, behaviour patterns and social relationships. The doctor might also believe that biological intervention could be useful and may prescribe medication such as Prozac, which is an anti-depressant drug that has a particular influence on the chemicals in the brain – one that is understood by the biological and chemical sciences. However, the psychological and biological levels of intervention are not mutually exclusive. Good doctors and therapists will consider the mode of action of the drug and any changes in behaviour and thought processes that it might trigger. They will know that the specific chemistry of the drug is only one factor in its efficacy, since the patient's beliefs and the therapist's attitudes to both the drug and patient might affect the outcome. The drug can affect chemicals in the brain in such a way as to influence positively the outcome of psychological therapy. This case exemplifies the approach that will be adopted in this chapter: the integration of biology and psychology, meaning that we are dealing with one unified system, having both biological and psychological aspects.

The biological psychology perspective advanced here rejects the exclusive reductionism expressed earlier by Crick, whereby that which is of interest to psychologists is described in terms of 'nothing but' the structure of our brains (MacKay, 1974). But, if we reject the idea that biology can explain everything, what is left? What exactly is this domain that is of peculiar interest to the psychologist? How might we relate it to the biology of the brain?

2.2 Analogies and emergent properties

How do we relate the phenomena of mental life to an understanding of the brain? The task can appear daunting, even to those who dedicate their lives to solving it. However, explanation in this area, as elsewhere, appears to be aided somewhat by appealing to analogies (MacKay, 1974). Take a look at Figure 4.1. What does it show? A series of dots or a meaningful sign? For some purposes, it might be described as a series of dots, formed on a white surface from ink which has a particular chemical composition. For other purposes, such as finding your way, it is more usefully described as a sign. It would be futile to argue over which is the more 'accurate' or 'better' description of Figure 4.1.

Figure 4.1   A series of dots or a meaningful sign?

Applied to our area of concern, what does the example in Figure 4.1 suggest? The discourse about the brain traditionally used by the biologist could be thought of as analogous to the pattern of dots; and that of thought, cognition and mind, traditionally used by the psychologist, as analogous to the meaningful sign. These are two different levels of description of the same underlying reality.

For another illustration, consider that water consists of two gases, hydrogen and oxygen. At one level, it might be described in terms of these constituents. At another level water may best be described as a liquid with particular distinct properties such as wetness and a tendency to flow. This example serves to illustrate an important principle, that of an **emergent property**.

Emergent property
A property exhibited by a combination of components, which is not evident when looking at the properties of the individual components alone.

When the gases oxygen and hydrogen combine, something new, with distinct properties, emerges – liquidity. The properties of liquidity are not evident when looking at the component gases, but are absolutely dependent upon them. The notion of emergent properties is a suitable motif for the present chapter. We could suggest that mental and behavioural phenomena arise from the properties of the physical brain in interaction with the physical and social environment. This raises an issue that has exercised many academics and which has deep implications for how we view ourselves and our fellow humans. We shall turn to this next.

2.3 Issues of mind-brain

Activity 4.1

Try asking some of your family and friends how they view the brain and the mind. How do they define each? How are they related? What is special about the brain and the mind in the context of an individual's personal identity?

Some people might describe the brain, but not the mind, in material terms. For instance, at autopsy, a brain can be weighed and its content analysed in terms of chemicals. The brain exists at a particular point in time and a place in space. Minds on the other hand are sometimes described as not following physical and chemical principles and as having some different mode of existence. This idea is closely associated with the views of the French philosopher René Descartes (1596–1650).

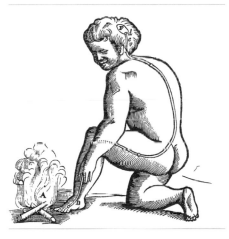

Figure 4.2 shows an example of behaviour discussed by René Descartes. Given a stimulus such as the heat of the flame, the body reacts in a predictable, 'reflex' way (in this case, to move a limb away from the heat).

Descartes was in the habit of spending time in the gardens of St. Germain-en-Laye, near Paris. He was fascinated by the automatons there. These were hydraulically activated statues of monsters, triggered into movement by a visitor stepping on a pedal. Given the

Figure 4.2 Behaviour as described by Descartes

stimulus, a monster would suddenly spring out of the bushes and squirt water into the faces of the visitors.

Descartes suggested that non-human behaviour (and some human behaviour) was like this: an automatic response to a stimulus. However, he suggested that over and above such stimulus–response mechanisms, humans have a reasoning mind (or 'soul') that could intervene and produce behaviour that was not automatic. Non-humans did not possess this and lacked immortal souls. The idea of **dualism**, a fundamental distinction between two aspects of human existence, mind and body, is associated most closely with Descartes. However, in studying brain and behaviour, very few psychologists or biologists now subscribe to dualistic principles in the tradition of Descartes. The majority opinion

Dualism
A philosophical perspective that draws an absolute distinction between the brain and mind.

rejects the idea that a mind can have an existence distinct from the physical brain.

In terms of emergent properties, biological psychologists would suggest that cognition, the mind, and conscious and unconscious awareness, all emerge from a certain combination of brain components operating in a particular way in interaction with an environment.

These philosophical considerations will be investigated in more detail in Chapter 4 of the second course book, *Challenging Psychological Issues*. Now it is time to turn to some basic biology, chosen for its relevance to understanding psychological phenomena.

Summary Section 2

- A reductionist perspective sees the possibility of reducing psychological phenomena to a complete explanation in terms of biological structures and processes, such as components of the brain.
- Although the present chapter will look to biological processes for an understanding of psychological phenomena, it will not attempt a reduction to biology.
- The philosophy advanced here – an integrative biological psychology perspective – is that there exist parallel and interdependent biological, psychological and social processes.
- The biological psychology perspective recognizes that explanation is a two-way process: physiological events depend, in part, upon psychological and social context.
- When components combine, something new, with distinct properties, emerges. Psychological phenomena might be described as emerging from the brain in interaction with the environment.
- Some theorists have suggested a fundamental dualism between material brain events and a non-material mind. However, these days within psychology, the mind is usually described as an emergent property of the brain.

3   Some basic biology

As with any new subject there are some basic concepts and terms that need to be understood. This section does not attempt to explain biology as a subject in its own right. Rather, it introduces just enough basic biology for you to understand the bases of a biological psychology perspective.

3.1 Cells - general and specialized

A fundamental principle in biology is that animals can be described in terms of the components that constitute the body. The body is composed of billions of very basic building blocks termed **cells**. Cells might be compared with the individual humans that form a society. Like people, there are variations in the function of different cells. Some cells, for example, form the structure of the skin and lungs. Mobile cells, in contrast, include red blood cells which transport oxygen, and specialist immune cells which are recruited to fight bacteria and viruses. Although there are differences in function, cells do have some common properties. As illustrated in Figure 4.3, each cell is surrounded by a cell membrane which, to some extent, separates the environment within the cell from the external environment. All cells require the nutrients and oxygen brought by the blood and a means of disposing of waste.

Cell
A basic building block of an organism.

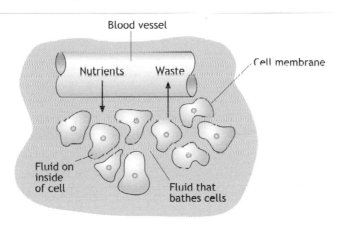

Figure 4.3   Some cells of the body (Source: Toates, 1998, Figure 2.1, p.25)

As psychologists, our principal interest amongst cells is in a particular type – the **neuron** – which serves the function of communication and control. Neurons form the basic building blocks of systems that are directly involved with behaviour. The network of all the neurons of the body, together with some closely associated cells, is termed the **nervous system.**

The nervous system will form a principal focus of this chapter and will be discussed further in Section 3.3. We shall be concerned with how variations in the functioning of the nervous system in individual people can be associated with differences in behaviour and the mind (for example, differences in temperament). Before we look at how neurons and nervous systems function, we will consider some broader, fundamental principles of biology.

Neuron
A type of cell that forms part of the nervous system and which is specialized for processing information.

Nervous system
The collection of cells in the body, such as neurons, that handles and processes information.

3.2 Physiology, motivation and behaviour

Through evolution, animals have emerged with physical and behavioural characteristics that maximize their chances of survival and reproduction. Viewed in this context, we can make sense of their behaviour by means of a functional explanation. This relates behaviour to its 'adaptive value' in evolutionary terms. Understanding such principles is essential when we ask – how much of human behaviour can be understood in terms of its evolutionary roots and its adaptive value? For example, it is not obvious how seemingly maladaptive behaviour such as drug-taking can be explained. However, a close look at adaptation provides a valuable context. Consider the following examples of the functions served by different behaviours.

An animal has mechanisms for locating and ingesting nutrients and water. These mechanisms take account of the external availability of food and the internal conditions (sometimes described as 'need states') of the animal. As a result, food tends to be selected at times that are appropriate for survival. Feeding **motivation** is aroused at these times. An animal such as a rat exhibits curiosity; it regularly explores its environment, paying particular attention to any changes. This maximizes its chances of locating sources of food.

Motivation
A tendency to engage in a particular type of behaviour, such as feeding.

Life is something of a juggling act in which humans, like other animals, balance conflicting requirements, such as whether to mate or feed, whether to flee, freeze or attack. Psychologists postulate a series of motivations (e.g. feeding, exploratory and sexual) which compete for expression in behaviour. These depend upon internal and external factors. For instance, energy deficiency increases the strength of feeding motivation. A system of prioritization is assumed to select which motivation is to gain expression. For example, feeding or mating would be interrupted by fear if a predator or potential attacker appears. Mechanisms of aggression and fear exist to protect the animal from danger. Evolution has been assumed to shape such processes in a way that has maximized survival and opportunities for reproduction (McFarland, 1976).

Homeostasis

Think about the psychological importance of maintaining body temperature. Excessive cold or heat occupies your conscious awareness and relentlessly goads you to take corrective action. The body can only function provided that conditions within it remain close to the optimal value, where the body functions best. For example, for a species such as a human, body temperature cannot depart far from 37°C if the individual is to survive. In the same way, neurons can only function within an optimal range of internal temperatures. For a similar example, the human body normally consists of some 69 per cent water, and this level is crucial to survival.

Variables such as temperature and body fluid level exhibit **regulation** (Cabanac and Russek, 1982). If there is a deviation of the value of these variables from the norm, action, described as **control**, is effected. Control of body temperature involves physiological actions such as sweating or shivering and behaviour such as building a shelter or moving into the shade. Control exerted in the interests of body fluid regulation involves changes in thirst motivation and drinking, and urine production.

The processes whereby physiological variables are regulated and corrective action is taken to keep them within close limits is termed **homeostasis** (meaning 'near to standing still'). We speak of 'homeostatic behaviour' such as drinking, feeding and seeking shelter at times of cold exposure. In humans, conscious awareness can be occupied by a negative emotion associated with, say, cold or thirst and thoughts of how to correct it. Correction of deviations from the optimal is usually associated with powerful pleasure, such as that of a person in the desert finding water.

Information from both the internal body and the external world is integrated in determining behaviour. For example, in deciding to feed, the brain is informed of both nutrient levels and the availability of food. The following section looks at some of the bases of this communication.

3.3 Communication and control

How is information communicated within the body and used in determining behaviour and mental states? For example, humans and other animals react to tissue damage by removing themselves from the source of damage. How is such information communicated? How is this behaviour mediated? The present section looks at two biological communication mechanisms: the nervous system and hormones.

Neurons and the nervous system

Neurons are specialized to convey and process information. Neurons come in many shapes and sizes as shown in Figure 4.4. Take note of the two components of the neurons in Figure 4.4 – the **cell body** and a long extension termed a **process**. Groups of neurons combine to form **neural systems** that perform a particular function, such as to arouse the motivation to seek food. Neural systems are of interest to psychologists since their role in a particular behaviour or cognition can sometimes be identified.

Regulation
The maintenance of stable conditions for bodily variables such as temperature.

Control
Action that is exerted in the interests of regulation.

Homeostasis
The tendency of certain parameters of the body to remain nearly constant and action to be taken when they deviate from their normal values.

Cell body
The cell body is the part of a neuron that contains the nucleus, amongst other things.

Process
A part of a neuron, an extension.

Neural system
A combination of neurons that serve a particular role.

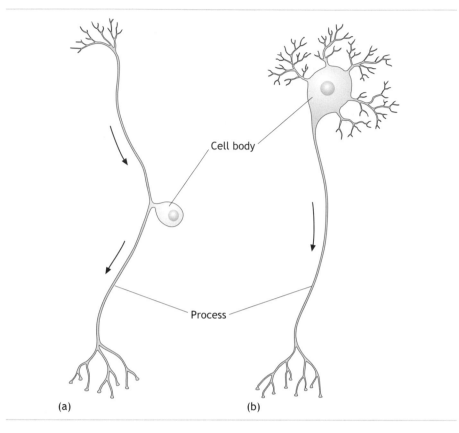

Cell body

Process

(a)   (b)

Figure 4.4   Neurons (a) with the cell body to one side of the main process and (b) with the cell body towards one end of the main process (Source: adapted from Martini *et al.*, 2000, Figure 13-10, p.340)

Spinal cord
A collection of neurons housed within the backbone.

Central nervous system
The brain and spinal cord.

Peripheral nervous system
The part of the nervous system that is outside the brain and spinal cord.

Most neurons are in the brain but, as Figure 4.5 shows, they are also found throughout the body, particularly in the **spinal cord**. The spinal cord is located within the spine and is surrounded by the backbone. It consists of a column of neurons, many of which extend throughout the length of the spinal cord. The brain and spinal cord together constitute the **central nervous system.** The neurons that are outside the central nervous system constitute the **peripheral nervous system**.

Neurons in the brain form the basis of our mental life. We can gain an insight into how they operate by looking at a simple reflex reaction. Figure 4.6(b) illustrates a segment of spinal cord and one role of some neurons located there. If a sharp object comes into contact with the skin of the foot, the tips of a number of neurons located at the skin

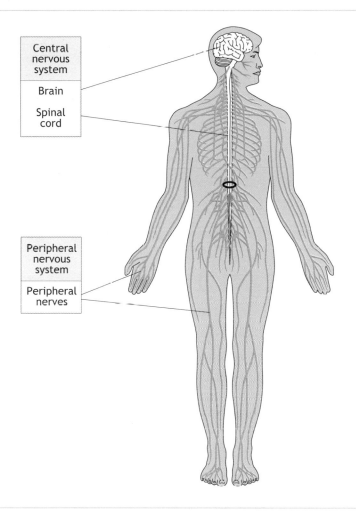

Figure 4.5   The nervous system (Source: adapted from Martini *et al.*, 2000,
Figure 13-1, p.330)

(represented by the single neuron, labelled 1) serve as **detectors** to
this damage. When these neurons are stimulated, as in the case of tissue
damage, an electro-chemical reaction occurs, setting up electrical activity in
these neurons (see Section 4.1 for further discussion). This forms part of
the communication network, with 'messages' transmitted towards the spinal
cord. At the spinal cord, the 'messages' are routed through neurons, such as
those labelled 2, 3 and 4 in Figure 4.6(b), towards muscles which cause the
reflex withdrawal of the foot from the sharp object. Within the spinal cord,
neurons also carry messages on tissue damage up to the brain, where they
contribute to triggering the sensation of pain.

Detector
A neuron or part of a
neuron that is sensitive to
events in the world, such
as touch or tissue
damage.

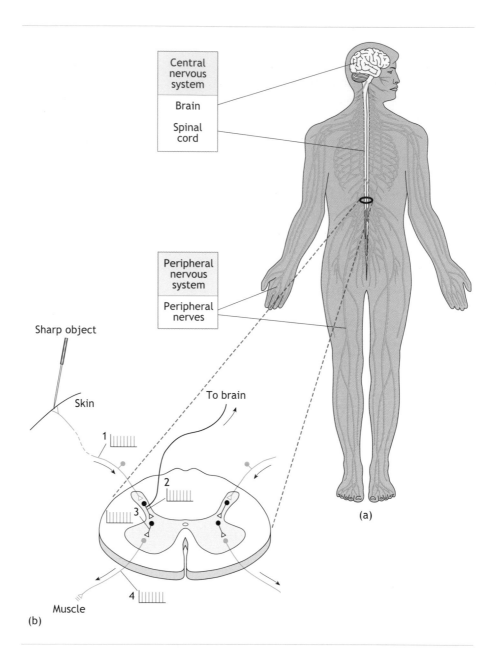

Figure 4.6   The (a) nervous system and (b) a section of spinal cord, showing the neuronal system involved in defence against tissue damage (Source: adapted from Martini *et al.*, 2000, Figure 13-1, p.330 and Toates, 2001, Figure 2.4b, p.25)

Hormones

Hormones are chemicals that exert many effects throughout the body. Some are only of peripheral interest to psychologists and will not be discussed here. However, certain hormones affect the nervous system and therefore have an influence on behaviour and mood. Reciprocally, the activity of the nervous system affects hormones. In this context, hormones are of central relevance to an understanding of the mind, cognition and behaviour.

Hormones are an example of 'chemical messengers'. To illustrate, Figure 4.7 shows how a **hormone** (1) is released into the blood at one site, such as a gland, (2) is transported to another site (termed a 'target'), (3) occupies receptors at the target organ and (4) in occupying them, changes the activity of the target organ (other modes of action of hormones also exist but are less relevant for our purposes).

Hormone
A chemical that is secreted into the blood at one location, is transported in the blood, and effects action at a distant site.

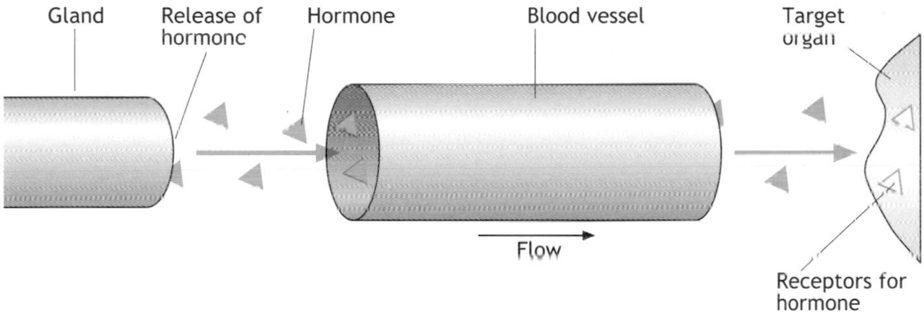

Figure 4.7   Hormones functioning as 'chemical messengers' (note that hormones fit particular receptors)

Hormones are a good example of the kind of dynamic interaction between biology and the social context that was introduced earlier in this chapter (Archer, 1994). Hormones play a role in effecting behaviour but, reciprocally, social context influences hormone levels. For instance, certain hormones increase the tendency of animals, including humans, to exhibit aggression. In non-human primate males, defeat in a competition for dominance can lead to a drop in the levels of the hormone testosterone (Rose, Bernstein and Gordon, 1975). In human males, winning in a competitive activity is associated with a boost in certain hormone levels (Archer, 1994).

So far we have looked at some links between biology and behaviour. In order to understand a number of other aspects of biological processes such as how characteristics can run in families, we now need to turn to the process of reproduction and evolution.

3.4 Reproduction and evolution

Activity 4.2

Stop for a moment and try to recall the principles of evolution discussed in Chapter 2. Think about what these principles require in terms of genetic transmission. For example, consider how it is that certain characteristics run in families. Hair and eye colour are obvious examples, but there is also evidence that temperament might, at least in part, be the outcome of something transmitted by biological means.

In order to understand the process of biological inheritance, it is necessary to look at the cells of the body. Cells, such as skin cells, heart cells and neurons, have a particular feature in common – they contain a component termed a **nucleus**. For a given individual, each cell nucleus contains 46 thread-shaped structures termed **chromosomes**. Each thread carries, what could be termed the unit of inheritance of information, genes (see Section 2 in Chapter 2 for a general discussion of genes). Figure 4.8(a) shows the structure of a generalized cell. Certain cells differ from this standard pattern. Egg ('ovum') cells produced by the female, and sperm cells produced by the male differ from other types of cells since they contain only 23 chromosomes, which are unpaired. These egg cells and sperm cells are collectively called **gametes**. For the sake of simplification, Figure 4.8(a) only shows three pairs of chromosomes and Figure 4.8(b) shows three unpaired chromosomes.

Nucleus
The component of the cell body of a neuron that contains the genetic material.

Chromosome
The structure within which genes are located.

Gamete
A generic term for egg cells of the female and sperm cells of the male.

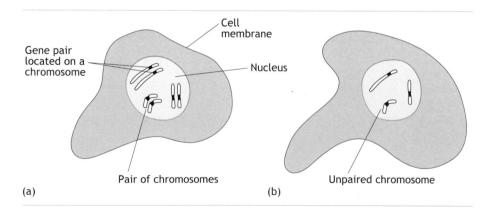

(a)   (b)

Figure 4.8   Cells showing nucleus and genetic material – (a) generalized cell and (b) gamete

The biological means of the inheritance of information from generation to generation relies on the combination of individual chromosomes within sperm cells and ovum cells to make a full set of chromosomes. At conception, two sets of 23 chromosomes, one from the female and one from the male, come together to give a full set of 46 chromosomes (see Figure 4.9). This forms part of what is termed **reproduction**. Each chromosome arising from the male finds its 'match' or 'pair' with a corresponding chromosome arising from the female. The genetic material of the new cell is not an exact replica of either the female or the male; bringing together cells from the female and the male yields a novel combination of genes. However, particular characteristics of each parent can manifest itself in the offspring as a result of genetic transmission.

An egg, once fertilized, has 46 chromosomes and is termed a 'zygote'. Shortly afterwards, the zygote divides into two and each division then grows to a full cell. These two then divide to give four cells and so on, until the new individual is fully developed. Each time a cell divides, the genetic material in its nucleus is copied, so that both cells have the same genetic information as in their precursor cell. This process is termed **replication**.

Reproduction
The coming together of sperm and egg cells and the production of a new individual.

Replication
The process of producing cells from the original precursor cell, the fertilized egg cell.

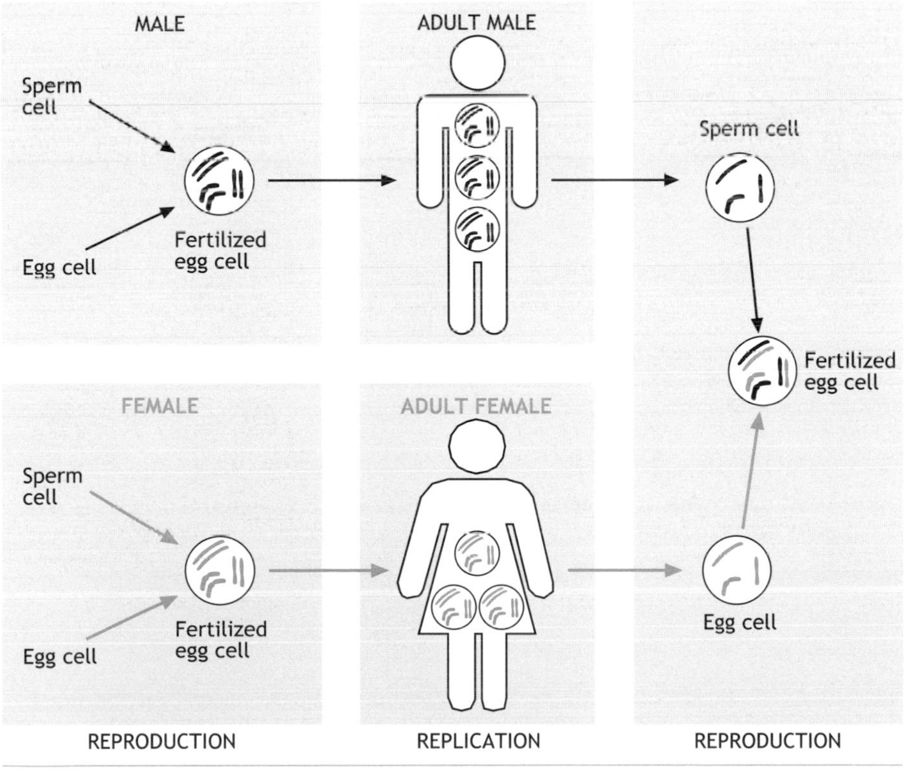

Figure 4.9   A sequence of the processes of replication and reproduction (Source: adapted from Toates, 1998, Figure 2.20, p.45)

Genotype and phenotype

How do *nature* and *nurture* act together in determining our behaviour and our mental life? This section will begin to answer this question.

Together with the environment (in all senses of the word), genes influence the structure and function of the body in terms of factors such as height, hair colour and the structure of the nervous system. In turn, the structure and function of the body influences behaviour.

Genes are responsible for the synthesis of complex chemicals termed proteins, which form an important part of the structure of the body. Differences between individuals in, say, temperament might arise in part from genetic differences, mediated via differences in the structure of the nervous system.

Genotype
The collection of all of the genes within the cell of a given individual.

Within a given individual, each cell contains an identical set of genes (apart from the fact that gametes have only one set). The collection of all the genes within each cell of an individual is termed its **genotype**. The genotype constitutes a source of information, which together with the environment, determines the development and structure of an individual. Genotype is determined at fertilization by the combination of genes that are contributed by the parents and it remains constant throughout life.

Differentiation
The changes that occur within cells during development, such that they come to serve particular roles.

Growth and development do not simply consist of building large numbers of identical cells by division. Rather, from the standard form, cells start the process of **differentiation** to form different types of cells with various functions. The timing and nature of differentiation depends, in part, on the properties of the genes within a given cell (see Section 2 in Chapter 2). At one time, genes were called the 'blueprints' for development, but this term is rightly unpopular these days (Gottlieb, 1998; Richardson, 1998). It suggests a fixed and predetermined course of development checked against coding instructions, which is not how things are. The expressions a 'source of information' for development or an 'influence' on development are more accurate since events in the body are also dependent on the external environment, for instance the availability of nutrients and the effects of behaviour itself on the environment. Gottlieb's model in Figure 4.10(a) demonstrates this concept. It shows the different levels of bi-directional influences on individual development. For example, the growing child effects action on the world by its behaviour, as in smiling at caregivers, and this evokes behaviour in others.

Genes interact with their immediate environment in the body. As illustrated in Figure 4.10(b), in this context 'immediate' means the fluid environment within the cell. Each cell interacts with neighbouring cells and the whole animal interacts with its surroundings. Strictly speaking, as represented in Figure 4.10(b), the genetic material within the cell and the external environment of the animal never come into direct contact in order to interact. The whole animal interacts with its external environment and genes interact with their cellular environment (Johnston, 1987).

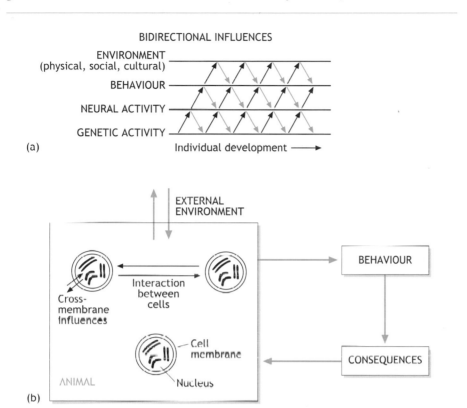

Figure 4.10 Dynamic 'gene environment' interactions underlying development – (a) Gottlieb's model and (b) a more detailed representation (Source: Toates, 2001, Figure 6.2, p.146)

Exposure to different environments, for instance those in which social interactions differ along a dimension of friendly to hostile, can have implications for how the process of development occurs. The actual structure or behaviour that appears as a result of the genotype interacting with the environment is termed the **phenotype**. Features of the phenotype change as a result of experience. For example, muscles strengthen with use and such things as joy, fear and aggression are learned by the consequences of behaviour (see Chapter 3). The genotype might be thought of as a kind of potential for development into a number of different phenotypes, and the end products also depend upon the environment experienced along the way. For reasons described in Chapter 2, some phenotypes will be at an advantage compared to others: they will reproduce more effectively. The genotype that contributed to such a phenotype will therefore tend to increase in frequency in the population, which is the basis of evolution.

Phenotype
The physical structure and behaviour of an animal that arises from the interaction of the genotype and the environment.

Role of genes

From the biology that has been presented so far, some important messages emerge for psychology. Discussions are sometimes couched in such terms as – is some behaviour *caused by* genes or the environment? Is nature *or* nurture the more important in determining a psychological characteristic such as intelligence? The notion of gene-environment interaction discussed above, shows that these are misleading dichotomies. The development of the nervous system and behaviour depends on both genes and the environment, and it is meaningless to refer to their relative importance. It is like asking – what is more important in determining the area of a rectangle, its length or its breadth? Or what is more important in baking bread, the ingredients or the oven?

If two individuals differ in a characteristic, is this due to differences in their genes or their environment? Even this question can be problematic since genetic differences between individuals might predispose them to find different environments. For example, genetically based differences in personality might underlie different tendencies to seek a quiet or noisy environment.

Of course, we cannot do controlled experiments on human genes and the environment in order to determine their relative effects. The complexity of the subject matter makes it difficult to even form theories. However, in the spirit of the earlier discussion, we can look at a simpler system that follows some similar principles and try to derive some insight that can be applied to the more complex example.

Consider Figure 4.11 (Rose, Kamin and Lewontin, 1984). There are two plots of soil, one rich in nutrients and one poor. Suppose that you put your hand into a sack of seeds and take out a handful at random. You put these seeds in the soil to the left, which is the rich soil. You take another handful of seeds at random and put these into the soil to the right of Figure 4.11, which is the poor soil. You keep the conditions, such as illumination, temperature and watering, constant over the two plots.

Rich soil   Poor soil

Figure 4.11 An example of the roles of genes and the environment (Source: adapted from Toates, 2001, Figure 2.15, p.34)

Note the differences between the two plots in the way that the plants grow. The underlying cause of these differences *between* the plants in the two plots would appear to be environmental (i.e. difference in the quality of soil) since there was a random allocation of seeds between the two plots. However, consider the differences among the plants *within* a given plot. Since the environment within a plot is constant, differences between the plants appear to be due to the genetic differences between them.

However, although genetic differences within a plot produce initial differences in plants, the plant itself can change its environment and that of neighbouring plants in the same plot. For example, a tall plant may cut out the light falling on a shorter plant, affecting the growth and development of the shorter plant. Although this shows the subtle complexity of gene–environment determination, this is not to deny the importance of genetic differences. However, the discussion in this section reveals the fallacy of assuming that because the differences within a population (plant or human) are *initially* genetically determined, so necessarily the differences between populations must also be genetically determined.

While the basis of the differences in environment within each plot in Figure 4.11 is genetic, the discussion reveals the danger of neat dichotomies. Human society and the psychological characteristics of its members are subject to even more complications of interpretation regarding the roles of genes and the environment than the plants in Figure 4.11. This will be discussed further in Chapter 5 of this book.

Having set the broad biological scene, the next section will focus on how the nervous system functions and its role in psychological phenomena.

Summary Section 3

- The body is made up of billions of small 'building blocks' termed cells.
- Motivation is said to underlie activities such as feeding and sex. Motivation is determined by a combination of internal and external factors.
- Some important variables such as body temperature are maintained within tight limits by a process termed 'homeostasis'. These variables are regulated. Action, described as control, is taken in the interests of regulation. Behaviour is one type of such action.
- One particular type of cell is the neuron. These cells communicate and process information by means of electrical signals.
- The collection of all the neurons in the body, together with some other cells, constitutes the nervous system.

- The central nervous system is composed of the brain and spinal cord.
- A hormone is a chemical means of communication, released at one location and carried in the blood to another.
- Genes interact with their immediate cellular environment and the whole animal interacts with the external environment.
- Rigid dichotomies in terms of the importance of either genetics or the environment should be avoided.

4   Neurons, neural systems and synapses

This section looks at neurons, how they communicate with other cells and how neural systems perform the roles that we associate with behaviour, the brain and the mind. For ease of explanation, we start by looking at events within individual neurons. By looking at the properties of neurons in the periphery of the body, we are able to gain a better understanding of how neurons operate. However, the principles that emerge are thought to be general ones, equally applicable to the brain. Remember that the activity within neurons underlies behaviour and, in turn, behaviour itself influences the activity of neurons.

4.1 Action potentials

The neuron is a cell specialized to transmit and process information. Look back to Figure 4.6(b) to see an example of this. Imagine a sharp object comes into contact with the tip of neuron 1. In Section 3.3 of this chapter, the reaction was described as 'setting up activity' in neuron 1. What does it mean to say that a neuron is 'active'?

If you were to take a very fine wire and spear an individual neuron, you would find that there is a small electrical voltage across the cell wall. In other words, the inside and outside are like two terminals of a miniature battery and a neuron has an electrical voltage or 'polarity'. If you did nothing else to disturb the neuron, you might well observe that it simply rests at this voltage indefinitely. Figure 4.12 shows the voltage of a neuron at rest. If a noxious stimulus contacts the tip of this neuron, you would observe a sudden and dramatic change in the electrical activity of the neuron. This change from the resting value and the return to it is termed an **action potential.**

Action potential
A brief and sudden change in electrical voltage in a cell and the means by which information is transmitted by neurons.

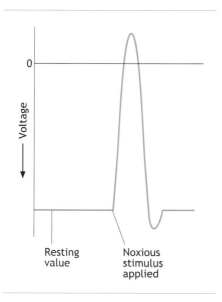

Figure 4.12 Electrical activity of a neuron

A property of an action potential is that once initiated, it travels down the length of the neuron. Figure 4.13 shows the 'propagation' of an action potential. Suppose that the stimulus is applied and the reaction of the neuron observed. As a frame of reference, let us call the time that the action potential arises at the tip, 'time zero' (t_0). A fraction of a second later, at t_1, the action potential is observed at location A. By t_2, it will have reached location B and by t_3 will be at the spinal cord. Action potentials travel rapidly, as evidenced by your speed of reaction to tissue damage.

The neuron shown in Figure 4.13, as well as neuron 1 in Figure 4.6(b), are examples of a class of neuron termed **sensory neurons.** These

Sensory neuron
A type of neuron that is specialized to detect information and convey it to the central nervous system.

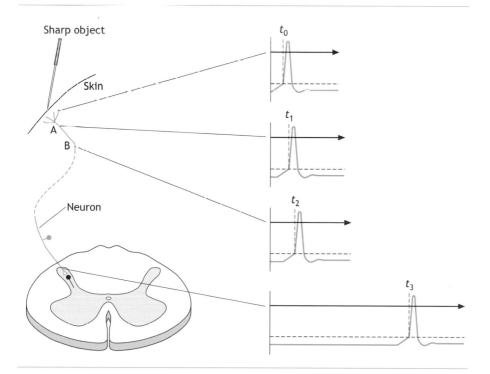

Figure 4.13 Transmission of an action potential (Source: adapted from Toates, 2001, Figure 4.9, p.87)

neurons are responsible for detecting events such as tissue damage or harmless tactile stimulation, and conveying information about the event to the central nervous system.

With reference to Figure 4.6(b), when the action potential reaches the end of neuron 1, it comes to an end. However, it can instigate events such that neuron 2 produces another action potential, which travels its length. In turn, this triggers an action potential in neuron 3. Finally, neuron 4 is activated. The existence of an action potential in neuron 4 excites the muscle. When it is excited, the muscle contracts and the limb is removed from the offending object. Neurons such as neuron 4, which trigger muscles, are members of the class termed **motor neurons**, the effectors of action.

Normally, tissue damage would not be expected to trigger just a single action potential in one neuron. Rather, it would trigger a series of them in a group of neurons. Sometime after one action potential has come to an end, another can be initiated. In other words, information is conveyed according to the frequency of action potentials in a neuron, each action potential being just like another.

Figure 4.14 illustrates how information can be conveyed by the frequency with which action potentials occur in a given neuron. There are neurons, termed 'cold neurons', with tips in the fingers and which are specifically

Motor neuron
A type of neuron that is specialized to convey information from the central nervous system to muscles.

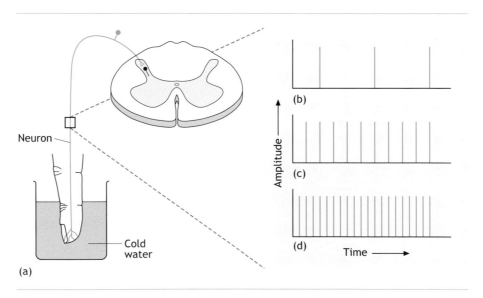

(a)

Figure 4.14 Encoding in terms of action potential frequency – (a) finger placed in cold water and sensory neuron sensitive to cold, (b) moderate cold encoded by a low frequency of action potentials, (c) lower temperature encoded by an increase in frequency of action potentials and (d) still colder temperature encoded by high frequency of action potentials (Source: Toates, 1998, Figure 2.6, p.32)

sensitive to cold. As the temperature of the tips of the neurons decreases, the frequency of action potentials in these cold neurons increases as shown in the three graphs in Figure 4.14. The message arriving at the spinal cord and subsequently conveyed to the brain concerns information on temperature encoded in terms of frequency of action potentials.

4.2 The synapse

Turn back to Figure 4.6(b) and look at the junction between two cells. How does activity in a neuron influence another cell? If you look carefully at Figure 4.6(b), you can see a minute gap between the cells. How is this gap bridged?

Figure 4.15 shows an enlargement of the junction between two neurons, termed a **synapse**. The principle of the organization of a synapse is a general one, whether it is in the brain or periphery. Synapses within the brain are of crucial importance for understanding our mental well-being and illness, since they can malfunction. An abnormality in a number of such synapses is thought to lie at the root of much psychological disorder, such as a disturbance of mood.

The principle under consideration in this section is how synapses operate. Look at Figure 4.15. You might like to imagine the neuron on the left to be neuron 1 of Figure 4.6(b) and that on the right to be neuron 2. With reference to the synapse, neuron 1 would be termed a 'presynaptic neuron' and neuron 2 a 'postsynaptic neuron', as shown in Figure 4.15.

Synapse
The junction between a neuron and another cell.

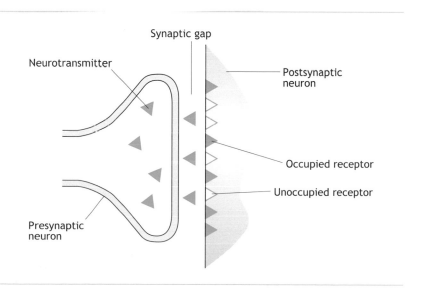

Figure 4.15 A synapse between a neuron and a second cell (Source: Toates, 2001, Figure 2.6, p.27)

Neurotransmitter
A chemical that is released from a neuron and influences a neighbouring cell.

Note the chemical transmitter substance ('messenger'), termed a **neurotransmitter**, stored at the terminal of the presynaptic neuron and the receptors for this chemical located on the surface of the postsynaptic neuron.

When an action potential arrives at the terminal of the presynaptic neuron, it releases neurotransmitters, which move quickly across the synaptic gap and occupy the receptors on the postsynaptic neuron. When this occurs, the electrical property of the postsynaptic neuron is altered. Thus, although the communication *within* a neuron is by electrical means, communication *between* the neurons occurs through chemical means (as shown in Figure 4.15).

Excitation
The effect that a neuron has on a neighbouring cell such that the second cell is more likely to exhibit action potentials.

The change caused by chemicals at a synapse can consist of **excitation** of the second neuron. This refers to either the appearance of action potentials in a neuron at rest, or an increase in activity to above its existing level for a neuron that is already active.

But, as Figure 4.16 shows, excitation is not the only effect that a neurotransmitter can have. Depending on the nature of the substance and the receptors that it occupies at the second cell, a neurotransmitter can exert **inhibition**. This means a suppression of activity. A given synapse can either be excitatory or inhibitory (but not both).

Inhibition
The effect that a neuron has on a neighbouring cell such that the second cell is less likely to exhibit action potentials.

At a psychological level it is not difficult to find examples of inhibition, captured by expressions such as 'a person is too inhibited to ask a question' or 'my inhibitions stood in the way'. How might such examples relate to the brain? In the absence of hard evidence, you should always

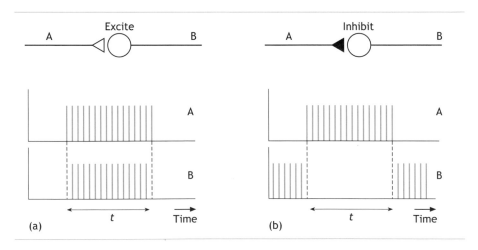

Figure 4.16   (a) Activity in neuron A excites activity in neuron B, and (b) activity in neuron A inhibits any activity that might otherwise exist in neuron B (some neurons, such as B in this case, are spontaneously active) (Source: adapted from Toates, 2001, Figure 3.1, p.53)

be cautious when speculating about the link between psychological events and brain processes. However, we know that the activity of neurons at one site in the nervous system can be inhibited by the activity of neurons at another site. For example, within one region of the brain, there might be the physical embodiment of the psychological experience of restraint exerted on behaviour, based upon rational calculation. This brain region might then exert inhibition on tendencies to aggression.

Figure 4.17 shows two synapses side-by-side. The specificity of the shape of the neurotransmitter and receptor, analogous to a key (neurotransmitter) fitting a lock (receptor), means that if a neurotransmitter from one synapse wafts across to another, it is without effect since it cannot engage with the receptors of the 'foreign' cell.

Neurons are characterized by the type of neurotransmitter that they store and release. For example, a neuron that stores and releases the neurotransmitter serotonin is described as 'serotonergic'. Imagine neuron 1 to be serotonergic in Figure 4.17. For the synapse between neuron 1 and 2 to be termed serotonergic, there would need to be a site for the release of serotonin from one cell and the next cell would need to have receptors for serotonin on the cell membrane.

Mental illnesses such as schizophrenia appear to be associated with abnormalities within certain types of neurotransmitter at particular regions of the brain. In schizophrenia, some parts of the brain are abnormally active and the person's attention is drawn to stimuli that would otherwise be ignored. Therapy can consist of chemical intervention to try to correct such abnormalities, such as reducing the overactivity in some parts of the brain.

The next section is designed to exemplify how neurons can combine to form neural systems serving a particular role.

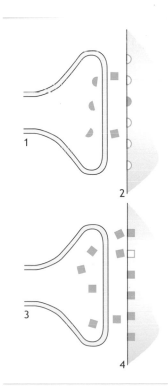

Figure 4.17 Two synapses employing different neurotransmitters – neuron 1 employs neurotransmitters that fit receptors on neuron 2 and neuron 3 employs neurotransmitters that fit receptors on neuron 4, but not on neuron 2 (Source: adapted from Toates, 2001, Figure 4.22, p.96)

4.3 Sensory detection and transmission – the visual system

How do we see the world around us? Most people see a world of colours, but those who are colour blind appear to see the world only in shades of grey. What is the difference between these two groups of people? Where does the difference lie – in the eyes or the brain? In understanding perception, we need to know what kind of information is sent from the eye to the brain. For example, how is the information coded to enable us to see colours? Our visual perception of the world has long been of interest to psychologists.

A knowledge of how the neurons in the visual system work is vital to understanding perception. Figure 4.18 shows a cross-section of the eye and a section through the retina. At the back of the eye on the retina, there is a mosaic of **receptor cells** which are sensitive to light. These cells are termed **rods** and **cones**. Like the cells described earlier in this chapter,

Receptor cell
A cell specialized to detect, for example, light.

Rod
A type of receptor cell specialized to detect light.

Cone
A type of receptor cell specialized to detect light.

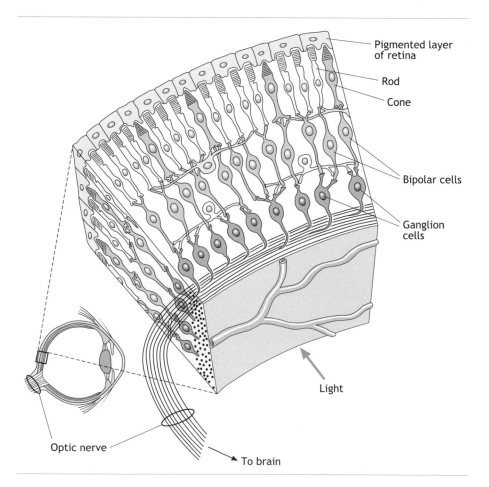

Figure 4.18 Cross-section of the eye and retina (Source: adapted from Martini *et al.*, 2000, Figure 18-22(a), p.690)

rods and cones also exhibit a small electrical voltage. When light falls on them, they change their electrical state: they are disturbed from their resting value. This change in electrical state is signalled to other cells (termed bipolar cells) within the retina, with which they form synapses. The bipolar cells then convey the signal to a third layer of cells in the retina, termed **ganglion cells**.

As shown in Figure 4.18, although ganglion cells are located partly within the retina, they have long processes that extend to the brain. An individual ganglion cell is something like the neuron shown in Figure 4.4(b). The bundle consisting of all these processes of ganglion cells leaving an eye is termed the **optic nerve**. A **nerve** is the collection of a number of processes of neurons forming a bundle, something like a cable, in the peripheral nervous system.

Receptive fields

Information is transmitted from the retina in the form of activity within the ganglion cells that constitute the optic nerve. There are many more receptors than there are ganglion cells and so, on average, a large number of receptors converge, through bipolar cells, to a given ganglion cell. This degree of convergence varies over the retina. For the region of retina shown in Figure 4.18, there is a low degree of convergence. What effect do receptors have on a given ganglion cell? In answering such questions on sensory systems, investigators often employ the expression **receptive field**.

A neuron within a sensory system can be characterized by its receptive field. As a general definition, the receptive field of a neuron is the area of sensory surface which, when stimulated, influences the activity of the neuron under investigation. For example, a particular type of sensory neuron (shown in Figure 4.13 and discussed in Section 4.1) has a receptive field at a particular point on the skin corresponding to its tip. Stimulation within this area excites the neuron. How do researchers establish what is the receptive field of a ganglion cell in the visual system?

Ganglion cell
A type of cell in the visual system, part of the route conveying information from receptors in the eye to the brain.

Optic nerve
The collection of neurons that convey information from the eye to the brain.

Nerve
A collection of neurons in the peripheral nervous system, rather like a cable made of a number of electrical wires

Receptive field
The part of a sensory surface, such as the retina of the eye, which when stimulated influences a neuron under investigation.

4.1 FEATURED METHOD

Invasive techniques: single unit recording

Technology has played a crucial role in understanding the brain and it has enabled researchers to relate brain activity to behaviour. For example, scientists are now able to gain a better understanding of the nervous system by looking at the activity of single neurons, in terms of their frequency of generating action potentials. In this way, the role an individual neuron plays in behaviour can sometimes be identified. Some of the techniques used in this type of research are described as 'invasive', in that it is necessary to 'invade' the nervous system with a piece of technology. Not surprisingly, the use of such techniques provokes controversy, and raises ethical issues.

Figure 4.19 shows the experimental apparatus and the subject in an invasive technique used to measure the receptive field of a retinal ganglion cell. An anaesthetized cat's head is held in position, pointing at a screen. A very fine microelectrode is implanted in a single ganglion cell in the optic nerve of the cat. The tip of the microelectrode detects the activity of a single ganglion cell. When the cell's activity is recorded while the eye is in complete darkness, a spontaneous activity level can be observed in the ganglion cell. By applying light stimuli to the retina the frequency of activity of the neurons in the visual system can be observed. This enables us to develop an understanding of the function of particular neurons in perception and allows us to describe the receptive field of a neuron.

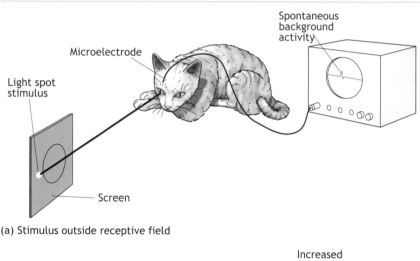

(a) Stimulus outside receptive field

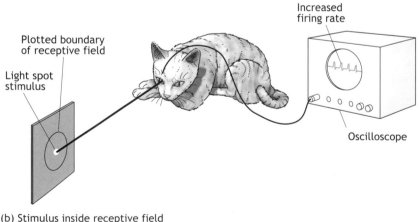

(b) Stimulus inside receptive field

Figure 4.19 Measuring the receptive field of a retinal ganglion cell – (a) light spot outside receptive field and (b) light spot within excitatory region of receptive field (Source: adapted from Greene, 1990)

As shown in Figure 4.19, the screen is explored with a small spot of light. Since the cat's head is held still, there is a one-to-one relation between the screen and the retina, so the scientist can map between them. The activity of the ganglion cell is observed as the spot of light is projected to different sites on the retina. In Figure 4.19(a), note the activity shown on the screen of the recording apparatus called an oscilloscope. Since the light spot is outside the receptive field, there is no change in activity from the spontaneous background level. In Figure 4.19(b) the light spot falls within the receptive field and the activity of the ganglion cell is recorded on the oscilloscope.

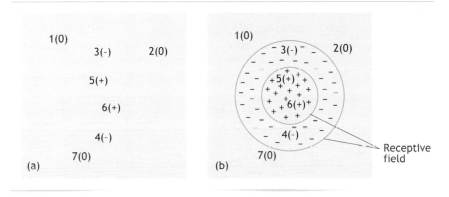

Figure 4.20 Defining a receptive field – (a) points plotted and (b) joining points together (Source: Toates, 1998, Figure 4.15, p.112)

Take a look at Figure 4.20(a). Suppose that first, the spot falls on location 1 on the screen. There is no change in frequency of action potentials recorded from the ganglion cell compared to darkness. By definition, location 1 is outside the receptive field of this ganglion cell so a zero (0) is placed at this location. Light falling at location 2 also has no effect and so similarly a zero is placed there. At location 3, the cell reduces its frequency of action potentials relative to the spontaneous level (darkness). Since it influences the activity of the ganglion cell, light falling here is, by definition, within its receptive field. Since the ganglion cell's activity is inhibited (i.e. a lower frequency of action potentials), the light is within the inhibitory region of the receptive field. Therefore, a minus sign is placed at 3. Similarly location 4 is within the inhibitory region. Imagine that when light is projected to location 5, the ganglion cell exhibits an increase in action potential frequency compared to darkness. Therefore, location 5 is within the excitatory region of the receptive field and a plus sign is placed at 5. The same effect is found at 6. Location 7 is outside the receptive field.

Suppose that we have completed an exploration of the entire retina, while recording from a given ganglion cell. Typically, if we join together all the pluses and join together all the minuses, what might emerge is shown in Figure 4.20(b) and Figure 4.21. This defines the receptive field of the ganglion cell. It consists of an excitatory centre (also termed an ON region) and an inhibitory surround (also termed an OFF region). A common type of receptive field consists of a

Centre-surround
A type of receptive field of ganglion cells in the visual system, such that light falling on the centre of the receptive field excites the cell and light falling on the surround inhibits it.

centre region which is excitatory, and a surround which is inhibitory. This is an example of **centre-surround** organization (Hubel and Wiesel, 1959; Livingstone and Hubel, 1988).

If the brain detects that the cell is exhibiting action potentials at a frequency higher than the spontaneous level, this is evidence for light within the excitatory centre region. This might be a distant star which floods just the centre region with light, while darkness

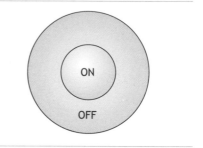

Figure 4.21 Receptive field of a retinal ganglion cell

corresponds to the outer region as shown in Figure 4.22(a). Conversely, if the ganglion cell's activity is suppressed to below the spontaneous level, this signals light falling in the outer, inhibitory region, as in Figure 4.22(b). What sort of stimulus might cause this reaction? A polo mint against a dark background and at a certain distance is one possibility. Figure 4.22(c) demonstrates that light covering the entire receptive field has little or no effect on the cell.

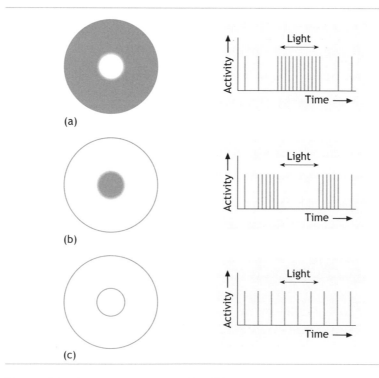

(a)

(b)

(c)

Figure 4.22 Response properties of an ON-centre − OFF-surround ganglion cell (a) to light in centre, (b) to light in surround and (c) to light covering all of the receptive field (Source: Toates, 1998, Figure 4.17, p.113)

4.4 Behaviour and mood – manipulations at the synapse

An assumption within biological psychology is that all features of our psychological life, such as our motivations, moods and emotions, have as their biological bases the activity of neuronal systems in the brain. For example, emotion alters as patterns of activity within particular neural systems change. Changes in the activity of synapses can cause changes in neural systems, which in turn affects behaviour, cognition and mood. Such changes can occur under certain circumstances:

(a) Disease can disrupt chemical transmission, as in the failure to produce a certain neurotransmitter. For example, Parkinson's disease is associated with difficulty in the instigation of action and motor control, and is caused by a loss of dopaminergic neurons (i.e. those that employ the neurochemical, dopamine) and a reduction in activity of those that remain.

(b) Drugs given on prescription (e.g. Prozac for obsessional neurosis and depression) target specific types of synapse, leading to a change in activity in certain parts of the brain, temporarily altering information processing by the brain. For example, a set of neurons whose activity forms part of the basis of fear, might show lowered activity as a result of the chemical manipulation.

(c) Drugs such as nicotine, alcohol, heroin and cocaine exert their effects by altering the activity of synapses in the central nervous system. Changes that occur at the level of synapses alter information processing, e.g. after drinking alcohol, a previously feared task is not ranked as so fearful.

Where a type of synapse shows malfunction, logic would suggest the possibility of chemical therapy; for example to supply an artificial form of the neurotransmitter employed there. When a neurotransmitter is released, it moves across the gap between neurons and is taken up by receptors before being inactivated. One means of inactivation is by a type of chemical termed an **enzyme** that is present at the synapse. If the enzyme itself is artificially inactivated then the neurotransmitter remains for longer at the synapse. Another process is shown in Figure 4.23. In the case of serotonergic synapses, inactivation of a neurotransmitter is caused by serotonin being taken back into the neuron from which it was released, a process termed **reuptake**. One way to artificially boost the activity at such synapses is to block reuptake, which increases the amount of neurotransmitter at the synapse and its activity at receptors. In Figure 4.23(b), the mood altering drug Prozac, targets serotonergic synapses and blocks reuptake. Serotonergic neurons appear to play a role in attention and mood, amongst other things.

Enzyme
A chemical that has an influence on another chemical.

Reuptake
The process of inactivation of a neurotransmitter by taking it back into the same neuron that released it.

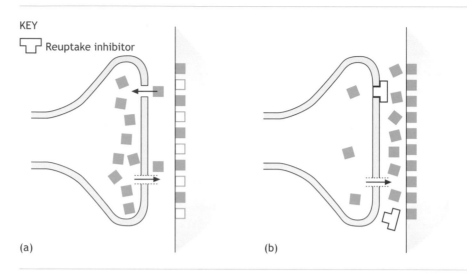

KEY

⊔ Reuptake inhibitor

(a)   (b)

Figure 4.23 Serotonergic synapse – (a) normal and (b) influence of Prozac (Source: adapted from Toates, 2001, Figure 4.27, p.99)

The drug cocaine acts at synapses. Amongst other effects, it blocks the reuptake of dopamine and thereby increases the amount of dopamine at synapses. Users of the drug describe the experience of its effect as euphoria or a 'high', implying that neural systems underlying pleasure have been affected by the changed activity at synapses.

However, since cocaine drastically and rapidly blocks the reuptake of dopamine, there is a net release over a period of time which is not compensated for by reuptake. Therefore, synthesis of dopamine within neurons cannot keep pace with the rate of removal and this results in depletion of dopamine from neurons. This then changes the activity within neural circuits to give a bias towards displeasure, which appears to be the biological basis of the 'crash' or 'down' (**dysphoria**) that follows cocaine taking. This state seems to contribute to the craving for more cocaine in an attempt to correct the displeasure.

The approach adopted here shows a useful aspect of the process of explaining psychological states by looking at biology. States such as euphoria and dysphoria can be associated with particular changes at a biological level. Drugs affect synapses that form part of neural systems involved in cognition, emotion, motivation and pleasure. However, drug-induced changes at synapses only make sense when interpreted in terms of the whole nervous system and conscious awareness. There is by no means a simple one-to-one link between a drug and the mental state of an individual. Antidepressants do not work for everyone. Psychoactive drugs such as heroin and cannabis often require repeated use and an appropriate social context to reveal and 'interpret' their effects. For experienced users, a totally inert chemical can sometimes create a similar effect to a specific drug if it is taken in anticipation

Dysphoria
A negative mood.

of the actual drug. For example, addicts who unwittingly take substances of no chemical potency often report psychoactive effects from using them.

There is an important psychological effect associated with the powerful pain-killing drug morphine. Morphine targets neurons in the central nervous system that are involved with pain. Some patients who expect to be given morphine sometimes feel pain relief simply on being injected with an inert substance, an effect termed a **placebo effect** (Wall, 1993). The link between these actions is an area of interest to biological psychologists.

Placebo effect
An effect obtained by an apparently neutral procedure, which owes its efficacy to a belief by the patient that a therapeutic intervention has taken place.

Summary Section 4

- Pulses of electricity termed 'action potentials' convey information within neurons.
- Sensory neurons convey information to the central nervous system and motor neurons convey information from it.
- Information is conveyed in terms of the frequency with which action potentials occur.
- A synapse is the point at which a neuron influences another cell. At a synapse, neurotransmitter is released from one neuron, crosses a junction and influences another cell. A neuron is characterized by the chemical that it synthesizes, stores and releases.
- Neurons can exert either excitatory or inhibitory effects, a given neuron exerting only one such effect.
- The retina is covered by a mosaic of light-sensitive cells termed rods and cones. Information on light detected at the retina is conveyed to the brain.
- Drugs can change the activity of synapses, for example by blocking the reuptake of a particular neurochemical.

5　The nervous system, cognition and behaviour

So far, a major part of the discussion has concerned the properties of neurons and how they combine to form neural systems. Implicit within the account was the notion that neurons are contained within the nervous system. This section looks at the whole nervous system, mainly the brain, and considers (a) how it can be described scientifically and (b) how its capacity to process information, the factor of most interest to psychologists, can be understood in terms of the systems of neurons that comprise it.

When we consider that the human brain has some 100 billion neurons with multiple connections between them, awe might seem the appropriate reaction. Can we gain an insight into how something so complex works and how it underlies cognition, the control of behaviour and consciousness? How do the properties of the whole depend upon the component cells? Looking at the systems of neurons that constitute the brain has provided a powerful means of insight. Our understanding still leaves much to be desired but there are various sources of information, such as study of the structure of the brain, carefully describing what is seen and looking at changes in behaviour that follow brain damage. Our starting point here will be with a reliable description of the brain.

5.1 Anatomical description

Hemisphere
One half of the upper part of the brain.

The brain is approximately symmetrical across its midline, something which you can appreciate in terms of its outward appearance. We therefore speak of left and right **hemispheres**. These terms are used with respect to the perspective of the individual whose brain is under discussion. In Figure 4.24, the left hemisphere is to your right.

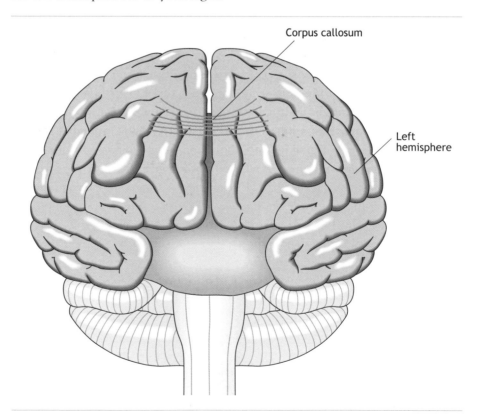

Corpus callosum

Left hemisphere

Figure 4.24 Anterior view of the human brain (Source: adapted from Martini *et al.*, 2000, Figure 15-10(b), p.391)

In Figure 4.24, note the outer appearance of the brain, formed by a creased structure, giving it the appearance of a walnut. This outer layer is termed the **cerebral cortex**. As shown in Figure 4.25, the brain is divided into a number of regions known as 'lobes': the temporal, occipital, parietal and frontal lobes. These lobes are known to serve different functions. For example, the occipital lobe is concerned with processing visual information and the temporal lobe is involved in, amongst other things, language.

Cerebral cortex
The outer layer of the brain.

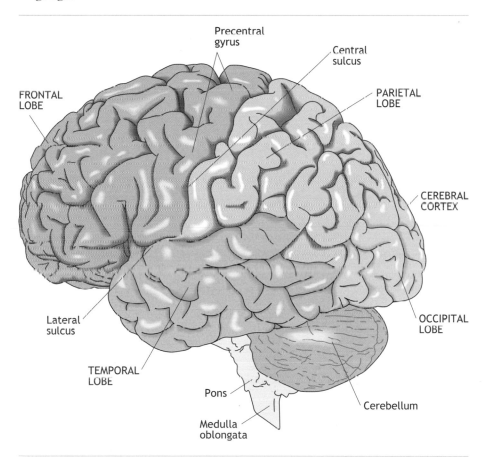

Figure 4.25   A view of the left hemisphere of the human brain (Source: adapted from Martini *et al.*, 2000, Figure 15-9(a), p.395)

The visual system

Figure 4.18 showed the retina and the ganglion cells that project information from the eye to the brain. This section briefly relates an understanding at the level of individual neurons to their location in the brain.

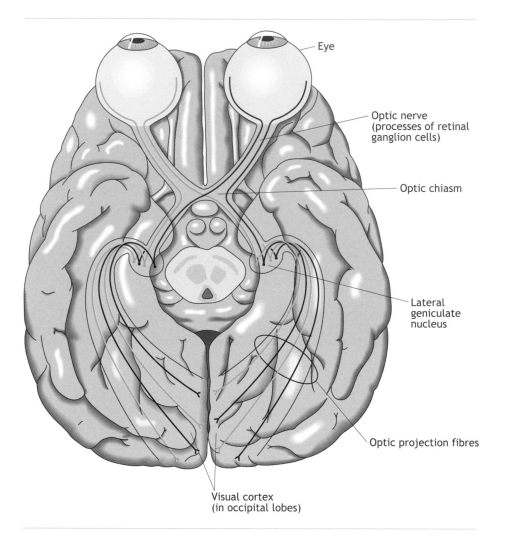

Figure 4.26 The visual system (Source: adapted from Martini *et al.*, 2000, Figure 15-23, p.407)

As represented in Figure 4.26, the processes of ganglion cells (forming the optic nerve) terminate at the brain structure known as the **lateral geniculate nucleus** (LGN). Anatomists have devised a very rich vocabulary for describing the brain. Let's dissect the expression 'lateral geniculate nucleus'. The term 'nucleus' is used with reference to sites throughout the brain and refers to a collection of the cell bodies of neurons at a particular location. The expression 'lateral' refers to a given location being away from the midline of the brain relative to another location (see Figure 4.27). By comparison, the medial geniculate nucleus (which, incidentally, processes auditory information from the ears) is nearer to the centre of the brain. Finally, the term 'geniculate', derives from the Latin name for knee, which is genu. Early anatomists felt that the LGN looked something like a knee.

Lateral geniculate nucleus
A part of the visual system that is a collection of cell bodies of neurons.

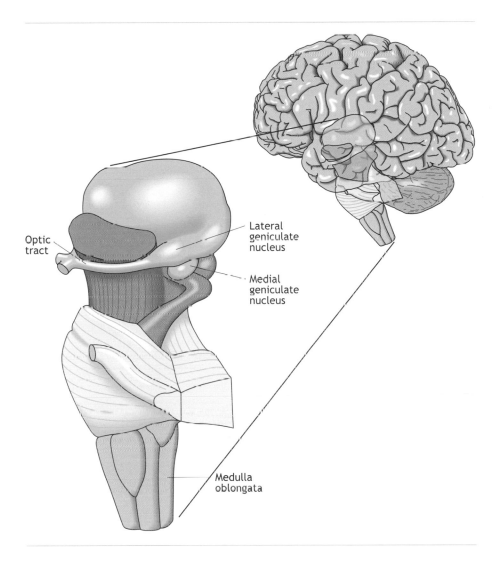

Optic tract

Lateral geniculate nucleus

Medial geniculate nucleus

Medulla oblongata

Figure 4.27 View of the lower part of the brain with a focus on the lateral geniculate nucleus and medial geniculate nucleus (Source: adapted from Martini et *al.*, 2000, Figure 15-16(a), p.400)

The neurons whose cell bodies are located in the LGN project processes to the visual cortex (see Figure 4.26), located at the occipital lobe, where further analysis of the visual world is performed.

5.2 Physiology and behaviour: sources of insight

This section examines some of the techniques used to investigate how the brain works and how its activity links with psychological phenomena.

Human brain surgery and electrical stimulation

In some cases, surgery has to be performed on the human brain, for example, to remove cancerous tissue. The behaviour of patients (e.g. performance on memory tasks) can then be compared before and after surgery. One particularly interesting surgical intervention for severe epilepsy was pioneered by Roger Sperry and his associates in California (Sperry, 1969). The basis of epilepsy is chaotic electrical activity amongst the neurons found in a particular part of the brain.

Corpus callosum
A bundle of processes of neurons which connect one hemisphere with another.

The two halves of the brain communicate through several routes, a principal one being the **corpus callosum**. Figure 4.28 shows a section through the midline of the brain, a slice through the corpus callosum.

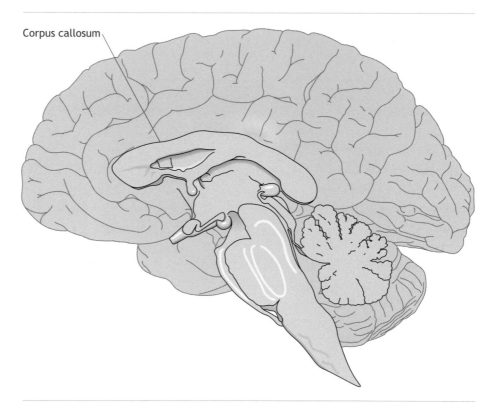

Corpus callosum

Figure 4.28 A view of the right half of the brain following a section of the brain through its midline (Source: adapted from Martini *et al.*, 2000, Figure 15-13(a), p.395)

Communication between the hemispheres is needed to integrate information throughout the brain. Unfortunately, epilepsy focused in one half of the brain also tends to influence the other half electrically, acting via the corpus callosum. The radical and daring surgery by Sperry consisted of cutting through the corpus callosum. The surgery did indeed restrain the epilepsy but what effect did it have on the rest of the mental and physical life of the individual? After the operation, the patients' epilepsy was much improved, but otherwise they appeared to be remarkably unchanged in their everyday behaviour, relative to that shown prior to surgery.

The surgery did however have some consequences. By targeting visual information to only one hemisphere, experimenters found a way of training the individuals on one task using just one hemisphere. On testing them, it was found that this learning was unavailable to the other hemisphere. One bit of information can be selectively presented to one hemisphere and different information to another. Each hemisphere could assimilate conflicting pieces of information. For example, a green light on a button would signal reward as far as the left hemisphere was concerned (and a red light would signal an absence of reward), but this information would be unavailable to the right hemisphere. Indeed, as far as the right hemisphere was concerned, a red light could be used to signal reward. On being set such tasks, patients were sometimes in conflict as to what to do, though whether their consciousness had been split remains a formidable problem.

Brain surgery can be performed on conscious humans since cutting the tissues of the brain does not evoke pain (there are no tips of neurons sensitive to tissue damage in the brain). In a classic study by Penfield and Rasmussen (1968), humans undergoing brain surgery for the removal of diseased tissue received electrical stimulation to different regions of their brains. Patients were asked to give reports on the conscious sensations evoked. For example, electrical stimulation of regions of the temporal lobe evoked vivid memories of incidents earlier in life. Such evidence enables theories on the biological bases of memory to be produced (and we will return to these in more detail in Chapter 8).

In some cases, for patients in chronic pain, electrodes are permanently implanted with their tips in regions associated with emotion. Patients can control stimulation of these electrodes and a decrease of pain is sometimes experienced. It is assumed that the stimulation alters the pattern of electrical activity within certain neural systems. It increases the electrical activity in neural systems associated with positive emotions and reduces activity in those associated with pain.

Accidental brain damage

One major source of evidence on the relationship between brain and behaviour has been the study of damage to the brain, for example caused by gunshot wounds or tumours. Another cause of damage is the blocking of a blood vessel within the brain or the breaking of a vessel (known as a 'stroke'), which results in a loss of the supply of fuel and oxygen to a part of the brain. Neurons in the location of the damage die and so any changes in behaviour suggest the contribution these regions usually make to normal functioning. A general term for damage to a region is **lesion**.

Lesion
Damage to a region of the brain, for example in an accident or in surgery.

There have been some famous cases of lesions that have illuminated brain and behavioural science, none more so than that of an unfortunate man named Phineas Gage (see Box 4.2).

4.2 *Accidental brain lesion*

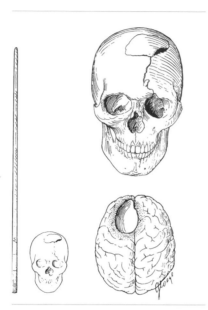

Figure 4.29 The accident of Phineas Gage (left, tamping iron and skull drawn to scale; top right, the skull; bottom right, the brain showing damage to the left frontal lobe)

Phineas Gage was employed as foreman of a gang of railroad workers, who were constructing a new railway line in Vermont in 1848. This involved using explosives to blast rocks out of the way for the line. One day an explosion went wrong and a tamping iron, 3 cm in diameter, passed right through his brain. Amazingly Gage survived the accident. However, the missile caused extensive damage to his left frontal lobe and some damage to his right frontal lobe (Macmillan, 1986; Damasio, 1996). Damage was particularly to the front part of the frontal lobe, termed the prefrontal lobe.

Gage subsequently showed little in the way of intellectual or linguistic impairment. However, marked changes were noted in his personality. Quite out of character, he became obstinate, egocentric and capricious and started to use foul language. Reconsidering Gage in the light of more recent evidence on the role of the frontal lobes, suggests that the parts of the brain concerned with emotional expression were previously held in check by the frontal lobes. This source of inhibition was disrupted by the damage.

Psychologists can also look at the circumstances under which the prefrontal cortex is most active in 'normal' participants. This method enables psychologists to construct theories on what this region does. The prefrontal cortex plays a role in, amongst other things, utilizing memories in the inhibition of behaviour, often in the face of competing tendencies to react to immediately present events. Following the accident, Gage showed a defect in his capacity to utilize emotional information concerning the more remote consequences of his actions (Damasio, 1996). Gage appeared to be emotionally in the 'here-and now', a victim of impulsivity.

A problem with basing our understanding of the brain on accidents is that they are 'one-off', uncontrolled phenomena. Damage is rarely to neat, circumscribed parts of the brain, and usually affects several areas simultaneously. Under ideal experimental conditions, scientists would employ a matched control group to analyse results and develop theories. In the case of human brain damage, there is no matched control group against which to compare the damaged brain.

There are additional difficulties in interpreting results when studying brain damage. For example, depending on the circumstances, other brain regions can take over some responsibility from the damaged region. The system might be fundamentally reorganized, and psychological function can be less disturbed than one might have first supposed. At a neural level, new communications between neurons can be formed. In some cases, such a process can offer hope to people suffering from brain damage.

If a part of the brain is damaged such that it is taken out of action, behaviour changes as a result. Strictly speaking, the working of the rest of the brain is revealed by the damage, and not the contribution or the role of the damaged part itself. An analogy can help to illustrate the problem (Gregory, 1966). Suppose that after removing a component from a radio, it emits a deafening howl. No one would assume that the normal function of the missing component is to suppress howling. When applied to interpreting the effects of brain damage, this analogy should encourage caution, but it does not negate the value of such evidence.

Experimental lesions

In a controversial approach, applied to non-human animals, scientists have damaged selected parts of the brain to investigate what effect, if any, this has on the brain. In what is termed the 'experimental group', clearly defined parts of the brain have been lesioned and the effect observed. A 'control group' of the same sex and age receives what are termed 'sham lesions' and the results compared for the two groups. Sham lesions consist of control animals being subject to some of the same surgical procedure as the experimental group, such as anaesthesia and cutting the skin, but the brain itself is not lesioned. The animals are killed and the brain of the subjects in the experimental group can be analysed to confirm the exact site of the lesion.

Stop and consider the ethics of performing such experiments on animals. Is it justified to inflict damage to an animal's brain if there is the possibility of gaining an insight into, for example, human psychiatric illnesses?

Experimenters do everything to minimize the discomfort of their subjects and there are strict laws on what can and cannot be done but the issue remains fraught.

Imaging the brain

In the last decades of the twentieth century, there were important advances in the techniques of forming images of the brain, both of its structure and the amount of blood flow to different regions. Advances in these techniques are continuing. Participants are studied as they engage in psychological tasks, which enables the activity of brain regions associated with the task to be measured.

4.3 FEATURED METHOD
Non-invasive methods for studying the brain's activity

In Featured Method Box 4.1, we explored how invasive techniques enable us to study individual neurons. These types of invasive techniques are obviously limited since they cannot be applied to humans. But, it is possible to gain a general impression of the function of different brain regions by using brain imaging techniques. These techniques are called 'non-invasive', since the nervous system is not disrupted by them (or is only minimally and temporarily disturbed).

Positron emission tomography (PET) is a non-invasive imaging technique. PET allows an image to be formed of the activity of different regions of the brain. It is based on the fact that differences in activity between brain regions are associated with variations in the flow of blood to them and their utilization of fuel (glucose and oxygen). Blood flow to a region varies with the activity of the neurons in the region itself. This gives researchers a possible index of the magnitude of local information processing at the regions observed. Comparisons can be made (a) within a given individual, between different regions of the brain and at various times, and (b) by looking at the same brain region in different individuals.

To instigate the technique, a radioactively-labelled substance termed a tracer is introduced into the body, either by inhalation or by using an injection (Myers, Spinks, Luthra and Brooks, 1992). The presence and location of the tracer is then monitored. A range of cells, such as neurons, employ specific chemical fuels for their energy needs, a principal one being glucose, a type of sugar. One variety of PET exploits the properties of an artificial substance similar to glucose, termed 2-deoxyglucose (2-DG). After the substance is introduced into the body, it enters neurons in the same way that glucose does. However, rather than serving as a fuel, the substance accumulates in the neurons. The brain regions in which

Positron emission tomography
A technique for forming images of the activity of the brain.

neurons are most active accumulate most 2-DG. After a time, the radioactively-labelled substance leaves the neurons and is lost from the body.

What can a PET scan reveal? Brain regions can be scaled according to their activity level, as shown in Figure 4.30 where regions involved in auditory and motor functions are indicated. By recording images of brain activity while research participants perform different tasks, researchers are able to formulate a hypothesis about the relationship between brain functioning, the different regions involved and psychological phenomena. A participant can be asked to perform a specific response, such as clenching a fist, or the participant may be asked to imagine a scene. Brain regions which play a part in either of the two activities – the organization of motor control of the hands or the formation of visual images – will then be activated.

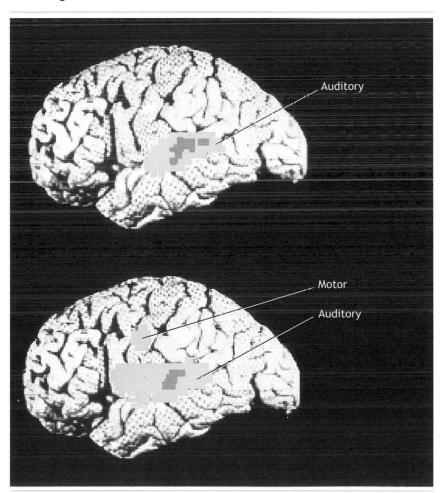

Figure 4.30 A PET scan showing (top) when there's activity in the auditory region and (below) when both auditory and motor regions are active.

PET scans can also reveal regions of the brain that are functioning irregularly. A PET scan of an individual with brain injury may show lower brain activity levels (compared with a control group) in certain brain regions when asked to perform a range of tasks. By identifying the regions of the brain that are affected by the injury, therapy can be investigated. It is also possible to monitor any improvements in the individual by using PET scans to note increases in activity in the part of the brain affected by the injury.

The PET scans of violent criminals have been compared with scans of control participants to look for differences in brain activity levels. The question posed in this type of research was whether regions of the brain known normally to exert restraint on action (e.g. the frontal lobes) are under-active in violent criminals. There is some evidence that this is indeed the case (Raine, Buchsbaum and LaCasse, 1997).

You have now looked at the properties of individual neurons and neural systems as well as how to relate these to an understanding of the whole brain. Some links between neurons, the brain and psychology have been indicated. The next section continues in this direction, but does so within a broader context by returning to material introduced early in the chapter.

Summary Section 5

- The brain is divided into left and right hemispheres, and its outer layer is known as the cerebral cortex.
- Surgical lesions of the corpus callosum have been shown to disrupt communication between the two hemispheres.
- Techniques for studying the brain include looking at the effect of brain damage, electrical stimulation, and forming an image of brain activity using positron emission tomography (PET).

6   Integration

This section shows how various sources of biological evidence can be brought together to give an integrated picture of influences on behaviour and how behaviour influences biology.

6.1 The control of behaviour

The present section considers the role of the brain in the control of behaviour, looking at both the external world and the internal physiology of the body. Figure 4.31 exemplifies just two of the many features of such control. Signals that arise in the brain, are conveyed down the spinal cord (neurons 1 and 2) to the muscles that control the legs and to the heart (neurons 3, 4 and 5).

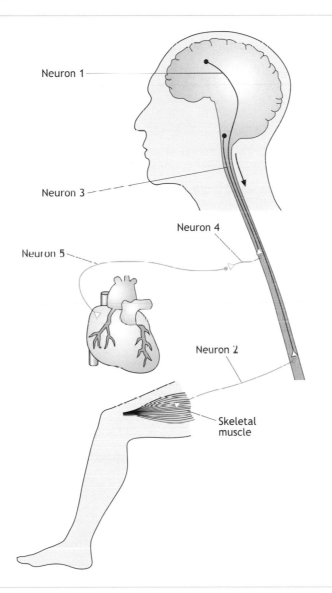

Figure 4.31 Control over external and internal environments (Source: Toates, 2001, Figure 3.3, p.55)

Imagine you are confronted with a runaway car. From adaptive considerations, it makes sense that your legs will be activated to move you as fast as possible. The legs require a large supply of blood in order to provide fuel to the muscles. This requires adaptive and coordinated internal adjustments of physiology, for example the heart beats faster and the internal 'plumbing' of the body is adjusted. Blood vessels at the muscles in the leg dilate to permit a larger flow of blood, and blood is diverted away from other body regions, such as the stomach, where the need is less acute. How are these actions effected? How is coordination between behaviour in the external world and the necessary internal adjustments achieved? Two branches of the nervous system are implicated – the somatic nervous system and the autonomic nervous system.

The somatic nervous system

Somatic nervous system
A division of the nervous system, which controls skeletal muscles.

Skeletal muscle
A type of muscle attached to the skeleton, which is responsible for moving parts of the body such as the arm.

Voluntary behaviour
Behaviour that is under our conscious control.

As shown in Figure 4.32, the **somatic nervous system** (soma means body in Greek) is the part of the nervous system that is responsible for action exerted on the external world. It controls what are termed **skeletal muscles**, such as those in the arms and legs. Skeletal muscles are used to effect our **voluntary behaviour** under conscious control by the brain. Figure 4.31 shows one such route of action. Neurons with their cell bodies in a region of cortex project processes down the spinal cord and communicate with motor neurons. In turn, their activity causes contraction of the skeletal muscle. For convenience we often dichotomize between reflexes and voluntary behaviour. However, in reality, most behaviour is made up of a combination of both.

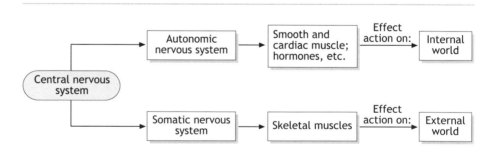

Figure 4.32 The central nervous system and the division of responsibility for action

Motor cortex
The part of the cerebral cortex which is responsible for organizing motor control.

A region of the cortex concerned with organizing motor control is termed the **motor cortex**. In Figure 4.33, a bizarre-looking figure is shown alongside the section of motor cortex. It represents the association between each part of the motor cortex and the part of the body over which it exerts some control. Imaging techniques can reveal the link between the activity of a given brain region and the region of body over which motor control is effected. Also, damage to a specific part of the motor cortex, as in a stroke, is associated with the corresponding disruption to motor control in particular regions of the body (e.g. loss of speech or use of the left arm). As you can see in Figure 4.33, the relative sensitivity of control of different regions of cortex varies. The fingers have a disproportionately large area of cortex devoted to them, indicative of the ability to resolve fine details in motor control through the fingers.

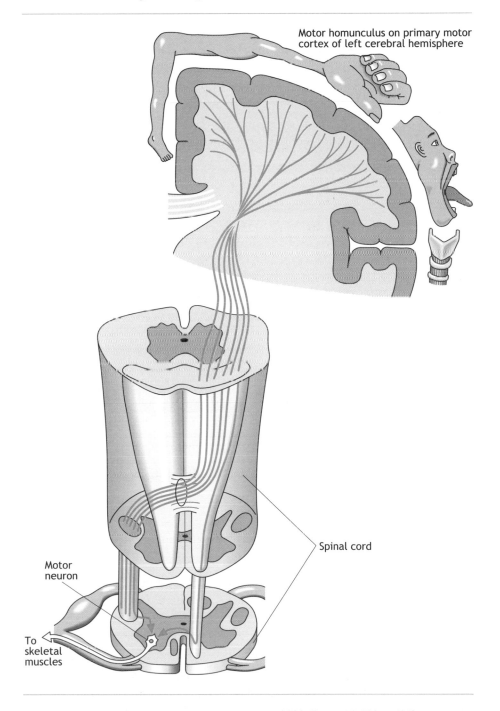

Figure 4.33 Motor control (Source: Martini et al., 2000, Figure 16-4(a), p.429)

The autonomic nervous system

Autonomic nervous system
Part of the nervous system which is responsible for exerting action on the internal environment, for example through smooth muscle.

The **autonomic nervous system** (ANS) is involuntary and is responsible for effecting action within the body itself, but not on the external world (see Figures 4.31 and 4.32). Again, the link between physiology and behaviour is two-way. Our emotions influence the physiology of the body and, in turn, emotions and moods depend upon feedback from the periphery of the body (e.g. activity by the immune system) (Damasio, 1996).

The ANS controls heart rate, the diameter of blood vessels throughout the body and the production of saliva, amongst other things. You do not have to make a conscious decision to accelerate your heart rate during an emergency or slow it down when you meditate, it happens automatically. Indeed, deliberately trying to target the ANS by voluntary control is extremely difficult. Try thinking of when you last blushed with embarrassment. Then think how futile or even counterproductive conscious attempts to counter this are. Blushing is caused by the dilation of blood vessels near to the surface of the skin of the face.

Cardiac muscle
Muscle in the wall of the heart which is responsible for its activity.

Smooth muscle
Muscle which is excited by the ANS, and is found in places such as the walls of blood vessels and the intestines.

Action is effected within the ANS by two types of muscle and by hormones. The two types of muscle are termed **cardiac muscle** and **smooth muscle**. Cardiac muscle is located in the walls of the heart and it effects the beating action of the heart. It exhibits a steady 'background' frequency of heartbeats. However, action within the ANS can either excite the heart to beat faster (e.g. in danger) or slow it down (e.g. when meditating). Smooth muscles are found in the walls of vessels, such as the gut and blood vessels. Their degree of contraction is changed by the activity of the ANS. The gut's smooth muscle programs ripples of contraction, which propel food along the gut. External influences can alter this, for example, when a state of anxiety provokes inappropriate and painful gut contractions.

The two principal hormones in the ANS are adrenalin and noradrenalin (termed respectively epinephrine and norepinephrine in the American literature). These hormones are released from the inner part of a gland situated just above the kidney, termed the adrenal gland (hence their name). The adrenal gland receives a rich supply of blood and so these hormones are secreted into passing blood and circulated throughout the body.

Sites of action of the adrenal hormones include receptors at the cardiac muscle. Their occupation of the receptors increases the heart's pumping action. From this, you might be able to suggest a possible logic behind a claim of the kind 'he is hooked on his own adrenalin'. This could imply that these hormones directly influence the brain. Or it could mean that we detect their influence less directly, for example on heart rate. Either way, sensation-seekers could be motivated to seek out situations that trigger such activation.

Under some conditions, adrenal hormones can be provoked into excessive secretion, inappropriate to adaptive requirements. For example, transient activation is clearly appropriate on some occasions, such as fleeing from a runaway car, but it would not be appropriate if you were stuck for four hours on a train that had broken down. There is little in the way of fighting or running that most of us would feel able to do under these circumstances. Instead, we sit with hormones and fatty substances pouring into our blood streams and forming deposits in our circulatory pathways, elevated heart rates, and groaning intestines. This represents the 'textbook' stress pathology of twenty-first century living; a maladaptive instance of the performance of an adaptive system, which will be discussed in the third course book, *Applying Psychology*.

6.2 The nervous system, development and behaviour

The nervous system changes over time as a function of the growth and the experiences of an individual. It is useful to view some of psychology's discussions in the light of this. For example, a heated debate has raged over human language. To introduce it, let us start with what is uncontroversial: in the adult human brain, regions of the temporal and frontal cortex of the left hemisphere are specialized to process language. We know this since (a) imaging techniques show them to be active during speech and processing the spoken word, and (b) damage to these regions has a particularly disruptive effect on language.

Turning to the controversy, on the one side were exponents of the idea that language is genetically determined by fixed structures 'pre-wired' into the left hemisphere of the brain (Chomsky, 1959). This gives the emergence of language a certain inevitability. Other theorists argued that language was learnt by a process of reinforcement (Skinner, 1957), much in the same way as learning to do anything else (see Chapter 3 of this book). These days, a compromise position appears to carry the most weight. There are parts of the brain which, given an appropriate linguistic context and exposure, preferentially develop into the biological bases of language. In the absence of such a context during development, these areas might be partly captured by other processing such as vision or touch (Elman, *et al.*, 1996).

6.3 Depression – an integrative view

Depression provides a very good example that enables us to draw together a number of the issues raised so far in this chapter, including that of development.

It could be argued that a combination of genes gives an individual a susceptibility to develop depression. However, it is not inevitable that the person will suffer depression since their early and later environment and lifestyle might cushion them against this. Conversely, a person with little genetic bias towards depression might suffer extremes of stress, that may, nevertheless lead to depression (Anisman and Zacharko, 1982).

If we identify that certain genes bias some individuals towards depression, how might this be manifest in the nervous system? The evidence on the efficacy of drugs such as Prozac points to the involvement of certain types of neurotransmitter in depression. Current theories suggest that there are abnormalities in neurotransmission within certain key neural systems such as the dopaminergic, serotonergic and noradrenergic. It is argued that a set of genes might bias an individual towards an abnormality in the density of receptors at a particular type of synapse.

Is depression biological or social? Such a dichotomy is unhelpful since it divides the world in a way that is not logical. Changes in synapses affect the way that we interpret events in the world. Conversely, events in the world, such as exposure to trauma, inevitably have consequences in the nervous system. Therefore, depression is bound to be both biological *and* social.

From a functional perspective, how could a nervous system with a bias towards depression have survived the evolutionary process? One possible argument is that depression is a pathological exaggeration of something that is basically adaptive. A phase of inactivity might serve to conserve resources and, for a social species, serve to deflect aggression or solicit sympathy. It is only when it is excessive that such a strategy is maladaptive.

6.4 Final thought

The chapter has indicated how an understanding of behaviour, emotion, motivation, cognition and the mind, including consciousness, might be enriched by insights from biology. A study of neurons, neural systems and the brain can provide explanations that dovetail with those derived from a psychological perspective. Having surveyed biological psychology and studied Chapter 2, you should be in a good position to take a critical stance towards both biology and its critics. We are not necessarily at the mercy of only our biology (complex psychological phenomena do not exist 'ready-made' in the genes), but neither do we have autonomy from it. A dynamic interaction between biological factors and social context emerges as the model having the most useful explanatory power.

Summary Section 6

- The somatic nervous system is responsible for effecting action on the external environment via skeletal muscle, whereas the autonomic nervous system effects action on the internal environment.
- Considering the brain in terms of genetics and development enhances our understanding of a number of issues, such as how language emerges and the dynamics of depression.

 Further reading

Cacioppo, J.T. and Berntson, G.G. (1992) 'Social psychological contributions to the decade of the brain', *American Psychologist*, vol.47, pp.1019–28.

Cacioppo, J.T., Berntson,G.G., Sheridan, J.F. and McClintock, M.K.(2000) 'Multilevel integrative analysis of human behaviour: Social neuroscience and the complementing nature of social and biological approaches', *Psychological Bulletin*, vol.126, pp.829–43.

Panksepp, J. (1998) 'Attention deficit hyperactivity disorders, psychostimulants, and intolerance of childhood playfulness: a tragedy in the making?', *Current Directions in Psychological Science*, vol.7, pp.91–8. These articles discuss the reciprocal interactive nature of biology and social context.

Davidson, R.J. (2000) 'Affective style, psychopathology, and resilience: brain mechanisms and plasticity,' *American Psychologist*, vol.55, pp.1196–214. Explores the role of imaging in psychological explanation including development.

Davidson, R.J., Jackson, D.C. and Kalin, N.H. (2000) 'Emotion, plasticity, context, and regulation: perspectives from affective neuroscience', *Psychological Bulletin*, vol.126, pp.890–909. Explores the role of the frontal lobes in behaviour.

Kalat, J.W. (2000) *Biological Psychology*, Pacific Grove, CA, Brooks/Cole.
Pinel, J. (2000) *Biopsychology*, Boston, MA, Allyn and Bacon.
Provides a good basic introduction to biological psychology, to advance the discussions of the present chapter.

Posner, M.I. and DiGirolamo, G.J. (2000) 'Cognitive neuroscience: origins and promise', *Psychological Bulletin*, vol.126, pp.873–89.
This article considers the role of brain science in cognitive psychological explanation.

Toates, F. (2001) *Biological Psychology: An Integrative Approach*, Harlow, Pearson Educational.
A useful introduction that assumes no prior knowledge of biology.

References

Ader, R. and Cohen, N. (1985) 'CNS–immune system interactions: conditioning phenomena', *The Behavioural and Brain Sciences,* vol.8, pp.379–94.

Albright, C.R. (2000) 'The "God module" and the complexifying brain', *Zygon*, vol.35, pp.735–43.

Allan, R. and Scheidt, S. (1996) *Heart and Mind: The Practice of Cardiac Psychology*, Washington, DC, American Psychological Association.

Anisman, H. and Zacharko, R.M. (1982) 'Depression: the predisposing influence of stress', *The Behavioural and Brain Sciences*, vol.5, pp.89–137.

Archer, J. (1994) 'Testosterone and aggression', *Journal of Offender Rehabilitation,* vol.21, pp.3–5.

Bateson, P. (1979) 'How do sensitive periods arise and what are they for?', *Animal Behaviour,* vol.27, pp.470–86.

Bolton, D. and Hill, J. (1996) *Mind, Meaning, and Mental Disorder: The Nature of Causal Explanation in Psychology and Psychiatry*, Oxford, Oxford University Press.

Cabanac, M. (1971) 'Physiological role of pleasure', *Science*, vol.173, pp.1103–7.

Cabanac, M. and Russek, M. (1982) *'Régulation et Controle en Biologie'*, Quebec, Les Presses de l'Université Laval.

Cacioppo, J.T. and Berntson, G.G. (1992) 'Social psychological contributions to the decade of the brain', *American Psychologist*, vol.47, pp.1019–28.

Chomsky, N. (1959) 'Review of "Verbal Behaviour" by Skinner, B.F.', *Language*, vol.35, pp.26–58.

Cohen, S. (1996) 'Psychological stress, immunity, and upper respiratory infections', *Current Directions in Psychological Science*, vol.5, pp.86–90.

Colman, A. (1990) 'Aspects of intelligence', in Roth, I. (ed.) *Introduction to Psychology, Volume 1*, East Sussex, Lawrence Erlbaum Associates/The Open University.

Crick, F. (1994) *The Astonishing Hypothesis: The Scientific Search for the Soul*, London, Simon and Schuster.

Damasio, A.R. (1996) *Descartes' Error: Emotion, Reason and the Human Brain*, London, Papermac.

Eccles, J.C. (1989) *Evolution of the Brain: Creation of the Self*, London, Routledge.

Elman, J.L., Bates, E.A., Johnson, M.H., Karmiloff-Smith, A., Parisi, D. and Plunkett, K. (1996) *Rethinking Innateness: A Connectionist Perspective on Development*, Cambridge, MA, MIT Press.

Fantz, R.L. (1961) 'The origin of form perception', in McGaugh, J.L. (ed.) *Psychobiology: The Biological Bases of Behaviour*, San Francisco, CA, W.H. Freeman.

Gottlieb, G. (1998) 'Normally occurring environmental and behavioural influences on gene activity: from central dogma to probabilistic epigenesis', *Psychological Review*, vol.105, pp.792–802.

Greene, J. (1990) 'Perception', in Roth, I. (ed.) *Introduction to Psychology, Volume 2*, East Sussex, Lawrence Erlbaum Associates/The Open University.

Gregory, R.L. (1966) 'The brain as an engineering problem', in Thorpe, W.H. and Zangwill, O.L. (eds) *Current Problems in Animal Behaviour*, Cambridge, Cambridge University Press.

Hubel, D.H. and Wiesel, T.N. (1959) 'Receptive fields of single neurons in the cat's striate cortex', *Journal of Physiology*, vol.148, pp574–91.

Johnson, M.H. (1997) *Developmental Cognitive Neuroscience: An Introduction*, Oxford, Blackwell.

Johnston, T.D. (1987) 'The persistence of dichotomies in the study of behavioural development', *Developmental Review*, vol.7, pp.149–82.

Kalat, J.W. (2000) *Biological Psychology*, Pacific Grove, CA, Brooks/Cole.

Livingstone, M. and Hubel, D. (1988) 'Segregation of form, colour, movement, and depth: anatomy, physiology, and perception', *Science*, vol.240, pp.740–49.

MacKay, D.M. (1974) *The Clockwork Image: A Christian Perspective on Science*, London, Inter-Varsity Press.

Macmillan, M.B. (1986) 'A wonderful journey through skull and brains: The travels of Mr. Gage's tamping iron', *Brain and Cognition*, vol.5, pp.67–107.

Martini, F.H., Timmons, M.J. and McKinley, M.P. (2000) *Human Anatomy*, Upper Saddle River, NJ, Prentice Hall.

McFarland, D.J. (1976) 'Form and function in the temporal organization of behaviour', in Bateson, P.P.G. and Hinde, R.A. (eds) *Growing Points in Ethology*, Cambridge, Cambridge University Press.

Milner, B. (1966) 'Amnesia following operation on the temporal lobes', in Whitty, C.W.M. and Zangwill, O.L. (eds) *Amnesia*, London, Butterworths.

Morton, J. and Johnson, M.H. (1991) 'CONSPEC and CONLERN: a two-process theory of infant face recognition', *Psychological Review*, vol.98, 164–81.

Myers, R., Spinks, T.J., Luthra, S.K. and Brooks, D.J. (1992) 'Positron-emission tomography', in Stewart, M. (ed.) *Quantitative Methods in Neuroanatomy*, Chichester, Wiley.

Penfield, W. and Rasmussen, T. (1968) *The Cerebral Cortex of Man,* New York, Hafner Publishing.

Plomin, R. and Rutter, M. (1998) 'Child development, molecular genetics, and what to do with genes once they are found', *Child Development*, vol.69, 1223–42.

Raine, A., Buchsbaum, M. and LaCasse, L. (1997) 'Brain abnormalities in murderers indicated by positron emission tomography', *Biological Psychiatry*, vol.42, pp.495–508.

Richardson, K. (1998) *The Origins of Human Potential: Evolution, Development and Psychology*, London, Routledge.

Rose, R.M., Bernstein, I.S. and Gordon, T.P. (1975) 'Consequences of social conflict on plasma testosterone levels in rhesus monkeys', *Psychosomatic Medicine*, vol.37, pp.50–61.

Rose, S., Kamin, L.J. and Lewontin, R.C. (1984) *Not in Our Genes*, Harmondsworth, Penguin.

Skinner, B.F. (1957) *Verbal Behaviour*, New York, Appleton-Century-Crofts.

Smith, W.S. and Fetz, E.E. (1987) 'Noninvasive brain imaging and the study of higher brain function in humans', in Wise, S.P. (ed.) *Higher Brain Functions: Recent Explorations of the Brain's Emergent Properties*, New York, Wiley.

Smythies, J.R. (1999) 'Consciousness: some basic issues – a neurophilosophical perspective', *Consciousness and Cognition*, vol.8, pp.164–72.

Sperry, R.W. (1969) 'Hemisphere deconnection and unity in conscious awareness', *American Psychologist*, vol.23, pp.723–33.

Stevens, R. (1996) 'Trimodal theory as a model for interrelating perspectives in psychology', in Sapsford, R., Still, A., Miell, D., Stevens, R. and Wetherell, M. (eds) *Theory and Social Psychology*, London, Sage.

Toates, F. (1998) 'Biological bases of behaviour', in Eysenck, M. (ed.) *Psychology: An Integrated Approach,* London, Longman.

Toates, F. (2001) *Biological Psychology: An Integrative Approach*, Harlow, Pearson Educational.

Wall, P.D. (1993) 'Pain and the placebo response', in Bock, G.R. and Marsh, J. (eds) *Experimental and Theoretical Studies of Consciousness*, Chichester, New York, Wilcy.

Weiskrantz, L. (1976) *Blindsight: A Case Study and Implications*, Oxford, Clarendon Press.

Commentary 4: Biological processes and psychological explanation

Every chapter so far has indicated that biological processes are central to the psychological processes it has been discussing. Chapter 1 ('Identities and diversities'), for example, argued that embodiment is an important part of people's identities and also that some kinds of damage to the brain can damage identities. Chapter 2 ('Evolutionary psychology') indicated that evolution depends on biological processes, including genetic transmission. Most aspects of learning (the subject of Chapter 3) depend on brain processes and evolutionary history. Later chapters (on personality, perception and attention, and memory) will also demonstrate the interdependence of psychological and biological processes. The chapter you have just read (Chapter 4, 'Biological processes and psychological explanation') focuses directly on how the central nervous system (which includes the brain) works and affects behaviour, emotions and cognition.

Theory

1 Most psychologists, but not all, take the view that biology is not *deterministic*; that is, biology, on its own, does not determine psychological processes. Instead, most believe that psychological phenomena are the result of *interactions* between biology and environments.

2 The issue of whether psychology can be reduced to biology has been, and to some extent continues to be, the subject of debate within psychology.

3 When different perspectives are complementary, such as biological and social explanations for depression, they can be used in conjunction with each other.

Methods

4 Biological psychologists predominantly use an outsider viewpoint. However, some recent neuroimaging techniques do use insider viewpoints as well, in that researchers ask people questions about their experiences as they record brain activity.

Themes

5 Biological psychology is concerned with the question of what makes all animals similar as well as what differentiates humans from non-human animals.

6 Both fixity and change (often referred to as stability and adaptation by biologists) are important in biological psychology.

■ Thinking about theory

Biological psychology is a *perspective* that argues that biological structures and biological processes underpin all behaviour, emotions and cognition. Since psychological processes depend on biology for their expression, there are fundamental issues regarding the role of biology as a tool in psychological explanation.

Perspectives at different levels of analysis

The first consideration is whether or not biology could be said to *determine* psychology. There are those who take an extreme position on this – believing that it does, and that ultimately biology, in some form, will fully explain all psychological phenomena. But most psychologists would claim that biology *alone* does not determine psychology. These psychologists, working in the biological psychology perspective, see psychological phenomena as the result of interactions between biology and environments. The same biological influences can have different effects in different social contexts, and contexts can in turn affect biology (e.g. stress can affect the functioning of the heart and of blood vessels). So there is a reciprocal relationship between them. This means that biological explanations alone are insufficient for psychological explanation and so psychology cannot be reduced to biology.

We have already seen that there are many perspectives in psychology and that they tend to guide how questions about subject matter are formed. So a biological psychologist might be expected to formulate a theory and ask questions about, say, depression, at the level of genetic inheritance, or the structure of synapses, or in terms of neurotransmitters. A social psychologist with an interest in clinical matters would, instead, formulate theories in terms of a depressed person's recent life events, social networks, relationships and general support. Both perspectives yield useful findings at these *different levels of analysis*. The different perspectives are complementary and, in terms of possible treatments, they could be used in conjunction with each other – for example, antidepressants *and* psychological counselling.

The meaning and implications of reductionism and different levels of analysis

In this book we are setting out a basic mapping of psychology, describing and discussing the different perspectives, their theories and methods. As we have already seen, there *are* questions to ask about whether and when different perspectives are in conflict or are complementary; and the second course book will discuss these issues in more depth. *Reductionism* is one way to deal with some conjunctions of different perspectives. For example, the phenomena described within a perspective at one level (such as the personal misery and social effects of depression) are explained in terms of the theories and phenomena of a different perspective at a lower level (e.g. neurotransmitters at synapses). The important point to grasp about reductionism, in a strict sense, is that it *privileges lower levels in a hierarchy of levels of explanation.* We can think about depression at the 'whole person' and social level, but it is the case that, whatever the social causes, these causes have their initial impact via biology. It is biology that initially creates the low mood as experienced, and depressed behaviour follows. (Note also that depressed behaviour and reduced social engagement will, in turn, have their effect on biochemistry, creating a spiral effect.) Clearly, if the explanation of depression is *only* in terms of biology – reduced to the biological level – then a great deal is missed. And biology is not the lowest possible level: biological processes could be explained in terms of chemicals, chemicals in terms of subatomic particles, and so on. The principle of reductionism can be applied to other hierarchies of explanation. In group psychology, the question is not usually about reduction to biology but about reduction to a lower level in a different sense. For example, can, or should, group phenomena be reduced to explanation at the level of individual behaviour?

The issue of whether psychology can be reduced to biology has been, and to some extent continues to be, the subject of some debate within psychology. But it is likely to be somewhat revitalized in the light of new technological developments such as molecular biology, the mapping of the human genome, and the techniques of neuropsychology. This is because the new techniques dramatically increase the literal visibility of brain structures and their activity, and hence their salience as biological causes and explanations. But it is important to realize that even these material data also have to be *interpreted* before they can be used as evidence.

Explanations at higher levels are not only less visible, but also much more complex to demonstrate. Chapter 4 has given examples of how different levels of analysis each have their own properties. It refers to the possibility that meaningful topics and experiences such as religion might be located in particular structures in the brain. But even if areas of brain activity can be demonstrated as relating to religious experiences, the meanings that these experiences have for individuals, groups and cultures cannot entirely be accounted for at the biological level. Another example is that things happen in groups that *cannot* happen with individuals, one at a time. A group has emergent properties such as cohesion and patterns of dependence that are difficult to demonstrate and study. And perhaps the most crucial emergent property of all is that of *meaning.* Perspectives such as psychoanalysis (discussed in Chapter 9), and social constructionism (one of the theoretical perspectives presented in Chapter 1) focus primarily on meanings and other symbolic data.

■ Thinking about methods

Multiple methods

A biological psychology perspective has different aspects, such as evolution, physiology, biochemistry, genetics and development. Not surprisingly, given that it has to account for a great many processes, it draws on a range of methods developed in disciplines such as chemistry, physics and neurophysiology and uses them with humans and other animals. A major part of biological psychology involves the study of the brain. Biological psychologists use invasive techniques to record the electric activity of single neurons to see how they react – for example, to light stimulation. They also stimulate neurons electrically and study the effects. And since neurons cannot function without chemical neurotransmitters, biological psychologists also study the activity of neurotransmitters in the brain using biochemical analyses.

For biological psychologists, brain damage has provided a means of finding out which parts of the brain are responsible for particular psychological functions, such as memory, perception and personality. However, using the metaphor of the brain as an engineering problem, if brain damage disrupts a psychological function this does not mean that that function was localized in the damaged part. It may simply be that the damage has disrupted connections within the brain. This raises the issue that using induction as a method of enquiry can be misleading and cautions us to recognize that, even in an area of psychology where we can directly investigate structure and function, theory and method allow us only to move towards understanding psychological issues, rather than furnishing us with 'the truth'.

Techniques for studying the brain, and debates about localization of function within it, have been much improved by the introduction, towards the end of the last century, of non-invasive brain-imaging techniques (e.g. positron emission tomography – PET). As in other areas of psychology, technological developments thus lead to exciting developments within the discipline. Another such example in biological psychology concerns the decoding of the human genome which was completed in 2001 and which is facilitating the study of genetic transmission, although, as we have seen, genes can only have their influence in the context of environments. For most of these techniques, psychologists can use the experimental method to compare the performance of different groups of people such as those with brain damage and those without, on various psychological tasks.

All the methods discussed above predominantly use an outsider viewpoint – although some recent neuroimaging techniques do use insider accounts since researchers ask people questions about their experiences as they record brain activity. They also predominantly use what we have called 'material data'.

■ Thinking about themes

Explaining ourselves as human

Biological psychology is concerned with the question of what makes all animals similar as well as what differentiates humans from non-human animals. Although it also discusses differences between people (e.g. in terms of brain damage or reactions to drugs), it is not concerned with what makes each human being unique. It is more concerned with documenting biological universals than with making individuals themselves the unit of analysis. However, biological psychology (like other areas of psychology) is dynamic and this emphasis may shift as non-invasive brain-imaging techniques make it more possible for the uniqueness of each person's neural connections to be explored.

Fixity and change

Biological psychology questions how animals (human and non-human) adapt to their external environment by changing *and* how they maintain themselves as stable organisms in equilibrium, through the process of homeostasis. So both fixity and change (often referred to as 'stability' and 'adaptation' by biologists) are important for survival.

   Some biological change is best thought of as development – unfolding over time. But organisms also learn, and in that way adapt to a wide range of environmental circumstances. The recognition that biology and environments (physical, social and cultural) affect each other and are always simultaneously present must lead to a rejection of a dichotomy between nature and nurture, for, as we have seen, complex interdependence between biology and environment begins *in utero* (the womb being a complex environment) and continues throughout life. Chapter 4 thus echoes one of the arguments put forward in the previous chapter that learning is simultaneously a cognitive, social, emotional and developmental process. The biological psychology perspective presented in the chapter argues that, in order to understand development, we need to examine both biological and social processes.

   The chapter that follows (Chapter 5, 'The individual differences approach to personality') builds on the material in Chapter 4 by considering possible biological origins of personality and discussing the role of genetics in the study of personality. But it also looks closely at the complexity of environments and the complexity of interactions between biological givens and the social world.

CHAPTER **5**

The individual differences approach to personality

Kerry Thomas

Contents

Aims

This chapter aims to:

- outline the individual differences approach to personality theory and the fundamentals of psychometric measurement
- consider the concept of personality as used in the individual differences perspective, in particular the notion of consistency of behaviour across time and situations
- present and evaluate three trait theories of personality
- give a short account of the correlational method and the principles underlying factor analysis
- outline theories that propose a biological basis for individual differences
- outline and evaluate methods for exploring the genetic contribution to individual differences in personality including the logic and the evidence of heritability studies
- outline the influence of environments on the development and the expression of personality
- revisit the concept of personality in terms of what the individual differences perspective does and does not address.

1 Introduction

'Personality' is a familiar idea so it is easy to assume that it is an unproblematic concept, but psychologists use the word in different ways. In ordinary language too, the word personality can refer to the different kinds of characteristics of people. We talk about some people having a 'charismatic personality', or 'not much personality'.

Activity 5.1

Think for a few minutes about how you use the word personality. What do you think the term means? Make notes and keep them until you get to the end of the chapter.

Comment

You may have thought of personality as something that sums up recognizable 'types'. This view implies that some people can be remarkably similar on certain dimensions, such as outgoingness or conscientiousness. Perhaps you thought of personality as something to do with consistency over time that enables you to predict what a friend might do in a particular setting. You could have considered personality to be a blend of many features that make up the uniqueness of a person. This might be an integrated whole or a more conflicting mixture of characteristics, rather more like the view of identities presented at the end of Chapter 1 in Section 5. You may, of course, hold all these opinions about what personality might be.

'Patterns of similarity' versus 'uniqueness' are two views of personality that are familiar in ordinary discourse, but they also underpin the formal study of personality. This chapter is concerned with the first, the view of personality that stands back from individuals-in-detail, looking instead for common dimensions of personality in order to make generalizations and comparisons. This is called the **nomothetic approach.** The word nomothetic means 'lawful' and this approach builds theories that apply universally – to everyone. These theories depend on rigorous attention to measurement and have to be set out clearly, so they can be tested. In contrast, the uniqueness view of personality concerns an in-depth analysis of individuals, studied one at a time, in all their complexity. This is called the **idiographic approach** and it has developed from the clinical tradition. It uses a case study method, where the intent is to give a comprehensive account of the behaviours, subjective experiences, feelings (i.e. affects) and lives of single individuals. The case studies of the psychoanalytic approach (which you will read about in Chapter 9) are an example of this way of thinking about personality.

Nomothetic personality research is part of a broader tradition of measurement of **individual differences** – differences in personality and across a range of psychological abilities from intelligence to manual skills (see Box 5.1).

Nomothetic approach
Builds testable theories that apply universally.

Idiographic approach
Studies individuals in depth and one at a time without generalizing.

Individual differences research
Identifies widely applicable dimensions of personality and other psychological abilities on which individuals' scores can be placed and compared with population norms.

Notice that there is a paradox here. Although nomothetic personality research seeks to make generalizations and establish the structure of personality for everyone, it is also known as the study of individual differences. The individual differences approach is not about exploring individuality: it sets about identifying universal dimensions for whole populations of people. Individuals' scores on these dimensions can then be used to discriminate between and compare people.

5.1 The origins of the individual differences tradition

Sir Francis Galton, 1822–1911

Francis Galton (1822–1911), a cousin of Charles Darwin, was probably the first person to research individual differences in a systematic, empirical way (Galton, 1884). His research focused on sensory and motor abilities, using these as building blocks for his theory of general intelligence. In 1884, at the International Health Exhibition in the South Kensington Museum, Galton set up a stall where visitors could have measures taken of visual, auditory and touch discriminations, reaction times and certain motor functions. He charged 3 pence for this battery of tests and more than 9,000 men and women took up his offer. Galton's sensory-motor approach to the measurement of intelligence was later abandoned in favour of direct tests of reasoning ability, which in turn led to the development of the first useful intelligence test by Alfred Binet and Theodore Simon in France in 1905. However, Galton had begun an important tradition of measurement called psychometrics: the collection of large amounts of data that describe the range and distribution of individual differences in populations; and the use of statistics to test hypotheses.

Galton's Anthropometric Laboratory at the International Health Exhibition South Kensington Museum (Science Museum) London

Psychometrics (mental measurement) rapidly gained ground as statistical techniques improved and particularly as computers became commonplace. (This is a good example of developments in technology leading to changes in research methods and theory building.) The use of psychometrics to examine individual differences has been crucial to the growth of psychology as an empirical and scientific discipline. Initially driven by education policies and recruitment into the military, increasingly sophisticated psychometric techniques developed over the course of the twentieth century. This has facilitated the development of all kinds of psychological tests and led to a highly profitable industry. There are now many established tests of aptitude, intelligence and personality which are used for research and in applied settings such as education, occupational testing for job selection, career counselling and in forensic psychology and clinical practice.

Psychometrics
Measures individual differences using tests constructed to high standards of reliability and validity.

This chapter focuses on the individual differences perspective on personality. The measurement of personality using formal questionnaires is outlined in Section 2. The individual differences perspective emphasizes similarity and difference in terms of **personality traits** like reliable or fun-loving, bipolar **trait dimensions** such as reliable–unreliable, or **personality dimensions** such as introversion–extraversion. In Section 2 we show that this kind of knowledge about personality is already encoded in ordinary languages and that 'commonsense' is the source of psychometric theories that describe the structure of personality. For example, ordinary dictionaries have been used as the source of trait adjectives since the earliest personality research. It was Galton who first suggested this, only about 20 years after his first attempt at the psychometrics of intelligence. Many of these original sets of trait adjectives are still recycled and widely used.

Personality traits
Adjectives that describe enduring characterisics of people that are used as the building blocks of personality theories.

Trait dimensions
Adjectival descriptors of people that are expressed as bipolar dimensions.

The individual differences approach goes beyond *descriptions* of personality to try to identify the *causes* of differences in personality. An outline of the ways in which personality traits might relate to individual differences in biological systems is given in Section 3, together with a discussion of the possible genetic contributions to personality.

Personality dimensions
Major bipolar features of personality that are widely applicable to people and form the structure of personality.

Section 4 will explore how environments affect both the *development* and the *expression* of individual differences in personality. Once the complexity of environments is acknowledged, and the influence that other people and social situations can have is taken into account, it becomes necessary to reconsider 'what personality is' and how it might relate to other concepts such as identity and role. This is explored in Section 5.

Summary Section 1

- Nomothetic personality research builds testable theories about people-in-general.
- Idiographic personality research studies unique individuals in depth.
- The individual differences perspective is a nomothetic approach to personality. It identifies psychological dimensions that are thought to apply either universally or widely within particular cultures.
- The individual differences tradition maps individual differences in populations and is based on the principles of psychometrics, which require rigorous measurement.
- The individual differences approach to personality uses personality traits which originate in ordinary language.

2   Trait theories of personality

This section gives an account of individual differences psychology as applied to the study of personality. It sets out the basic features of trait psychology and describes three trait theories of personality.

2.1 From common-sense to trait psychology

The common-sense theories that people use to describe others and attribute motives are called implicit personality theories.

Activity 5.2

1 Identify someone you know slightly and write a short description of their personality.

2 Think of someone you know extremely well and write a description of this person's personality.

3 Write a short description of your own personality.

Limit your time to 15 minutes maximum. Keep what you write down to use later in the chapter.

Comment

Your descriptions in Activity 5.2 will almost certainly have used personality trait labels. Since you do not know the person well, your answer to (1) will probably be the shortest. You may have had to go beyond your direct experience and draw on implicit knowledge of people-in-general. Rather than using specific traits you might have used a broad, summary 'type' as your descriptor. To answer (2), you probably used traits that you attribute on the basis of experiences of this person's behaviours, attitudes and 'talk'. Because you know this person well, you might have made your description into more of a story, giving *reasons* for how the person behaves and explaining inconsistencies (e.g. 'He's a warm person but it doesn't always show because he is rather shy').

Many people do not spend much time reflecting on their own personality so question (3) might have been the most difficult. You probably used personality traits again, but you may have written down inner feelings, motives and values, and given more reasons and life event 'causes' than for (2). If you are aware of inconsistencies in your own personality you might have given quite complex explanations of why this might be.

Activity 5.2 is likely to have demonstrated that you have a trait-based implicit theory of personality, even if you are not usually aware of it. **Implicit personality theories** reveal other common-sense aspects of personality. For example, you will almost certainly find that your implicit notion of personality is built on the idea that the people you are describing are consistent, across time and across situations. Almost all approaches to personality are based on consistency – the idea that people's personalities are inner dispositions that lead them to behave in consistent ways and maintain, over time, a consistent orientation to the world and other people. Without this underlying idea of consistency the notion of personality seems to vanish, leaving people's behaviour unpredictable and perhaps no more than fluctuations of states – hormones and neurotransmitters, or reactions to the situations they find themselves in. Psychologists make a distinction here between **trait** and **state**. For example, a trait of anxiety is a characteristic that is persistent over years and likely to be expressed in a wide variety of settings. A state of anxiety could be short-lived and be evoked by a particular situation like a job interview. Whether or not personality *is* stable over time and whether or not people *are* consistent in what they do across different situations are empirical questions that have been studied and are discussed later.

Most personality theories also assume some degree of coherence within personality, meaning that certain aspects of a person's personality 'hang together'; again this can be demonstrated by implicit personality theory.

Implicit personality theories
Lay theories about personality that people use to attribute motives and to describe themselves and others.

Trait and state
Differentiates personality traits that persist over time from mood states that are transient and more dependent on situations.

Activity 5.3

1   The personality characteristics below are from descriptions of two real people. Try to sort them into two trait clusters, each of five traits.

   modest; gregarious; risk-taking; helpful; trustworthy; active; compliant; energetic; assertive; soft-hearted

2   Try to think of appropriate names for the two clusters.

Comment

You were probably able to group these traits into two clusters, demonstrating that in everyday life we are aware that not all combinations of traits are equally likely. Grouped into two clusters, the original descriptions were (a) energetic; gregarious; active; risk-taking; assertive and (b) modest; helpful; compliant; trustworthy; soft-hearted. According to implicit personality theory, people do not expect someone who is gregarious and risk-taking to be compliant. Most people, in a given culture, make similar assumptions about how personality traits fit together. They use these common patterns of **trait clusters** to make intuitive predictions about the motives and behaviour of other people. Were you able to think of a meaningful name for each cluster? This might not have been so easy. The individual differences approach to personality establishes *empirically* which traits cluster together, but the task of 'naming' them in a way that adds something to the understanding of personality is difficult. Researchers have named the two clusters in Activity 5.3 extraversion and agreeableness respectively.

Trait clusters
Personality traits in individuals that have been found commonly to group together.

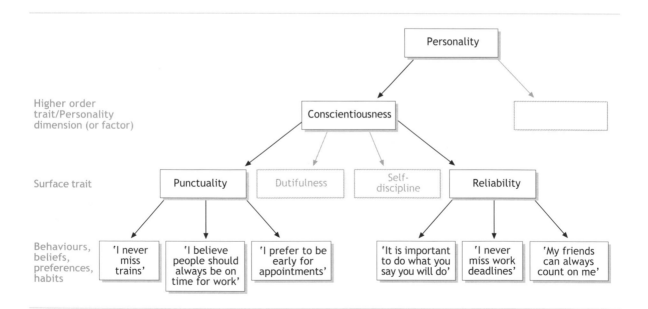

Higher order trait/Personality dimension (or factor)

Surface trait

Behaviours, beliefs, preferences, habits

Figure 5.1   A diagram of a proposed hierarchical structure of personality

Activities 5.2 and 5.3 suggest that, according to implicit personality theories, personality has a hierarchical structure (see Figure 5.1). At the lowest, most specific and observable level, are people's behaviours ('what they usually do'), their expressed feelings and preferences, and their openly stated beliefs. These can be grouped and described by **surface traits**. For example, 'I believe people should always be on time for work' and 'I prefer to be early for appointments', can be described by the trait 'punctuality'. Surface traits cluster together into **higher order traits**. In this example, punctuality would cluster with reliability, dutifulness and self-discipline forming the higher order trait or personality dimension that has been labelled conscientiousness.

Formal **trait theories of personality** mirror implicit personality theories. They all begin with the **lexical hypothesis** which is that what appears in natural language must have some meaningful relationship with personality as actually encountered in everyday life. Trait theories are *descriptions* of personality structure that have *emerged* from questionnaires filled in by a large number of participants. Responses from large samples are necessary because individual differences research aims to use statistics to go beyond the samples tested and describe the lawfulness and the commonalities of personality *at the level of populations*. The questions asked of individuals may be about personality traits or behaviours, beliefs or preferences. Sometimes the respondents are asked about themselves (self-reports); sometimes they are asked to rate other people that they know well (peer reports). Usually the format of questions is either forced choice ('I am punctual': true–false) or a rating scale of three or five points ('She is reliable': strongly agree, agree, don't know, disagree, strongly disagree.) The use of closed-format questionnaires (as opposed to open-ended questions) produces standardized data that can be combined across all respondents. It is this process of aggregation that makes it possible to use statistical techniques to search for patterns and establish the dimensions of personality.

There are several trait theories and they differ in the number and nature of personality dimensions that they specify. These dimensions are commonly referred to as **factors**, a 'shorthand' technical term derived from the statistical method of **factor analysis** by which they are established. The most commonly arrived at structure for personality has five factors or dimensions. Keep in mind that the structures that have been put forward in trait theories are **hypothetical constructs**. They do not exist in a material sense and they are provisional: their validity and usefulness have to be continually tested against people's manifestations of their personalities, such as overt behaviour, and the jobs they choose.

Surface traits
Ordinary language descriptors of personality that encompass what people do and express.

Higher order traits
Personality traits that encompass clusters of surface traits.

Trait theories of personality
Propose a hierarchical structure for personality built from traits and clusters of traits.

Lexical hypothesis
Personality descriptors in ordinary language relate in a meaningful way to personality as encountered in everyday life.

Factors
Technical term for empirically established personality dimensions.

Factor analysis
Statistical technique for establishing personality dimensions.

Hypothetical constructs
Psychological constructions used in theory building and hypothesis testing.

2.2 Three trait theories of personality

Cattell

Raymond B. Cattell, 1905–1998

Inductive approach
Focuses on the collection of data unconstrained by theory allowing patterns, relationships and eventually theories to emerge.

Raymond Cattell (1905–1998) was born and educated in the UK but spent most of his life researching trait psychology in the USA. He collected vast amounts of data over many decades and believed that it was from this empirical material that theory would emerge. This is known as an **inductive approach**. Cattell established a 16 factor (including one intelligence factor) structure to describe personality and constructed several psychometric personality tests to measure the 16 factors. The most well-known and robust of Cattell's tests is the 16PF (Sixteen Personality Factor Questionnaire). This version has been widely used in research, occupational selection and clinical practice for several decades.

Cattell believed that personality is too complex to be represented by a small number of dimensions. Figure 5.2 shows all 16 factors and some of their trait representations. In line with this idea of complexity, Cattell always advocated using **personality profiles** (see Figure 5.2) which give an individual's scores on all of the 16 factors. This way of illustrating the results of the test shows immediately where the individual's scores are extreme or more average.

Personality profile
Visual or numerical representation of an individual's positions on a set of personality dimensions.

Cattell used his psychometric tests to test hypotheses about personality development and consistency across the age-span. He also tested his theory and its measuring instruments to see if they were valid predictors of people's behaviours in the 'real world'. Thus, from an inductive starting point, Cattell moved to theory building, refining his personality tests and finally testing hypotheses in an **inductive-hypothetico-deductive spiral** (see also Chapter 2, Section 5.1).

Inductive-hypothetico-deductive spiral
Cyclic process whereby theories that emerge from data are used to generate testable hypotheses and then new data that are fed back into the cycle.

Figure 5.3 shows the mean levels for the 16PF factors taken from different occupational groups (Cattell and Kline, 1977). If you examine this figure together with the factor descriptions in Figure 5.2, there does seem to be some validation of the 16 factor theory in terms of the characteristics that might be expected in these different careers.

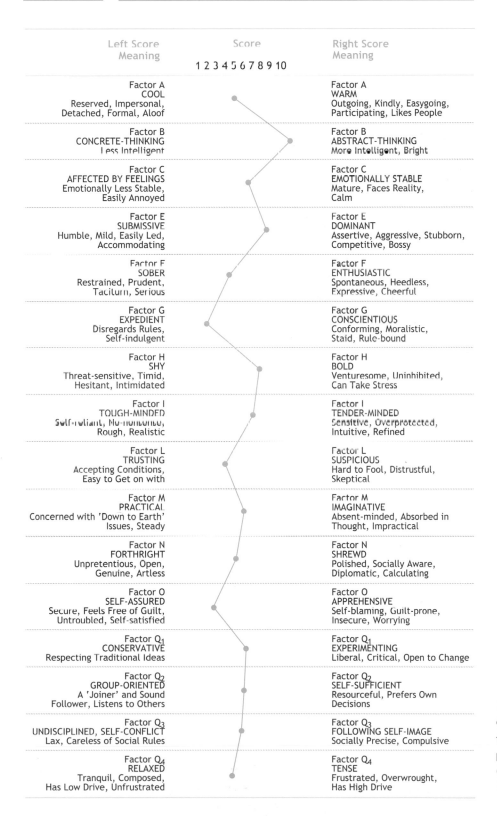

Left Score Meaning	Score	Right Score Meaning
	1 2 3 4 5 6 7 8 9 10	

Factor A
COOL
Reserved, Impersonal, Detached, Formal, Aloof

Factor A
WARM
Outgoing, Kindly, Easygoing, Participating, Likes People

Factor B
CONCRETE-THINKING
Less Intelligent

Factor B
ABSTRACT-THINKING
More Intelligent, Bright

Factor C
AFFECTED BY FEELINGS
Emotionally Less Stable, Easily Annoyed

Factor C
EMOTIONALLY STABLE
Mature, Faces Reality, Calm

Factor E
SUBMISSIVE
Humble, Mild, Easily Led, Accommodating

Factor E
DOMINANT
Assertive, Aggressive, Stubborn, Competitive, Bossy

Factor F
SOBER
Restrained, Prudent, Taciturn, Serious

Factor F
ENTHUSIASTIC
Spontaneous, Heedless, Expressive, Cheerful

Factor G
EXPEDIENT
Disregards Rules, Self-indulgent

Factor G
CONSCIENTIOUS
Conforming, Moralistic, Staid, Rule-bound

Factor H
SHY
Threat-sensitive, Timid, Hesitant, Intimidated

Factor H
BOLD
Venturesome, Uninhibited, Can Take Stress

Factor I
TOUGH-MINDED
Self-reliant, No-nonsense, Rough, Realistic

Factor I
TENDER-MINDED
Sensitive, Overprotected, Intuitive, Refined

Factor L
TRUSTING
Accepting Conditions, Easy to Get on with

Factor L
SUSPICIOUS
Hard to Fool, Distrustful, Skeptical

Factor M
PRACTICAL
Concerned with 'Down to Earth' Issues, Steady

Factor M
IMAGINATIVE
Absent-minded, Absorbed in Thought, Impractical

Factor N
FORTHRIGHT
Unpretentious, Open, Genuine, Artless

Factor N
SHREWD
Polished, Socially Aware, Diplomatic, Calculating

Factor O
SELF-ASSURED
Secure, Feels Free of Guilt, Untroubled, Self-satisfied

Factor O
APPREHENSIVE
Self-blaming, Guilt-prone, Insecure, Worrying

Factor Q_1
CONSERVATIVE
Respecting Traditional Ideas

Factor Q_1
EXPERIMENTING
Liberal, Critical, Open to Change

Factor Q_2
GROUP-ORIENTED
A 'Joiner' and Sound Follower, Listens to Others

Factor Q_2
SELF-SUFFICIENT
Resourceful, Prefers Own Decisions

Factor Q_3
UNDISCIPLINED, SELF-CONFLICT
Lax, Careless of Social Rules

Factor Q_3
FOLLOWING SELF-IMAGE
Socially Precise, Compulsive

Factor Q_4
RELAXED
Tranquil, Composed, Has Low Drive, Unfrustrated

Factor Q_4
TENSE
Frustrated, Overwrought, Has High Drive

Figure 5.2
Cattell's 16 personality factors, showing a personality profile (Source: Cloninger, 1996, p.96)

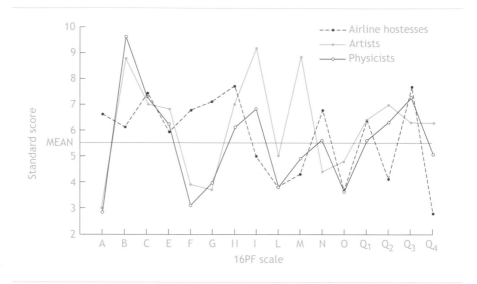

Figure 5.3   Mean scores obtained on the 16PF by three occupational groups (Source: Cattell and Kline, 1977, p.304)

Despite the practical success of the 16PF and Cattell's view that a large number of factors is necessary to describe personality adequately, his model has lost favour to five factor versions of personality structure. Two versions of five factor theory will be outlined next. Although these versions may look very similar, they are the outcome of different research agendas.

Costa and McCrae

Paul J. Costa Jnr and Robert R. McCrae

The five factor model of Costa, McCrae and colleagues is most easily remembered by the mnemonic OCEAN, the acronym for the names of the factors: Openness, Conscientiousness, Extraversion, Agreeableness and Neuroticism. These five factors and the traits associated with them are shown in Table 5.1. (This model is often referred to as the 'Big Five' but this name should, more properly, be kept for Goldberg's model which is discussed later.)

Table 5.1 **The five factors of Costa and McCrae's trait theory of personality, showing examples of traits associated with each factor**

Neuroticism:	anxiety, angry hostility, depression, self-consciousness, impulsiveness, vulnerability
Extraversion:	warmth, gregariousness, assertiveness, activity, excitement-seeking, positive emotions
Openness:	fantasy, aesthetics, feelings, actions, ideas, values
Agreeableness:	trust, straightforwardness, altruism, compliance, modesty, tender-mindedness
Conscientiousness:	competence, order, dutifulness, achievement striving, self-discipline, deliberation

Source: Matthews and Deary, 1990, p.27

Costa and McCrae arrived at their model in a pragmatic way. They realised that five similar factors had emerged in many Western studies of personality over several decades, and that similar factors were also 'buried' in other research, including Cattell's work. They set out to unify the findings by choosing the most commonly found and most robust set of five factors. They then designed a questionnaire to improve measurement of these five factors. Their main personality inventory is the NEO-PI (Costa and McCrae, 1992). (The acronym NEO is derived from three of the factors, neuroticism, extraversion and openness, and it also implies 'new'.) Personality inventories like those of Costa and McCrae, and Cattell are not just collections of questions, they are highly refined **psychometric tests**, constructed to rigorous standards of reliability and validity (see Box 5.2).

Psychometric tests
Psychological tests that are based on rigorous psychometric properties and related to population norms.

5.2 FEATURED METHOD

Psychometric tests

Personality questionnaires, intelligence tests and other aptitude tests are commonplace in many cultures. They are used for selection for jobs and education and for monitoring educational progress. Many tests have been developed for clinical diagnosis. The tests are products of the close links between individual differences psychology and psychometrics and have special psychometric properties that distinguish them from the majority of questionnaires, surveys and attitude scales that are used in psychology and other professions such as market research.

Psychometric tests are constructed in a series of steps. Costa and McCrae's development of the NEO-PI is a good example of this process. They used documented research (theories of the structure of personality and the questions used by many researchers to arrive at these structures) to clarify the constructs (the five personality dimensions) they intended to measure and to provide questions for the initial stage of test construction. A psychometric test sets out to measure a well-defined construct and its measurement must be both reliable and valid. A test must be reliable before there is any point in considering its validity. If a test has **reliability**, i.e. gives virtually the same results (for each individual) time and again, it must be measuring something. **Test validity** is the extent to which a test or a measurement measures what it is intended to measure.

Test reliability
The extent to which a test gives the same result for an individual over time and situation.

Test validity
The extent to which a test measures what it purports to measure.

Costa and McCrae would have worked and re-worked their NEO-PI until, for each of the five dimensions, people's scores were virtually the same on two separate occasions (**test–retest reliability**). They also needed to ensure that all the traits 'hung together' for each dimension, and showed internal consistency, which is another form of reliability. For example, individuals who achieved high scores on dutifulness would also get high scores on competence and self-discipline.

Test–retest reliability
The extent to which a test gives the same score for an individual on two occasions.

In addition, Costa and McCrae would have had to demonstrate that the NEO-PI is valid. Table 5.1 demonstrates **face validity**. You can see that the items make ordinary sense and appear to relate to personality. **Construct validity** refers to the relation between a theoretical construct (what a theory states) and what is actually being measured. Costa and McCrae believe that there are five factors and that each is something different. So, if during the development of the NEO-PI they had found that virtually everyone with high scores on conscientiousness also got very similar high scores on extraversion, neuroticism and agreeableness, they would have known that something was wrong because the sub-scales were not differentiating between the dimensions. Either the measuring instrument was not valid or the theory mistaken. Another way of assessing the validity of a test is to compare the measures obtained using the test against the measures obtained in research that uses other instruments

Face validity
When test items can be seen to make sense and relate to the construct being measured.

Construct validity
The extent to which a test measures the construct it claims to measure.

to measure the same theoretical construct. This is called **convergent validity**. For example, Costa and McCrae might have compared findings for their extraversion sub-scale with scores obtained by the same individuals on Eysenck's well-known test for extraversion (see Section 3.1). The **criterion validity** of a test can best be assessed when the measures produced by a test are compared with a clear 'external' criterion such as overt behaviour. Cattell's 16PF test shows some degree of criterion validity in that certain factors relate to job choice (see Figure 5.3). Construct validation is a never-ending task, concerned with the coherence of a theory and the adequacy of tests that support it.

Psychometric tests are used to obtain scores for individuals that then allow these individuals to be compared with others. But, if an individual's score is to have any meaning, the test itself must be calibrated. It has to be administered to a large number of people who form a representative sample of a recognizable population to establish the test norms. These may be different for different populations such as male and female, and different age groups.

Psychometric tests are expensive to construct. They are researched by psychologists but usually published by companies who restrict their use and make charges. The charges cover development costs and produce profit. The restrictions are important for several reasons. First, if tests are widely available then people can practise and learn to manipulate their scores. Second, because these tests have particular psychometric properties that require professional interpretation, if they are used by those who have not been sufficiently trained, scores may be wrongly interpreted and the results could be misleading. Third, the administration, confidentiality and feedback to participants of psychometric tests often involves sensitive ethical issues. But there are those who believe that easier access to tests is important. In research, for example, access to other researchers' test materials can be important for the continuity and consistency of investigations. One personality theorist (Goldberg) has organized an Internet–based collection of personality trait items which is not restricted.

Convergent validity
The extent to which two independent tests give the same scores for the same construct.

Criterion validity
The extent to which the scores on a test equate with scores on an established test or predict an external criterion such as behaviour.

Costa and McCrae and their colleagues have used their personality tests to explore the stability of personality over time and across the age-span. Costa and McCrae (1988) have shown that adult (over the age of 30 years) personality is stable, at least over a six year period. Before adulthood, personality has more fluidity (Costa and McCrae, 1994; McCrae and Costa, 1994). Typically, between the late teenage years and the age of 30 years scores decrease for neuroticism, extraversion and openness, and increase for conscientiousness and agreeableness. After the age of 30 years, the same trends are present but the changes are smaller. This has been found for participants in a variety of European cultures (McCrae *et al.*, 2000). But what does this increase in stability mean? Do people become more immune to the moulding effects of their environments? Do environments and does life become less variable? Or is it that people become used to describing themselves in particular ways? It is important to note that sometimes people do change significantly in response to life events such as a change in career or marital status, or accidents and illnesses (Helson and Stewart, 1994). It is interesting to consider the possible connection between the personality change that happens alongside life changes and notions of flexible identity, which you read about in Chapter 1.

Costa and McCrae's measuring instruments (and others, like the 16PF) have been translated into several languages and used in diverse cultures and language groups to explore whether the five factors of personality can be considered universal. And there is evidence that, across cultures and language groups, 'personality' can indeed be described in terms of the same five factors. But, since these instruments originated in English language lexicons, 'personality' as encoded in English has been *imported* into other cultures. This approach to cross-cultural research (essentially 'from the outside') is called the **etic approach**. In this case it rests on the *assumption* that the *same* personality traits and hierarchical structures that have been established in English are relevant in other cultures and language groups. The work of Goldberg, discussed below, questions this assumption.

Etic approach
Imports concepts, theories, meanings and tests from one culture to collect data and test hypotheses in another.

Goldberg

Lewis R. Goldberg

Goldberg and his associates (Goldberg, 1981) have also arrived at a five factor model called the Big Five (see Table 5.2 below). If you compare Tables 5.1 and 5.2 you will see that Goldberg's model looks very similar to that of Costa and McCrae. Goldberg's model has an 'intellect' factor whereas Costa and McCrae have an 'openness' factor. These domains are similar but the meaning is not identical. But there is a more important difference between the two five factor models: Goldberg's *agenda* is different from the pragmatic approach of Costa and McCrae.

Table 5.2 The 'Big Five' factors and associated personality traits found in English

Domain	Subcomponent	Example terms in English	
		Positive pole	Negative pole
Extraversion (I)	Assertiveness	assertive	weak
	Activity-adventurousness	daring	unadventurous
	Unrestraint	talkative	shy
	Sociability	cheerful	unsociable
Agreeableness (II)	Warmth-affection	affectionate	cold
	Generosity	generous	selfish
	Gentleness	agreeable	harsh
	Modesty-humility	modest	egotistical
Conscientiousness (III)	Orderliness	organized	sloppy
	Reliability	responsible	undependable
	Industriousness	ambitious	lazy
	Decisiveness	decisive	inconsistent
Emotional stability (IV)	Insecurity[a]	relaxed	insecure
	Emotionality[a]	unemotional	excitable
	Irritability[a]	undemanding	irritable
Intellect (V)	Intellect	intelligent	unreflective
	Imagination	creative	unimaginative
	Perceptiveness	perceptive	short-sighted

[a] These subcomponents are labelled by their negative rather than positive pole.

Source: Saucier et al., 2000, p.2

Goldberg and his colleagues are still searching for the main dimensions of personality-as-encoded-in-different-language-groups, *using each language's own, unabridged lexicons.* This is called the **emic approach** ('from within') to cross-cultural research. With each new language studied, Goldberg is testing the lexical hypothesis that, in all cultures, people communicate about the most important personality attributes for human transactions and that these attributes will become part of their language. The more languages that yield the same personality dimensions, the more likely it is that those dimensions are universal (Somer and Goldberg, 1999).

Emic approach
Is based on concepts, theories, meaning and tests that originate from within the culture in which the research is conducted.

Suppose that Goldberg and his colleagues studied virtually all known language groups and found the same five dimensions, what would this mean? It would suggest that these five factors are universal for human transactions. It might also suggest that, because they are universal, they have a biological origin, that there is some 'genetically-based personality hardware' (Saucier et al., 2000, p.27). This is called the biogenic assumption. But it could also mean that regularities in human environments and/or social groups have led different cultures to encode the same systems of describing personality and behaviour. This is called the sociogenic assumption. Both of these possible origins could have been selected for by evolutionary processes. But if differences were found between language groups, then cultural influences must be at work. In this case, the dimensions discovered in different languages might reflect the culture-specific meanings and values attributed to transactions and/or the construction through talk of 'what is important about other people'. If differences do exist across cultures it is most likely that universal biological factors provide the constraints on which cultural forces have acted (Bruner, 1990).

What have Goldberg and his colleagues discovered? The results are not yet clear and there are methodological difficulties, but some trends are emerging. Goldberg's 'Big Five' factors are numbered according to their dominance in the English language where there are a lot more personality trait adjectives associated with factor I (extraversion), factor II (agreeableness) and factor III (conscientiousness). These first three factors tend to be the most easily replicated in other languages. All five personality factors are found in Northern European languages (e.g. English, German and Dutch). Although a fairly similar structure is found in Czech, Russian, Hungarian and Polish, only the first three factors are clear in Romance languages like Spanish and Italian. In Filipino, factor IV (emotional stability) splits into two, and in Hebrew, factor I (extraversion) and factor IV (emotional stability) both split (Saucier *et al.*, 2000). Researchers have found that the deviations are not language-specific so it seems that other regularities in personality-as-encoded-in-language are emerging. It may be that only two or three factors are widely replicable, suggesting that only two or three dimensions of personality are universal and the others vary across cultures.

An example of the possible impact of culture on personality is illustrated by research on Turkish, another language outside the Indo-European language group (Somer and Goldberg, 1999). The Big Five were replicated, although the Turkish factor V seemed to be much closer to Costa and McCrae's 'Openness' than Goldberg *et al.*'s English factor V characterized as 'Intellect'. Somer and Goldberg suggest that the Turkish factor V might be mirroring cultural polarities in terms of openness to new experiences and progressivism rather than intellect, especially since: '[Turkish] culture ... faces both East and West ... Whereas in most modern Western societies ... one would not expect large personality differences related to traditionalism versus modernity, the opposite may be true in Turkey, especially among Turkish youth who are caught up in such cultural conflicts' (Somer and Goldberg, 1999, pp.432–3).

Goldberg's approach to the dimensions of personality is important because it attempts to link two very different domains. These domains are (a) evolutionary psychology and the ideas of biology in interaction with physical and social environments and that dimensions of personality are selected for by evolutionary processes, and (b) cultural expression of personality and the possible elaboration of dimensions of personality through everyday talk about the 'important dimensions of being a person'. Buss has pointed out that the Big Five 'summarize the most important features of the social landscape' (Buss, 1997, p.334). He suggests that surgency (extraversion), agreeableness and conscientiousness (trust) are likely to be very important in group life, perhaps mapping onto the social significance of hierarchy and dominance, and cooperation and willingness to form reciprocal alliances. Of the three trait models outlined here, it is only the work of Goldberg and his colleagues that pays attention to the social and cultural aspects of commonalities in personality.

2.3 Evaluating trait theories of personality

Trait theories have succeeded in mapping individual differences in personality for populations – within their own definition of personality. This tradition of research has led to advances in psychometrics and the development of psychological tests, which in turn have facilitated additional research. Traits have been shown to be stable over time and there is some evidence for their existence across cultures. External validation (through criterion validity) of trait theories suggests that measures of individual differences can predict a range of behaviours. But, there are some obvious problems.

Why are there different versions of trait theory, with different numbers and kinds of factors?

The theories are not as different as they seem. Trait psychology illustrates how researchers have a degree of *choice* about exactly how to proceed and how to *interpret* their findings. This is illustrated in Box 5.3 which outlines the kinds of data analyses on which the trait theories are built.

Analysing individual differences: looking for patterns and correlations in data

When research teams investigate personality structure they start by collecting a large amount of data. These are the scored responses to questionnaire items, often as many as a hundred or more items per questionnaire, collected from hundreds of people. The researchers have in front of them a mass of variability. What they are faced with can be thought of as a puzzle. How can this variability be reduced and simplified so that it makes sense? Essentially, the task involves looking for patterns of similarity or clusters of 'things that go together' or that *correlate*. These clusters then have to be named in a meaningful way.

The underlying *technique* is that of correlation, which measures how closely pairs of variables (individuals' scores for punctuality and reliability) move together over a large number of people. If most people who have high scores on punctuality also have high scores on reliability (or if most people have low scores on both) then, for that population, it can be said that the two variables correlate highly. (As you might expect, this is what is usually found empirically.) If, and this is less likely, when people have high scores on punctuality they are just as likely to have high, medium or low scores on reliability, then the two variables do not correlate (the variables are independent of each other). The strength of a correlation is given by a statistical **correlation coefficient**, 'r'. If there is a perfect positive correlation, then r = I; if there is no correlation at all (i.e. the two variables 'move' independently of each other), then r = 0. If the variables move together, but in opposite directions, then r is negative: we could imagine a negative correlation with a value of, perhaps, r = −0.8 for the variables reliable and lazy since we would expect that the higher someone's score on reliability, the lower would be their score on laziness. A correlation of r = −I would be a perfect negative relationship, as one variable goes up the other always goes down (e.g. this must, by definition, be the case for scores on reliability and unreliability). You will be learning more about correlations in the next methods week and you will find more details about correlation as a statistical technique in *Statistics Without Maths for Psychology* (Dancey and Reidy, 2002).

Figure 5.1 shows a small number of behaviours and beliefs that could cluster into the surface traits of punctuality and reliability. Many more behaviours and beliefs could have been tapped using a questionnaire. By looking for correlations between all possible pairs of behaviours/beliefs the data could be simplified. In this process, the actual answers to the questionnaire items about behaviour at the lowest level in the pyramid, are summarized and replaced by a much smaller number of surface traits. The researchers have to give each of these surface traits a meaningful name. By repeating the process, the surface traits can be shown to cluster into a much smaller number of dimensions (factors) which can be given meaningful names such as conscientiousness. This is a process that necessarily involves legitimate approximations and interpretations.

Correlation coefficient
A statistical index of the strength and direction of the relationship between variables.

Over the decades, advances in statistical techniques and computational tools have simplified this process. More than one statistical route to such simplification exists. The generic name for techniques that reduce and simplify data into clusters is factor analysis.

In Cattell's theory, there are 16 factors and in others there are five factors. But in Cattell's theory, the factors themselves correlate and can be grouped into a smaller number. Cattell could have *chosen* to create a smaller number of **secondary factors** out of the 16 **primary factors**. This is where the researcher's ultimate research goals and beliefs come into the process. Cattell believed that personality could be better accounted for if he retained more complexity in his data and stopped the clustering process lower down the pyramid, keeping the 16 primary factors. Many other researchers have disagreed and have *chosen* to search for overlaps between primary factors and reduce them to a smaller number of virtually independent (called orthogonal) secondary factors. Cattell's 16 primary factors can be reduced to eight secondary ones, of which five have been frequently replicated. These five factors are similar to those of the five factor models. While Cattell's 16 factor model stops at a relatively low level in the hierarchy, Eysenck's three factor model goes right to the top of the hierarchy to find an answer to the question, 'how many factors can account for personality?'

Primary factors
The first and largest set of factors or dimensions that emerge in factor analysis and can themselves sometimes be simplified further.

Secondary factors
Dimensions or factors found in factor analysis by looking for relationships between primary factors.

Researchers can choose different question items and use long or short questionnaires with different formats. The personality dimensions that emerge from factor analysis depend directly on the specific questions asked. Researchers can choose different statistical procedures to reduce the variability of their data; and at each stage of the simplification process they can choose different 'names' to use and thus give different meanings to their findings. There isn't just one trait theory because, whilst all trait theorists have been looking for a reasonable 'solution' to the puzzle, there isn't just one answer.

Researchers' choices are driven by their preconceptions about personality and by their research goals. Cattell wanted to retain complexity and use it to research his view of personality. Costa and McCrae wanted to summarize and regularize all the findings to date so they chose a model that could account for most research findings. Both Cattell's 16 factor version and Costa and McCrae's five factor version are *perpetuated* by the psychometric tests that they have generated, because the questionnaire items in the psychometric tests are selected deliberately to measure the factors already chosen for each theory.

In contrast, Goldberg and his associates are not looking for a single 'correct' model of personality structure because they are primarily interested in possible cross-cultural differences. They continue to search for factors that reflect the full range and *frequencies* of traits as they are encoded in different language groups. They are looking beyond the Big Five to see if important dimensions have been missed. Saucier and Goldberg (1998) give examples of individual differences that do not relate significantly to any of the Big Five: for example, differences related to sexuality, and encoded in terms like prudish, coy, promiscuous, and differences described by adjectives that refer to maturity, physical characteristics and gender. They have suggested that the prime contenders for extending the Big Five might be attractiveness, religiousness and, perhaps, negative valence (evil, good-for-nothing, wicked, disgusting).

Trait theories are 'only' descriptions. Do they explain personality?

A common criticism of trait theories is that they *describe* personality but do not *explain* it. For most theorists (e.g. Cattell, Costa and McCrae), traits are descriptors, and they also represent a construct that might, one day, explain the behaviours that the trait describes, in terms of causal biological processes. Nevertheless, hypothetical constructs like traits and trait-based personality dimensions can lead to important research and be validated without necessarily being reduced to a lower level of analysis, i.e. to biological explanations. For example, Goldberg and his associates are primarily concerned with personality description.

However, some psychologists believe that causal explanations *should* be grounded in biology, and that ultimately personality should be explained in terms of neurophysiology and genetics. In the next section we begin to examine the biological causes of personality and ask whether personality can be thought of as inherited.

Summary Section 2

- Trait theories of personality mirror the implicit personality theories of common sense.
- The idea of consistency is central to the concept of personality.
- Trait theories propose a hierarchical structure for personality.
- Personality is measured using closed-format questionnaires that permit aggregation of data and statistical procedures including factor analysis to search for emergent patterns.
- Trait theories differ in the number and nature of the personality dimensions (or factors) they propose for the structure of personality.
- Trait theories measure personality using psychological tests that have psychometric properties including reliability and validity.

- The 16 factor theory of Cattell and the five factor theory of Costa and McCrae both claim to describe the universal dimensions of personality, but they also imply that these dimensions will eventually be explained biologically.
- Goldberg's Big Five model describes personality as encoded in Northern European languages and is part of a project seeking to establish whether these dimensions are universal or different across cultures.

3   Biology and personality

This section moves to a different level of analysis and a search for the *causes* of personality. Are there universal dimensions of biological difference that can explain dimensions of personality? If personality *can* be linked to biology, then how much of personality might be explained by inherited factors? An important theme for many areas of psychology is trying to understand the interacting influences of genetics and environments. In this section we begin to examine the effects of nature and nurture with respect to personality.

3.1 The search for the biological causes of individual differences in personality

The brain is an extremely complex and interactive system. This means that psychologists who have tried to map individual differences in personality onto individual differences in brain structure or function, have started with a simple *model* of just two or three key neural subsystems, described in terms of either anatomy and/or biochemistry. Gray (1987) made it clear that such a model is a **conceptual nervous system** and certainly does not reflect the full complexity of the biology. In such a model, key subsystems in the brain need to be linked to fundamental behavioural functions such as managing arousal levels, approach/avoidance, learning, novelty seeking, and sensitivity to reward versus punishment. These in turn have to be related to measurable individual differences in personality. Eysenck was the first psychologist to attempt this kind of theory (Eysenck, 1967). Although the evidence for the biological underpinnings of his theory is weak, it has generated considerable personality research and it has remained a dominant theory.

Eysenck's methods of establishing and measuring personality dimensions were exactly the same as those of the trait theorists. (You will find that

Conceptual nervous system
A simple, hypothetical model of an aspect of the nervous system used to explore relationships between brain, behaviour and personality.

Hans Jurgen Eysenck, 1916–1997

Type theory
Suggests personality is based in biology which is treated as the determinant of type which in turn leads to traits.

many texts treat his theory as a three factor model of personality.) But Eysenck called his theory a **type theory** because he believed that type is *determined* by biology, type then *determines* traits and traits *determine* behaviours, from simple habits to social attitudes and political affiliations. He proposed that people can be categorized into four types using just two main personality dimensions, extraversion–introversion (E) and neuroticism–emotional stability (N), as shown in Figure 5.4. Examples of traits associated with extraversion and neuroticism are shown in Table 5.3.

Eysenck later added a third dimension called psychoticism–superego strength (P). Despite their clinical sounding names, Eysenck claimed that both neuroticism and psychoticism are normal personality dimensions that measure a predisposition and not a psychiatric disorder. His basic psychometric test for measuring personality in terms of E, N and P is the Eysenck Personality Questionnaire (EPQ), one of the most widely used measures of personality for several decades.

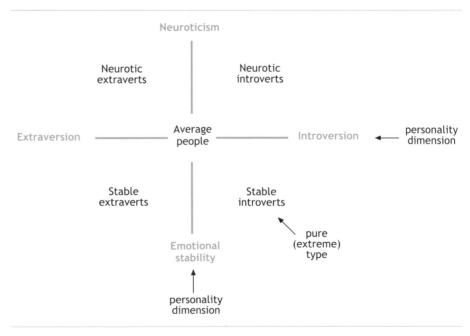

Figure 5.4   Eysenck's personality dimensions and personality types
(Source: Roth, 1996, p.385)

Table 5.3   The three factors and associated personality traits of Eysenck's model of personality

Neuroticism	anxious, depressed, guilt feelings, low self-esteem, tense, irrational, shy, moody, emotional
Extraversion	sociable, lively, active, assertive, sensation-seeking, carefree, dominant, surgent, venturesome
Psychoticism	aggressive, cold, egocentric, impersonal, impulsive, antisocial, unempathetic, creative, tough-minded

Source: Matthews and Deary, 1998, p.25

According to Eysenck, extraversion–introversion is caused by individual differences in cortical arousal, controlled by the **ascending reticulocortical activating system (ARAS)** which is thought to be involved in alertness and arousal. He proposed that there are genetically determined individual differences in the ARAS which affect the usual levels of arousal experienced. He proposed two mechanisms to link ARAS to personality.

First, he suggested that introverts are chronically over-aroused from birth, and so they behave in a way that *reduces* their arousal level; they avoid extra stimulation, resulting in typical introverted behaviour. In contrast, extraverts are chronically under aroused, and so tend to behave in a way that *increases* their arousal level, looking for more stimulation and excitement. Second, Eysenck proposed a relationship between arousal levels and ease of conditioning and hence learning. Eysenck saw a parallel between a 'weak nervous system' (one that is easily conditioned) and the chronic over-arousal associated with introversion, implying that introverts should be relatively easy to condition. He claimed that, since it is extraverts who have a low level of arousal, they would be less easy to condition than introverts.

Eysenck proposed that the biological basis of the neuroticism–emotional stability dimension lies in individual differences in the activity of the **limbic system** which organizes emotional response. He suggested that neuroticism is concerned with reactivity, emotionality and sensitivity to stress; those who are low on the neuroticism dimension being emotionally stable. Eysenck did not pay much attention to the psychoticism dimension or its grounding in biology.

Eysenck's work is an important example of theory building. It encompasses several different levels of analysis, linking genetics and subsystems in the brain through basic psychological processes such as learning, arousal and emotional reactivity to behaviours ranging from specific habits to social attitudes. There is widespread *psychometric*

Ascending reticulocortical activating system (ARAS)
A part of the brain that controls cortical arousal.

Limbic system
Part of the brain that organizes emotional responses.

evidence for Eysenck's three factor structure of personality. There is also *physiological evidence;* for example depressant drugs, like alcohol, make introverts less aroused and make them behave more like extraverts while stimulant drugs, like coffee, make extraverts behave more like introverts. *Behavioural evidence* has provided some limited support for predictions about how extraverts and introverts learn and how they react to performing tedious manual tasks in the laboratory.

Eysenck believed that individual differences in brain structure and functioning are inherited and, therefore, that a significant part of personality is genetically determined. Perhaps more than any other theorist, he stressed the inevitability of certain paths of development for each personality type, particularly for those at the extremes of the personality dimensions. Nevertheless, he acknowledged that personality becomes more diverse in terms of behaviour as individuals experience the interaction of their basic type with the realities of everyday life in the social world.

A major criticism of Eysenck's work lies in its failure to establish the biological basis of E and N (Zuckerman, 1991). There is some evidence of differences in cortical arousal in extraverts and introverts, but also some that is conflicting. It now seems to make little sense to suggest a functional separation between the arousal system and the limbic system since they are closely interconnected (Eysenck, 1998). There is also little evidence for the neural basis of neuroticism and psychoticism.

Other psychobiological models have been proposed. Gray (1991) believes that the subsystems most important for personality are sensitivity to reward (reward seeking) and sensitivity to punishment (inhibition and anxiety); and that links between brain functions and personality primarily concern the traits of impulsivity and anxiety – both of which, in some form, appear in all trait theories.

Activity 5.4

Take a few minutes to refer back to Table 5.1 (Costa and McCrae), Table 5.2 (Goldberg) and Table 5.3 (Eysenck). Make a note of the dimensions that include sensation/excitement-seeking, lack of restraint and impulsiveness.

Comment

The two major dimensions of Gray's model are impulsivity and anxiety. In all the personality models anxiety (or inhibition or insecurity) is associated with the neuroticism/emotional security dimension. But, as you have seen, there is confusion about impulsiveness — which is an important variable, particularly for certain personality disorders. Some empirical findings support Gray's model, others support Eysenck's.

Currently, there is little clear evidence linking measures of personality to specific models of psychobiology. Zuckerman (1995) believes that it is not brain anatomy but neurochemistry and associated physiology which are the most likely links with personality and most likely to be inherited. He suggests that neurotransmitters such as serotonin, dopamine and noradrenalin, also known as norepinephrine, enzymes such as monoamine oxidase (MAO) and the hormones that control them will be found to be the key mediators: 'We are not born as extraverts, neurotics, impulsive sensation-seekers or antisocial personalities, but we are born with differences in reactivities of brain structures and levels of regulators like MAO' (Zuckerman, 1995, p.332). He then asks the really crucial question – *how* do these very basic biological differences direct our choices from amongst all those available in the environment?

3.2 Three approaches to studying the inheritance of the biological basis of personality

Psychologists have long been fascinated with the idea that individual differences in personality, and aptitudes of many kinds, are inherited. But, at the outset, it is crucial to understand that genetics *alone* can never be more than a part of the story.

   People (and other animals) are essentially adaptive and adaptation happens in environments. It is meaningless to question whether a personality trait or an aptitude is 'caused by genetics' or 'caused by environments' because both (nature *and* nurture), *in interaction*, are essential to life and development. From very soon after conception, and certainly before birth, the genotype has its effect on the developing organism *within an environment* to produce the phenotype, and it is impossible for genetics to have an effect without an environment (see Chapter 4).

   There are at least three empirical approaches to research on the inheritance of the biological basis of personality.

Molecular genetics

Molecular genetics is a branch of the broader field of behaviour genetics; it is based, at least in part, on biological data – at the level of DNA and positions on chromosomes. Molecular genetics encourages behaviour geneticists to identify the genes that influence individual differences in personality. An example is the tentative finding that neuroticism can be linked with the neurotransmitter serotonin, which in turn can be linked with a particular gene (Goldman, 1996; Lesch *et al.*, 1996). With the advent of the Human Genome Project this is likely to be a rapidly expanding field and there is a vast array of possible effects waiting to be explored.

The study of temperament

Psychologists have focused on *demonstrating* genetic contributions to personality by studying the consistency of a range of behaviours and emotional reactions from birth through to the teenage years. This is the study of temperament. Buss and Plomin (1984) define temperament as the subset of personality traits that are genetically inherited. They have identified three basic temperaments: emotionality, activity and sociability (EAS). They believe that these three temperaments, observed in childhood, will predict personality in adult life. This view of temperament has some overlap with Eysenck's type theory of personality. Buss and Plomin's three temperaments are shown in Table 5.4.

Table 5.4   **The EAS components of temperament**

Temperament component		
Emotionality		
	Fear	Sympathetic activation
		Apprehension, worry
		Fear face
		Escape, avoidance
	Anger	Sympathetic activation
		Transient hostility
		Angry face, pout
		Angry aggression
	Distress	
Activity		Tempo
		Vigour
		Endurance
Sociability		Tendency to affiliate
		Responsivity when with others

Source: Buss and Plomin, 1984

If temperament is to be used to study the possibility of inheritance of at least some aspects of personality, then it needs to be assessed as early in life as possible, to minimize the influence of environmental factors, and its consistency monitored over several years. This requires **longitudinal studies**. Kagan and his colleagues have spent many years studying just two temperaments observable in infants and children – *cautiousness* (inhibited) and *boldness* (uninhibited) (Kagan, 1994). In one project, Kagan observed 600 children at four months old and later at two years old. About 40 per cent started at four months of age with a relaxed reaction to

Longitudinal studies
Research designs that monitor psychological variables over long periods of time to chart development and change.

stimulation (a loud noise or a cotton swab dipped in dilute alcohol placed under their noses) and at the age of two, two-thirds of these children were still 'uninhibited'. Some of the children, however, changed their initial orientation. In another study (Kagan *et al.*, 1988), inhibition at 21 months was still observable in about 50 per cent of the children aged between 12 and 14 years, although 15 per cent had substantially changed.

When temperament is studied in neonates (infants and small children), it is relatively easy to observe and measure simple behaviours (such as frequency of crying, time spent sleeping, amount of physical activity, approach or avoidance tendencies) over quite long periods of time and at regular intervals. And it is relatively easy to conduct simple experiments, where the children are introduced to novel situations or briefly separated from their mothers to provide information about children's reactions to stimuli and situations.

There are always important ethical issues to consider when infants and young children are the participants in psychological studies. Since they cannot give informed consent to take part, this must be obtained from their parents and guardians. These studies on temperament involve mildly unpleasant stimuli and short separations from parents. Look back to the BPS guidelines in Section 2.4 of the Introduction and examine this research against the criteria.

Another way to study temperament involves parents' diaries of their children's behaviours, reactions and moods and other reports made at the time or from distant memory by parents and teachers. Most of these methods of studying temperament can be quite rigorous, but there is evidence that for parental questionnaires and diary data other factors are involved. There can be memory failures or parents may *construct* their children's temperaments and personalities in terms of their own personal ideals and social values. It is likely that quite a large proportion of the variability in the classification of children's temperament is due to parents' perceptions and projections. However, despite such limitations, it seems that there is substantial consistency in temperament through childhood and into adult life. But does this necessarily mean that it is genetic and due to biological differences that operate from birth? Consistency can be constructed from birth by a self-fulfilling prophecy of 'what (or whom) this child is like' that exists in the environment. We shall return to the effects of environments in Section 4.

Behaviour genetics: estimating heritability

Psychologists and behaviour geneticists have tried for decades to estimate the relative contributions of genetics and environment to a range of individual differences, including temperament, personality traits and intelligence. This is the study of heritability. The logic that underpins the design of studies in this tradition is based on:

- *knowing* the birth relationships (genetic relatedness) between people (parent, sibling, twin, non-related adopted sibling), which defines the proportion of genes that they have in common;
- *measuring* the trait or aptitude in question;
- *making comparisons* between groups with different levels of genetic relatedness in terms of what would be predicted from the genetic overlap and what is actually found empirically.

The genetic component is called **heritability**: the extent to which genetics are responsible for the variability in a trait in a population. (Heritability is a statistical concept and estimates of heritability do not provide information about particular individuals.)

The most commonly used design in behavioural genetics is the comparison between pairs of identical twins, **monozygotic twins** (MZ) and **dizygotic twins** (DZ). The idea is that if genetic factors explain variation in a personality trait, for example, neuroticism, then MZ twins who share all their genetic material, should be more similar in score than DZ twins, who only have half of their genes in common. Researchers use various formulae to convert associations between and within twin pairs into a 'heritability' estimate. This estimate refers to the proportion of variation between individuals in neuroticism that can be attributed to genetic influence. In fact, empirical studies have shown that, for neuroticism, despite sharing all their genes, correlations between MZ twin pairs are approximately r = 0.3, thus the observed heritability is about 0.3 or 30 per cent.

Heritability is expressed as a proportion, either as a percentage or as a decimal. When an estimate for heritability is quoted, it *automatically implies* a corresponding value for the environmental contribution – where the heritability estimate is 30 per cent, the environmental contribution would be 70 per cent, although some allowance has to be made for measurement error since no measures are perfect. Note that the influence of the environment is almost invariably *inferred* and not measured. Only rarely have attempts been made to measure aspects of the environment and these tend to be parental recollections of raising their children or indices of quite gross aspects of the environment.

Comparing MZ and DZ twins makes an assumption about their environments, namely that for each twin pair (whether MZ or DZ), the

Heritability
The proportion of variability in a trait or psychological measure within a population that can be accounted for by genetic inheritance.

Monozygotic twins
Twins who develop from a single fertilized ovum that has divided and who therefore have identical genes.

Dizygotic twins
Twins who develop from two fertilized ova and who therefore have different genes.

environment was the same. This is called the 'equal environment assumption'. But MZ twins may show more similar personality traits than DZ twins because they share more similar environments as well as having the same genes. MZ twins are likely to be treated more similarly and make closer bonds than DZ twins. Behaviour geneticists arrived at a research design that was *assumed* would avoid this problem. They make comparisons between MZ twins reared together (i.e. in the same family) and MZ twins reared apart (i.e. in different families). But this comparison still rests on the assumption that 'being brought up in the same family in a shared environment' provides the *same* environment (and the same experience of the environment), and therefore that, insofar as the environment has any impact, sharing a family environment would make twins (and other siblings, including adopted siblings) more alike. Similarly, being brought up in different families was assumed to make MZ twin pairs (and other siblings) more different. Empirical research using such 'reared together' (MZ<u>T</u> and DZ<u>T</u>) and 'reared apart' (MZ<u>A</u> and DZ<u>A</u>) designs depends on twins being separated at birth, a condition which has not always been met. The research has produced some unexpected findings. In Section 3.3 and again in Section 4 we will discuss some of these findings and return to the assumptions on which they are based.

The logic of heritability requires knowledge of genetic relatedness but studies need not be confined to **twin studies**. **Family studies** compare findings for family members of different degrees of relatedness such as siblings, half-siblings, cousins, parents and children. **Adoption studies** include non-related siblings who have been adopted; these permit comparisons between full siblings (with 50 per cent genetic overlap) and adopted siblings (with 0 per cent genetic overlap), all brought up in the same family.

Most of the basic research on heritability has used twin studies. Up to the mid 1970s these studies were quite small scale because suitable twin pairs were difficult to find. Since then, the methods of assessing heritability have dramatically improved for two reasons. First, much larger samples of twins became available. In Sweden and Finland the births of twins have to be recorded centrally with accurate medical records that distinguish between MZ and DZ twins. Using these records, it has been possible to design twin studies based on large (sometimes thousands), representative (population-based) samples of twins reared together and those documented as reared completely apart.

Second, improved statistical techniques and computer technology have made it possible to carry out larger studies which, while based on the same logic, involve testing the fit between empirical findings and mathematical projections. These kinds of studies are what make up a large

Twin studies
Studies on heritability that often use comparisons between monozygotic and dizygotic twins because their genetic relatedness is known.

Family studies
Studies on heritability that use comparisons between family members because their genetic relatedness is known.

Adoption studies
Studies on heritability that use comparisons between family members, adopted children because their genetic relatedness is known.

Behaviour genetics
Large-scale,
mathematically
modelled studies of
relationships between
genetics and behaviour.

part of **behaviour genetics**. Using greatly enhanced statistical techniques, modern behaviour geneticists have also been able to re-analyse batches of older studies that have attempted to estimate heritability and also to make detailed comparisons between studies.

3.3   Interpreting the findings of behaviour genetic studies

The findings from heritability studies suggest that most temperaments and personality traits are associated with quite high levels of genetic influence. For example, extraversion–introversion, and the EAS dimensions of temperament have estimates of heritability of the order of 50 per cent or more. For neuroticism–emotional stability, the estimates are usually lower, around 30 per cent. However, research findings are often contradictory and controversial because the explanatory power of heritability designs depends on strong assumptions that are not always met.

Early research using small twin samples, recruited by word-of-mouth and advertising, was often biased since twins who were reared apart were quite often brought up by relatives and, therefore, remained in contact with each other. More recently, twins reared apart have searched for each other and been reunited. Finding such reunited pairs to take part in research, by using the media or by advertising, may introduce substantial biases. For example, it is the successful reunions that get most media attention and, possibly, these are the ones between the most-alike twins. Often, these reunited twins have spent several years together before the researchers take their measurements. Rose *et al.* (1988), in a very large study of adult Finnish twins who had left home, found that MZ twins

Monozygotic twins

continued to have substantial contact on a daily or weekly basis, far more than the DZ twins. Thus measures (taken in adulthood) of traits may well have reflected continuing social support for their similarity.

One of the most crucial biases present in many of the studies is the time of separation of twins. An early, influential study of twins reared apart by Shields (1962) was based on only 44 twin pairs. Several of these twin pairs were only separated after a number of years and, on average, twin pairs were reared apart for only 11 years of their first 18 years of life. Some other studies have done better; for example, in the study by Lykken (1982), the twins were separated before their first birthday. But in a large, careful study by Pedersen *et al.* (1988), 18 per cent of the twins were separated *after they were five years old*. And we are not told the exact age at separation for the other 82 per cent.

This is a good example of how assumptions differ across fields of psychology. In the world of twin studies, heritability, and mathematical modelling, a definition of 'reared apart' can mean many things. Separation at less than one year or between one year and five years seems to be considered acceptable for modelling the relative contributions of heritability and environmental influence. Psychologists who work with different models of the person might argue that a great deal of psychological development has already crystallized by 6 months or 1 year, and certainly by 5 years of age.

Pedersen *et al.* (1988) obtained their sample of twins using the Swedish Twin Registry, and ensured that the twins who had been reared apart really did not know each other. They identified 328 pairs of twins who were reared apart (A), 99 MZA pairs and 229 DZA pairs; and 372 pairs of twins reared together (T), 160 MZT pairs and 212 DZT pairs. They also matched the pairs of twins reared together with pairs reared apart in terms of variables like age, gender and country of birth. In this study, the estimate of heritability of neuroticism was found to be 0.25.

Given the design weaknesses discussed above, perhaps it is to be expected that estimates of heritability are often conflicting. On closer examination, twin studies commonly use different measures of personality traits. For example, in the Pedersen *et al.* (1988) study, a short form of the Eysenck Personality Inventory was used, possibly being less accurate than measures used in other research and so the estimate of heritability might be less reliable. (Also, in this study the twins were much older than in most research.) Eaves *et al.* (1989) re-analysed all the twin studies up to 1976 and found the estimate of heritability of neuroticism to be 0.29, whereas Loehlin and Nichols (1976) studied a sample of about 800 twins and found the estimate of heritability of neuroticism to be 0.53. In 1992, Loehlin re-analysed all the findings from around the world that had used behaviour genetic designs to assess the heritability of the five factor personality traits. In this re-analysis (see Table 5.5) the estimate of heritability of neuroticism was 0.31. This study showed that the estimates of heritability of all five factors was quite high. Most commonly, although not in Loehlin's work shown in Table 5.5, extraversion is the trait that gives the largest estimate of heritability.

Table 5.5 **Estimates of the heritability of personality factors from the five factor model**

Personality factor	Heritability
Extraversion	0.36
Agreeableness	0.28
Conscientiousness	0.28
Neuroticism	0.31
Openness	0.46

Adapted from Loehlin, 1992
Source: Cloninger, 1996, p.67

Loehlin's 1992 study, like several others, shows a surprising but well-documented finding that the effect of the so-called shared environment (i.e. the effect of being brought up in the same family) appears to have little or no influence on temperament or personality. This is strongly counterintuitive and goes against much research concerning the impact of early environments, carers, family life and upbringing regimes on personality development.

As we shall see in the next section, in many respects children brought up in the same family do not have the same environment. And as children from the same family, twins or otherwise, get older and experience school, peer groups and friends, this too is a form of non-shared environment. The impact of life outside the family on personality is explored by Harris (1995).

This section has shown that the biological components of temperament and personality are inherited to a quite substantial degree. But the genetic contribution still accounts for less than half of the variability in personality measures. The remainder, apart from error, is due to the influence of environments. What are these environmental influences and how do they operate? Questions like these will be the focus of the next section.

Summary Section 3

- Personality *can* be studied at the biological level of analysis, although, to date, the findings are far from clear.
- Attempts to explain personality at the biological level start with simple models of the brain. These involve (1) key subsystems of anatomy or biochemistry which are linked to (2) behavioural functions of survival value and (3) can be translated into individual differences in personality. To date these models have proved to be too simple to give good accounts of the biological basis of personality.
- Biological explanations of personality strongly suggest that part of personality is genetically determined.
- Genetic and environmental factors always *interact* to produce their effects.
- The possible contribution of genetics to personality can be studied empirically through (1) molecular genetics, (2) temperament in children and (3) the twin, family and adoption studies of behaviour genetics.
- Heritability studies depend on assumptions that are frequently not met.
- Heritability is an estimate which assigns a percentage of the variation in test scores to genetic components in a population.
- Current best estimates of the heritability of personality and temperament are of the order of 20 to 30 per cent.

4 Personality and environments

Although heritability studies attempt to estimate the relative contributions of genetics and the environment, the effects of nature and nurture on personality are joint and inseparable. Continuous *interactive processes* between the organism and its environment begin at conception and continue after birth with a massive increase in the complexity and diversity of environments. These environments are physical, and made up of 'other people' and the meanings they carry and create. It is the process of interaction between *reactive* organisms and infinitely variable, *reactive* and meaningful environments that brings about the explosion of individual diversity.

The focus of this section is on the importance of environments for understanding the *development* and the *expression* of personality.

4.1 A closer look at environments and their role in early personality development

Trying to understand environments and their role in personality development is a task that has been defined very differently by the various perspectives in psychology. Individual differences psychologists have usually described environments in terms of broad 'dimensions', rather as they define personality itself. These 'dimensions' include the socio-economic status of the family, education levels of the parents, neighbourhood in which the family lives, parents' relationship, mother's well-being, and perhaps the tone of the 'regime' of child rearing such as controlling or relaxed. In line with this broad-brush approach, behaviour geneticists *assumed* that children brought up in the same family would be in exactly the same environment. But research shows that being brought up in the same family, by the same parents, does not necessarily make MZ or DZ twins more similar than those who are brought up in different families.

There is now collaboration between individual differences psychologists, behaviour geneticists and developmental psychologists to explore this finding that environmental influences on infants and children *within the same family* serve to make them different in terms of their temperaments and personalities and general adjustment (Dunn and Plomin, 1990; Hetherington *et al.*, 1994). There are a range of reasons why shared environments are **non-standard environments**.

Non-standard environments
Environments of siblings growing up in the same household which vary in subtle ways and are experienced as different.

First, each child *experiences* the environment differently, perceiving what goes on around them through the lens of their individual temperament and personality. It is to this idiosyncratic experience of the environment that they learn to adapt.

Second, children and even infants have ways of selecting, acting on and modifying their environments, creating their own environmental niches. It is easy to think of environments as just 'being there', exerting an influence on passive recipients. But, children choose and shape aspects of their family environment and their parents' behaviour from a very early age, in line with their temperaments. Children with different temperaments seek out different aspects of their environments; and different children also have different meanings for their parents and different effects on them.

They thus receive different treatment from them. So each child has the capacity to create its own environment and potentiate diversity.

Third, each child's environment (in the same family) *is* different. Families *do* change over time. Economic factors change, living conditions change, parents' relationships change, sometimes there is separation and divorce. One of the most powerful sets of environmental factors within the family concerns siblings. A child born into a family where there are already four siblings has a very different social world from a child who is first born. Birth order itself has been found to be an important factor in personality development, as have sibling personalities and the nature of sibling dynamics (Brody, 1996; Dunn, 2000).

Parents *do* treat their children differently, sometimes in quite obvious ways but certainly in a variety of subtle and pervasive ways that add up to a considerable force for diversity. Children's personalities are shaped by subtle systems of reward and punishment (from parents and other people), most of which operate below the level of consciousness for both parents and children. These are known as processes of **social learning.** Chapter 3 illustrated the power of the stimulus and reward properties of environments to shape behaviours. But it is important to realize that systems of reward not only shape learning but also communicate meanings – they inform the child what is of value and what is not. The earliest family environment attributes meanings and creates meanings for each child and, in this sense, *at least a part of the child's personality is constructed by interaction and talk within the family.*

Social learning
Takes place in social contexts that provide reward contingencies and models for information.

Siblings may be treated the same simply because they look the same. MZ twins are a special case of this. In some families the similarities between MZ twins are emphasized at every opportunity; in others it is the differences that are exaggerated. These contrast effects were demonstrated in Loehlin's review of twin studies (1992) where MZ twin pairs were more likely to have different levels of extraversion if brought up in the same family than if brought up in different families. There is also evidence of contrast effects for the childhood temperaments of shyness, inhibition and activity.

Apart from twins, some families have a culture in which differences between their children are treated and talked about as undesirable, where an emphasis is placed on everyone being alike and everything being equal. In other families, individuality is encouraged and siblings can be assigned roles within the family group, such as 'the energetic one' or, the 'quiet one'. These different roles may be equally acceptable but they may be assigned punitively to force value-laden contrasts between children. Family systems that attribute meanings and values to temperaments and personality traits can be a healthy process, however they may also be limiting for the development of the child's personality. Often, these attributions relate to the caregiver's own personality, perhaps being unconscious projections of the caregiver's own personality or attempts to *label* the child as very different. Parents' perceptions of their child's temperaments will influence how they and everyone else behave towards the child, and perhaps the child's subsequent development. This illustrates just how difficult it is to separate the parents' personalities from those of their children.

It is often the psychoanalytically influenced developmental researchers who have studied the effect of the earliest 'other people' environments in most detail. For example, Stern (1985) has described the underlying *meaningfulness* of the process through which a mother tries to modulate her baby's temperament. **Tuning**, according to Stern, is a maternal response to a baby's mood that neither exactly matches the baby nor is misattuned. Tuning falls between the two extremes. It can give infants an experience they can use to learn to regulate themselves and it can also be part of the mother's unconscious or semiconscious *shaping of the baby's personality*. This is illustrated in the following extract in which Stern describes observational research where the mother is an engaged participant.

Tuning
Maternal responses to an infant's mood that provide an experience that the infant can use to self-regulate its mood.

| 5.4 | *Learning self-regulation of temperament: an example of mother and child interaction* |

Sam's mother was observed characteristically to just undermatch the affective behaviours of her ten-month old son. For instance, when he evidenced some affect and looked to her with a bright face and some excited arm-flapping, she responded with a good, solid, "Yes, honey" that, in its absolute level of activation, fell just short of his arm-flapping and face-brightness. Such behaviour on her part was all the more striking because she was a highly animated, vivacious person.

In our usual fashion, we asked our routine questions – why she did what she did when she did it the way she did it – for each such interchange. Her answers to the first questions – why, what and when – were quite expected and unremarkable. When we asked her why she did it the way she did it, more was revealed. In particular, when asked if she had intended to match the infant's level of enthusiasm in her response to him, she said "no". She was vaguely aware of the fact that she frequently undermatched him. When asked why, she struggled toward verbalizing that if she were to match him – not even overmatch, but just match him – he would tend to focus more on her behaviour than on his own; it might shift the initiative over from him to her. She felt that he tended to lose his initiative if she joined in fully and equally and shared with him. When asked what was wrong if the initiative passed over to her some of the time, she paused and finally said that she felt he was a little on the passive side and tended to let the initiative slip to her, which she prevented by undermatching.

When the mother was asked what was wrong with the child's being relatively more passive or less initiatory than she at this life phase, she revealed that she thought he was too much like his father, who was too passive and low-keyed. She was the initiator, the spark plug in the family. She was the one who infused enthusiasm into the marriage, decided what to eat, whether to go to the movies, when to make love. And she did not want her son to grow up to be like his father in these ways.

Both mother and we were surprised to find that this one piece of behaviour, purposeful slight misattunements, carried such weight and had become a cornerstone of her upbringing strategy and fantasy. Actually, it should not have been surprising. After all, there has to be some way in which attitudes, plans and fantasies get transposed into palpable interactive behaviour to achieve their ultimate aim. We happened to uncover one such point of transposition. Attunement and misattunement exist at the interface between attitude or fantasy and behaviour, and their importance lies in their capacity to translate between the two.

One of the fascinating paradoxes about her strategy is that left alone, it would do exactly the opposite of what she intended. Her underattunements would tend to create a lower-keyed child who was less inclined to share his spunk. The mother would inadvertently have contributed to making the son more like the father, rather than different from him. The lines of "generational influences" are often not straight.

Source: Stern, 1985, pp.211–13

This extract provides a vivid illustration of the potency of the maternal environment. This mother is shaping her son's affective responses and creating an important part of his personality. She is also beginning the process of constructing a personality for him, in her fantasy and talk. Sam is learning to regulate his 'natural' emotional state. Babies are not only born with different temperaments but with different capacities to self-regulate their temperaments. Derryberry and Rothbart (1988) believe that individual differences in capacities for self-regulation of temperament are crucial for the development of personality traits.

4.2 Environments and the expression of personality

The idea of consistency seems to be the hallmark of 'personality', but *do* people behave consistently across different settings and environments? There is empirical research that supports quite high levels of consistency of behaviour (in terms of personality traits) when participants are observed in similar settings across several occasions, *providing the behaviour that is being observed is central to the trait in question.* But there is also plenty of everyday experience that suggests that people behave, think, and feel differently in different settings and with different people. For example, someone who is low in conscientiousness may well show various kinds of unreliability and unpunctuality across a range of different, but broadly 'work' settings, but would never miss a flight to a holiday destination. Is this inconsistency? Another example might be someone who scores highly on extraversion, and gets invited to lots of weddings. Would it be surprising to find that the person behaves like an introvert during marriage ceremonies, but like an extravert at receptions? Is this person being inconsistent by behaving differently in the two settings? Does this mean that the person's behaviour is not a function of his/her personality?

    The argument that behaviour is under the influence of the environment – the range of situations that people encounter – was first put forward by Mischel (1968) who claimed that all trait psychology is misconceived. This point of view is known as **situationism** and a classic study by Hartshorne and May (1928) is often quoted in its support. They investigated whether children would behave honestly or dishonestly under conditions where discovery seemed (to the children) impossible. When it was advantageous to cheat, many children did so, but not necessarily consistently. Hartshorne and May concluded that traits like honesty and cooperativeness do not consistently control behaviour and that what people do is largely influenced by situational factors. This study is problematic because children are known to think about 'honesty' rather differently from adults and their conception of what is 'moral' changes as they grow older. But the study seemed to show that the children were being influenced by the rewards offered in a certain situation. They were behaving instrumentally. Similarly, the person who is never late for holiday flights could be seen as exhibiting behaviour driven by rewards and costs rather than a personality trait. It seems obvious that there must be some point at which the salient features of a situation will outweigh trait-driven habits. Perhaps what would be more indicative of consistency and personality traits would be the same behaviour every time the same situation is encountered. Does the extravert *always* party exuberantly at wedding receptions *and* at other

Situationism
The idea that personality is not consistent but that behaviour is under the control of environments and situations.

celebrations? Some psychologists stress that in order to explain behaviours, interactions between inner dispositions and situations have to be taken into account.

The quiet, introverted behaviour of the extravert personality at Western wedding ceremonies is hardly a surprise. It doesn't seem necessary to do away with the idea of the extravert's inner disposition: most people would immediately understand the person's behaviour as being under the influence of the **social norms**, or scripts of how to behave at a solemn ceremony. In general it is important to have some understanding of the *extent* to which behaviour is the result of inner dispositions (traits) or the rules, roles and required skills of social behaviour.

The word 'personality' is derived from the Latin word persona, which means a mask. But if a great deal of 'what people do' depends on the situation, in what sense can there be 'real' personality as opposed to a social persona? Is social behaviour grafted on to one's 'real' personality? This might be understandable in the case of a clearly prescribed social behaviour like waiting one's turn at the doctor's surgery. But what about role behaviour like that of 'parent' or a long lived-in occupational role such as 'police officer' or 'scientist'? How might a personality theorist draw a line between the demands of the role and personality? What is the difference between what 'we really are' and what 'we often do'? What people do for long periods of time usually becomes part of their *identity* (see Chapter 1), but does it become integrated into personality or change trait scores? Some roles are easily adopted and easily left behind. Everyone can take the role of patient when consulting the doctor and no-one would suggest that this brief role has a long-term impact on personality or identity, whereas chronic illness and long-term 'being a patient' certainly change identity and can change personality traits.

Role-taking, in particular, is a mysterious process often requiring subtle knowledge that people seem to be able to mobilize and enact quite easily. Sometimes taking a role seems to involve identification, really 'becoming' the role. People's facility for role-taking is often used by psychologists to explore social processes. One famous role-play study carried out in the USA by Zimbardo (1975) not only demonstrates the force of role-taking but dramatically illustrates some of the unresolved questions about interactions between roles, situations and personality. This study also raises considerable ethical issues. Box 5.5 presents a collage of extracts from Zimbardo's own website on the Stanford Prison Experiment (1999) together with a commentary.

Social norms
Expectations and prescriptions in the social and cultural context that influence behaviours and values.

5.5 The Stanford prison experiment

Philip G. Zimbardo

Probably the most famous psychological study that involved role-play is Zimbardo's (1975) investigation of the effects on the behaviour of college students of adopting the role of prisoner or guard in a mock prison created in a university department. So powerful was the effect of role-play and the situation, that the planned two-week study was stopped after six days. (This research was outlined in the discussion on ethics in Section 2.4 of the introductory chapter.) The 'prisoners' had become demoralized and showed signs of extreme stress. Some of them were depressed and others were substantially out of touch with reality. The 'guards' behaved in authoritarian and aggressive ways and some of them became sadistic. Zimbardo describes how he himself and the 'prison consultant', although not consciously role-playing, were also drawn into authoritarian and quite cruel behaviour.

The participants in the study were volunteers who responded to an advertisement in the local paper asking for volunteers for research on the psychological effects of prison life. There were more than 70 applicants. They were given personality tests and diagnostic interviews to eliminate those with medical and psychological problems, a history of crime and drug abuse. The 24 college students who were selected to take part were paid $15 a day. In light of what happened, it is worth wondering how good these selection procedures were. Or did they fail to measure salient aspects of personality that were mobilized in the study?

> On all dimensions that we were able to test or observe, they [the chosen participants] reacted normally. Our study of prison life began, then, with an average group of healthy, intelligent, middle-class males. These boys were arbitrarily divided into two groups by a flip of the coin. Half were randomly assigned to be guards, the other to be prisoners.
>
> We began with nine guards and nine prisoners in our jail. Three guards worked each of three eight-hour shifts, while three prisoners occupied each of the three barren cells around the clock. The remaining guards and prisoners from our sample of 24 were on

call in case they were needed. The cells were so small that there was room for only three cots on which the prisoners slept or sat, with room for little else.

Less than 36 hours into the experiment, Prisoner #8612 began suffering from acute emotional disturbance, disorganized thinking, uncontrollable crying, and rage.

Levels of identification with the role had already reached the point where personality seemed to be affected.

In spite of all of this, we had already come to think so much like prison authorities that we thought he was trying to 'con' us - to fool us into releasing him. [...] During the parole hearings we also witnessed an unexpected metamorphosis of our prison consultant as he adopted the role of head of the Parole Board. He literally became the most hated authoritarian official imaginable, so much so that when it was over he felt sick at who he had become – his own tormentor who had previously rejected his annual parole requests for 16 years when he was a prisoner.

Here Zimbardo is observing that the prison consultant, who had himself been a prisoner many years before, was identifying with (had 'become') another person. This sounds more like a temporary change of personality than either a role or a change of identity.

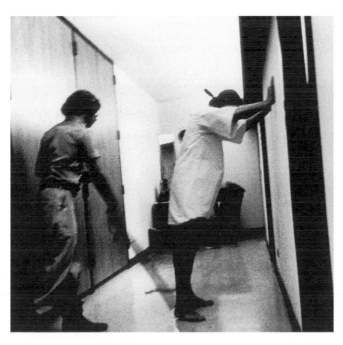
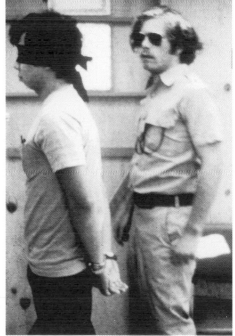

'Prisoners' and 'guards' in the Stanford Prison Experiment

There were three types of guards. First, there were tough but fair guards who followed prison rules. Second, there were 'good guys' who did little favours for the prisoners and never punished them. And finally, about a third of the guards were hostile, arbitrary, and inventive in their forms of prisoner humiliation. These guards appeared to thoroughly enjoy the power they wielded, yet none of our preliminary personality tests were able to predict this behaviour.

The prisoners even nicknamed the most macho and brutal guard in our study 'John Wayne.' [...] Where had our 'John Wayne' learned to become such a guard? How could he and others move so readily into that role? How could intelligent, mentally healthy, 'ordinary' men become perpetrators of evil so quickly? These were questions we were forced to ask.

[...] it became clear that we had to end the study. We had created an overwhelmingly powerful situation – a situation in which prisoners were withdrawing and behaving in pathological ways, and in which some of the guards were behaving sadistically. Even the 'good' guards felt helpless to intervene [...] we had learned through videotapes that the guards were escalating their abuse of prisoners in the middle of the night when they thought no researchers were watching and the experiment was 'off.' Their boredom had driven them to ever more pornographic and degrading abuse of the prisoners. [...]

Christina Maslach, a recent Stanford Ph.D. brought in to conduct interviews with the guards and prisoners, strongly objected when she saw our prisoners being marched on a toilet run, bags over their heads, legs chained together, hands on each other's shoulders. Filled with outrage, she said, 'It's terrible what you are doing to these boys!' Out of 50 or more outsiders who had seen our prison, she was the only one who ever questioned its morality. Once she countered the power of the situation, however, it became clear that the study should be ended.

(Zimbardo, 1999)

What was going on in this study? Can role-taking explain the extreme behaviours observed? The situation in which these participants found themselves exerted a profound effect. And perhaps the extreme behaviours were driven by personality traits that were normally hidden and/or controlled. Perhaps this extreme situation simply permitted the *expression* of these personality traits. There were individual differences at work. For example, not all the guards behaved badly and only a few were overtly sadistic – although the others didn't stop them. According to Zimbardo, all his would-be participants had been thoroughly screened for psychological disturbance and for personality variables. Only one of the traits measured at the start of the study predicted any of the behaviours observed – measures of authoritarianism predicted the prisoners who would survive best in the extreme situation. But these participants volunteered for a study known to be about prison life. Did they self-select in terms of their personalities? Or in terms of their fantasies? Why didn't Zimbardo's personality tests at least pick up the potential for high levels of sadism? (Three out of 24 of the selected participants were overtly sadistic during the study.) Perhaps sadism wasn't measured, although Eysenck's psychoticism scale, if used, might have picked up a propensity to sadism. Sadism as a personality trait is probably not talked about much in cultural life and Goldberg has shown that negative evaluative words are limited in ordinary lexicons in several cultures and therefore do not feature highly in trait psychology. This is one of the suggestions for extending trait models beyond the Big Five.

Zimbardo's study raises questions about personality that the individual differences approach has difficulty in answering. The final section will review some of the questions about conceptualizing personality that have surfaced in the chapter, some that are addressed by individual differences psychology and some that are not.

Summary Section 4

- Environments have a considerable and complex effect on the development of individual differences in personality and individuality.
- So-called shared environments are non-standard in that each child experiences, adapts to and actively creates his/her own unique environment.
- Environments contain reward contingencies that shape personality. They also carry family and wider cultural values and meanings that can construct personality in social interactions.
- The consistency of behaviour implied by trait psychology can be disrupted by social norms and by role-taking. Sometimes role-taking facilitates the expression of personality traits.
- The individual differences approach to personality does not address possible relationships between personality, social persona, role and identity.

5 Review: conceptualizing personality

This chapter began with the idea that personality is a familiar concept, but more complicated than it might at first appear; and you were invited to think about what you believed 'personality' means. This section explores some complications associated with the concept of personality.

Activity 5.5

Find the notes you made for Activities 5.1 and 5.2(3) at the beginning of this chapter and the answers you gave to the 'Who am I?' questions in Activity 1.1 of Chapter 1 ('Identities and diversities'). Refer back to these notes as you read this last section. Think about whether you have changed your opinions about the concept of personality since you made the notes for Activity 5.1.

Suppose you began with the notion of 'personality' as denoting types of people, personality traits and resting on the idea of consistency of behaviour. If so, then the individual differences view of personality will have bolstered your initial opinion. If you wrote about personality, or temperament, as being something we have that belongs to us, is biologically based and inherited to some degree, then your view will have been supported by individual differences theory and research. But it is unlikely that this perspective encompasses *all* that you listed as the features of personality; there are other ways of thinking about personality.

In your list for Activity 5.1, and perhaps in your description of your own personality in Activity 5.2(3), you may have linked consistency to integration, the idea that a person's personality is somehow unified. The individual differences approach suggests that we think of personality as a stable *profile* of traits or dimensions, or in Eysenck's terminology a 'type'. But does this mean that personality is a unitary synthesis of traits? Or do we perhaps roll out different traits in different environments as if we have **modular personalities**? Does consistency mean *always* being the same, *always* doing the same thing in the same or similar situations? Zimbardo's experiment demonstrated how social situations can have a powerful effect on behaviours. It is difficult to explain what happened in that study in terms of traits and consistency.

You may have stressed, right at the beginning, that people's personalities are full of contradictions. Refer back to your description of your own personality in Activity 5.2(3). From your insider viewpoint on your

Modular personality
The idea that personality is not unitary, coherent and consistent but has different facets that are mobilized in different situations.

personality, you may have been thinking 'behind' personality traits. If you wrote 'I am reliable and conscientious', you might also have been aware of the conflict that you experience in being that way. Conflict might be a significant part of your personality, but it is difficult to tap when using a questionnaire and it doesn't feature in the individual differences perspective. It is this kind of inner conflict that is central to psychoanalytic views of personality (see Chapter 9). Conflicts and contradictions also form a part of identities and identity formation, especially according to the social constructionist view (see Chapter 1). Perhaps people have fragmented personalities, keeping some aspects hidden most of the time. Although this would not accord with the individual differences view, it could help to explain what happened in the Zimbardo study.

At the beginning of this chapter you might have stressed the diversity of people's personalities. Understanding and explaining individuality is certainly not the focus of the individual differences tradition. But most individual differences psychologists acknowledge that, whilst the basics of personality type might be inherited, constraining, and relatively fixed, nevertheless environments and experiences are a crucial source of individual diversity as people learn and adapt. Section 4 showed that personality development involves elaborate interactions between temperament, self-regulatory capacities and personality and the contingencies existing in the environment. A crucial part of this process involves meanings and the attribution of personality by other people and by more general cultural forces. Perhaps a significant part of personality is socially constructed, created through conversation, interaction and feedback from other people. (Remember that the starting point for individual differences research on personality was the 'words we use' to describe other people.) There are parallels here with the concept of identity and the discussion of social constructionism in Chapter 1.

Activity 5.6

Examine your responses to Activity 5.2(3) and take a few minutes to compare these with your answers to the 'Who am I?' questions from Activity 1.1 in Chapter 1. How similar are these two lists? Do they imply equally 'consistent' or 'contradictory' versions of you? Do the two questions elicit different kinds of answers?

Comment

It seems that attempts to examine how people behave, feel and present themselves in the social world, and how they experience themselves, invite the use of terms like 'role', 'identity' and 'self'. While these terms are related to personality, they are also rather different. Your answers to the identity question in Activity 1.1 may have been more about what you 'do' and your roles, even if this word was not used; and these answers were almost certainly more located in your social environment. Personality theories tend to focus on individuals in a much more bounded sense. It is as if we think of personality as 'just there' inside us, a bit like having lungs or a heart, relatively solid and contained and not very open to social influences. In contrast, 'identity' connects us to the rest of the world and is more permeable and fluid. The biology and trait building blocks of the individual differences view of personality particularly indicate this, certainly in comparison with the ideas of identity projects and identity shifts discussed in Chapter 1.

In the Zimbardo study, one of the distressed 'prisoners' (not quoted in Box 5.5) said that he felt he had lost his identity. This sounds well beyond role-taking. Could identity have changed so quickly? In this extreme situation, the participant was stripped of physical and social support for his identity and his usual 'reality'. But did his personality change? This seems a bit more difficult to accept. The prison consultant, who had been a 'real' prisoner many years before, felt as if he had 'become' someone else. Again this doesn't sound like a personality change. Perhaps identity *was* involved. However, he did not 'become' his former identity but, instead, another significant person who had aroused very strong feelings in him. This suggests a more psychoanalytic explanation in terms of **identification** with the aggressor. It seems that we learn how to 'be' others with whom we have had important interactions. In Freudian theory, power-related and perhaps frightening interactions seem to be particularly conducive to identification. From a psychoanalytic perspective what happened to the prison consultant (and perhaps the most abusive of the guards) was identification rather than role-taking or identity change. In psychoanalytic terms, this *would* be thought of as an expression of a part of personality. In psychoanalytic theory, internalized figures of significant others are considered to be part of the self, and available to be expressed as modules of personality. This level of fluidity is not compatible with the individual differences approach.

Perhaps you mentioned in Activity 5.1, or with respect to your own personality, that personality is multifaceted and fluid; that personality can undergo development, and sometimes dramatic change. People seem to have mixed feelings about this possibility, wanting to be 'themselves' and stay the same but also wanting to be able to change and re-invent themselves. There are similarities here with research on identities. In contrast, the individual differences view of personality and its empirical findings give strong support to the stability of personality, once it is established, along with its resistance to change.

You may also have stressed that we have some degree of control over the personalities we become – that we can exercise conscious reflection and change ourselves. This is not part of the individual differences

Identification
Hypothetical process by which individuals experience some temporary merging with another or 'becoming' an aspect of another person.

tradition but it is something that you will meet in Chapter 9 which addresses the 'whole person' – the organization of personality, individuality, subjective experiences and how processes of change can be promoted.

Further reading

Allen, B.P. (2000) *Personality Theories: Development, Growth and Diversity* (3rd edn), Boston, MA, Allyn and Bacon.
This contextualizes each personality theory within the life and times of the theorist.
Cloninger, S.C. (1996) *Personality: Description, Dynamics, and Development*, New York, W.H.Freeman and Company.
This provides extra detail on personality and personality research. Its author has an engaging style and unusual organisation of topics that creates a strong storyline.
Dunn, J. and Plomin, R. (1990) *Separate Lives: Why Siblings Are So Different*, New York, Basic Books.
In this book Dunn and Plomin addressed the unexpected finding of behaviour genetics research – that early experiences in our families appeared to have little effect on the development of our personalities.

References

Brody, G.H. (ed.) (1996) *Sibling Relationships: Their Causes and Consequences*, Norwood, NJ, Ablex.

Bruner, J.S. (1990) *Acts of Meaning*, Cambridge, MA, Harvard University Press.

Buss, D.M. (1997) 'Evolutionary foundations of personality', in Hogan, R., Johnson, J. and Briggs, S.R. (eds) *Handbook of Personality Psychology*, San Diego, CA, Academic Press.

Buss, A.H. and Plomin, R. (1984) *Temperament: Early Developing Personality Traits*, Hillsdale, NJ, Lawrence Erlbaum.

Cattell, R.B. and Kline, P. (1977) *The Scientific Analysis of Personality and Motivation*, New York, Academic Press.

Cloninger, S.C. (1996) *Personality: Description, Dynamics and Development*, New York, W.H.Freeman and Company.

Costa, P.T. and McCrae, R.R. (1988) 'Personality in adulthood: a 6-year longitudinal study of self-reports and spouse ratings on the NEO

Personality Inventory', *Journal of Personality and Social Psychology*, vol.54, pp.853–63.

Costa, P.T. and McCrae, R.R. (1992) *NEO PI-R Professional Manual*, Odessa, FL, Psychological Assessment Resources.

Costa, P.T. and McCrae, R.R. (1994) 'Set like plaster? Evidence for the stability of adult personality', in Heatherton, T.F. and Weinberger, J.L. (eds).

Dancey, C. and Reidy, J. (2002) *Statistics Without Maths for Psychology* (2nd edn), Harlow, Pearson Education.

Derryberry, D. and Rothbart, M.K. (1988) 'Arousal, affect and attention as components of temperament', *Journal of Personality and Social Psychology*, vol.55, pp.958–66.

Dunn, J. (2000) 'State of the art: siblings', *The Psychologist*, vol.13, pp.244–9.

Dunn, J. and Plomin, R. (1990) *Separate Lives: Why Siblings Are So Different*, New York, Basic Books.

Eaves, L.J., Eysenck, H.J. and Martin, N.G. (1989) *Genes, Culture and Personality: An Empirical Approach*, Austin, TX, University of Texas Press.

Eysenck, H.J. (1967) *The Biological Basis of Personality*, Springfield, IL, Thomas.

Eysenck, M.W. (1998) 'Personality', in Eysenck, M (ed.) *Psychology: An Integrated Approach*, London, Longman.

Galton, F. (1884) 'Measurement of character', *Fortnightly Review*, vol.36, pp.179–85.

Goldberg, L.R. (1981) 'Language and individual differences: the search for universals in personality lexicons', in Wheeler, L. (ed.), *Review of Personality and Social Psychology, Vol.2*, London, Sage.

Goldman, D. (1996) 'High anxiety', *Science*, vol.274, p.1483.

Gray, J.A. (1987) *The Neuropsychology of Anxiety: An Enquiry into the Functions of the Septo-hippocampal System* (2nd edn), Cambridge, Cambridge University Press.

Gray, J.A. (1991) 'Neural systems, emotion and affect', in Madden, J. (ed.) *Neurobiology of Learning, Emotion and Affect*, New York, Raven Press.

Harris, J.R. (1995) 'Where is the child's environment? A group socialization theory of development', *Psychological Review*, vol.102, no.3, pp.458–89.

Hartshorne, H. and May, M.A. (1928) *Studies in Deceit*, New York, Macmillan.

Heatherton, T.F. and Weinberger, J.L. (eds) (1994) *Can Personality Change?*, Washington, DC, American Psychological Association.

Helson, R. and Stewart, A. (1994) 'Personality change in adulthood', in Heatherton, T.F. and Weinberger, J.L. (eds).

Hetherington, E.M., Reiss, D. and Plomin, R. (1994) *Separate Social Worlds of Siblings: The Impact of Nonshared Environment on Development*, Hillsdale, NJ, Lawrence Erlbaum.

Kagan, J. (1994) *Galen's Prophecy: Temperament in Human Nature*, London, Free Association Books.

Kagan, J., Resnick, J.S. and Snidman, N. (1988) 'Biological bases of childhood shyness', *Science*, vol.240, pp.167–71.

Lesch, K.P., Bengel, D., Heils, A., Sabol, S.Z., Greenberg, B.D., Petri, S., Bejamin, J., Muller, C.R., Hamer, D.H. and Murphy, D.L. (1996) 'Association of anxiety-related traits with a polymorphism in the serotonin transporter gene regulatory region', *Science*, vol.274, pp.1527–31.

Loehlin, J.C. (1992) *Genes and Environment in Personality Development*, Newbury Park, CA, Sage.

Loehlin, J.C. and Nichols, R.C. (1976) *Heredity, Environment and Personality: A Study of 850 Sets of Twins*, Austin, TX, University of Texas Press.

Lykken, D.T. (1982) 'Research with twins: the concept of emergencies', *Psychophysiology*, vol.19, pp.361–73.

McCrae, R.R. and Costa, P.T. (1994) 'The stability of personality: observations and evaluations', *Current Directions in Psychological Science*, vol.3, pp.171–5.

McCrae, R.R., Costa, P.T., Ostendorf, F., Angleitner, A., Hebíčková, M., Avia, M.D., Sanz, J., Sánchez-Bernardos, M.L., Kusdil, M.E., Woodfield, R., Saunders, P.R. and Smith, P.B. (2000) 'Nature over nurture: temperament, personality and life span development', *Journal of Personality and Social Psychology*, vol.78, no.1, pp.173–86.

Matthews, G. and Deary, I.J. (1998) *Personality Traits,* Cambridge, Cambridge University Press.

Mischel, W. (1968) *Personality and Assessment*, New York, Wiley.

Pedersen, N.L., Plomin, R., McClearn, G.E. and Friberg, L. (1988) 'Neuroticism, extraversion and related traits in adult twins reared apart and reared together', *Journal of Personality and Social Psychology*, vol.55, pp.950–7.

Rose, R.J., Koskenvuo, M., Kaprio, J., Sarna, S. and Langinvainio, H. (1988) 'Shared genes, shared experience, and similarity of personality: data from 14,288 adult Finnish co-twins', *Journal of Personality and Social Psychology*, vol.54, pp.161–71.

Roth, I. (ed.) (1996) *Introduction to Psychology*, East Sussex, Lawrence Erlbaum Associates/The Open University.

Saucier, G. and Goldberg, L.R. (1998) 'What is beyond the big five?', *Journal of Personality*, vol.66, no.4, pp.495–524.

Saucier, G., Hampson, S.E. and Goldberg, L.R. (2000) 'Cross-language studies of lexical personality factors', in Hampson, S.E (ed.) *Advances in Personality Psychology, Vol. 1*, Philadelphia, PA, Taylor and Francis.

Shields, J. (1962) *Monozygotic Twins Brought Up Apart and Brought Up Together: An Investigation into the Genetic and Environmental Causes of Variation in Personality*, London, Oxford University Press.

Somer, O. and Goldberg, L.R. (1999) 'The structure of Turkish trait-descriptive adjectives', *Journal of Personality and Social Psychology*, vol.76, no.3, pp.431–50.

Stern, D.N. (1985) *The Interpersonal World of the Infant: A View from Psychoanalysis and Developmental Psychology*, New York, Basic Books.

Zimbardo, P. (1975) 'Transforming experimental research into advocacy for social change', in Deutsch, M. and Hornstein, H. (eds) *Applying Social Psychology*, Hillsdale, NJ, Lawrence Erlbaum.

Zimbardo, P.G. (1999) *Stanford Prison Experiment: A Simulation Study of the Psychology of Imprisonment Conducted at Stanford University*. [on line] http://www.prisonexp.org [accessed 22 March 2001]

Zuckerman, M. (1991) *Psychobiology of Personality*, Cambridge, MA, Cambridge University Press.

Zuckerman, M. (1995) 'Good and bad humors: biochemical bases of personality and its disorders', *Psychological Science*, vol.6, no.6, pp.325–32.

Commentary 5: The individual differences approach to personality

The focus of Chapter 5 is personality in terms of traits and types – a measurement approach. This perspective on personality has always been associated with a search for the biological bases of individual differences and their possible inheritance. In this sense, Chapter 5 builds on the biological psychology approach presented in the previous chapter.

Theory

1 The psychometric/individual differences perspective *measures* personality, *describes* personality structure, and tries to *explain* the origins of personality in terms of biology, including genetics.

Methods

2 Personality and identity (the subject of Chapter 1) are both concerned with 'who we are'. However, whilst most identity theorists use a holistic approach, personality theorists in the psychometric, individual differences perspective focus on measurable aspects of people.

3 The individual differences perspective takes an outsider viewpoint on personality that privileges the *measurement* of behaviour. However, sometimes researchers also use some self-reports from their participants.

Themes

4 The individual differences perspective seeks out the ways in which humans are different from each other, but in terms of their positions on the *same* broad dimensions of personality, rather than the ways in which each person is unique.

5 Individual differences psychology is concerned with fixity in the sense of the consistency and stability of temperament and personality over time. Nevertheless, personality is not genetically *determined* and unchangeable but is open to different paths of development, expression and some degree of change influenced by environments, especially other people.

6 Nature *and* nurture and their relative contributions to personality are central to the individual differences approach. And there is a great deal of debate about how these different influences should be theorized.

■ Thinking about theory

By the end of Chapter 5 the range of perspectives in current use in psychology has been clearly demonstrated. Personality can be studied from different perspectives (you will meet the psychoanalytic and humanistic perspectives in Chapter 9), but in this chapter it is individual differences psychology, part of the psychometric tradition, that is discussed.

The psychometric tradition

Psychometrics has a long tradition. It began with Galton (around 1884) and from the beginning it was associated with the biologically-based theories of evolution and heritability that were especially popular at that time. Psychometrics, therefore, always had a connection, sometimes not a very savoury one, with the measurement and comparison of abilities and intelligence and eugenics. Towards the end of his life the psychometrician, Cattell, was about to be awarded a Gold Medal for Life Achievement in Psychological Science by the American Psychological Association. But his connections with the eugenics movement and some of his early publications received adverse publicity and he withdrew himself from consideration for the award. You can track the psychometric tradition on *EPoCH*.

As a tradition, psychometrics and individual differences psychology – whether in relation to personality, intelligence or other aspects of psychological measurement – has tended to develop and use its methods for practical applications as well as pure research. The commentaries following Chapters 3 and 4 pointed out that the psychology of learning and biological psychology both produce applications that can be used to help alleviate problems. Chapter 5 also points out that psychometric personality questionnaires are frequently applied in everyday settings: for clinical diagnosis, job selection, and for monitoring educational progress. You may well have encountered psychometric tests yourself in one of these contexts.

It is possible that the psychometric tradition may be revolutionized in the future by the use of the Internet to reach global samples and measure a very wide range of individual differences and explore diversity.

Complementary perspectives on personality

As you have seen in Chapter 5, the psychometric, individual differences perspective has both *described* personality structure and tried to *explain* personality at the biological level by asking whether it is individual differences in biology that cause individual differences in personality. Trait theorists began by describing personality, but several of them also used (or implied) a lower level of analysis in their search for the biological underpinnings of their theories, thus combining different levels of analysis. In other words, the biological psychology perspective is used in a complementary way to explore what might be the biological basis for personality traits and types. Some theorists, notably Eysenck, have attempted to synthesize the two different perspectives into a unified theory of personality.

The biological perspective (in this case, genetics) has also been used in conjunction with the psychometrics and individual differences perspective to study heritability. This is because the individual differences view of personality aims to connect personality to genetically transmitted predispositions that have survival value – a link also with the evolutionary psychology perspective. Recent developments in biology, especially molecular genetics, are therefore important for personality theorists.

In Chapter 5 we have focused on one perspective but demonstrated the complementary use of another in trying to understand personality. However, as part of the evaluation of the individual differences view, yet other perspectives have been alluded to that do not sit so easily alongside individual differences. In the final section of Chapter 5 there was reference to some similarities between personality (as a broad concept) and identity. But none of the three perspectives on identity discussed in Chapter 1 could be said to be complementary with the individual differences perspective. There are two other psychological perspectives, not yet covered, that are relevant to theorizing personality but which also are not complementary, and could be said to *conflict* with the individual differences view. These are psychoanalysis and humanistic psychology, which you will meet in Chapter 9 of this book.

■ Thinking about methods

The individual differences approach to personality is as much concerned with theory *building* as theory *testing*. In Chapter 5 we saw that Cattell started with an inductive approach to data collection – looking for patterns and the emergence of theory and then testing hypotheses, thus using an inductive-hypothetico-deductive spiral. This process, which you also saw illustrated in Chapter 2 ('Evolutionary psychology') is a version of the cycle of enquiry described in the Introduction. Both the inductive-hypothetico-deductive spiral and the cycle of enquiry illustrate how research and theory can enrich and inform each other in an *iterative* process. This means a series of repetitions whereby insights from one part of the process are applied to and fed back into understandings of other parts of the process.

Focus on whole people or on aspects of people? An outsider viewpoint or insider accounts?

The concepts of personality and identity have some issues in common. In particular, both are concerned with 'who we are'. Most identity theorists approach this in a holistic way, being concerned with 'whole people' and their lives, motivations, experiences and what they *say* about themselves. Many identity theorists take an insider viewpoint – which is the viewpoint that tends to be associated with a holistic approach. However, some identity theorists, notably those who work in SIT, make sense of 'who we are' from an outsider viewpoint. In contrast, personality theorists working in the individual differences perspective focus on *aspects* of people – particular dimensions of their behaviour and feelings – and they almost always take an outsider viewpoint, which privileges the *measurement* of behaviour. Sometimes they use some self-reports (an insider viewpoint) from their participants, but even when they use these kinds of data their concern is not with individual 'whole people' and their inner experience; the aim is to make statements about people-in-general. So, although the study of personality and identity share some issues, the kinds of theories, methods and data they use diverge.

■ Thinking about themes

Explaining ourselves as human – similarities and differences between people

The individual differences view of personality described in the chapter you have just read is concerned with common dimensions of personality. It focuses on the ways in which humans are different from each other, but in terms of their positions on the *same* broad dimensions, rather than the ways in which each person is unique. Yet, given that psychometric tests are administered to individuals, identify differences between groups of individuals, and give individuals their own 'test scores', the individual differences approach does not treat humans as entirely undifferentiated.

Fixity and change

The most commonly asked questions about personality are probably those about fixity and the possibility of change. Is personality fixed? Does it change with age and life experiences? What influences act on the development of personality? Is it possible to change personality through conscious effort? These questions, after all, lie at the heart of psychological therapies.

In Chapter 5, traits and temperaments have been shown to be relatively consistent over time – that is, relatively fixed. But the idea that personality is something we arrive with at birth, genetically determined and unchangeable, is clearly not the case. Heritability studies have shown that environments and social contexts have a profound impact on personality development. Environments also have an impact on personality as we *express* it. As you saw in Section 4 of Chapter 5, people do not express the same aspects of their personality across all situations. There is fluidity in personality, certainly as observable from the outside by other people, although perhaps not as we experience our own personality from within.

Nature and nurture

Personality is one of the topics in psychology where debates about nature and nurture have always been at the forefront. Research within the psychometric, individual differences perspective has shown that genetics do have an influence on personality, but that personality is not genetically *determined* and unchangeable. Personality is open to different paths of development, expression and some degree of change influenced by interaction with environments, especially other people. Relatively recent research affecting personality theory concerns fine-grain definitions of environment. For example, at one time it was assumed that children brought up in the same family would have the same environment, but more detailed attention to environments has shown that this is not the case. Infants and children actively help to create their own unique environments in subtle ways. Environments are much more complex and have a more complex effect on the development of individual differences in personality than was previously recognized.

As in Chapters 4 ('Biological processes and psychological explanation') and Chapter 2 ('Evolutionary psychology'), the individual differences chapter takes an *interactionist* view of the influences of genetics and environment. Indeed, this is the chapter that most clearly lays out what is currently understood in psychology about the effects of nature *and* nurture in this case with respect to personality.

The next chapter (Chapter 6, 'Perception and attention') continues the discussion of people as biological entities. However, again you will find demonstrations of how the everyday tasks of perception and attention are affected by the social and cultural contexts in which they take place.

Index

Acknowledgements

Grateful acknowledgement is made to the following sources for permission to reproduce material in this book:

Introduction

Text

Box 2: adapted from: 'Ethical Principles for Conducting Research with Human Participants 2000', pp.7–11, *Code of Conduct, Ethical Principles and Guidelines*, The British Psychological Society.

Illustrations

p.7: Charles Darwin, © English Heritage Photographic Library, Sigmund Freud, © Sigmund Freud Copyrights/Photo: Mary Evans Picture Library, Wilhelm Max Wundt and William James, © Bettmann/CORBIS; p.14: © Sigmund Freud Copyrights/Photo: Mary Evans Picture Library; p.17: Courtesy of the Centre for Brain and Cognitive Development, Department of Psychology, Birkbeck College, London; p.18: Geoff Tomkinson/Science Photo Library; p.23: Mike Levers/Open University; p.28: still from the Stanford Prison Experiment © 1999, Courtesy of Professor Philip Zimbardo; p.29: Courtesy of Mrs. A. Milgram.

Chapter 1

Text

Box 1.6: Keith, L. (1994) 'Tomorrow I'm going to re-write the English language', *Mustn't Grumble: Writing by Disabled Women*, The Women's Press Limited.

Illustrations

p.49: from *The Emptiness of the Image,* by Parveen Adams, Routledge, 1996, plate 18, Onmipresence IV, Courtesy of Orlan; p.50: *(top left)* Toby Melville/PA Photos Ltd, *(top right)* Martin Keen/PA Photos Ltd, *(bottom left)* John Birdsall Photography, *(bottom right)* Stefano Cagnoni/Report Digital; p.54: Ted Streshinsky/CORBIS; p.59: Courtesy of Professor Marcia; p.62: Courtesy of Professor W.P. Robinson, University of Bristol; p.66: from *A Class Divided, Then and Now,* William Peters, Yale University Press, 1987. Photo: Charlotte Button for ABC News. © 2001 ABC Photography Archives; p.70: Courtesy of Professor Gergen; p.74: *(top left)* CBS TV (Courtesy Kobal), *(top right)* William Conran/PA Photos Ltd, *(bottom left)* Clarence S. Bull (Courtesy Kobal), *(bottom right)* Cannon (Courtesy Kobal);

p.75: *(top left)* Warner Bros. (Courtesy Kobal), *(top right)* Murdo McLeod, *(bottom left)* John F. Stevenson/Hulton Archive, January 1938, *(bottom right)* Hulton Archive; p.83: illustration by Wong Sai Ming from *What It's Like To Be Me*, ed. Helen Exley, Exley Publications, 1981, p.80; p.84: John Birdsall Photography.

Chapter 2

Figures

Figure 2.1: reprinted by permission of the publisher from *Good Natured: The Origins of Right and Wrong in Humans and Other Animals* by Frans B.M. de Waal, Cambridge, Mass.: Harvard University Press, Copyright © 1996 by Frans B.M. deWaal

Illustrations

p.108: *(top left)* Frans Lanting/Minden Pictures, *(top right)* Shehzad Noorani/Still Pictures, *(bottom left)* Mike Levers, Open University, *(bottom right)* Martha Holmes/BBC Natural History Unit Picture Library; p.109: *(left)* Astronomical watch, *c.*1790 by George Margetts, Photo: Science & Society Picture Library, *(top right)* NSAS/Science & Society Picture Library, *(bottom right)* Science & Society Picture Library; p.112: T.Buck, Custom Medical Stock/Science Photo Library; p.115: *(top)* Source: G.P.Darwin on behalf of the Darwin Heirlooms Trust, © English Heritage Photo Library/Jonathan Bailey, *(bottom)* Mary Evans Picture Library; p.116: from *Evolution*, Life Nature Library; p.118: *(top)* The Jane Goodall Institute, UK, *(bottom)* Frans Lanting/Minden Pictures; p.121: Michael W. Tweedie/Science Photo Library; p.129: 'Lowenmensch', © Ulmer Museum, Ulm, Photographer, Thomas Stephan; p.131: Karl Amann/BBC Natural History Unit Photo Library; p.132: Keith Scholey/BBC Natural History Unit Photo Library; p.138: All photos, Reprinted by permission of Paul Ekman; p.139: From I. Eibl-Eibesfeldt, *Human Ethology*, 1989 Aldine de Gruyter, New York. Reproduced by courtesy of Professor Dr Eibl-Eibesfeldt; p.142: Associated Press; p.143: Associated Press; p.145: Popperfoto; p.147: Lee Frost/The National Trust.

Chapter 3

Text

pp.206–7: Mercer, N. (1995) *The Guided Construction of Knowledge: Talk Amongst Teachers and Learners*, Multilingual Matters Ltd. Copyright © 1995 Neil Mercer.

Figures

Figures 3.2 and 3.6: Toates, F. (1995) 'Animal motivation and behaviour', in Roitblat, H. and Meyer, J.-A. (eds) *Comparative Approaches to Cognitive Science*, MIT Press; Figure 3.4: Toates, F. (1998) 'The biological bases of behaviour', in Eysenck, M. (ed.) *Psychology: An Integrated Approach*, Pearson Education Limited. Copyright © Addison Wesley Longman Limited 1998, reprinted by permission of Pearson Education Limited; Figure 3.5(a): O'Keefe, J. and Nadel, L. (1978) *The Hippocampus as a Cognitive Map*, Oxford University Press; Figures 3.7 and 3.8: Bruner, J.S., Goodnow, J.J. and Austin, G.A. (1956) *A Study of Thinking*, John Wiley & Sons, Inc. Reprinted by permission of the author.

Illustration

p.203: John Walmsley Photography.

Chapter 4

Figures

Figures 4.3, 4.13, 4.14, 4.16, 4.17, 4.20, 4.22, 4.23, 4.31: Eysenck, M. (ed.) *Psychology: An Integrated Approach*, Addison Wesley Longman Limited 2000, reprinted by Pearson Education Limited; Figures 4.4, 4.5, 4.6, 4.18, 4.23, 4.24, 4.25, 4.26, 4.27, 4.28, 4.33: Martini, F.H. *et.al.*, *Human Anatomy*, © Addison Wesley Longman Limited 2000, reprinted by Pearson Education Limited; Figure 4.10: Gottlieb, G. (1997) 'A systems view of psychobiological development', in Magnusson, D. (ed.) *The Lifespan Development of Individuals: Behavioural, Neurobiological and Psychosocial Perspectives: A Synthesis*, Cambridge University Press; Figure 4.15: Toates, F., *Biological Psychology: An Integrative Approach*, © Frederick Toates 2001, reprinted by permission of Pearson Education Limited; Figure 4.30: Photo: Wellcome Department of Cognitive Neurology/ Science Photo Library.

Chapter 5

Text

pp.326–7: from *The Interpersonal World of the Infant* by Daniel N. Stern. Copyright © 1987 by Basic Books, Inc. Reprinted by permission of Basic Books, a member of Perseus Books, L.L.C.; pp.330–2: Zimbardo, P.G. (1999) Extracts from *The Stanford Prison Experiment: A Simulation Study of the Psychology of Imprisonment*, Professor Philip G. Zimbardo, University of Stanford.

Figures

Figure 5.2: Adapted by permission from the 16PF ® Test Profile. Copyright © 1956, 1973, 1982 by the Institute for Personality and Ability Testing, Inc., PO Box 1188, Champaign, IL, 61824–1188, USA. All rights reserved. '16PF' is a trademark belonging to IPAT; Figure 5.3: Reprinted from *The Scientific Analysis of Personality and Motivation*, Cattell & Kline, 'Mean scores obtained on the 16PF by three occupational groups', page 23, (1997) by permission of the publisher Academic Press, London.

Tables

Tables 5.1 and 5.3: Matthews, G. and Deary, I.J. (1998) *Personality Traits*, page 27, Cambridge University Press; Table 5.2: Saucier, Hampson and Goldberg, 'Big five subcomponents found in English and German', (1999) *Advances in Personality Psychology*, ed. Sarah E. Hampson, Taylor and Francis Books Limited; Table 5.4: Buss, A.H. and Plomin, R. (1984) 'Temperament component', *Personality Traits*, Matthews, G. and Deary, I.J., Lawrence Erlbaum Asociates, Inc; Table 5.5: Loehlin, J.C. *Genes and Environment in Personality Development*, vol. 2, copyright © (1996) Reprinted by Permission of Sage Publications.

Illustrations

p.292: *(top)* From Karl Pearson, *The Life, Letters and Labours of Francis Galton*, 1914 (Vol. 1, p.242), Photo: Mary Evans Picture Library, *(bottom)* From Karl Pearson, *The Life, Letters and Labours of Francis Galton*, 1914 (Vol. 11, p.371), Photo: Mary Evans Picture Library; p.298: Courtesy of the Cattell family; p.300: *(left)* Courtesy of Professor Paul T. Costa, *(right)* Photo: Bill Newhall, Courtesy of Dr Robert R. McCrae; p.304: Courtesy of Professor Lewis Goldberg; p.312: Courtesy of Mrs S. Eysenck; p.320: *(left)* Photo: Bettman/Corbis Images, *(right)* Photo: Phil Noble/PA Photos Limited; p.330: Courtesy of Professor Philip Zimbardo; p.331: *(left and right)* Still from Stanford Prison Experiment: Humiliation, © 1999, Courtesy of Professor Philip Zimbardo.

Every effort has been made to trace all the copyright owners, but if any has been inadvertently overlooked, the publishers will be pleased to make the necessary arrangements at the first opportunity.